THE NATIVE AMERICANS OF THE
TEXAS EDWARDS PLATEAU,
1582–1799

TEXAS ARCHAEOLOGY AND ETHNOHISTORY SERIES

THOMAS R. HESTER, EDITOR

The Native Americans of the Texas Edwards Plateau, 1582–1799

MARIA F. WADE

MAPS BY DON E. WADE

UNIVERSITY OF TEXAS PRESS

AUSTIN

The publication of this book was assisted by a University Cooperative Society
Subvention Grant awarded by the University of Texas at Austin.

First edition, 2003

∞ The paper used in this book meets the minimum requirements of
ANSI/NISO Z39.48-1992 (R1997) (Permanence of Paper).

ISBN 0-292-79156-9

LIBRARY OF CONGRESS CATALOGING-IN-PUBLICATION DATA
Wade, Maria de Fátima, 1948–
The Native Americans of the Texas Edwards Plateau, 1582–1799 /
Maria F. Wade ; maps by Don E. Wade.
p. cm. — (Texas archaeology and ethnohistory series)
Includes bibliographical references and index.
ISBN 0-292-79156-9 (hardcover : alk. paper)
1. Indians of North America—Texas—Edwards Plateau—History.
2. Edwards Plateau (Tex.)—History.   I. Title.   II. Series.
E78.T4 W24   2003
976.4′8701—dc21
2002012928

Contents

Figures

Foreword

THOMAS R. HESTER

During the sixteenth through the eighteenth centuries, several major Spanish expeditions traversed the Edwards Plateau canyon lands of central Texas. The region was occupied by a large number of Native American groups who lived by hunting and gathering. Although earlier studies have tended to lump these groups under a generalized rubric, such as "Coahuiltecan," it is now clear that there was remarkable diversity. Through exhaustive ethnohistoric research, Maria Wade has revealed the complex nature of these groups and their interaction both with other Native Americans and with the Spanish. Careful use of primary archives, coupled with her knowledge of the nuances of the Spanish language of this era, has permitted her to compile a resource that will be used by scholars for generations to come.

The Native American peoples of the early historic period in the Edwards Plateau, for the most part, have their roots in central Texas prehistory. For at least 11,500 years, the Edwards Plateau was occupied by hunters and gatherers, who left behind a rich archaeological record. Maria Wade's ethnohistoric research is part of a rapidly expanding body of knowledge that has revealed, in the last few years, a very complicated cultural record. For example, at the Gault site in Bell County, Michael B. Collins has directed the excavations of a major occupation of the Clovis culture, dating to the late Pleistocene. From Clovis times to the end of what archaeologists refer to as the Paleoindian period (around 8,500 years ago), researchers have documented an increasing population, the emergence of modern climates, and the beginnings of regional cultural patterns. However, the bulk of the archaeological record in the region derives from the long-lived Archaic period. Hunter-gatherer occupation and food-processing sites are very common, and there is a bewildering array of chipped stone tools, especially projectile points. Earth oven cooking of sotol bulbs and other plant resources resulted in the formation of thousands of "burned rock middens," explored through a number of new techniques exemplified by the research of Stephen L. Black. Central Texas archaeologists who study this long span of time, which lasted well over 7,000 years, have investigated hundreds of sites, published many reports and monographs, and worked out much of the detail on the culture history, stone-tool technology, and diet of the Archaic hunters and gatherers. However, when it comes to such issues as territoriality, political and social organization, linguistic diversity, seasonal use of campsites, or many other details of human behavior, we are almost wholly at a loss for any useful information. Much the same can be said for the last phase of antiquity, the Late Prehistoric, from 300 to 1,300 years ago. To be sure, we have better detail on daily life, as cultural remains are generally better preserved from archaeological deposits that are comparatively recent. We are fascinated by the spread of a set of material-culture traits (Perdiz arrow points, end scrapers, perforators, beveled knives, bone-tempered pottery) known as the Toyah horizon, beginning around A.D. 1250 and lasting up to the beginning of Spanish missions of the eighteenth century. Some scholars have referred to this constellation of distinctive artifacts as derived from a "folk" or a "people," but other researchers believe that the traits diffused during a time when bison-hunting was an important activity among many hunters and gatherers. This is an example of important anthropological issue to which Wade's ethnohistory makes a new contribution.

Though this brief summary does not do justice to the many recent accomplishments of archaeologists studying the prehistoric Edwards Plateau, it emphasizes that fieldwork and analysis of the preserved cultural remains can go only so far. We run the danger of imposing our own ideas of what prehistory may have been like—rather than what it was really like. Or we can apply ethnographic analogies about hunter-gatherer cultures in other regions to our interpretations, but this also is risky business. What central Texas archaeologists have needed for the last several decades is a scholarly and comprehensive scrutiny of the historic records left by the Spanish explorers of the sixteenth to eighteenth centuries, specifically the documents of the expeditions that explored the Edwards Plateau and adjacent areas. We have needed detailed information on the distribution of various animal species, the nature of the terrain and its vegetative cover, the presence (or absence) of water, and, most of all, a focused and innovative look at the Native American peoples who lived in this landscape. Maria Wade has provided all of this in the present book.

It should be clear that Wade is building on the hard work of earlier ethnohistorians interested in central Texas, especially W. W. Newcomb and T. N. Campbell. Newcomb's work, first synthesized in his *Indians of Texas,* was invaluable for its time, though today much of the information there has been eclipsed by later research—much of it by Newcomb himself. Of note are his studies of the Wichita and the Tonkawa (the latter in collaboration with Campbell). For example, the Tonkawa research, as published in a volume of the *Handbook of North American Indians* (Smithsonian Institution) used historical documents to indicate that the Tonkawa came into Texas late in the seventeenth century from a presumed homeland in Oklahoma (Wade addresses this issue in regard to the appearance of the Tonkawa in central Texas). This is of particular importance to archaeologists, as for many years there has been some effort to link the Tonkawa to the Toyah horizon noted earlier. T. N. Campbell and his daughter, T. J. Campbell, have spent countless hours—and many years—mining the microfilms and other ethnohistoric resources for every detail they could find on the Indians of central and southern Texas and northeastern Mexico. Campbell has synthesized these data in several papers, especially related to southern Texas, but has never done an overarching study of the historic Indians of central Texas. On the other hand, all one has to do is to flip through the pages of the *New Handbook of Texas* to realize how many hundreds of Native American groups have been identified, indeed rescued, from the thousands of scribbled pages of Spanish documents studied by Campbell. Both Newcomb and Campbell have done much of the "leg work" that made it possible for Maria Wade to provide this integrated review of the early historic Native Americans of the Edwards Plateau. Campbell's counsel was invaluable to Wade, but he wisely turned her loose, with her incredible energy, inquisitive and critical mind, and barely controlled impatience, to scour the Spanish archives and to extract detail and fashion new interpretations of broad scale.

To be truthful, I am intimidated by this book. I have read drafts of it, and its original dissertation format, over several years. Each time I picked up a few pages, I learned something entirely new about the Edwards Plateau and its Native populations. With each chapter or partial chapter, I was struck by the amount of information—presented either as hard data or as an observation that assimilated many pieces of data—that will permit archaeologists, anthropologists, and historians, as well as zoologists and botanists, to better understand the environmental and cultural dynamics of the Edwards Plateau. Though other scholars have made note of the links between the Native peoples of the Edwards Plateau and those of other regions, as far flung as El Paso, East Texas, or deep into northern Mexico, this volume provides much new information on the mechanisms of these relationships and coalitions. Furthermore, one of Wade's major goals was to approach this research from the perspective of the Native speakers documented in the Spanish archives. Such an approach gives us a much better understanding (in reality, a first understanding) of how the Indians manipulated the Spanish, formed and then dissolved large population aggregates, and reacted to the events unfolding around them. It has become rather popular in anthropological circles to speak of the Spaniards as "oppressors" who were "resisted" by the doomed Native peoples. Certainly there is some truth to that. But, from what Wade has found, it seems that most of the peoples of the Edward Plateau were much more worried about the "oppression" of the invading Lipan Apaches than the more easily manipulated Spanish.

The careful reader will gain insights into hunting technologies, seasonality, territoriality, social structure, political coalitions, and many of the topics that I noted earlier in this Foreword. These will cause many scholars to reevaluate their perspectives about late prehistory and even earlier times. There are also new vistas of the Edwards Plateau terrain, vegetation, and fauna of three hundred years ago, well before farmers and freeways forever altered it. Central Texas of the sixteenth to eighteenth centuries has been buried in the archives, and it is only through Maria Wade's dedicated efforts that we are now able to explore it.

Acknowledgments

This book started with my dissertation, which was completed in 1998 at the University of Texas, Austin. Since that date, I have done a great deal more research, which has resulted in the complete revision of some of the key historical events discussed in this book. The dissertation, as well as this book, represents a commitment to unravel Native American history that was spurred and nurtured by the work and guidance of Thom Campbell. No doubt his scholarship and questions shaped my research, but what he taught me about intellectual humility and intellectual generosity goes beyond any single work: it takes a lifetime to honor, and I intend to do so.

This book is enhanced by beautiful maps, and those would not have been possible without the help of my husband, Don Wade. He translated my research in elegant pictorial fashion and he read and edited endless drafts. He too has fallen under Campbell's spell, and his commitment to Native American history is as strong as mine.

Nevertheless, this book might not have been published had it not been for the vision and trust of Thom Hester and Theresa May. In different ways, their support and efforts were pivotal to this publication; again, their acts speak for their commitment.

Many other people, in multiple ways, contributed to this work. Elizabeth and Karl Butzer favored me with their friendship and helpful suggestions, as did Carole Smith, T. J. Campbell, Jim Neely, and Sam Wilson. Several staff members of the University of Texas Press guided me through the intricacies of a finished manuscript: I am grateful to all.

The nature of the work required extensive archival research and heavy reliance on the knowledge and kindness of the staff of several archival repositories. Special thanks are due to Adán Benavides and the staff of the Nettie Lee Benson Latin American Library (Austin); John Wheat, Ralph Elder, and Ned Brierley at the Center for American History (Austin); and Kinga Perzynska and Susan Eason at the Catholic Archives of Austin. The assistance of Nancy Brown at the Spanish Colonial Research Center, University of New Mexico, was invaluable.

I would like also to express my gratitude to Grant Hall and William Foster, who reviewed this book for the publisher. Not only were they kind to my efforts, they took the time to make suggestions and improve its final outcome.

A book is never a solitary endeavor: it is always, at some level, the thoughts, words, and acts of others. I have benefited from the help and labors of others, but I am solely responsible for any errors committed.

M.F.W.

Introduction

THE OBJECTIVE

Ethnohistory, as a field of study, has the singular position of being at the intersection of the disciplines of anthropology, history, and archaeology, taken in their broadest sense. Ethnohistory came of age because of a blind spot in the practices of anthropology and history. It emerged to fill the void that existed between anthropological and historical studies because of their failure to document the changes in Native life that occurred during the colonial encounter.

The archival text is the material base of ethnohistoric studies, but these texts were produced by the colonizing nations and present a biased view of historical events. Because ethnohistorians have to base their interpretations of history on the colonizer's documents, it is easy to slide into a perspective that subsumes Native history to European history.

The guiding objective of this work was to study the Native American groups that, between 1582 and 1799, lived in and utilized the physiographic region called the Edwards Plateau and related geographic areas. The evidence was obtained mainly from primary archival documents mostly generated by colonial Spain, but a few French documents were also used. Although the work is based on European recorded history, it attempts to reverse the usual perspective: it uses the role the Spanish and French played in Native history as a catalyst to analyze events in the history of Native Americans in Texas and Coahuila.

In disentangling the threads of Native American history from the fabric of colonial history, a great deal of primary archival research was necessary. In the process many documents were found that fill lacunae and clear up misunderstandings about the early Franciscan work south and north of the Rio Grande. The letters of Fr. Larios and his companions are unique and invaluable sources on the Native groups and the environment. Among the documents found are a few pages of a diary of the Bosque-Larios expedition that appear to have been written not by Fernando del Bosque, but by Fr. Juan Larios.

But probably the biggest archival surprise was the material uncovered while researching the Mendoza-Lopez expedition. Apart from the confirmation, by a Native American, of contacts in Texas (1650) among the Spanish, the Jumano, and the Tejas, a new and very different version of the diary of the Mendoza-Lopez expedition was found. When compared with the other known versions of the diary, this version, which I assume to have been penned by Mendoza, raises fundamental questions about all other previous interpretations and introduces a great deal of historical uncertainty about the events surrounding the expedition. The archival material that relates to this expedition should impress upon the reader the ephemeral quality of historical interpretation and the absolute need for continued research.

As a result of the methodology practiced, this work reveals information about the ethnic identities of the Native groups that lived in and used the Edwards Plateau and related areas, their physical environment, and their sociocultural behavior.

OVERVIEW

The history of the Spanish colonization of Texas in the seventeenth century is intimately connected with the events that took place in other areas of northern New Spain, particularly in Coahuila and even in New Mexico. After Cabeza de Vaca, Coronado, and the De Soto–Moscoso penetrations in the sixteenth century, no concrete effort to conquer or contact Native populations was undertaken within the territory that would become modern Texas.

In the seventeenth century, the first Spanish *entradas* into west-central Texas resulted primarily from the efforts of Native groups on both sides of the Rio Grande to establish autonomous settlements and evade Spanish control over their lives. The early Christianizing endeavors of the Franciscan friars from Coahuila stemmed from those Native moves to settle, which began in Saltillo in 1658. Likewise, the first contacts (1630–1654) between New Mexico Franciscans and the Jumano groups in central Texas were the consequence of invitations by the Jumano to the Spanish to visit their lands and were grafted onto long-term trade relationships between Natives and Spanish.

The *entradas* from Coahuila and from New Mexico eventually resulted in conquest expeditions, respectively the 1675 Bosque-Larios expedition and the 1683–1684 Mendoza-Lopez expedition. These Spanish expeditions proved inconsequential to later full-fledged Spanish conquest endeavors in Texas, but they caused misgivings and disappointments among the Native populations contacted, and they soured future relations between Natives and Spanish.

The Franciscan mission-settlements established during the last two decades of the seventeenth century for Native groups that lived south and north of the Rio Grande were worthy religious efforts that produced a very mixed record. In times of conflict or economic stress, most Native groups accepted the refuge and help those enclaves provided, but few remained long enough to satisfy the Church and justify the Crown's investment. The conflicts among the various Franciscan provinces, the civilians, the military, and the Native groups, particularly over the control of the Native labor force and the usufruct of lands, did little to improve the mission record.

This book provides a timeline that spans the period between 1686 and 1750. The timeline has two functions: (1) it establishes historical context and highlights events that affected the Native groups studied, and (2) it is designed to reflect the importance of the actions of singular individuals within the long-term perspective of the sequence of events.

The arrival of the Apache in the seventeenth century preceded the actual establishment of Spanish settlements in Texas and proved to be the essential element in changing the Native human landscape in the territory. The two newcomers, Apache and Spaniard, wrestled for the bodies and souls of local Native groups, forcing them into submission or mission life: either way, the Native groups made alliances that compromised their ethnic and cultural identities.

We are far from deciphering the history of the Apache groups in Texas, and this book makes only a minor incision into a problem festering with assumptions. The Spanish political and military decisions made during the last four decades of the eighteenth century make the colonial history of the Apache east of the Medina River (Texas) and west of the Medina River (Coahuila) considerably different. The policy of Native mutual destruction advocated and practiced by Spanish officials, together with the private economic interests of individuals who supplied weaponry and gifts that fueled the wars among Apache, Comanche, and Norteños, created a collusion of interests that strangled the Apache. But the die had been cast: it would be up to the Comanche and the Norteños to impress upon the Spanish the dangers of unholy alliances.

The completed research permits the identification of twenty-one Native groups that occupied the Edwards Plateau region between 1673 and 1700. It is beyond the scope of this work to identify all the groups that lived in the Edwards Plateau after the onset of the eighteenth century.

Statements by the Jumano captain, Juan Sabeata, confirm that Jumano groups occupied the lands east of the Pecos and immediately west of the Colorado River, certainly from 1650 through 1684, and very probably from 1630 through the end of the 1690s. The evidence from the ethnohistorical record places Jumano groups within the geographic area normally considered as the heart of the archaeological Toyah culture during some of the time when the Toyah cultural manifestations are thought to have flourished. This fact does not necessarily mean that Jumano groups were associated with the Toyah archaeological manifestations, but their presence in the area raises the question of their association with the Toyah culture.

THE GEOGRAPHIC AREA OF STUDY

All recorded contacts between Native populations and the Spanish within Texas between 1630 and 1684 took place in the general area of the Edwards Plateau. The physiographic region of the Edwards Plateau is a section of the Great Plains Physiographic Province as defined by Carr (1967). The definition of the physiographic area follows closely the geologic definition of the Edwards Plateau by Sellards, Adkins, and Plummer (1954).

Despite the fact that the Spanish *entradas* and expeditions traveled through a large portion of the Edwards Plateau, the historical conjunctures that connect those events were rooted in other areas of New Spain. Thus, in cultural terms the Edwards Plateau links Texas to territories closely connected with its history, such as New Mexico and the Mexican territories of Coahuila, Nueva Vizcaya, and Nuevo León. The historical connections between the Plateau and the regions to the north and southwest are clearly confirmed by the fact that those were the entry points of the early Spanish colonial expeditions.

For most of the time span covered in this work, Texas did not exist as a political entity. The events that took place within the modern Texas territory have to be addressed by freeing the landscape from its modern political boundaries.

METHODOLOGY AND CONVENTIONS

METHODS AND ARCHIVES

The history of Native Americans in Texas usually has been treated as incidental to the history of the European colonial powers that occupied the Native lands. Such an approach, facilitated by the very nature of the historical records, has primarily produced a broad-stroke picture of the groups that occupied Texas and easternmost Coahuila in the early historic period. The production of a seamless history is appealing, but detrimental to research. Researchers and students alike often assume that the history of Texas and its people has already been unraveled and thus desist from further inquiry. That perception could not be further from the truth, particularly as it regards Texas Native groups.

The Native groups discussed in this work fall under the cultural assignation of hunters and gatherers, and their social structures and cultural achievements were (and often still are) viewed as simplistic. The archival information about these groups is fragmentary, disjointed, and reflective of the lack of value attributed by Europeans to the social and cultural practices of these groups. It is therefore argued that in order to study, analyze, and understand the behavior of the Native populations, the focus of research has to be the micro- or subtle event that is often taken for granted. The micro-event is often no more than an isolated document, a sentence, a word, or even the absence of a word. Once these singular and subtle pieces of evidence are considered for their potential importance, the researcher attempts to locate corroborating evidence to build and support an ethnohistoric interpretation.

The majority of historical documents that include information about Native American groups do not deal with Native issues. The documents only mention Native groups in passing, and the information transmitted is framed by the contextual knowledge possessed and assumed by the historical recorder and his contemporaries. Each document is a deliberate link in a chain of continuous events, experiences, and discussions that the modern ethnohistorian often cannot reconstruct. It is by piecing together information scattered throughout the documentary record, and placing it in context, that a mosaic can be constructed and a pattern discerned. Often there is not enough evidence to anchor a pattern, and the best that can be achieved is a delineation of possibilities with assumptions grafted onto the slim evidence.

The archival text should be treated by the researcher as a historical fact in itself. The life history of a document should be considered in the assessment of the historical evidence it contains. Letters between individuals produce a series of historical moments and relationships. The interpretation of these moments is made not only out of the various interrelated texts, but also out of the ambiguities created in the texts by marginal notations, corrections, and opinions.

TEXTUAL INTERPRETATION

The Spain that colonized the Americas was an empire composed of many countries, which later became independent nations. The presence in New Spain of Castilians, Catalans, Basques, and Galicians as well as Italians, Portuguese, French, and Greeks — just to name a few — introduced many languages and dialects in the colonies under the linguistic umbrella of Spanish.

Language differences in the European countries that provided most of the documents considered in this study were, and continue to be, marked, politicized, and culturally very important. These language differences, and the particular cultural and environmental backgrounds that went along with them, affected what people heard and recorded, how they perceived the landscape, and what comparative models and cognitive maps they brought to bear on their descriptions of peoples and landscapes in the New World.

Regional differences within continental Spain were, and are, considerable. Vowels and consonants had, and have, different values; words present different spellings; and nouns and verbs for daily objects and activities are often quite dissimilar. Recorders and official scribes inscribed their social and linguistic background on the text. Most important, the mother language of the recorder affected the way he heard and recorded the names of Native groups.

Language differences are important when translating and interpreting archival documents, but they are probably easier to detect than differences in background. When and where individuals grew up could have considerable repercussions for their perception of the physical landscape. This becomes a serious problem when trying to relate the observer's descriptions to the environment of today, especially when dealing with such features as hills, creeks, rivers, and springs. The change in the environment, coupled with personal perceptions and cultural reference terms, leads to many conditional statements.

Documents were copied several times for different reasons and by different scribes, often with very different backgrounds. In some cases, when a document bearing the signature of the writer of the document is not available, it is difficult to tell which copy was the first one to be made from the original. Whatever errors appear in the first copy will persist. It is easy for a scribe to skip words, lines, or paragraphs, or change spellings, because the script was hard to read or because the spellings were considered incorrect at a later time. In this case, the corrected copies are said to be "castigated," from the Latin root meaning "to cut" (Jed 1989: 8, 12). Often these copies are certified to have been corrected and to be like the original. This, however, does not guarantee that the information in the document is pristine, and the certified copy may actually have been "castigated" and therefore not a faithful rendition of its original.

Some of the documents consulted were originals written on paper, while others were in microfilm form, photocopies of the original documents, or typed transcripts. All these types of documents, except typed transcripts, pose similar problems in terms of textual treatment. Typed transcripts are one step farther removed from the original, especially because it is often quite clear the transcriber was not familiar with the historical material and was thus prone to making errors.

TERMINOLOGY

It seems premature and unwise to place the Native groups that dwelled in northeastern-most Coahuila and modern Texas under the umbrella of "bands" or "tribes." Individually, these anthropological concepts carry specific sociocultural implications that may be inadequate to describe the social organization of the groups dealt with in this study (e.g., Firth 1958; Service 1958). The concept of group—two or more individuals who view themselves as constituting an aggregate—has the conceptual and anthropologic plasticity to allow researchers to designate such socially related aggregates as groups, and thus facilitate research for additional information about the nature of their social structure. The concept of group is both sufficient for the purpose of research and necessary in order to avoid misconceptions (e.g., Lee 1985: 54–57).

The concept of group encompasses two other dimensions that are particularly relevant for ethnohistorians, anthropologists, and archaeologists. There is a crucial conceptual difference between the group that is felt (the aggregate of individuals who see themselves as members of the group) and the group that is observed (the entity perceived by the observer, be it in the historic document, the ethnographic field setting, or the archaeological site). For this reason, among others, information obtained from Native American sources is always privileged over information provided by Europeans whose sources are not identified.

The concept of ethnicity has both singular and plural dimensions. At these two levels it articulates the individual to the community, and the community to the individual, through a sense of belonging expressed socially, culturally, and spiritually. The ethnic name is a synthetic and communal expression of real and perceived social ties, as well as accepted rights and duties. In reality, ethnicity is a cognitive map of belonging.

The word *Native* appears capitalized throughout the text because it is used with the same grammatical and lexical value as *Portuguese* or *English*. It denotes citizenship not in a country, but in a continent—the Americas. The word *Indian* is shunned because it results from a historical and geographic error committed by Columbus.

NATIVE NAMES

Group names that appear in the body of the text are transcribed as they appear in the original documents. Variation in the spelling of Native names *is not a mistake,* but reflects the variation that appears in the historical documents. All Native group names are shown in the *singular,* except for a few Native groups that have been consistently known by their Spanish appellatives (for example, the Manos Prietas). The word *Tejas* (with a *j*) refers to the Caddo groups of east Texas; all references to the Texas territory use the word *Texas* (with an *x*). Exceptions to this rule are found in translations and quotations. Whenever possible, the word *nation* has been replaced by the word *group*.

Many Spanish proper names and nouns vary widely in spelling and in the use of diacritic marks. Because modern linguistic conventions did not apply to the documents consulted, this work reproduces the variation that exists in the archival documentation.

MAPS AND ROUTES

The maps (figures) that accompany the text include most of the places mentioned, except for those that could not be located or could not be accommodated due to limitations of space. To maintain clarity and legibility, places mentioned and included in maps in earlier chapters often are excluded from the maps of later chapters.

The translation, tracing, plotting, and mapping of the routes of the Spanish expeditions researched for this work (Espejo, Castaño de Sosa, Fr. Manuel, Bosque-Larios, and Mendoza-Lopez) followed specific guidelines and assumptions. The first guideline considers that distance and direction of travel constitute objective information, while description is subjective and generally depends on the perceptions and cultural background of the recorder. An exception to this is the presence of major, perennial landmarks or unique landscape features. Unique landmarks or features were used as anchor points in plotting the routes; otherwise, distance and direction of travel overrode physical features. Routes were adjusted if recorded landmarks had a high probability of being recognized; routes were not adjusted for environmental information that was not unique or perennial.

The second guideline considers that when the recorder used cardinal points (north, east, west, and south), the route taken could be within 45 degrees on either side of that cardinal point. If the recorder provided intermediate cardinal points (northeast, etc.), the direction of travel could vary 22.5 degrees on either side of the direction recorded. If the recorder discriminated further on the direction of travel (north-northeast, etc.), the actual direction could be 11.25 degrees on either side of that provided.

It has been assumed that prior to the widespread availability of horses, the primary constraint on the best and shortest routes for foot travelers was the availability of water sources. Most expeditions, if not all, used Native guides. These guides would be familiar with the location of water sources, but their water requirements for travel would be far less stringent than those of Spanish expeditions traveling on horseback. Horseback travel would require not only a different type of water source, but also the availability of adequate pasture. Native guides adjusted their routes to these constraints, as Sabeata made clear (Appendix). The routes used by travelers riding horses would be somewhat different from those used by foot travelers. In general, shorter, flatter, and less forested routes would be preferred. Once these routes were established, they would tend to be followed in later times by other expeditions and as stagecoach and railroad routes.

The problem of the determination of the value of the Spanish league through time is a thorny one (e.g., Anderson 1925; Chardon 1980; Haggard 1941: 78–79). However, after the seventeenth century the legal league (*legua legal*) was generally used throughout colonial Spain (Chardon 1980: 138, 144 Table 1). The "old" Spanish league is equivalent to 2.63 English statute miles, while the later Spanish league is equivalent to 2.59 English statute miles. Thus, like most authors, I have used the value of 2.6 miles to the Spanish league. For clarity and consistency, miles and leagues are expressed in numerals throughout.

TRANSLATION

To translate archival documents is to translate between cultures and across time, and the danger of misreading or misinterpretation is ever present. This danger increases exponentially when the documents report Native statements that are already the result of multilingual translations. Awareness of the danger does not diminish the potential pitfalls, nor should it preclude translation. Except when noted, all translations are my responsibility. It is not a responsibility that I took lightly nor one that I could evade: that's the nature of a commitment.

It is my hope that this book serves the community of researchers on Native American history and aids in their work. Also, it is my sincere wish that the facts uncovered during this project will make Native Americans—and all Americans—proud.

Note to the Reader

The documents translated, paraphrased, and summarized in this book span almost 150 years. The Spanish (and French) texts produced during this period reflect deep changes in colonial paradigms, personal worldviews, and cultural and linguistic backgrounds as well as phonetic and lexical variations exhibited by a language searching for uniformity and standards. Add to these difficulties the physical condition of the documents, particularly the faded and almost illegible copies, and it becomes easy to understand why most scholars and translators choose to file away textual edges and produce a cohesive and seamless text, leading the reader to assume a textual clarity and transparency of meaning that are frequently illusory.

These problems are most evident in the translations of source material published during the late nineteenth and early twentieth centuries, because that was a period of frenetic efforts to make known a history hereto unknown or disregarded. Scholars (and their translators) such as Bancroft, Bolton, and Castañeda (not to single out anyone but to name just the most prominent) provided historians, anthropologists, and ethnohistorians not just with translated texts but also with intellectual leadership. Later, few scholars revisited or questioned the original translations and so reproduced, indefinitely, whatever errors, omissions, and misconceptions were present in the earlier works. Also, the clarity of the original texts, their immediacy, and the correctness of interpretation made by earlier scholars were (and are) taken for granted. Eugene Bolton would certainly be the first to question such research practices.

Unlike other scholars I chose to treat the archival documents in this book by keeping as close to the actual text as possible, and to maintain the language "flavor" and textual idiosyncrasies of each writer. This effort extends to phonetic, lexical, and grammatical choices. This practice results in texts whose structure feels awkward and foreign (as it should). Texts that I have paraphrased or summarized will, as far as possible, keep close to the word choice of the original writer, particularly if the words relate to cultural information (i.e., *tejado* dwellings versus *zacate* huts) or controversial issues (such as Fr. Manuel's trip to Texas).

As for the documents that I translated for the first time, or that I re-translated (specifically the travel diaries), I elected to translate the text by retelling it as an outside observer (participant-observer). This device allowed me to reorder the sentences and contextualize the subject being discussed without changing the information provided. This strategy also let me interject the travel diaries and hopefully produced a more fluid narrative without smoothing the incongruencies of the original text. To give the reader a concise idea of problems and the strategies I adopted, below is an example of the Mendoza-Lopez diary transcribed from the transcription available in the Center for American History:

== *En veinte dias del dho mes y hano llegamos a heste paraxe que por nombre se le puso nra. S^{ra} del transito ques en el rio del norte q* [corrected in ink and replaced with the word *que*] *con su lomeria hase un potrero y las hegas* [corrected in ink and replaced with the words *sus begas*] *habundantes de pasto y leña dista del paraxe de nra. S^{ra} de la soledad hocho leguas poco mas oy meno parte* [corrected in ink and replaced with the words *o menos y en partes*] *tiera doblada y en medio ahi un ohjo Caliente y ase el dho ojo el dho rio hes la tierra yntratable poblada de halgunas rancherias el habrebadero es bueno en lo alto de una loma yse colocar una Sta crus y para que mexor corte* [corrected in ink and replaced with the word *coxte*] *lo firme ante mi con los testigos de mi asistencia en dho dia mes y haño.* == (Mendoza 1684 p.40)

My translation, which omits the closing formula of most diary entries (y para que mexor . . . mes y haño), is as follows:

*The party traveled southward and reached a spot they named Nuestra Señora del Transito, about 8 leagues (20.8 miles) distant from N.S. de la Soledad. The place was on the Rio Grande. A range of hills framed or defined the pastureland, with abundant low-lying pastures and plenty of wood. In some areas the land was rough (**doblada**). Between [the two named places or the range of hills?] there was a hot spring that made the river [actually the water of the spring ran into the Rio Grande, since the spring did not make the Rio Grande]. The water source (**habrevadero**) was good. The land was intractable. There were some **rancherías** of settled people. Mendoza had a cross placed on top of a hill.*

There are language discrepancies between the diary entry in Províncias Internas (transcribed above) and the copy in Historia v. 298 that I followed. Some of these discrepancies reflect changes in spelling (*hace, intractable, conste, año*), and cases of interchangeable consonants such as *b* and *v* and *g* and *x* (*parage, vegas, abrevadero*).

To some this attention to detail may seem unwarranted, but it is through such practices that the researcher comes to know the writer and can detect statements that appear out of character. That is how I knew it was unlikely that version L had been written by Juan Dominguez Mendoza.

ONE

A Move to Settle

SETTING THE STAGE

Until the mid-seventeenth century the Crown of Spain had shown little interest in the territory today known as Texas. The expeditions of Pánfilo Narvaez (1527–1536), Francisco Vazquéz de Coronado (1540), and Hernán de Soto (1541) provided the Crown with information about the lands that were to frame, roughly, the modern state of Texas. The sporadic Spanish contacts with the lands and the Native peoples in Texas (Chamuscado-Rodríguez, Castaño de Sosa, and Espejo-Luxán)[1] had been directed at New Mexico, not Texas.

On the other hand, the northeastern region of modern Mexico had been actively settled by Spanish colonizers and by displaced Native populations who had either reached an agreement with the Spanish, like the Tlaxcaltecans, or been made an offer they could not refuse. The northern towns of Saltillo and Monterrey were well established by the mid-seventeenth century, whereas the Villa de Almáden (modern Monclova), established by Luis de Carvajal y de la Cueva circa 1590, succumbed more than once to the hazards of the frontier.

Not much is known about the Native groups that occupied the area of Monclova and the regions north and east of this town. There is evidence that the Native groups that frequented the areas immediately south and north of the Rio Grande had fallen prey to slave-raiding parties as early as 1581, if not earlier. Some of the events that took place during the forays of Castaño de Sosa and Antonio de Espejo testify to the fears already felt by the Natives in the areas along and north of the Rio Grande. Slave raids in Coahuila and across the Rio Grande were expensive, dangerous, and not sanctioned by the Spanish Crown unless justified as punitive actions against the Natives. For example, in September 1607, Francisco de Urdiñola led an expedition to the area between the Río Sabinas and the Rio Grande to punish the Quamoquane. According to various individuals who participated in the conflict, many Quamoquane were killed and many others were imprisoned or agreed to work in the haciendas and mines in Saltillo, Parras, and Patos (Garcia 1608; Urdiñola 1608).

Mining operations and landed estates needed a malleable and inexpensive labor force:

that justified the risks faced by the Spanish during these punitive raids. Native Americans were not willing slaves, and those who worked for the Spaniards did not want to be confined and demanded payment for their labor. The conflict generated by the Spanish need for a workforce and the conditions under which the Native workforce was willing to labor did not follow a single linear trajectory. There were historical moments when the Natives helped the newly arrived conquistadors, moments when they rebelled against the pressures and the demands placed on Native populations, and moments when the parties reached a mutual understanding. However, the natural progression of the colonization process and the increasing numbers of Spanish colonizers meant the inexorable occupation of Native lands, the reduction of Native territories and resource areas, and an exponential increase in the need for cheap Native labor. The following narrative begins with one of the historical moments when Native groups, squeezed by the Spanish demands for labor and fatigued by the labor conditions imposed on them, attempted to find a legal solution to their woes.

EVENTS

1658

In March 1658, Miguel de Otalona, war captain and judge in Saltillo, heard testimony from army personnel and the citizenry of Saltillo relative to a request made by four Babane and Jumano to establish a pueblo for their people. The Babane had been laboring at the Hacienda de San Ysidro de las Palomas and had been part of the *encomienda*[2] of Ambrosio de Zepeda since its inception. Ambrosio de Zepeda was deceased at the time of the request, and in 1656 his widow rented the hacienda to Captain Diego de Montemayor from Monterrey (Valdés et al. 1997–1999: 9, 18). The Jumano had been part of the *encomienda* of Pedro de Bega, who brought them from Coahuila. At the time of the request, the *encomienda* belonged to Joan de Farias (Morales 1658; Otalona 1658; P. Ximenes 1658). These Natives had visited Viceroy Duque de Albuquerque[3] to present their request, and the Viceroy ordered the matter investigated (Otalona 1658).

Testimony of various witnesses shows that the request made by the Babane and Jumano charged that the *encomenderos* of Saltillo rounded up Natives in Coahuila for their *encomiendas*, imprisoned the children of Native workers to force their parents to remain in the haciendas, and did not pay the Natives for their work. In the request to establish a settlement, these Native Americans begged the Viceroy to provide them with fifteen Tlaxcaltecan families in order that both groups could settle and be Christianized together. Some of the Spanish witnesses testified that they had been in the province since around 1618 and that they had known the Babane and the Jumano for a long time (Morales 1658; Otalona 1658). News of the petition for settlement caused ripples of anticipation among Native groups in various areas of New Spain and raised fears among farmers and miners (Morales 1658). Local Spanish officials and *encomenderos* objected vehemently to this petition. Their arguments were that (1) these Natives had no pueblo and no Native following, since they had always been *encomendados;* (2) the Natives wished to gather in a pueblo only to return to their barbaric customs and be free to commit all sorts of depredations without fear of punishment; (3) the *encomenderos* provided for all the Natives' physical and spiritual needs, which would not be met if they were in a pueblo; (4) if they were allowed to leave Saltillo they would retire to the mountains, where the *encomenderos* could not reach them; and finally, (5) if these Natives left, others would follow, and the province would be ruined, since the *encomenderos* did not have a labor force to work the farms. If that occurred, they would have to abandon the province. The farmers of Saltillo collectively sent a petition to Viceroy Duque de Albuquerque, and the matter was closed (Aguirre et al. 1673b; Otalona 1658).

This attempt to establish an autonomous Native settlement took place some fifty years after the arrival of the Tlaxcaltecans in the area and the establishment of their pueblo of San Esteban de Tlaxcala.[4] This first move for settlement initiated by Native groups of hunters and gatherers had to be inspired by the realization of the possibilities offered by the Tlaxcaltecan agreement with the Spanish. The request made to the Viceroy for fifteen Tlaxcaltecan families, who would participate in the establishment of the pueblo, leaves little doubt that either the local groups were co-opting the Tlaxcaltecan arrangement with the Spanish, or they were trying to establish satellite pueblos created on the legal basis of a modified Spanish-Tlaxcaltecan charter.

The archival information presently available permits some inferences about the way the request was presented and about its representatives. First, the four Natives involved in the petition represented other unnamed groups who wanted to settle. Apparently the three Babane involved in this request were part of a group of no more than six or seven remaining Babane ((Morales 1658). Both the Babane and the Jumano represented the sole survivors of a larger group of *encomendados* whose members had perished due to the difficulty of their living conditions and the strife between their group and other groups with which they had been housed. Second, the only non-Native mentioned in the proceedings, who was chosen by the Natives as their protector, was Antonio Aleman, a mule driver who had worked for the *encomienda* of Ambrosio de Zepeda from 1654 through 1658 (Otalona 1658).

From the 1658 proceedings it appears that the legal basis for the Natives' petition was their poor treatment and the lack of payment for their labor. On the other hand, the Spanish refusal was founded on the insubstantial Native following (*sequito*) of the petitioners and on the recognized necessity of a controllable and cheap labor force to guarantee the economic survival of the province. The outcome was never in doubt.

1673–1674

For the next fourteen years, Don Marcos, a Babane (Fr. Talavera's letter as transcribed in Gómezgil 1997: 150–151), continued to pursue the matter, and in 1673 the issue was resurrected. In April 1673, Don Marcos, a Jumano, appeared before General Echeberz y Subiza in Saltillo to request settlement in a pueblo. Don Marcos was accompanied by his brother, Don Lacaro Agustin, a Jumano, and by Don Marcos, a Babane. Echeberz y Subiza appointed Fr. Juan Larios, who had recently arrived in the province, as interpreter of the proceedings because of his proficiency in the Mexican (Nahuatl) language (Echeberz y Subiça 1673). Echeberz y Subiza told Don Marcos the Jumano to bring the Natives of his group and following (*nación y séquito*) to discuss the settlement. Don Marcos replied that there were only three people left of his group. Those who sent him to request a pueblo were the Bobole and their allies (*y otros agregados suios*), who lived in the province of Coahuila and the Valley of Buffalo (Agustin 1673).

Echeberz y Subiza convened a meeting of prominent citizens to evaluate the merits of the request and to provide information on the character and intentions of the petitioners. Most of the military and church officials testified that they knew Lacaro Agustin and the other petitioners, and that it was not a bad idea to establish a pueblo for them in Coahuila. The area had promising mining possibilities and needed to be explored, but it would be essential to place a presidio in the area. They were of the opinion that it would not be easy to sustain a pueblo in Coahuila because of the many rebel and non-Christian peoples who inhabited it, and because the Natives were not accustomed to labor for their sustenance, but survived on what the earth provided. Furthermore, they stated, it would be difficult to control the Natives and prevent their return to a sinful and barbaric way of life (Salaçar 1673).

Nicolas Flores, one of the witnesses, declared that he had known Lacaro Agustin since he was a boy and that Lacaro had been raised in Saltillo. He had no Native following except for his brother, or uncle (Don Marcos), who was a party to the petition (Flores 1673). Captain Domingo de Menchaca declared that he knew Agustin and the other Natives. He testified that when he was in Coahuila, before the Spaniards abandoned the area, he had seen many *rancherías* of people who spoke the same language and had the same customs (*de la misma lengua y costumbres*) as those who were petitioning to gather in a pueblo (D. Menchaca 1673).

On June 30, 1673, the petitioners were led to believe that their request would be granted. Lacaro was told to bring before Echeberz y Subiza the Natives who were a part of the request for settlement (Echeberz y Subiça 1673a). Don Lacaro stated that he would get the Bobole and their allies (*agregados*) to come in person and "state their needs as kin that they all were since they understood each other in a mother language and were all natives of the province of Coahuila" ("y juntos pidiriamos do que nos combiese como parientes que somos todos pues nos entendemos en una lengua materna originarios de la dicha probincia de cohaila") (Aguirre et al. 1673a). Lacaro included in the group of petitioners the Bobole, Baia, Contotore, and Tetecore and half of the Momone. Two other very large groups were also joining: the Gueiquesale and the Tiltic y Maigunm. At the next meeting Don Lacaro was accompanied by a Christian Gueiquesale captain by the name of Don Esteban, two non-Christian captains, and twenty-eight Bobole and Temmanar (Aguirre et al. 1673a; Agustin 1673a).

Don Lacaro stated that the Bobole had more than three hundred warriors and that they had been in Coahuila since time immemorial (*desde tiempo ymmemorial*). The Bobole declared that they had lost many people in wars and could not maintain their *ran-cheria* unless they congregated with other groups. Lacaro added that the Bobole had always been loyal to the Spaniards. He stressed the help given by the Bobole to the Spanish during the battle that Don Fernando de Azcué fought against the Cacaxtles[5] and their allies in 1665 (Echeberz y Subiça 1673a). The intervention of fifty Bobole warriors gave the victory to Azcué and made possible the chastisement of the Tetecore and Contotore. (For another version of this conflict, see Chapa and Foster 1997: 55–56.) Don Lacaro also mentioned that the other nation joining in the petition (Gueiquesale or Catujano?) was from the east and that he did not know the boundaries of its lands (Aguirre et al. 1673a; D. Menchaca 1673).

On August 3, 1673, Don Lacaro testified once more before Echeberz y Subiza. He brought along Don Esteban, a Gueiquesale, Don Miguel, a Teimamare, the Bobole captain, a non-Christian, and several other companions. They all declared their wish to settle in pueblos and have the Spaniards establish a presidio and live in the area of Coahuila (Echeberz y Subiça 1673a).

After all the testimonies, the consensus was that Don Lacaro Agustin was a manipulative ladino who incited other groups to rebellion, and that he had nothing to do with the help given to Fernando Azcué. General Echeberz y Subiça asked the Town Council (Cabildo) for a decision on the affair. The Cabildo declared that it was very convenient and useful to establish the pueblo requested by the Natives if the town had the military force and resources to guarantee its survival. Since the creation of such a pueblo would strain the town's resources and cause its ruin, the request was denied (Aguirre et al. 1673, 1673a; Echeberz y Subiça 1673a, 1673b).

In September 1673, Fr. Larios traveled to Guadalajara accompanied by twenty Native Americans (Ardenol 1673a). This group of Natives came to plead their case for settlement before the Audiencia de Guadalajara on behalf of twenty-four groups. Among the Native visitors were Don Lazaro Agustin, Don Marcos, and a Native named Juan. These Native ambassadors were protesting the offenses committed against them by the *encomenderos*, including the use of military force by the officials in Saltillo to prevent Fr. Larios and the Native groups from moving into Coahuila (Ardenol 1673a: 40–42). During their three-month sojourn in Guadalajara the Native Americans were housed at the Convent of San Francisco, where eight Natives were publicly and solemnly baptized. The last of the baptismal ceremonies took place on November 27, 1673 (Ardenol 1673a: 37–38). The following day, Fr. Larios, Fr. Peñasco, Fr. Manuel de la Cruz, and the Natives returned to Saltillo.

The trip to Guadalajara resulted in part from a formal complaint made by Captain Francisco de Barbarigo against the Alcalde Mayor of Saltillo, Juan de Maya. In response to the complaint, the Audiencia de Guadalajara sent Don Martin Moreno, Don Antonio Balcarcel, and Don Miguel Thomas de Ascoide to Saltillo to investigate the charges (Ardenol 1673a: 46). In December 1673, these men testified to the conflicts they had witnessed in Saltillo and to the tense situation among the friars, the Native Americans, the *encomenderos,* and the Saltillo authorities. Balcarcel, who held personal talks with the Native representatives, stated that together the twenty-four nations mustered about 3,700 warriors and over 12,000 people ("y reducido a numero alto ser tres mil y setecientos yndios de armas en que se supone y reconosse este testigo seran mas de dose mill almas") (Ardenol 1673a: 43).

When Fr. Larios returned to Saltillo with Fr. Francisco Peñasco and Fr. Manuel de la Cruz in November 1673, he had been granted official permission to missionize in Coahuila (Ardenol 1673; Mohedano 1673). The inquiries ordered by the Audiencia de Guadalajara apparently led to a change of attitude. On December 12, 1673, following orders from the governor of Nueva Vizcaya, Maestro de Campo Don Joseph Garcia de Salcedo ordered Captain Francisco de Elizondo, Justicia Mayor de Saltillo, to travel to Coahuila to give possession of the lands requested and granted by the Crown to Don Marcos the Babane and his allies the Tetecore, Huiquechale, Obaya, and Contotore (Elizondo 1674: 65–66). On December 30 the Natives who had returned from Guadalajara pledged peace and were given thirty *fanegas*[6] (seventy-seven bushels) of corn and five heifers (Barbarigo 1674: 102). Despite these events, in December the governor of Saltillo ordered presidial troops to subdue nine rebel Native groups. On December 29 the troops vanquished the rebels, took their possessions, and reduced the males to slavery (Larios 1674a: 136).

On January 12, 1674, Captain Francisco Elizondo departed for Coahuila with thirty men to establish pueblos for Don Marcos the Babane and for his allies (Elizondo 1674: 65). When Elizondo arrived at Nuestra Señora de Guadalupe (Monclova), 35 leagues (91 miles) from Saltillo, he learned that the friars and the Natives had moved further inland because of the high incidence of smallpox. Elizondo sent a courier to inform Fr. Larios that he would wait four days to meet them and to give official possession of the lands to the Natives (Elizondo 1674: 66). By January 24, Elizondo had not heard from Fr. Larios, and he decided to search for the friars. He continued northward to Santa Cruz de las Peñuelas, halfway between the Nadadores and the Sabinas rivers. From Santa Cruz he traveled about 14 leagues (36.4 miles) northward to a place where he was intercepted by two Xicocoge, who informed him that Don Marcos, his allies, and the friars were on the Río Sabinas (Elizondo 1674: 67). Elizondo's party proceeded to the Río Sabinas. On January 26, they stopped 60 leagues (156 miles) north of Saltillo upon being met by two Natives who carried a letter from Fr. Larios. Larios reported that on January 22 he had arrived at a *ranchería* of the Bobole, Gueiquechale, Tiltic and Mayhuam, and other allied groups. These groups were camped about 10 leagues (26 miles) beyond the Río Sabinas and east toward the Rio Grande because they were suffering from smallpox. Since Elizondo's deadline had expired, and Fr. Larios did not wish to forsake the sick, he stayed with them, but promised that as soon as the epidemic subsided he would place the Natives in pueblos and inform Elizondo (Elizondo 1674: 68–69).

However, when Fr. Larios learned from his couriers that Elizondo had not departed for Saltillo he traveled 4 leagues (10.4 miles) further to San Ildefonso, where he arrived January 23 (Elizondo 1674: 68; Larios 1674: 111). Captain Elizondo proceeded 14 leagues north of the Río Sabinas and joined Fr. Larios and several Native captains at San Ildefonso de la Paz. On January 28, according to Elizondo, they were visited by the captains of the Gueiquechale, Bobole, Manos Prietas, Pinanaca, Obaya, Babaymare, Zupulame, Omomone, and Xicocoge. Fr. Larios, on the other hand, states that they were visited by the principal "leaders" of the Gueiquechale, Bobole, Xicocoge, Obaya, Xiupulame, Manos Prietas, Bacorama, Omomone, and Baniamamar and later by the Mescale, Jumee, Cabesa, Contotor, Tetecora, Bausari, Manos Coloradas, Teimamar, and others (Barbarigo 1674: 112). These Natives were interviewed with the help of Don Marcos and Don Lasaro Agustin, who spoke Castilian, Mexican, and apparently the languages of those groups (Elizondo 1674: 69). They reiterated their wish to settle, but stated that, for the moment, they were divided into several groups because of the epidemic and the lack of food. Fr. Larios reported that they subsisted on mescal, the tuna of the prickly pear, small nuts and oak acorns, fish, deer, and buffalo. They lived in round huts lined with straw and covered with buffalo pelts skillfully prepared to be impermeable to water (Barbarigo 1674: 112). Some of the people were on the Rio Grande, 20 leagues (52 miles) from San Ildefonso, hunting and jerking buffalo meat. Many others were in various spots looking for food while several warriors guarded their belongings at the place where they had congregated with Fr. Larios (Elizondo 1674: 69–70). The following day (January 29) Elizondo counted the people: there were 543 adult women and children and 106 warriors. Fr. Larios baptized 63 Native children and buried an elderly woman.

Captain Elizondo notified Don Marcos and his allies to gather on the Río Sabinas to take possession of the lands they had selected. Don Marcos made it clear that the number of people to be settled far exceeded those present. He stated that he needed more time to gather those who were settled ("com mas gente de la suya de la que esta en aquella parte que la de demas esta fixos y an menester mas tiempo para salir a ella") (Elizondo 1674: 71). After the religious ceremonies Elizondo gave the Native captains their staffs and admonished them to remain peaceful. He also told them to share their food with the friars because the latter had no Spanish foods and were eating mescal ("y acudiessen a su corriente con algun sustento de sus comidas por quanto se allan sin ningun de las de los espanoles comiendo mescale") (Elizondo 1674: 71–72).

On February 1, 1674, Elizondo reported that he had given to Don Marcos and his allies the lands along the course of the Río Sabinas above and below a divide between hills that is next to the river, and beyond and northward of the place they called "where the Tetecores were killed" (Elizondo 1674: 74). The lands extended about 8 leagues north-south from the divide and downstream to a small hill shaped like a hat, which is located at the crossing of the path that led to the San Ildefonso settlement. This pueblo, which was 14 leagues (36.4 miles) south of San Ildefonso, was called Santa Rosa de Santa Maria (de la Cruz 1674; Elizondo 1674: 74–75). As a sign of possession the Natives pulled grass, dug dirt, sprinkled water on the earth, and marked with stones the square area where the church was to be built.

Captain Elizondo, clearly at the behest of Fr. Larios, made several recommendations to ensure the success of the enterprise. First, he asked that no Spaniard be allowed to enter that area, particularly those from Saltillo and Nuevo León, because the Natives abhorred the citizens of those areas due to the punishments and deaths they caused the Natives.

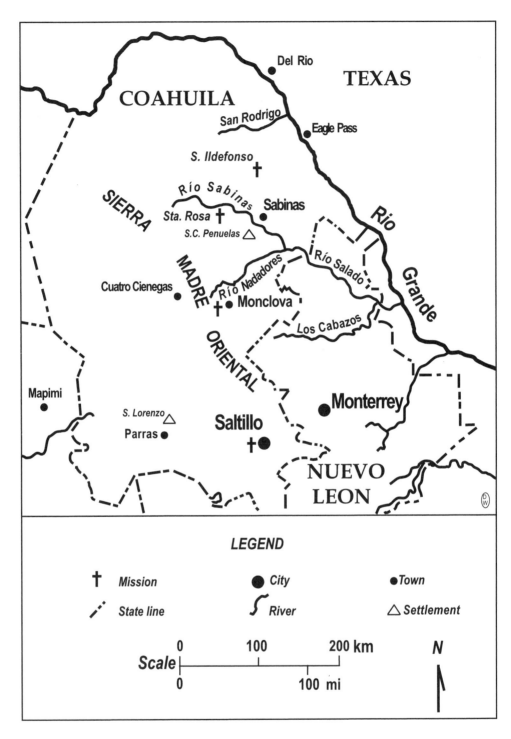

FIGURE I.I
Map of Coahuila showing places mentioned in the text.

Second, he asked that no Spaniard be allowed to hunt buffalo in the area. This was a very sensitive issue among the Natives and they defended their hunting rights by the force of arms ("por ser materia mui sensible para ellos, y que afuerza de armas defienden de otras naciones"). Third, he asked that no Native be again subjected to *encomienda* since the *encomenderos* did not reduce them, but only exploited them (Elizondo 1674: 72–73), and fourth, that the missionaries be provided with food, seed, and farming utensils. On March 2, 1674, Fr. Larios sent a letter, accompanied by testimony of their missionary work, to the Commissary General in Guadalajara. This letter was hand-carried by Fr. Peñasco, who traveled to Guadalajara to request help for the new conversions in Coahuila (Larios 1674).

The events surrounding the establishment of the mission-settlement of Santa Rosa were also reported by Fr. Manuel de la Cruz (1674). According to his report, on February 9, 1674, Fr. Larios and Fr. Peñasco went to Saltillo to report on their *entrada* in Coahuila. Fr. Manuel remained in Coahuila with only 178 Obaya and Bobole because 512 Gueiquesale asked to leave the area due to the serious epidemic of smallpox afflicting them (*muy enfermos de biruelas*). The Gueiquesale promised to return by the half-moon of March. The Obaya and a number of the Bobole, who remained with Fr. Manuel, but who were also suffering from smallpox, traveled with the friar to another area 5.5 leagues (13 miles) southwest of the Río Sabinas, where Fr. Manuel founded the mission-settlement of Santa Rosa de Santa Maria. The pueblo was near a beautiful spring and the area had many nut trees (*nogales morenos*), pines, and white cottonwoods (*alamos*). Fr. Manuel and his Native companions built a chapel from tree branches and *zacate* (green grass) and a dwelling for the friars. On March 20 Fr. Larios and Captain Barbarigo arrived at Santa Rosa with much-needed food and other supplies for the three thousand Natives congregated in the area (Barbarigo 1674a; de la Cruz 1674).

On September 15, 1674, Fr. Larios (Figueroa Torres 1963: 67; Larios 1674a: 135; 1674b: 145) confirmed that between January and February 1674, the friars had established two mission-settlements[7] (*poblaciones*): S. Ildefonso de la Paz, located 14 leagues (36.4 miles) north of the Río Sabinas, 20 leagues (52 miles) south of the Rio Grande, and over 70 leagues (182 miles) from Saltillo; and Santa Rosa de Santa Maria, located 80 leagues (208 miles) north of Saltillo and 40 leagues (104 miles) west of the Rio Grande. The two mission-settlements were established principally for the Gueiquezale and the Bobole, but in them were aggregated thirty-two different Native groups. Twenty-two other groups from Nueva Vizcaya and Nueva Galícia had also declared peace and were joining the friars (Larios 1674a: 135). At S. Ildefonso there were 512 Gueiquesale and 178 additional Natives, some of whom were Bobole, Obayo, Tiltique, Tiltiquimayo, Pinanaca, and Mayhuam (de la Cruz 1674; Steck 1932: 6). Information from the various documents indicates that the Babane, Bobole, Gueiquesale, Obayo, and Manos Prietas were present at Santa Rosa and at San Ildefonso during the spring of 1674.

The friars reported that the conditions at the mission-settlements were very bad: they had little to eat but mescal and roots, and their tattered robes would soon force them to wear buffalo and deerskins (de la Cruz 1674; Steck 1932: 16–17). Captain Barbarigo stated that the friars sent him donkeys to be returned with flour and ground corn, but when the friars ran out of these foods they ate roots of *lechugilla*,[8] *tule*,[9] and *sotol*[10] (Barbarigo 1674a; Figueroa Torres 1963: 96). Although it is clear that the conditions were not good, especially for the Natives affected by smallpox, the friars' reports seem to reflect more their own difficulties than those of the local inhabitants, particularly because the Native groups actually supplied the friars with food (Elizondo 1674: 71–72).

On March 20, 1674, when Fr. Larios arrived at Santa Rosa and realized that the Bobole had left the settlement, he asked Fr. Manuel to find them and persuade them to return to the pueblo. On March 22, Fr. Manuel departed Santa Rosa and traveled 12 leagues (31.2 miles) to an arroyo where the Bobole were camped. Six days later Fr. Manuel returned to Santa Rosa with the Bobole. One day after his arrival Fr. Larios ordered him to the north side of the Rio Grande to look for the Gueiquesale, and Fr. Manuel left the following day (March 30 or 31?) (de la Cruz 1674: 119–120).

In his letter of May 29, 1674, Fr. Manuel described his trip to the north side of the Rio Grande. The letter makes it clear that he was reluctant to make the trip (de la Cruz 1674). He left with five Bobole and traveled northward for four and a half days and covered about 40 leagues (104 miles) to reach the Rio Grande. The group crossed the Rio Grande in two stages. The crossing was difficult and disturbed the horse or mule Fr. Manuel was riding. After crossing the Rio Grande Fr. Manuel traveled eastward for three days and arrived near a mountain the Natives called Dacate,[11] a word that in Castilian meant "noses" ("camine al salir del sol dejando de ir acia el norte y a los tres dias llege junto de una sierra q. los yndios llamam dacate q. en nuestro edioma es lo proprio q. narices") (de la Cruz 1674: 120). Near Dacate Fr. Manuel was intercepted by a Native who warned him to leave that path because the Patagua-Ocane and Catujane were coming to arrest him and kill his companions. These groups had been told to do so by a devil that appeared to them in visible form ("y me dijo q. dejase aquel camino porq. los yndios Pataguas-Ocanes y catujanes abisados de un demonio q. se les aparece en forma bisible"). Fr. Manuel changed course toward the north and hid in an arroyo for three days, surviving on reed roots ("y despidiendose de mi bolbi a caminar acia a el norte y escondido en un aroyo estube tres dias") (de la Cruz 1674: 120). While in hiding he sent one of the Bobole guides to reconnoiter the land. On his return the guide reported that the Bobole who were missing from Santa Rosa were camped about 6 leagues (15.6 miles) upstream and northward on the same arroyo.

Pleased with the news, Fr. Manuel left his hiding place at about midnight and arrived at the Bobole camp around 9:00 A.M.[12] The Bobole informed him that the Gueiquesale "leader" was staying, with all his people, 8 leagues (20.8 miles) distant from the Bobole camp. Fr. Manuel told the Bobole how he had been warned about the hostile attitude of the Patagua-Ocane and Catujane. The Bobole appeared to be rather astonished and immediately sent scouts to survey the land while Fr. Manuel sent a Bobole to warn the Gueiquesale. Upon learning of his plight, Don Esteban left camp with such haste that he reached the Bobole camp before sunset. Don Esteban brought along ninety-eight warriors[13] well supplied with bows and arrows, and displaying body decoration for war. They

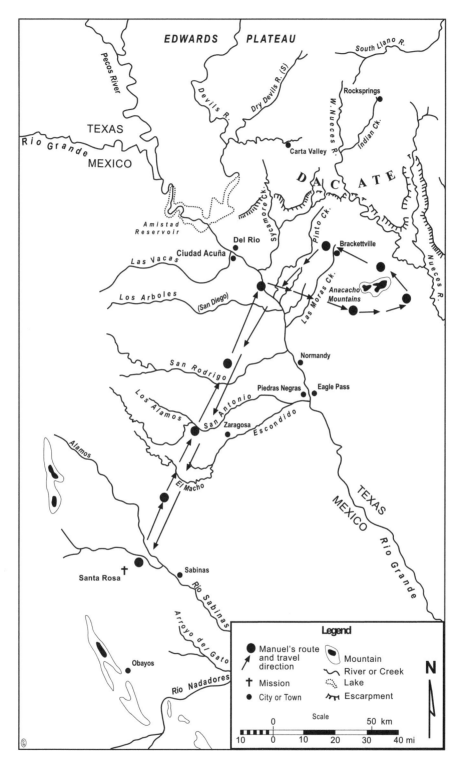

FIGURE I.2
Route of the 1674 trip of Fr. Manuel de la Cruz.

were wearing only a small piece of deerskin (*gamuça*) over their sexual organs and a hide shield (*adarga de cuero*). Their arms and chests were decorated with streaks of red, yellow, and white. On their heads they had crowns made of mesquite leaves and others of leaves of *estofiate silvestre* (a medicinal herb). Above the crowns of leaves they wore beautiful feathers. When the Gueiquesale arrived at the Bobole camp they sat down and Fr. Manuel embraced Don Esteban, who asked Fr. Manuel the reason for his visit. Fr. Manuel declared that he had come to look for them and to find out why the Gueiquesale had not returned to Santa Rosa. Don Esteban reassured Fr. Manuel that he and his people wished to be Christians, and stated that as long as Fr. Manuel had come for them they would depart with him (de la Cruz 1674: 21).

Meanwhile, the scouts who had gone to patrol the land reported that the enemies were still pursuing Fr. Manuel and that they had 180 warriors. Upon receiving such news all the Natives got very excited and told Fr. Manuel to stay in the camp (*rancho*) with the women and children while the warriors proceeded to meet the enemy. Fr. Manuel refused their offer, stating that he would not abandon his brothers. Considering Fr. Manuel's decision proof of his friendship, they declared that they would rather die than abandon him. Fr. Manuel, Don Esteban, and 147 bowmen left the Bobole camp about 10:00 P.M. and traveled until they detected the enemy. Then they stopped, and at sunrise appraised each other's forces. The Gueiquesale and Bobole warriors recognized the superiority in numbers of their adversaries. Fr. Manuel showed them Christ's image (a cross or picture of Christ on the cross) and told them God would help them. The last thing the warriors did before battle was to prepare their bows. Then with a horrific noise they attacked the enemy with great valor. Unable to resist, the enemy abandoned the field and hid in the Sierra Dacate. The Gueiquesale and the Bobole killed seven men and captured four women and three boys, whom they did not kill due to Fr. Manuel's intervention.

After their victory the Bobole and Gueiquesale showed the surrounding area to Fr. Manuel, telling him the names of the arroyos, mountains, and hills ("y muy alegres me llebaran por toda aquella tierra ensenandomela y diciendome los nombres de los arroyos, sierras y lomas") (de la Cruz 1674: 22). They returned to the Bobole camp and the following day Fr. Manuel left with the Bobole to join the Gueiquesale *ranchería*. They traveled two days through beautiful prairies (*caminando dos dias por unas ermosas lanadas*) (de la Cruz 1674: 22). The prairies they traversed, as well as all the land Fr. Manuel had crossed on the north side of the Rio Grande, were very bountiful and covered with countless buffalo. The streams had plenty of fish, shrimp, and turtles (de la Cruz 1674: 22).

Fr. Manuel was well received at the Gueiquesale *ranchería*. The Gueiquesale women put on a dance, as was their custom, to express their pleasure with the friar's visit, and the following day they all departed. There were 733 people, counting children and adults. Fr. Manuel stated that he had spent twenty-one days north of the Rio Grande. The group crossed the Rio Grande in two stages at a wide and beautiful crossing. Fr. Manuel reported that the river water reached only the belly of the animal he was riding. At this crossing in the middle of the river, there was a sandy island with beautiful beaches (de la Cruz 1674: 22).

After crossing the Rio Grande they traveled for two days and reached an arroyo where 166 Pinanaca and Tiltiqmaya were camped. The Natives welcomed Fr. Manuel and the women prepared a feast in his honor. The following day they continued their journey, traveling seven days through beautiful lands and arroyos until they reached a river they called Río Nueces. Fr. Manuel explained that the river was so named because the trees produced a great quantity of large nuts. From the Río Nueces they traveled one day to a spring located in a marsh between some hills. Here they found 82 Babusarigame, who welcomed the friar. The following day they all departed for Santa Rosa. Both male and female children ran ahead of the friar, gathering small beadlike fruits that grew in thick bushes. With great joy they brought them to the friar, saying in their language, "Here, father, these are for you to eat" (de la Cruz 1674: 123). Fr. Manuel accepted them and thanked God for this blessing. After crossing several beautiful and wide plains and many pleasant arroyos the group reached a stream located about 10 leagues (26 miles) from Santa Rosa. The Native travelers were tired and asked to rest there two or three days. Fr. Manuel proceeded to Santa Rosa, where he met Fr. Larios and Captain Barbarigo.

The day after Fr. Manuel's arrival they finished an adobe church, which had a sacristy and a *zacate* (grass) dwelling for the friars. On that same day, Fr. Peñasco arrived from Guadalajara, having tried, unsuccessfully, to see his Franciscan superiors and obtain support for the mission-settlements. Three days later Fr. Manuel accompanied Barbarigo to Saltillo to request food donations. Captain Barbarigo, personally aware of the difficulties the friars were experiencing, gave Fr. Manuel flour and corn. After two days in Saltillo, Fr. Manuel returned to the pueblo with food supplies (de la Cruz 1674: 123).

Fr. Manuel closed his letter with an appeal to his Franciscan superiors for help with supplies as well as a vehement request for action against the *encomenderos* who would not set the Natives free to settle their lands. Fr. Manuel reported an incident that had just taken place: two male and two female Natives had left the Hacienda de Patos, owned by Don Agustin Echeberz y Subiza, the future first Marques de Aguayo. Upon learning of their departure, Don Agustin sent three people in pursuit who hunted down the Natives as if they were runaway slaves (*como se fueran esclavos fugitivos*). Fr. Manuel concluded by saying that, if the actions of the *encomenderos* were not curbed, all their missionary work among the Native populations would be lost (de la Cruz 1674: 124).

In July, Fr. Peñasco wrote to his superiors from Saltillo to relate the events that occurred during May and June. From Fr. Peñasco's letter it appears he left Guadalajara April 10 and arrived at Santa Rosa May 10, 1674 (Barbarigo 1674a: 130). Eight days after his arrival at Santa Rosa (May 18), Fr. Larios sent him in search of the Manos Prietas (Peñasco 1674: 127). Fr. Peñasco found them 4 leagues (10.4 miles) north of the Rio Grande and about 50 leagues (130 miles) from Santa Rosa. The Manos Prietas offered him buffalo meat, which they had in quantity. Fr. Peñasco asked them to move closer to Santa Rosa in order that he could catechize them, and they agreed to do so within eight days (Peñasco 1674: 127).

Meanwhile, the Manos Prietas told Fr. Peñasco about another group, the Giorica (Yorica), who lived 8 leagues (20.8 miles) closer to the interior (*mas adentro*). Fr. Peñasco dispatched two ambassadors (*dos embaxadores*) to the Yorica to inform them of his presence. The Yorica told the ambassadors they did not want to leave their land, where they were doing very well and had plenty of food and supplies ("q. no querian salir a parte alguna por allarse mui bien en aquella tierra, adonde no les faltaba la comida, y sustento necesario") (Peñasco 1674: 127). Undaunted, Fr. Peñasco dispatched another ambassador to make it clear that he was not trying to persuade them to leave their land, but to teach them about God. Fr. Peñasco added that if his words made sense to them they should come and embrace God; otherwise they should stay where they were because God did not force people to serve him. The Yorica treated the third ambassador with more affection than they had the first two and gave him a Quezale (Gueiquesale) boy they kept captive. Furthermore, they told the ambassador that in two days' time they would come to see Fr. Peñasco, which they did (Peñasco 1674: 127).

The Manos Prietas, their bodies festively decorated, met the Yorica on the way. Later they held a dance for the Yorica as a sign of peace and exchanged bows and arrows to solidify the peace commitment ("una danza, o baile, q. es señal de paz, y trocaron unos con otros arcos y flechas para maior firmeza de la paz") (Peñasco 1674: 127–128). The following day Fr. Peñasco told them that God and the King wanted them to settle and be peaceful. With that intent, the King would give them corn to plant and oxen to sustain themselves. He stated that the friars were sent by God and the King to teach them the Christian doctrine and to defend them against those Spaniards whom the Natives intensely disliked because of the reports they continually received of the tyrannical behavior suffered by those closer to the Spaniards: "defenderlos de los españoles (aquien tienen notable aborrecimiento, por las noticias que les dan de las tiranias que usan con los de la tierra afuera)" (Peñasco 1674: 127; parentheses in the original).

The gift of the Gueiquesale boy marked a particular occasion and was matched by the elaborate reception prepared by the Manos Prietas for the Yorica. The care taken in the preparation of the reception implies that these two groups may not have been well acquainted or were not on good terms before this date. This assumption is reinforced by the Manos Prietas's offering of bows and arrows to the Yorica. The offering of the boy constituted a particularly friendly gesture to erase previous conflicts, and a shrewd political move, indicating that the Yorica knew of the close relationships between the Manos Prietas and the Gueiquesale and between those groups and the Spanish. The ritualized dance, the exchange of bows and arrows, and the offering of the young boy also imply that both groups recognized and accepted similar hospitality and friendship rituals.

Persuaded by Fr. Peñasco, about 300 Yorica departed with him and the Manos Prietas for Santa Rosa. About 70 Yorica remained behind to care for some of their people who were sick, with the understanding that as soon as they recovered they would join their kinfolk (Peñasco 1674: 128). Fr. Peñasco stated that at Santa Rosa the friars had gathered about 3,200 people, who were settled in radii of 2, 3, 5, and 7 leagues (5.2, 7.8, 13, and 18.2 miles). At the time (June) they were subsisting on the large, productive tuna (prickly pear) fields in the area, but, as Fr. Peñasco pointed out, if the friars did not get other food supplies before the tuna ran out, all the Natives would leave in search of sustenance.

Disillusioned and hungry, they would tell the friars that the friars had wronged them by convincing them to gather at Santa Rosa and promising food without delivering (Peñasco 1674: 128).

In July Barbarigo wrote a letter to the Franciscan Commissary that confirmed the problems facing the friars at Santa Rosa. Barbarigo, who returned to Saltillo with Fr. Manuel on May 22, 1674, reported that the friars needed three more religious workers to be able to handle so many people, particularly because they could not remain together due to the lack of food. The friars were obliged to follow the Natives, who moved every three or four days to look for food. They would set up a *ranchería,* but when there were no more roots to be had, hunger forced them to move again. For this reason, the friars often stayed apart 20 to 30 leagues (52 to 78 miles). Barbarigo reported that despite the laws, the *encomenderos* were continuing to enslave the natives (Barbarigo 1674a: 133). In late July or early August (when the tuna ran out?), the mission-settlement of Santa Rosa was robbed and destroyed by Native groups, but the friars remained in the area.

In September 1674, Fr. Larios was planning to establish four other settlements to accommodate the large number of people who wished to settle. These settlements were to be located in Mapimi, San Lorenzo, San Pedro, and Cuatro Cienegas. The families who were going to occupy these settlements were expected to move in by November 1674 (Larios 1674a: 138). Given this program, Larios was understandably desperate for funds as well as food and other supplies. Fr. Larios was aware that Don Antonio de Balcarcel had been appointed Alcalde Mayor of Coahuila, and it appears that Fr. Larios wanted to have these settlements in place before Balcarcel took office.

On October 31, 1674, Fr. Dionisio de San Buenaventura stated that he and Fr. Esteban Martinez had arrived at Santa Rosa in early August to work with Fr. Larios. When they reached Santa Rosa the place had been abandoned and destroyed, and about six hundred Natives had moved 15 leagues (39 miles) farther inland. The two friars joined them while awaiting Fr. Larios, who had gone to see the governor of Parral (Figure 3.1) to request the release of the men, women, and children the governor had imprisoned in December 1673 (de San Buenaventura 1674: 141; Larios 1674a; 1674b: 143). Fr. Dionisio reported that Balcarcel was to take office in November. The friars were so apprehensive about the Natives' reaction to this new *entrada* in Coahuila that they had gathered in Saltillo to see what transpired and to get food donations (*limosna*) (de San Buenaventura 1674: 142). Their preoccupation was justified: Balcarcel's *entrada* with a group of Spanish settlers would be disquieting for the Native groups, who had just received title (*merced y título de tierras*) (Elizondo 1674: 65) to lands around the area of the town of Nuestra Señora de Guadalupe (Monclova).

On November 18, 1674, Balcarcel left Saltillo to occupy his post as Alcalde Mayor of Coahuila, and on November 23 he arrived at Monclova. Balcarcel was welcomed by a delegation of sixty Natives belonging to the Bobole, Yorica, Xicocole, Gusiquesale (Gueiquesale), Catujano, and Jacafe. Ruins of a previous European settlement could be seen in the area. Balcarcel cleared the ground, erected some buildings, and started work on the acequia and the church. By December 6, the settlers were planting wheat (Portillo

1886: 68–69). On December 8, 1674, Balcarcel reestablished the town, which was already known as Nuestra Señora de Guadalupe. The town's lands had a radius of 6 leagues (15.6 miles). Near the town Balcarcel later founded the Native pueblo of San Miguel de Luna (Portillo 1886: 69). This pueblo was originally intended for several Native groups, but shortly after its establishment it became home only to the Bobole, the Gueiquesale, and some of their allies.

On November 28, 1674, Fr. Larios and Fr. Manuel went in search of the Bobole and their allies who were at the Río Sabinas. Fr. Larios stated that in February (1675) he planned to travel to the north side of the Rio Grande to visit Don Esteban, who was there with all his people. He was also sending another friar to the Catujano to continue to catechize them and to make arrangements for the trip Balcarcel was to make north of the Rio Grande (Larios 1674b: 149).

On December 20, 1674, Fr. Larios and Fr. Manuel de la Cruz brought before Balcarcel Juan de la Cruz, a Bobole; Francisco, a Gicocoge; and a non-Christian Yorica, who, with their people, were gathered on the Río Sabinas. These Natives declared that for some time they had been requesting help from the authorities in Mexico and Nueva Viscaya. With that intent, some had traveled to Guadalajara and were pleased that finally their petitions for religious and material support were being heard (Portillo 1886: 71–72). They all expressed the wish to settle in pueblos.

On December 30, 1674, Fr. Larios provided his Franciscan superiors with a *Memoria* (Larios 1674c) that included the names of the groups that had pledged obedience to the Crown as of that date. His letter recapitulates some of the events of the year that was about to close. Fr. Larios reported on the unhappy events at Santa Rosa, where only Don Esteban, the Gueiquezale, and Don Marcos, the Babane, had remained. Don Esteban was very sick, and it appears that Don Marcos and some of his people, mostly ladinos,[14] were responsible for the destruction of Santa Rosa: they had taken all the things from the sacristy and set fire to the *jacale* (grass hut) of the friars (Larios 1674b: 144–145).

Fr. Larios went on to explain why Native groups moved so frequently and why the friars were compelled to follow them. He stated that because they were very numerous and lived on gathered roots and on hunted animals, in about fifteen days they depleted the area where they camped, and were forced to move to other areas. Thus, the friars could not erect permanent buildings and stay with the Native groups in one place. They were like gypsies who did not have permanently located dwellings ("en quince dias atalan la tierra donde se hallan de rayces y luego les es fuerça levantar su ranchería y andarse a otro paraje, y desta suerte no nos es possible hacer mansion en parte alguna con ellos, porque son como gitanos q. no tienen vivienda situada") (Larios 1674b: 144).

In his *Memoria* (Larios 1674c) Fr. Larios listed the coalitions, their "leaders," and the Native membership of each. The Bobole coalition, under Captain Joan de la Cruz, included the Bobole proper and the Xicocosse, Jumane, Bauane (Babane), Xupulame, Yorica, Xianco cadam, Yergiba, and Bacaranan (Larios 1674c). Although there is no later list for the Bobole coalition, the Bagname, Bibit, Geniocane, Gicocoge, Jumee, and Yorica are mentioned as allies of the Bobole in 1675 (Portillo 1886: 128).

The Gueiquesale coalition, under Don Esteban, included the Hueyquetzale (Gueiquesale) proper and the Manos Prietas, Bacoram, Pinanacam, Cacaxte, Coniane, Ovaya, Tetecora, Contotore, Tocaymamare, Saesser, Teneymamar, Codam (Oodam?), Guiguigoa, Eguapit, Tocamomom, Huhuygam, Doaquioydacam, Cocuytzam, Aquita doydacam, Babury, Dedepo, Soromet, and Teymamare (Larios 1674c).

The third coalition was under Don Fabian and included the Mayo, Babusarigame, Bamarimamare, Cabesas, Bauiasmamare, Colorado, Pies de Venado, Igo quib, and Toque (Larios 1674c). The members of this coalition acknowledged the authority of Don Esteban. The fourth and last coalition group was under the influence of Captain Miguel, a Catujano, and included the Catujano proper and the Bahanero, Chacahuale, Toarma, Masiabe, Madmeda, Mabibit, Milihae, Ape, Pachaque, Tilyhay, Xumez, Garafe, and Mexcale (Larios 1674c).

Fr. Larios's lists, as published by Alessio Robles (1938: 232, 242) and Griffen (1969: 88), differ from the original: some Native names are shown with a different spelling, and the Xumez are omitted from the Catujano list. From the events of 1658 and 1673, it is clear that these groups stated their allegiance to Fr. Larios and established these coalitions sometime before the arrival of Balcarcel.

After Balcarcel took possession of Monclova he received a series of Native ambassadorial delegations that came to pledge obedience and declare their intent to be peaceful and settle in pueblos. Balcarcel's offer to establish Native pueblos under Spanish leadership and with Spanish economic and military help, which matched the Natives' desire for settlements and continued the work of the friars, met with overwhelming Native response. Balcarcel was unprepared for the response, particularly because the number of people involved was much greater than anticipated. He had neither the economic nor the military resources to accommodate all the Native people willing to settle. Also, these ambassadorial delegations continued to arrive at Monclova to discuss the conditions of settlement, and the small Spanish settlement was overwhelmed with the continuous flow of Native Americans. Spanish settlers, fearful of the Native presence, began to leave the area (Portillo 1886: 130).

The lists of Native groups provided by Fr. Larios include groups that did not appear before Balcarcel to pay homage, and were not included in the lists given by Juan de la Cruz, Don Esteban, or Captain Miguel. Don Fabian does not appear as the spokesman for a coalition in the later lists. Don Esteban came in the name of his group and as representative of the following groups: Manos Prietas, Bocora, Siaexer, Pinanaca, Escabaca, Cacaste, Cocobipta, Cocomaque, Oodame, Contotore, Colorado, Babiamare, and Taimamare (Portillo 1886: 77). Captain Miguel, a Christian Catujano, appeared on behalf of his group and as representative of his allies the Tilijae, Ape, Jumee, Pachuque, and Toamare (Portillo 1886: 81). Later, Captain Miguel brought before Balcarcel the captains of the Bajare, Pachaque, and Jumee (Portillo 1886: 96). Also, it appears that the early allies of Don Marcos, the Babane (Elizondo 1674), were all members of the Gueiquezale coalition, except for the members of the Babane proper, who were members of the Bobole coalition.

On January 18, Balcarcel welcomed Francisco, a Bagname, who was accompanied by eighteen warriors; three women; Mapo, a Bagname captain; and Yosame carboan, a Siano captain[15] (Portillo 1886: 83–84). On January 26, 1675, Balcarcel received the visit of Pablo, a Manos Prietas, who was accompanied by eight members of his group, the Gueiquesale, BapacoraPinanaca (Bacopora and Pinanaca), and Espopolame (Portillo 1886: 85–86). On April 22, 1675, Balcarcel received Don Salvador, a Bobosarigame, who came accompanied by Don Bernabe, a Contotore, and by Don Esteban, who was, by then, called Capitán Grande by the other Natives (Portillo 1886: 95–96).

This series of ambassadorial delegations provides some information about Native power relationships and the various coalitions and their member groups. The order of appearance before Balcarcel is as follows: the Gueiquesale and their allies; the Catujano and their allies; the Contotore; the Bagname and the Siano; and the Manos Prietas, who came as allies of the Gueiquesale and with two groups allied with the Gueiquesale (Bacora and Pinanaca). The Manos Prietas also brought along the Espopolame, not mentioned in the coalition of Don Esteban, but recorded as Xupulame, a member of the Bobole coalition, in December 1674. The Manos Prietas had alliances, or friendship ties, with groups belonging to the Gueiquesale and the Bobole macro-spheres of influence. This indicates a primary alliance (micro-social) with the Xupulame (and probably other groups), and an alliance with the Bobole at a macro-social level. The Manos Prietas alliance with the Gueiquesale appears to have been also a primary alliance. The same would hold true for the alliance between the Bacora and the Pinanaca (micro-social) and the alliance of the Bacora, the Pinanaca, and the Gueiquesale (macro-social). Quite possibly, these alliances were restricted to certain spheres of social and economic interaction.

The next round of ambassadorial delegations started with the Catujano and their allies, followed by the Bobosarigame (who came accompanied by Don Esteban and Don Bernabe, a Contotore), followed, once again, by the Catujano and their allies. Don Bernabe appeared to be an adjunct to Don Esteban, a Gueiquesale. The Bobosarigame, who in December 1674 appeared within the following of Don Fabian, accepted Don Esteban's authority, quite likely via the Contotore. This implies a closer relationship between the Bobosarigame and the Contotore (micro-social), and an alliance between both these groups and the Gueiquesale at a macro-social level.

The Catujano brought before Balcarcel the captains of the Ape, Tilijae, Bajare, Jumee, and Pachaque. Only the representative of the Toamare, listed as a Catujano ally in January, did not visit Balcarcel. In their visits to Balcarcel the Catujano representatives were never accompanied by the Gueiquesale or the Bobole. This confirms the independence of the Catujano coalition from the other two coalitions.

Two other groups visited Balcarcel: the Bagname and the Siano, who asked to be settled with the Bobole. They do not appear to have considered the Gueiquesale their friends or to have had an alliance with them. Their relationship to the Catujano, if there was one, could have been via the Bobole. Being inhabitants of the Dacate area, as they stated, they were probably being squeezed by the peoples of Don Esteban's coalition, as indicated by the statements made by the people encountered by the Bosque-Larios expedition (Chapter 2). Some of the Catujano groups (Ape, Jumee, and Bibit or Mabibit) seem to have had a closer relationship with the Bobole, likely via the Yorica. These series of interlocking ties at various structural tiers and within micro- or macro-coalitions reflect the particular and timely concerns of each group. Quite likely such concerns determined the lifespan of specific coalition arrangements and the membership in those arrangements.

The process of aggregation through coalitions and alliances is noted among the prehispanic Tlaxcaltecans (Corona 1988: 66–69). Although in the Tlaxcaltecan case Corona refers to "clans" and "tribes," he points out that the political structure was organized around an individual, who was viewed as the supreme expression of the community and was the eldest or the strongest in political and military terms. This individual would establish close relations with other "chiefs" of the same ethnic group or, alternatively, establish alliances to achieve a broad coalition to defend the ethnic and territorial viability of the group (Corona 1988: 68).

Similar processes were at work in precontact California. Discussing issues of multilingualism, Silver and Miller (1997: 212–215) state: "[T]ribelets were strongly connected with each other by both formal and informal interlocking links, and stable trade and military alliances often involved communities that were members of various language groups. Alliance structures occurred throughout the precontact California area from west to east and from north to south. In addition, there were communities that served as cross-tribelet interface centers, sometimes involving several hundred to several thousand people in intense sociopolitical and economic interaction" (214). Unfortunately, these authors provide only general sources (223) to substantiate these comments, making it difficult to compare specific groups and cases.

It is important to note that Balcarcel was first visited by the principal captains of these coalitions, who spoke for their members: only after the first contact did they introduce to Balcarcel some of the other captains of the member groups in the coalition. This process may indicate a hierarchical chain of responsibilities, although not necessarily classic leadership roles as normally conceived for groups with a tribal or segmentary social organization.

In April 1675, Pablo, the Manos Prietas captain, was sent by Don Esteban to get Fr. Larios. Don Esteban, who was at San Ildefonso, was worried about the Ervipiame (Yrvipias) because they had killed five people belonging to the Gueiquesale coalition. In retaliation for that attack, the Gueiquesale attacked the Ervipiame, killing their captain and eight of his people. As proof of their victory, the Gueiquesale obtained a well-made wooden staff that belonged to the Ervipiame captain. In the battle the Gueiquesale retrieved three females of the Yorica and Bapocora groups who had been captured by the Ervipiame. Pablo stated that the Ervipiame lived very far away from Monclova (Portillo 1886: 79, 85–86).

The sequence of conflicts between the Gueiquesale and their allies and the Ervipiame shows the continuation of a problem that existed the year before, when Fr. Manuel witnessed a battle between these groups (Portillo 1886: 78–79). Whatever the problems at issue, they had not been resolved. If the Ervipiame were trying to infringe on the territory held by the Gueiquesale and their allies, they had not yet succeeded. If the situation was reversed, the Gueiquesale had not succeeded in displacing the Ervipiame. It appears, however, that the Gueiquesale were getting the upper hand. Regardless of the final outcome of the conflict, smaller and weaker groups in the area would have to establish alliances with one of the principal parties. Despite the actions of the Spanish, which may or may not have contributed to the conflicts, the notion of static and stable populations north or south of the Rio Grande before the encroachment of the Apache should not be entertained.

On April 25, 1675, the parochial church of Nuestra Señora de Guadalupe was inaugurated. Fr. Peñasco and Fr. Dioniso de San Buenaventura counted the people at San Miguel de Luna and found 182 adult males, 78 adult women, and 135 boys and girls of all ages. Two fourteen-year-old females were baptized after they explained the intricacies of the mystery of the Holy Trinity (Balcarcel 1675; Portillo 1886: 98). The following day Balcarcel officially founded the Native pueblo of San Miguel de Luna. The pueblo leadership was given to the Bobole and the Gicocoge even though other groups, including the Ape and the Gueiquesale, were congregated there (Portillo 1886: 97–100).

On April 29, 1675, Captain Pablo, a Manos Prietas, arrived to settle at San Miguel de Luna with 232 of his people: 120 warriors, 65 adults (*indios grandes*), and 47 boys and girls. He informed Balcarcel that he had left, ready to depart, all the people who wanted to be settled. Their numbers were so great that they extended from Monclova to both the south and the north banks of the Rio Grande (Portillo 1886: 103–105). Balcarcel must have been petrified. San Miguel de Luna was already overflowing, and even charismatic leaders like Juan de la Cruz and Don Esteban were hard-pressed to maintain peace. According to Balcarcel (Portillo 1886: 164), the Bobole, under Juan de la Cruz, were not interested in sharing San Miguel de Luna except with their closest allies. The alliance of the Bobole, the Gueiquesale, and the Spaniards held the balance of power and was key to the peace that kept other groups at bay. Spanish settlers, fearful of the presence of so many Natives, had fled the area (Portillo 1886: 165). Balcarcel quickly recognized the potential for conflict if all these people were allowed to stay at San Miguel de Luna.

On April 30, Balcarcel declared that because of the request for settlement made by Captain Pablo of the Manos Prietas, the peoples of the Rio Grande area, Francisco of the Bobosarigame, Captain Sianoque, and others, as well as the need for peace and quiet in the province, it was better to visit the Native groups in their own lands. That very day Alferez Fernando del Bosque and Fr. Juan Larios departed with orders to go from the Río de Nadadores to the Sierra Dacate and other areas that might be convenient to visit for the benefit of the Crown and the Natives.

REFLECTIONS

The 1658 request to settle did not happen in a vacuum. The Babane and Jumano, who had been brought to Saltillo to work as *encomendados,* had seen their numbers dwindle.

Faced with the decimation of their kinfolk, the remaining Babane and Jumano and their allies attempted to reach an agreement with the Spanish authorities that could afford them privileges similar to those enjoyed by the Tlaxcaltecans.

The petitioners based their request on the unfair labor treatment they were experiencing and the bondage imposed on their families. Wisely, they included in the petition a request for Tlaxcaltecan families with whom they would establish the pueblo. However, they were unable to show a substantial number of Native petitioners, or to garner the support of people in power, particularly influential churchmen. More important, perhaps, they could not show that their members had, at any time, helped the Spanish military against other Native groups and that such help had been crucial to the outcome of a military conflict. The notion that the Natives' plight could take precedence over the needs of the *encomenderos* and the economic stability of the province could not be conceived.

Nevertheless, Don Marcos, the Babane, persisted, and in 1673 he and his allies tried again. It was no accident that the petitioners bypassed the authorities in Saltillo and appealed to the Audiencia de Guadalajara, since Monclova was under the bishopric of Guadalajara and the civil jurisdiction of Nuevo León until 1687. It is likely that Fr. Larios was behind that crucial decision. On the other hand, in 1673, the Natives demonstrated a substantial Native following and, more important, they provided proof of the help given by the Bobole to the Spanish in a specific battle against the Cacaxtle in 1665. This fact may explain why the Bobole headed the request for settlement. The manner in which the request was formulated probably reflects Fr. Larios's sophistication and legal maneuvering. But the initiative, staying power, and foresight belonged to the Native groups.

The request for settlement made in 1673, if not the one in 1658, demonstrates the remarkable consensus among large numbers of groups and their cohesion around the initiative. The establishment of coalitions that operated at various tiers of the social and political structure was the connective mechanism between groups. The malleability and resilience of the coalition agreements depended on (1) influential and persuasive Native spokespersons, (2) the proficiency of Native ladinos in the culture of the colonizer, and (3) the capacity of ladinos to function in the Native milieu, as well as their charisma coefficient among the various groups of hunters and gatherers.

The trips of Fr. Peñasco and Fr. Manuel de la Cruz to the north side of the Rio Grande stress the fact that, at this time, the territory of Coahuila included modern Texas. Researchers who deal with historical events involving both sides of the Rio Grande in terms of modern political boundaries truncate the geographical and historical context. The journeys of these friars provide information on group alliances, specific locations of groups, and resources. Fr. Manuel's trip places the Bobole and the Gueiquesale in the southwest area of the Edwards Plateau escarpment, while the Manos Prietas were south and west of these groups and nearer to the north bank of the Rio Grande.

The Bobole and the Gueiquesale spent a considerable amount of time in large *rancherías* north of the Rio Grande and were engaged in conflicts over territory and resources with the Catujano, Ervipiame, Ocane, and Patagua. The control of certain areas may refer principally to the usufruct of resources present in those locations at specific times, such as tuna fields or buffalo herds. The Manos Prietas, on the other hand, appear to have traveled to the north side of the Rio Grande to hunt buffalo, but they did not remain there for prolonged periods of time.

In March and April 1674, the Ervipiame were probably located near the headwaters of the Dry Devils River and the West Nueces River, and northeastward from the Bobole and Gueiquesale *rancherías*. In 1674, the Ervipiame were at war with the Gueiquesale and the Bobole. In 1675, they were at war with the Ape, Bacopora, Bobole, Gueiquesale, and Yorica, and they may have been allies of the Ocane and Patagua. The battle that Fr. Manuel witnessed may have been, in part, the result of disputes over buffalo-hunting rights. In fact, Don Esteban Gueiquesale stated that the Ervipiame captain wanted to have Fr. Manuel brought to his presence to reprimand him for trespassing on Ervipiame land (Portillo 1886: 79). If the battle was fought in part for that reason, it implies that the Bobole and the Gueiquesale may also have been considered trespassers.

In 1674 the Yorica were certainly living on the north side of the Rio Grande, about 31.2 miles north and east of the river. After they established (or reestablished) peace with the Manos Prietas and the Gueiquesale, the Yorica maintained friendly relations with those groups and with the Bobole. It is possible that their rapprochement to the Gueiquesale and their allies brought about their problems with the Ervipiame in 1675 or, conversely, that the Yorica were seeking allies to shore up their defenses against the Ervipiame and their allies.

The picture that emerges from the Spanish archival documentation pertaining to this stream of events indicates that the majority of the groups involved had considerable populations, were organized in broad multiethnic coalitions, and controlled sophisticated information networks. The evidence also indicates that some Native groups controlled and defended specific geographic areas and the harvesting of resources within those land areas. A reshuffling and bid for control of some of those areas and resources may have been under way. This realignment, which appears to have been a major source of conflict between group coalitions, was caused in part by the Spanish colonization policies, and sometimes by the well-intentioned work of the friars.

The influence of the *encomenderos* and the persistence of the *encomienda* system as a system of unfree labor are demonstrated throughout the archival documents on which this narrative is based. Regardless of the laws promulgated, the practice continued because haciendas and mines required a cheap labor force to prosper. Those needs subverted, and sometimes co-opted, the intent of the missionaries. As an example, the extraordinary efforts made by Fr. Larios and his companions on behalf of the Native groups ultimately led to the reestablishment of a Spanish settlement in Monclova.

Nonetheless, the initiatives of the friars provoked a wide response among a multitude of Native groups whose motives, expectations, and level of acculturation were diverse. Although they all agreed with the need to establish autonomous settlements, few were fully cognizant of the changes required by a settled life. Later, as we shall see, the fissures between expectations and reality became apparent and caused deep disillusionment for the friars as well as for the Native Americans.

The appointment of Don Antonio Balcarcel as Alcalde Mayor of Coahuila was the catalyst for the Bosque-Larios expedition into modern Texas territory. Faced with the overwhelming response of Native groups to the settlement project, and without appropriate resources to see it through, Balcarcel ordered Fr. Larios and his lieutenant, Fernando del Bosque, to travel to the north side of the Rio Grande, survey the land, count the people, and tell the Native people on the north side of the Rio Grande to remain in their lands and not to move into Monclova.

TWO

The Bosque-Larios Expedition

THE ARCHIVAL SOURCES

The diary of the Bosque-Larios expedition used in this chapter was transcribed by Portillo (1886, 1984). In a few instances, which are noted in the text, Bolton's (1916) translation of the diary had to be used because particular entries or sentences were not included in Portillo's transcript. I do not know the location of the original used by Portillo. Some of the archival documents dealing with the events preceding the expedition were also obtained from Portillo. In a few cases, I found the original Spanish documents later transcribed by Portillo (1886). From that slim evidence, Portillo's transcripts appear to be faithful to the original. A few things in Portillo's transcripts do not make sense, but in the absence of the original documentation, no evaluation can be made of the correctness of the statements. I am responsible for all translations of Portillo's transcripts presented in this work, and all information derived from Portillo or Bolton is duly referenced.

SETTING THE STAGE

The events described in the previous chapter set the stage for the expedition of Fernando del Bosque and Fr. Juan Larios to the north side of the Rio Grande. The explicit objectives of the expedition were to survey the land, assess its resources, count the Native people, and develop some idea of their demographic distribution. Behind that clear mandate was the need to convince the groups who had been invited to settle in the Monclova area to remain in their own lands.

The orders given by Don Antonio Balcarcel for the Bosque-Larios *entrada* specified that Bosque, Fr. Larios, and Fr. Dionisio de San Buenaventura were to be accompanied by (1) ten Spaniards, (2) the Bobole captain Juan de la Cruz, his lieutenant (Alferez), and twenty Bobole warriors, (3) one hundred Gueiquesale warriors, and (4) Don Lazaro Agustin, the Bobole governor of San Miguel de Luna. The diary names only five Spaniards, including the two friars, as members of the expedition. If all the individuals mentioned took part in the expedition, the party included at least 143 people.

The number of Spanish men-at-arms present in the area was very small. To accomplish the survey and conquest of the north side of the Rio Grande the Spanish needed the help of Natives to serve as soldiers, guides, and interpreters. Don Lazaro was chosen because he knew the groups to be visited and he was to serve as interpreter, a role he had performed since 1673. Don Lazaro was ladino in Castilian and Mexican (Portillo 1886: 105, 168). In his role as leading interpreter, Lazaro conducted most of the interviews Bosque had with Natives. The expedition included another interpreter, named Pascual, of unknown ethnic affiliation. It is possible that Pascual was a Gueiquesale or belonged to a group of the Gueiquesale coalition.

The issue of language interpretation is crucial to the understanding of the events that took place during the expedition as well as the relationships among the Native groups. Most discussions between the Spanish and the Natives took place through interpreters, who frequently performed multilingual translations of Castilian, "Mexican" (Nahuatl), and the languages of the various Native groups. Don Lazaro had been, and would remain, a pivotal character in the events and dealings between Natives and Spanish. From archival documents we know that he was a Jumano captain. As a Jumano and Bobole, Lazaro certainly spoke the language or languages spoken by these two groups. Also, in 1673 Don Lazaro stated that he spoke the same mother language as the Contotore (Chapter 1). The documents Portillo transcribed (1886: 71, 79–85, 91, 96, 103–105, 113, 116–117, 121, 175) permit the assumption that Don Lazaro spoke a language intelligible to the Catujano, Jumee, Bibit, Manos Prietas, Pinanaca, Teneimamar, Yorica, and Xaeser, or, conversely, the languages of all these groups. The diary makes it clear that this common language, if there was one, was not Mexican. It is also reasonable to assume that Lazaro spoke or knew the languages spoken by the Bagname and the Jeapa (Ape).

The Xoman, Terecodam, Teaname, and Teimamar were interviewed in their language and (or) Mexican, but Don Lazaro had the help of Pascual, the other interpreter. If we consider the Xoman as Jumano, Don Lazaro would be expected to speak the language of his own ethnic group. Thus, one may assume that Lazaro did not speak the language(s) of the Terecodam, Teaname, and Teimamar and that he needed help with the language(s) spoken by the Gueiquesale and the Bobosarigame.

Bilingualism and multilingualism were prevalent among most Native American groups as well as among hunting and gathering societies in other parts of the world (e.g., Kratz 1981, Payne 1990). Silver and Miller (1997: 207–253) review the evidence for language diversity in various Native American societies and emphasize the relations between language diversity and exogamy, prestige acquired through proficiency in several languages, similarity of culture coupled with high linguistic diversity, and the practice of sending young men to another community in order to learn its language and customs. Discussing the Yurok from California, Silver and Miller (1997: 213) report that the Yurok and their neighbors sometimes would converse for hours, during which time each person spoke only his own language. Although they understood each other's language, and even though they may have been able to speak it, *they chose not to do so*. This example is as illuminating as it is humbling, particularly given the scarcity of linguistic evidence for Native groups in Coahuila and Texas.

The trip accomplished the objectives set out by the Spanish. It is unclear how the groups that had been invited to move into Monclova interpreted the reversal of Spanish policy. Nonetheless it may be safe to assume that such reversal discredited the Spanish, particularly regarding the Native groups on the north side of the Rio Grande, which had had limited contact with the Spanish before these events.

THE TRIP

DAILY TRAVEL LOG

All translations of diary entries are mine. Generally, each entry ends with the location of the camping stop as I determined it (Figure 2.1) and is followed by a short commentary. To preserve the ambiguities in the Spanish text, no effort was made to make the translation grammatically correct in English. Although the text is not rendered in the first person singular, but as reported by an outside observer, the contents of the diary are completely and faithfully rendered. All comments placed in square brackets are my interpolations.

April 30, 1675, Day 1

*The group traveled down the river of Monclova toward the north for about 6 leagues (15.6 miles) and reached a spot on the river which Bosque named San Felipe de Jesus. Bosque was told that the place was called Pajarito (**que dijeron llamarse lo de Pajarito**). Bosque stated that he saw no signs that the spot had ever been occupied by anyone and took possession for King Charles II of Spain. He placed a tall wooden cross on the spot. He walked over the riverbank, saw plenty of fish, and caught some. (Portillo 1886: 106–107)*

Comments: This spot seems to have been about 1.5 to 2.5 miles east-northeast of the railroad siding of Las Adjuntas.[1] The daily travel documents are signed by Bosque, Ambrosio Berlanga, and Diego Luis Sanchez, and sometimes by the two friars. Bosque placed a wooden cross in almost every spot where they made camp. The placement of the cross symbolized the act of taking possession in the name of God and King. Although the cross is a Christian symbol, it was appropriated by some Native groups. Its prevalence in Native cultural manifestations, as reported by the Spanish, raises the question of the resonance of the symbol among Native Americans. It is possible that the name Pajarito (small bird) was used by the Native populations, although it is not a Native word.

May 1, 1675, Day 2

The group departed San Felipe de Jesus and traveled 10 leagues (26 miles) toward the north, arriving at San Francisco del Paso on May 2. (Portillo 1886: 107–108)

Comments: The travel log for this day, or at least part of the day, covers some ground traveled on May 2. It is probable that the party traveled to the junction with the Río Nadadores (4 leagues or 10.4 miles) on May 1, spent the night there, and traveled the

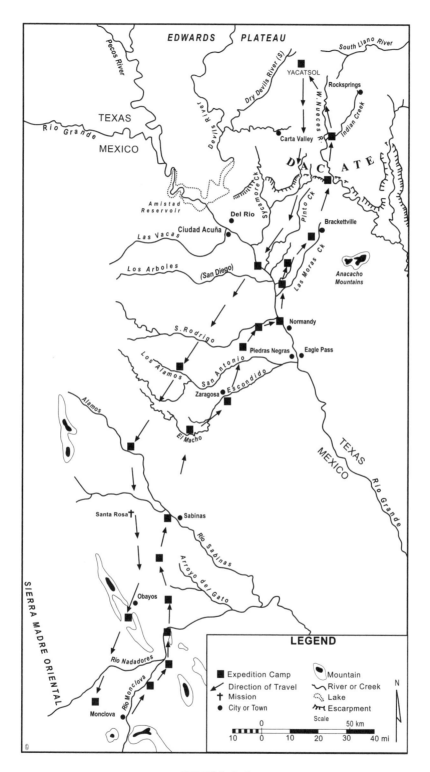

FIGURE 2.1
Route of the 1675 expedition of Fr. Juan Larios and Lieutenant Fernando del Bosque.

remaining distance (6 leagues or 15.6 miles) on May 2. The argument for this assumption is that they would have to overnight on May 1, and the document gives the two distances separately in the May 2 entry.

May 2, 1675, Day 3

The party traveled downstream on the Río Monclova 4 leagues (10.4 miles), more or less. The direction was northward. They kept on their right and to the east large hills (serros grandes). After passing these hills they reached the junction of the Monclova and Nadadores rivers.

The party traveled 6 more leagues (15.6 miles) downriver and toward the north, reaching the river pass. They arrived at this spot, which Bosque named San Francisco del Paso, on May 2. He found San Francisco del Paso uninhabited and took possession of the place for the King, placing a tall wooden cross on the riverbank. He walked over the land, noting cottonwoods (alamos) and great quantities of mesquite (mucho monte de mesquite) on the banks of the river. The river carried a lot of water and the party caught large catfish, bream, mojarras, tortoises, mud-turtles, bobos, and eels.[2] (Portillo 1886: 107–108)

Comments: The spot was probably due east of Puente Negro (a bridge).[3] As stated above, this part of the trip is assumed to have taken place on May 1. The river pass and the location of San Francisco del Paso was north of the Cerros de las Burras and southwest of Agua Buena, near the junction of the Río Salado de Nadadores and the Arroyo El Aura.[4] In a report about the state of the Coahuila missions prepared in 1679, Fr. Manuel de la Cruz (1679) stated that the Río Nadadores carried abundant water and could be forded only in a few places.

May 3, 1675, Day 4

There is no travel entry for this day. See the comments below.

May 4, 1675, Day 5

The party left San Francisco del Paso, crossed the Río Nadadores, and continued northward 4 leagues (10.4 miles). They kept a large chain of mountains oriented south-north on their left. They reached a stream (arroyo), which seemed to be running west to east. The arroyo carried water, and the Natives said that it was called Toporica in their language. Bosque took possession of the spot, named it Santa Crus, and erected a tall wooden cross.

On the same day the party left Santa Crus and traveled northward about 4 leagues (10.4 miles), keeping the same mountain chain on the left. They reached a stream at the foot of a hill that faced another small hill with a peak shaped like a nipple. The arroyo had running water and a growth of reeds (tular). Bosque took possession, placed a tall wooden cross on the spot, and named it Santa Catalina Martir. Bosque found the place unoccupied. The Catholic doctrine was taught to the Natives. (Portillo 1886: 108–109)

Comments: Toporica was probably 2 miles, more or less, northwest of the modern village of Santa Cruz and El Muerto Lake.[5] Santa Catalina Martir must have been near El

Sauze on the Arroyo del Gato.[6] The mountain chain on the left would be the Obayos and Hermanas mountains. The mountains run northwest-southeast, but from the viewpoint of someone riding a horse the orientation of south-north would not be incorrect. The name of the stream, or area, is given as Toporica. This toponymic could be given in the Bobole, the Gueiquesale, or even the Jumano language.

The first set of 4 leagues from San Francisco del Paso to Santa Crus was probably traveled on May 3, while the second set of 4 leagues from Santa Crus to Santa Catalina Martir was covered on May 4. This assumption is based on the two distinct diary entries for this day, both with naming ceremonies. The topography locates Santa Catalina Martir at El Sauze. If, however, the party traveled more northwesterly and more parallel to the Obayas and Hermanas mountains, Bosque would have been nearer to the Minas de Berroteran on the same arroyo. If Bosque was traveling more easterly, he could have been on the Arroyo del Gato, facing Agua Dulce Peak. Regardless of the exact spot, Bosque was evidently between modern (1980) highways 9 and 53.

May 5, 1675, Day 6

*The party left Santa Catalina Martir and traveled about 6 leagues (15.6 miles), keeping the same large mountain range to the left. They reached a large and beautiful river with many trees, such as large cedars, cottonwoods, and mesquite (**monte de mesquite**). The prairie lands were covered with green grass (**sacate**). Bosque found the place unoccupied and placed a tall wooden cross on the spot. He named the place San Antonio. The Natives told him that the river was called Río de las Sabinas [juniper or cyprus trees?], and that in their language it was called Muero. The river was rich in fish of all sorts. The party caught **piltontes**, bream, and catfish. The doctrine was taught to the Native Americans. (Portillo 1886: 109–110)*

Comments: Bosque was about 5 miles upstream of the modern town of Sabinas near San Jose de Cloete, and about 3.5 miles southeast of the modern hamlet of San Antonio.[7] As mentioned above, it is likely that *muero* is also a Bobole word. However, a female child was baptized at Mission S. Francisco Solano in 1706. The child, who was six years old and classified as Jumano, was given the Native name Mueracuba, and the Spanish name of Nicolasa. The mother of the girl was a non-Christian Jumano. Bosque states that the Río Sabinas was called Muero in a Native language. This raises the possibility that *muero* is actually a Jumano word or that the Bobole and the Jumano spoke the same language. Whether the word *muero* referred to the river, the trees (*sabinas*), or both is not clear.

May 6, 1675, Day 7

There is no travel log entry for this day.

May 7, 1675, Day 8

*Bosque departed San Antonio de las Sabinas and traveled toward the north about 12 leagues (31.2 miles). He reached a watering place (**aguaje**), which he was told was called San Ildefonso*

*(Ilefonso). The place was deserted and Bosque noted two grass huts (**jacales**) almost completely ruined. Bosque took possession and placed a tall wooden cross on the spot. (Portillo 1886: 110)*

Comments: San Ildefonso was quite possibly on the arroyo El Macho, west of the modern town of Allende, but existing information is insufficient to state its location with confidence.[8] The site of San Ildefonso is important because of the events preceding this journey, and the actual location of several Native groups during the period of 1674–1675. The spot Bosque reached on May 7 is apparently the same San Ildefonso mentioned in earlier documents. The argument for this conclusion is based on the following facts: (1) the place had been named before and was not renamed by Bosque; (2) the place bore the same name used by Fr. Larios for the area where he worked in 1673–1674; and (3) the ruins of two huts in the area could correspond to the church and sacristy built by Fr. Larios in 1674. Bolton (1916: 294) reached the same conclusion. Nonetheless, it is disturbing that Bosque did not mention that he was acquainted with the place: after all, he was a member of the group that established the mission-settlements of Santa Rosa and San Ildefonso in 1674. When the Marqués de Rubí traveled through this area in 1767, the spring and marshy area were still called San Ildefonso.

May 8, 1675, Day 9

*Bosque departed San Ildefonso and traveled toward the north about 7 leagues (18.2 miles). The party reached a copious water source. The place was surrounded by wide plains, and in the middle there was a large area of mesquite (**mucho monte de mesquite**). Bosque was told that the area was called in a native language **cocomarque jojona**. He found the spot unoccupied and took possession, naming it Señor Juan Evangelista. Bosque placed a tall wooden cross on the spot. Fr. Larios taught doctrine to the Native Americans. (Portillo 1886: 110–111)*

Comments: The site of Sn. Juan Evangelista on the Río Escondido seems to have been near the modern town of Zaragoza.[9] The problem of translating the expression *monte de mesquite* is a relevant one. Bolton translates the exact same Spanish expression both as "mesquite trees" (1916: 292) and as "mesquite brush" (1916: 294). The difference between these two landscapes is considerable, as anyone knows who has traveled westward through the Edwards Plateau from San Sabá to Brady. I think that *monte de mesquite* refers mostly to mesquite brush or small trees and not to large mesquite trees.[10] The Native expression *cocomarque jojona* could be Bobole or Jumano (see above). Among the following of Don Esteban Gueiquesale was a group called Cocomaque (Portillo 1886: 77). It is not clear if there is a relation between the toponymic and the name of the ethnic group.

The location of Sn. Juan Evangelista may be shifted to the plains away from the Río Escondido, which today flows intermittently. Bosque referred to a copious water source, but the current status of the river probably reflects the effects of extensive use of its waters for irrigation upstream from Zaragoza.

May 9, 1675, Day 10

*The party left Sn. Juan Evangelista and traveled toward the north about 6 leagues (15.6 miles) through plains with mesquite brush (**monte de mesquite**). They reached a marshy area (**aguaje de sienega**) with reeds that was located between some small hills with small oak trees (**monte de ensinal**). Bosque found the place unoccupied and took possession, naming it San Reymundo de Peña Forte (or Fuerte) de Fuertes Aires. He placed a tall wooden cross on the spot, and Fr. Buenaventura taught the doctrine to the Native Americans. (Portillo 1886: 111)*

Comments: This place is best located between the El Encino and San Rodrigo rivers, possibly southwest of the village of Papatote and about 17 miles west of Piedras Negras.[11] *Monte de ensinal* has been translated as an area of small oak trees on the assumption that *monte* refers to small trees and brushy areas.

May 10, 1675, Day 11

*Bosque left San Reymundo and traveled about 3 leagues (7.8 miles) toward the north. They arrived at a river running west to east, which the Natives said was called Agua Asul. The river was very beautiful and carried many fish of all kinds. There were many cottonwoods, willows, mesquite, and **guisaches**. The plains were covered with very green grass (**sacate mui verde**). Bosque found the place unoccupied, took possession, placed a tall wooden cross on the spot, and named it Río de San Josefe. The friars preached the doctrine to the Native Americans. (Portillo 1886: 111–112)*

Comments: The Río de San Josefe is most likely the current Río Rodrigo, and the spot where they set up camp was about 2.5 miles northeast of Paso de las Mulas and about 15 to 18 miles northwest of Eagle Pass.[12]

May 11, 1675, Day 12

*On this day the party left Río de San Josefe and traveled northward about 3 leagues (7.8 miles), traversing some plains covered with green grass and a profusion of mesquite brush (**monte de mesquite**). They arrived at a very wide river carrying a lot of water. The river seemed to run west-east. The riverbed was more than 400 varas (1,111 feet) wide.[13] The Native Americans said that this river was called Río del Norte. Bosque stated that he found the place unoccupied **except** for Native **rancherías**. He explained that the **rancherías** were composed of grass hut dwellings (**chosas de sacate**) built after Native custom. The party traveled upstream trying to locate a passable ford. The Natives decided to cross at a place where the river made three forks (**tres brasos de agua**). They forded the first branch that had a width of more than 200 varas (555 feet), and a depth of 1.5 varas (4 feet). For those on horseback, the water reached above the stirrup and near the hind bow of the saddle. They built a raft of poles to cross to the middle of the river where there was a small island with a variety of willow trees. The banks of the river were very pleasing, and the river supported many fish such as catfish, **piltontes,** very large turtles, and clams (**almejas**). The party did some fishing. The friars taught the Christian* *doctrine to the Native Americans. Bosque took possession of the place, placed a tall wooden cross on the spot, and named it San Buenaventura. (Portillo 1886: 112–113)*

Comments: The party reached and crossed the Rio Grande probably about 2 miles west of modern Normandy, Texas, and 1 mile north of El Moral, Mexico.[14] Bosque considered a territory unoccupied if it did not have buildings or the remains of buildings that revealed a previous European presence. In other entries in the diary he considered the lands he traversed unoccupied and mentioned no Native dwellings. On the banks of the Rio Grande he acknowledged the presence of dwellings, but took possession of the lands for his King in the manner of a conquest. Because of his perception of what was or was not occupied it cannot be said that the lands he traversed before had no Native inhabitants. It probably can be assumed that he did not see organized and congregated dwellings before those on the Rio Grande. This landscape was "written as uninhabited [and] unpossessed" (Pratt 1992: 51) not because it exemplified a narrative of anticonquest (Pratt 1992: 38–68), but precisely because it was a conquest that assumed *only* no previous European ownership or occupation.

May 12, 1675, Day 13

There is no entry for this day in the diary.

May 13, 1675, Day 14

*Bosque left the Río San Buenaventura del Norte (Rio Grande) and traveled toward the north about 4 leagues (10.4 miles). The party reached a stream (**arroyo**) between some hills where they met fifty-four Native warriors (**indios de arco y flecha**) of the Yorica and Jeapa groups. These heathen Natives were carrying **tersios (or tercios)** of jerked buffalo meat.[15] Don Lazaro Agustin was the interpreter, since he knew their language and Castilian. Many questions were posed to these Natives. They stated that they had been hunting buffalo and preparing meat (**aser carne**)[16] for the sustenance of their families and **rancherías**. They were forced to travel this far because they had nothing to eat near their settlements. They declared that their groups were numerous, but they could not give a number. They wished to be Christians and settle in a pueblo. They had not tried to reach the Spaniards for fear of their enemies, and that was also the reason they wandered so far [to look for food]. They reported that their enemies had killed one of their own: the act had been perpetrated by the Ocane, Pataguaque, and Yurbipame [Ervipiame]. To demonstrate their obedience to the King they would accompany Bosque to where the nations of the Sierra Dacate[17] and Yacatsol were located (**indios de la sierra Dacate y Yacasole**). Meanwhile they would send emissaries to the **rancherías** of their people in order that they would come out to a place where all could receive the Christian doctrine [Day 17]. Bosque named the place San Gregorio Nasianseno. (Portillo 1886: 113–114)*

Comments: Quite likely San Gregorio was located on Las Moras Creek about 5 miles east of the Rio Grande in Maverick County.[18] Bosque did not take possession of San Gregorio Nasianceno, nor did he place a cross there. The Yorica and Jeapa warriors were hunting away from their land. They were carrying, on foot it appears, loads of jerked buffalo meat. Jerked meat is supposed to be prepared by the Native women in settlements or temporary hunting camps (Fletcher and La Flesche 1972, vol. 2: 344–345); therefore, one would expect the women to have been present in a camp nearby. Regarding the availability of buffalo and their seasonality patterns, it should be noted that by this date (May 18), these buffalo hunters had already obtained and prepared their meat supplies, which indicates the presence of buffalo herds in the area in early May.

In December 1674, Fr. Larios stated that he and two other friars planned to travel in February 1675 to the north side of the Rio Grande to make preparations for this very expedition (Chapter 1). The encounter with the Yorica and Jeapa was no accident: they knew the Spanish were coming and used the opportunity to discuss the problems they were experiencing with other groups that impeded access to their kinfolk, to the Spanish, and to essential subsistence resources. The case of the Yorica is particularly relevant because in 1674, when Fr. Peñasco persuaded them to move to Monclova, they at first refused and stated that they were doing very well in their lands, where they had plenty to eat. One year later they complained about difficulty in traveling and access to resources.

Despite the fact that the Gueiquesale coalition appears to have controlled access to certain areas in the Edwards Plateau, these warriors made a specific complaint against the Ervipiame, Ocane, and Pataguaque. We have no information on the Ervipiame, but the Ocane and Pataguaque were members of the Catujano coalition no later than October 1675 (Chapter 1). This is all the more interesting because in December 1674 the Ape (Jeapa), the Mabibit (Bibit), and the Xumez (Jumee) were members of the Catujano coalition (Chapter 1). This implies, first, that the Ocane and Pataguaque joined the Catujano coalition sometime after May 1675, and second, that the Yorica, Jeapa, Bibit, and Jumee (see below) were having problems with members of the Catujano coalition by mid-1675. It appears that a significant realignment of groups and allegiances was taking place during 1675.

The Yorica were never mentioned by a Native American as members of the Catujano coalition. It was Bosque who stated that the Yorica, Bibit, and Jumee belonged to the followings of the Bobole and the Catujano/Tilijae (Portillo 1886: 128). Bosque's statement is correct if we restate it by saying that the Yorica belonged to the following of the Bobole, while the Ape, Bibit, and Jumee were within the coalition of the Catujano-Tilijae. The other possibility is that one or more of these groups belonged to the Tilijae micro-coalition and to the Catujano-Tilijae macro-coalition. Bosque's statement further indicates the nature of the relationship between the Bobole and the Catujano-Tilijae: they were closer to each other than they were to the Gueiquesale and their allies.

The Yorica and Jeapa warriors stated that they would send messengers to call their kinfolk out of their *rancherías* to meet the Spaniards on the way. The text does not mention meeting Yorica and Jeapa peoples again. Further north, however, at San Bisente Ferrer, the Spanish met the Jumee and Bibit. As will be shown, these were the people to whom the Yorica and Jeapa sent messengers, and were therefore their kinfolk. As for the ethnic identity of the Jeapa, Campbell (1988: 141) believed the Jeapa to be the Ape, and I concur.

The Yorica, Bibit, Jeapa, and Jumee were allied at one level of organization (micro-social). The alliance of the Yorica, Jumee, Bibit, and Ape may have been a regional one, based on geographic location and possibly on long-standing social ties. The Yorica were allied with the Bobole at a micro-level of social organization, and very probably they were the liaison group for the macro-coalitions of the Bobole, the Catujano, and, possibly, the Gueiquesale. In May 1674, the Yorica sent a young male Gueiquesale as a gift to the Manos Prietas. Quite possibly this gift was an indirect gift to the Gueiquesale, because the Gueiquesale were closely allied with the Manos Prietas (Chapter 1). Later documents confirm this interpretation in that the Gueiquesale and the Manos Prietas were together at the same mission (Chapter 3).

The interlocking of the two macro-spheres of influence of the Bobole and the Catujano-Tilijae (Day 23), the first north of Monclova and the second east of Monclova, placed the quadrumvirate Yorica, Bibit, Jumee, and Ape with allies in both macro-spheres. The connecting element (the broker group) in this interlocking of influences would have been the Yorica. If this analysis is correct, these alliances facilitated the relationship of these four groups within both macro-spheres of influence, but would also have obligated them to the alliances made by those groups.

The interlocking of these two coalitions increased the influence of the Bobole and Catujano-Tilijae vis-à-vis the coalition of Don Esteban, which had been reinforced by the groups of Don Fabian (Chapter 1). The Yorica, Bibit, Jumee, and Jeapa complained about their difficulties in traveling and procuring food, particularly buffalo. Their access to hunting areas may have depended on these interlocking alliances. As we shall see, the control over the northern areas that Bosque traversed was in the hands of the groups that belonged to the following of Don Esteban, a Gueiquesale. The connecting element for the Bobole, the Catujano-Tilijae, and the Gueiquesale appears to have been the Yorica, who made a peace alliance with the Gueiquesale via the Manos Prietas (Chapter 1). Quite possibly the Manos Prietas enjoyed a mediating position similar to the Yorica's.

There is one more element to this puzzle, and that is the enmity between the Gueiquesale and the Ervipiame, which was shared by the Bobole, Yorica, Ape, Bibit, and Jumee, as well as by the Pinanaca and the Bacora (Chapter 1). Since the Ape, Bibit, and Jumee no longer appeared as members of the Catujano-Tilijae coalition in October 1675, and the Ervipiame were grouped with the Ocane and the Pataguaque (or Patagua) as their enemies, it may be that the chief incentive to maintain the liaison among the three macro-coalitions was the threat posed by the Ervipiame and their allies. Taking the Yorica as an example, what appears to have started as an effort to gain favor with the Gueiquesale and their allies in 1674 soon escalated into a conflict in which smaller groups were forced to take sides. By the middle of 1675 the conflict between the Gueiquesale and the Ervipiame may have involved all three major coalitions and led to group realignments.

May 14, 1675, Day 15

Bosque left San Gregorio Nasianseno accompanied by the usual retinue, plus the Yorica and Jeapa warriors. They traveled 3 leagues (7.8 miles) toward the north and reached a water *source in a plain without trees, but with mesquite brush (**monte de mesquite**). He found the place unoccupied and took possession of it by placing a tall wooden cross on the spot. He named it San Bisente Ferrer. The Christian doctrine was taught to the Native Americans. At San Bisente Ferrer both Natives and Spaniards hunted buffalo for their sustenance. [Portillo's transcription (1886: 115) says that they killed two buffalo (**dos sibulas**). Bolton's translation (1916: 298) says that they killed three buffalo bulls and two buffalo cows.]*

Bosque described the appearance of the buffalo and stated that their meat was very tasty. He stated that the shape [form] of the animal was very ugly. Although the buffalo were bigger, they resembled cows and bulls. The hair was very shaggy, the withers were so high and their necks so very short that they appeared humpbacked. The head hair was very shaggy and it covered their eyes to the point that they could not see well. The horns were short and thick, but like those of a bull. The hips and haunches were like those of a hog and the tail was bare, except for some long bristles at the end. The hoofs were cloven and from the knees to the shoulder they had a lot of bristle-like hair similar to that of he-goats. The females were like the males but had four teats. They faced the observer standing sideways like wild hogs with their hair raised. They were the same size as cattle. (Portillo 1886: 115–116)

*While at San Bisente Ferrer, Bosque was visited by Juan, a Bibit captain, and by a captain of the Jumee group who had not been baptized. Juan was a Christian baptized in Saltillo. Don Lazaro Agustin was the interpreter for these interviews because he knew their language and Castilian. They were asked many questions and stated that for a long time they had wished to be Christians. Some of their people had traveled to Saltillo where they became Christians [were baptized], but others had not because it was very far and the people could not travel. Many of their people had died of smallpox without having been baptized. They wished to receive baptism and be settled in a pueblo, but they had not been able to do so or join the rest of the people of their group because of other barbarous groups who would kill them. They brought with them 105 people counting adults and children. Of these, 55 were male adults who carried [or could carry] weapons, and the remainder **women and boys** (Portillo 1886: 116; emphasis mine). [Bolton (1916: 298) does not refer to 55 male warriors, but mentions that "[t]he people whom they brought numbered 105 large and small, including women and children."]*

At the same locale, six Native heathen warriors, of the Pinanaca, Xaeser, and Teneinamar, appeared before Bosque. [Bolton (1916: 299) shows a different spelling for the last group—Tenimama—and includes a fourth group, the Cocoma.] These individuals belonged to the following of Don Esteban, a Gueiquesale. The interpreter was Don Lazaro Agustin, who knew their language and Castilian. They declared they came on behalf of their people to reaffirm the allegiance given to the King of Spain, in their name, by Don Esteban. They were waiting to become Christians and be settled in a pueblo (Portillo 1886: 116–117). [Bolton (1916: 299) includes a sentence at the end of the entry for this day that is not included in Portillo. Bolton says that the four captains stated that "all their people and others remained in the Sierra de Matoat."]

Comments: San Bisente Ferrer was located between Las Moras Creek and Cow Creek south or southwest of Brackettville.[19] The Bibit and the Jumee complained that they could not travel through certain areas to see the Spaniards, as the Yorica and the Jeapa had done (Day 13), reflecting the conflicts with their neighbors. It is likely that the number of people who came to see the Spaniards reflected the Native losses to disease and the inability of the sick to travel.

No girls were counted for the Bibit (Mabibit) or the Jumee.[20] When Cabeza de Vaca stayed with the Mareame in 1533–1534, he mentioned (1971: 49–50, 52) that the Mareame and the Yguase practiced female infanticide. This is the only time that Cabeza de Vaca referred to such a cultural practice during his travels in Texas, and it is also the only time that Bosque and Larios did not include young females in the people they counted. This is not conclusive evidence that the Bibit, the Jumee, and possibly the Yorica were culturally related to the Mareame and the Yguase. It is also not conclusive evidence that, 142 years later, female infanticide was still being practiced. However, it is the only evidence of a possible connection between these two (perhaps three) groups and the specific cultural practice reported by Cabeza de Vaca.

The Bibit and Jumee were separated from other members of their groups due to internecine strife between Native groups. This pattern of forced geographical division of ethnic groups that lived in the Edwards Plateau occurred prior to the southward moves of the Apache. The statements of the Mabibit, Jeapa, Jumee, and Yorica, but particularly the Mabibit and the Jumee, constitute good evidence that the same or related Native groups lived in different areas, either by choice or as a result of local conflicts.

The visit of the Pinanaca, Xaeser, and Teneinamar (or Tenimama) captains confirms the connections among the following of Don Esteban in the south and those north of the Rio Grande. All these groups were included in the coalition of Don Esteban. According to the documentation issued by Balcarcel's *entrada,* only the Pinanaca (and possibly the Cocoma) had ambassadorial groups or representations south of the Rio Grande. Neither the Saesse (Xaeser) nor the Teneinamar visited Balcarcel at Monclova, even though the Teimamar (as Temmanar and not Teneimamar) had been in Saltillo in 1673 during some of the negotiations for settlement (Chapter 1). It is not clear if the Temmanar, Teimamar, and Teneimamar were three different groups, or if the last two names represent different spellings of the same group name. The fact that these groups hunted buffalo in the area and their silence about difficulties in traveling appear to confirm their control over the area as members of the Gueiquesale coalition.

The Cocoma, included by Bolton but not by Portillo, were not among the group members of the following of Don Esteban, the Bobole, Don Fabian, or the Catujano-Tilijae. However, a group by the name of Cocomaque appears on the list of Don Esteban (Portillo 1886: 77), and the place Bosque named Sn. Juan Evangelista was called in a Native language Cocomarque jojona (Day 9). The location of the Sierra Matoat could be in the series of high hills and sierras west-northwest of Zaragoza. It was near this area that Bosque found the Pinanaca and the Bacora on his return trip (Day 33).

The problem of the discrepancies between Portillo's transcription and Bolton's translation has been addressed before (Introduction). The influence of scribes, copyists, transcribers, translators, and historians in the spelling of names and in the alteration of the overall text should not be forgotten. Both versions mention the killing of only a few buffalo. Probably, the Spanish and Native Americans were hunting at what were the southwestern limits of the buffalo range at the time.

Bosque's description of the buffalo is accomplished by comparing it with European livestock. The description exemplifies a phenomenon that should be kept in mind: descriptions of landscapes, fauna, and flora are almost always made with reference to the known universe of the observer-reporter. The reporter is cognizant that he is conveying information to others not familiar with the environment or the animals he is describing. Thus, descriptive language is manipulated to draw a representation commensurable with the universe known to the audience.

May 15, 1675, Day 16

Bosque left San Bisente Ferrer and traveled northward about 4 leagues (10.4 miles). The party reached a river, which the Natives said was called, in their language, Ona, which in Castilian meant "salty" (or "salt pond" [salina]). Bosque took possession and placed a tall wooden cross on the spot. He named the place San Isidro Labrador. The locale had many groves of oak and mesquite and plenty of buffalo. The land had good pastures and the river abundant fish. Bosque found the place uninhabited. (Portillo 1886: 117–118)

*In this spot, and on the same day, Bosque was visited by the captains of the Xoman, Tereodan, Teaname, and Tumamar (Portillo 1886: 118) or Teimamar (Bolton 1916: 299), together with their people. The interpreters for these groups were Don Lazaro Agustin and Pascual because they understood their language, Mexican, and Castilian. These captains were questioned extensively, and one by one. They declared they were heathen, without knowledge of God or the true way to salvation. They had been in the dark about God, and their wives and children wished to become Christians and be baptized. They wished to settle in a pueblo as Christians. Although they were old and would not enjoy the benefits of such change, their children and their descendants would be raised as Christians. They rendered obedience to King Carlos and declared themselves, from that day onward, friends of the Spaniards. Bosque welcomed them and assured them of the Spanish friendship. He ordered them to be peaceful (**y les mandé bibiesen quieta y pasificamente**), and to attend the doctrine wherever it was more convenient for them, considering how far their settlements were located [from Coahuila], and the conflicts between the various groups which caused them to kill each other. He noted that there was not enough food to sustain all the people while awaiting his Majesty's decision, and told them to remain at peace while the King decided where to settle them. The captains, through the interpreters, affirmed that they would comply. Soon afterward the people of these groups began to arrive and devotedly kissed the sleeves of the robes of the priests. They asked to be allowed to offer alms (**limosna**) of what they possessed as thanks to God for having shown them the way: one placed on the ground a piece of animal fat (**sebo**), another a piece of rendered fat (**manteca**), and others skins or pelts of animals that they used to make clothing, as covering for themselves, or to sleep on. (Portillo 1886: 118–119)*

Comments: San Isidro was probably on Elm Creek about 6 miles west of Brackettville.[21] It is difficult to know to what language the word *ona* should be attributed. The

Xoman, Tereoodam, Teaname, and Teimamar spoke their language and probably Mexican, as the record shows. Still, since the principal interpreter spoke Bobole, it is likely that the word is from the language spoken by the Bobole. This, however, is an assumption. Nonetheless, the phonemic similarity between *jojona* (Day 9) and *ona* is intriguing.

More than 1,300 people gathered at this spot, and such a group would have required substantial resources. The abundance of buffalo indicates that the party were able to hunt enough buffalo in the area to satiate the number of people present. It may also indicate that the Spanish visit had been scheduled during a buffalo hunt.

The Xoman, Tereodam, Teaname, and Teimamar were questioned separately. It was probably necessary to conduct separate interviews because some of these captains spoke only their own language, while others may also have spoken Mexican. Don Lazaro Agustin, who did know Mexican, did not speak, did not wish to speak, or needed help with the other language, or languages, being spoken, since he was assisted by Pascual. Pascual may have spoken the language (or languages) of one or more of the four captains and translated it to Mexican for Lazaro Agustin, who in turn translated the conversation into Spanish. This is the only instance, on this trip, in which the Mexican language is said to have been used. By "Mexican" is meant Nahuatl, or, alternatively, a corrupt form of Nahuatl used as lingua franca in the west.[22]

There are important discrepancies between the Portillo and Bolton versions of this diary entry. Referring to the Xoman, Tereodam, Teaname, and Tumammar (Teimamar), Bolton (1916: 300) includes the sentence "that in their lives they [never] had seen Spaniards." Bolton (1916: 300) also includes a footnote that reads: "Both my transcript from the original and the Portillo version omit the negative, but I feel confident from the sense that it [the negative] is intended." The sentence Bolton refers to in his footnote does not appear in the Portillo transcript I consulted (1886: 118–119).

Portillo (1886: 119) transcribes the following: "*no aber con que sustentar tanta gente.*" Bolton (1916: 300) correctly translated this as "because they have nothing with which to sustain so many people." The translation, in context, seems to indicate that these people did not have enough food to sustain themselves where they were. This statement contradicts Bosque's remark about the abundance of buffalo. Bosque's sentence relates to the pueblos the Spanish planned to establish in and around Monclova, and their inability to support them while awaiting the King's decision (Portillo 1886: 161, 165). Bosque was referring to the reason why he was making this trip: to assess the viability of settling all these groups around Monclova and supplying them with food.

Regarding the giving of alms, actually a gift-giving ceremony initiated by the Native Americans, Bolton (1916: 301) says that "some [gave] a piece of tallow, others skins of animals of the kind with which they clothe themselves or cover themselves and in which they sleep." The reference to *sebo* and *manteca* in Portillo's version (1886: 119) shows the use of animal fat not rendered (*sebo*), and the use of fat prepared by a rendering process (*manteca*). The distinction between the two types of animal fat indicates not only different processes and practices of fat-rendering, but the likelihood that these animal by-products were used in different ways. The ceremony of gift-giving to expected guests is noteworthy. The gifts were not given individually, but placed on the ground (*echando en el suelo*) as offerings to all those who were present.[23]

The statements made by the captains of the Xoman, Tereodan, Teaname, and Teimamar about their wish to settle show that the decision was well thought out. The move to settle was for the sake of their children and grandchildren. They were too old to benefit from the change, but they thought it would favor their offspring. The sense of continuity and history is patent in their speech. It is a move to adapt to new historical circumstances and make the most of situations that were affecting their way of living. This was not a solution of last resort, nor was it a case of a few individuals entering a Catholic mission. Although their acts were certainly conditioned by colonial circumstances, it was their decision, their agency, to change their living conditions.

May 16, 1675, Day 17

*While the party was still at the place and river of Santo Isidro, they set up a portable altar to say mass. At the sound of a small bell, all the people came to attend mass, which was sung by the Commissary for the Missions, Fr. Juan Larios. After mass, the Natives asked the priest for baptism. They were told, by the interpreter, that they could not receive baptism until they knew the doctrine. To console them, the friar baptized 55 breast-feeding babies and the Spaniards were the godparents (**compadres**) of those baptized. After the teaching of doctrine, the Spanish proceeded to count the people. Within the group of the four captains [Xoman, Tereodan, Teaname, and Teimamar] there were 425 warriors (**indios de arco y flecha**), and 747 women, boys, and girls of all ages. The total is 1,172. Bosque placed Fr. Juan Larios in possession of his office and the administration of the post of San Isidro, complying with the royal orders and provisions. (Portillo 1886: 119–120)*

While they were at this spot a Gueiquesale captain, who had not been baptized, presented Bosque with a Spanish boy who appeared to be about twelve years of age. The boy was tattooed with a black line that ran from the forehead to the nose, and one row of round designs in the shape of the letter O on each of his cheeks. The boy had several rows of Os on the left arm, and one line of Os on the right arm. The Gueiquesale captain was questioned through Don Lazaro Agustin, who spoke his language and Castilian. Helping Don Lazaro in the interpretation was Pascual, who also knew the Gueiquesale's language.

The Gueiquesale captain was asked where he got the boy. He responded that the Cabesas [a Native group] had told him that many years ago they had gotten the boy and other captives from Yndee, near Parral [Figure 3.1]. The Cabesas gave the boy to his [the Gueiquesale captain's] mother and she raised the boy. He stated that, although he loved the boy like a brother, he would give him back to the Spaniards, on this spot, as a sign of friendship. He wished the boy to be returned to his parents. The boy was not questioned to find out about other Spaniards being held by the Natives because he could not speak Spanish. The Gueiquesale captain was asked if there were more young Spaniards among them. He replied that all he knew was that at the time the Cabesas brought this boy they had brought another young male and a young girl. The other male youngster was killed with arrows. He was made to stand up to be shot. When the boy realized he was about to die, he picked up a cross which he held while he prayed. He prayed until he died. The Spanish girl was kept as a servant, but one time, when the Cabesas went on a raid to steal and kill, one of their own got killed in the fray. They took the girl and shot her with arrows until she died. They left her body uncovered in a given place. Two years later they went by the same spot and found the body of the girl. The body was as they had left it, untouched by animals and without decay. Because of this, they transported her body to a cave where they left it. He did not know anything else except that the girl had long hair. He stated that this was the truth. (Portillo 1886: 120–121)

Diary Entry for Version B

There is another version of the events of this day. In this second version of the diary, Version B, the writer, very likely Fr. Juan Larios, stated that

*San Isidro is about 70 leagues (182 miles) from Monclova and about 16 to 20 leagues (41.6 to 52 miles) from the Rio Grande crossing (Bosque 1675). On May 16, Bosque officially placed Fr. Larios in charge of his ecclesiastic duties. After a portable altar had been set up, mass was sung. The people of the Xoman, Theodoran [Tereodan], Teaname, and Teimamar, together with the people of the Jume, Mavivit, and Oricas, who came to meet the Spaniards on the way, attended mass and the teaching of doctrine. Bosque counted the people of the first four groups and found 425 warriors and 740 women, boys, and girls, who in their lifetime had seen Spaniards. They also counted the Jume, Mavivit, and Orica and found 159 people, of which 59 were warriors. The total was 1,331 people, young and adult. After declaring that they had lived without the knowledge of God, the people of the first four nations asked to be baptized. Fr. Larios, through the interpreters, told them they could not be baptized until they knew how to pray. To console them, and since Larios knew them (**y como conocidas**), he told them he would baptize some of the infants (**criaturas de pecho**). First Fr. Larios baptized the son of a captain, and then Fr. Dionisio baptized another 54 infants. The people of these four nations were very pleased and asked permission to make a gift of some of their goods. Some gave pieces of fat (**sebo**), others pieces of rendered fat (**manteca**), others pelts which they used for sleeping and others pelts with which they covered themselves. Through the interpreter they stated that they were doing this to thank God for the good they were receiving in becoming Christians.*

Comments: Version B does not include any information about the Gueiquesale captain or the offering of the Spanish boy. This version confirms that the Mabibit and the Jumee were the people mentioned by the Yorica as their people. The Jeapa are not mentioned. However, the people counted by Bosque were:

Yorica and Jeapa: 54 warriors
Bibit and Jumee: 55 warriors and 50 people
Total: 159 people (109 warriors and 50 people).

Fr. Larios, in Version B, states that there were 59 warriors and 100 people for a total of 159 people. This number referred to the Orica, Mabibit, and Jumee. It seems an unlikely coincidence that the two totals would be the same unless they referred to the same group of people. The discrepancy is in the warrior count. There are several scenarios that could justify the discrepancy, but there is no proof to validate any of them. Nevertheless, it is difficult to envision a group, or groups, that would have 109 warriors for only 50 people—a very unusual warrior/nonwarrior ratio (see below). These groups had recently suffered a smallpox epidemic: that alone could have created the imbalance. It is also possible that most of the people were not present to be counted, or that the group possessed more males than females (Day 14). If the total of 159 reflects the total of the people encountered, then it appears that the Jeapa were also counted in the total. On the other hand, the majority of the Yorica had moved to Coahuila with Fr. Peñasco (Chapter 1), which could explain the absence of nonwarriors among the Yorica, though not the Jeapa. If this is the case, then there were indeed 54 Yorica and Jeapa warriors and 105 Mabibit and Jumee individuals. Version B also confirms that Fr. Larios knew the Xoman, Teorodam (Tereodan), Teaname, and Teinamar and that, contrary to Bolton's interpretation (1916: 300), they *had seen Spaniards* before.

The Tereodan and the Teaname do not appear in the lists of the followings of Don Esteban, Juan de la Cruz, or the Catujano-Tilijae. The Tumamar are not listed either, but the Teimamar are listed with the following of Don Esteban. Later in the journey, at San Pablo Ermitano, Bosque mentioned these four captains as part of the following of Don Esteban the Gueiquesale (Portillo 1886: 125). The Jumano, as Jumano and not Xoman, were listed within the Bobole coalition in December 1674, while the Xoman were listed with the following of Don Esteban in 1675. This raises the issue of whether the Xoman were the Jumano proper, a group allied with the Jumano, or a group unrelated to the Jumano.

In the process of counting the Native people, the separation of warriors, adult women, and adolescents is always maintained. Of the 747 women and adolescents, at least 55 were breast-feeding infants. The remainder consisted of 692 women and male and female adolescents. It seems clear that males who were not warriors were considered to be boys. The criteria used to classify female individuals as adult women or girls are not specified. Because the Spanish separation is always made in terms of warriors and adult women, boys, and girls, it is not possible to determine how the Native groups classified the individuals and the boundaries for age grades. The Spaniards were interested in recording the total population as well as the number of warriors, because these were either potential allies or potential enemies. Bosque stated that the Spaniards were the godparents of the Native infants baptized at San Isidro. Bosque used the Spanish word *compadres*. As godparents (*padriños*) of the infants, the Spaniards became *compadres* of the baptized childrens' parents.

There is a fair possibility that having 100 warriors was viewed as a threshold that defined the viability and importance of a group in terms of its military capabilities. The Xoman, Tereodan, Teaname, and Teimamar had 425 warriors. Jean Gery (Chapter 5) counted the people of his Native friends as eleven times 100 (Marmolejo 1688). Don Esteban attacked the Ervipiame with 100 warriors, and 100 Gueiquesale warriors were ordered to accompany the Bosque-Larios expedition. Further research may confirm this pattern and probably explain the subordination of groups, such as the Bobole to the Gueiquesale, in battle situations due to their fighting forces. The ratio of warriors to non-warriors for the Teaname, Teimamar, Tereodan, and Xoman is 1 to 1.8, and the ratio for the Orica, Bibit, Jumee, and Jeapa could be either 2.2 to 1 (109 warriors and 50 people) or 1 to 1.7 (59 warriors to 100 people).

The appearance of a Gueiquesale captain on this spot is noteworthy. First, although Bosque visited the Natives of the following of Don Esteban who lived toward Dacate (Portillo 1886: 125), the Spaniards did not meet any other Gueiquesale. At this time of the year the other Gueiquesale were at San Miguel de Luna (Portillo 1886: 93, 165, 176, 178), at San Diego near the Obayas Mountains (Bolton 1916: 306), or traveling with Bosque. The Gueiquesale captain stated that "he will [sic] give the boy to the Spaniards in this place (en este lugar)" (Portillo 1886: 121). The statement is significant. There are at least three possibilities to be considered: (1) the Gueiquesale captain could give the boy to the Spaniards only on that spot because it was not safe to travel with the boy to other areas, and the following day the Spanish group would be at Dacate; (2) the gift of the boy, as a sign of friendship, had particular meaning on that spot where other gift-giving ceremonies were held, and was meant to establish a scale of importance in gift-giving; or (3) the exchange of the boy had only recently been completed. Let me explain the reasons for the last scenario.

On January 19, 1675, Fr. Larios (Figueroa Torres 1963: 92; Larios 1675) informed Fr. Francisco Treviño, the General Commissary, that he, Larios, had made extensive inquiries among all the groups in the region, but had been unable to locate the slave (esclavo). Fr. Larios assumed that the slave might have been eaten (lo hubiesen comido, porque así son los barbaros), but assured the Commissary that he would pursue the quest. Fr. Larios stated that on the date of his letter to the Commissary, all the Native groups were gathered on the Rio Grande, and he would use that opportunity to make further inquiries. Fr. Larios also said that Don Esteban had such high regard for him (Larios) that, if necessary, Don Esteban would take the slave from those who held him by the force of arms. This makes it clear that Fr. Larios had asked for the boy upon request from the Franciscan General Commissary.

On January 26, 1675, Pablo, a Manos Prietas, traveled to Monclova to guide Fr. Larios to Don Esteban, who awaited the friar between San Ildefonso and the Rio Grande. On March 20, when Fr. Larios (Portillo 1886: 93) reported back to Balcarcel, he said that Don Esteban had been given a Spanish boy. This boy and his brother had been captured by the Cabesas and the Sibulo (Cibolo) in the past. At present (March 20), the boy was with a group called the Colorados.

The boy had been tattooed (or marked) with a black line from the forehead to the nose and had a tattoo resembling a beauty mark on the cheek above the line of the beard.[24] The reason for this particular tattoo was the belief that the boy was a wolf. The boy appeared to be eighteen to twenty years old and did not speak Castilian because he had been taken as a child. Don Esteban wanted to give him back to the Spanish so that he could learn the Christian faith and the Castilian language. Fr. Larios testified that he had seen the boy (Portillo 1886: 93). The Spanish boy given to Bosque by the Gueiquesale captain on May 16 was almost certainly the same boy mentioned by Don Esteban to Fr. Larios, and also mentioned by Fr. Larios to Balcarcel on March 20, 1675.

There is no question that this was a planned act. It is likely that Don Esteban used his influence to obtain the boy from the Colorados, and that such a gift was meant to mark a particular occasion[25] and was timed to coincide with the visit of the Spanish to the north side of the Rio Grande. If, indeed, this interpretation of events is correct, Larios's request of the boy made the gift particularly significant, outranking other offerings given at San Isidro. Furthermore, in December 1674 (Chapter 1), Fr. Larios stated that he intended to travel to the north side of the Rio Grande in February 1675 to make arrangements for the Bosque-Larios trip. Fr. Larios returned to Monclova on or about March 20, at which time he informed Balcarcel about the Spanish boy.

May 17, 1675, Day 18

There is no entry for this date.

May 18, 1675, Day 19

Bosque left San Isidro and traveled 8 leagues (20.8 miles) more or less toward the north. They reached a place and a small river, which the Natives said was called Dacate. He found the place unoccupied and took possession of the spot, naming it San Bernardino. He placed a tall wooden cross on the spot. A Geniocane captain, who had not been baptized, came to see Bosque. He stated that he and his people would be waiting for Bosque at a spot further northward to receive the Christian doctrine. He said that he could not travel any further south with his people, because of the multitude of enemies that lived in between, who did not let them travel to seek aid. The Geniocane stated that this was the reason that led them to fight and kill one another. Bosque stated that he had personally witnessed these problems. (Portillo 1886: 122)

Comments: San Bernardino was most likely on the southwest bank of the West Nueces River, about 17 miles north-northwest of Brackettville and about 4.5 miles south-southwest of Black Mountain.[26] Bolton translates "*la muchedumbre de enemigos que tenian de por medio*" (Portillo 1886: 122) as "the multitude of enemies on the way" (Bolton 1916: 303). This translation does not connote the way the Geniocane were sandwiched between enemies. The fact is that the Geniocane captain did not bring his people south to Dacate because he could not travel to the limitrophe area of Dacate—the southern edge of the Edwards Plateau. Control of that physiographic feature prevented access to the buffalo hunting grounds on the plains to the south.

The Bagname captains Francisco and Mapo, and the Siano (Sana) captain Yosame carboan, who came to visit Balcarcel at Monclova, declared that they came from a mountain range (*sierra*), which in their language was called Dacate. These groups were not mentioned among the following of Don Esteban. When they declared to Balcarcel their wish to be settled, they did not mention Don Esteban, but instead affirmed their wish to be settled with the Bobole (Portillo 1886: 83). Presumably the Bagname and the Siano were in the same situation as the Geniocane, sandwiched between the friends of the Gueiquesale and other enemies further to the north on the plains forming the top of the Edwards Plateau.

May 19, 1675, Day 20

There is no entry in the diary for this day.

May 20, 1675, Day 21

*The party left San Bernardo [Bernardino] and traveled northward about 8 leagues (20.8 miles) within the same district. The Geniocane came to meet them on the way, and together they traveled to their **rancheria** or settlement located on an arroyo between some hills. The place had many stocks of red grapes. The grapes were large like the ones in Castilla. There were many other grapevines. Bosque took possession of the place and erected a large wooden cross on the spot. He named the place San Jorje. Fr. Buenaventura taught the doctrine to the Natives. (Portillo 1886: 122–123)*

Comments: Quite likely San Jorje was about 2.5 miles northeast of the West Nueces River and in the valley of Indian Creek.[27] The settlement of the Geniocane was further inland than the beginning of the area designated as Dacate, but within the same district. There is a discrepancy between the texts of Portillo and Bolton. Bolton (1916: 303) does not mention that the grapes were red (*ubas cimarronas*), and describes the fruit as wild grapes. It is very likely that these were indeed wild grapes, but Bosque differentiates *cepas* from *viña*. (Portillo 1886: 123). The text implies that intentional pruning, or what appeared to be purposeful pruning (*cepas*), had been done to the vines in order to produce strong stock, especially because he noted the size of the fruit. It is possible to argue that these were mustang grapes and that the vines were intentionally manipulated to produce larger fruit (see also Foster 1995: 259; Tous 1930: 4–24).

May 21, 1675, Day 22

On this day an altar was set up and Fr. Buenaventura said mass, which was attended by the Geniocane and by other groups present. After mass, Fr. Larios taught the doctrine to the Native Americans. The Geniocane were counted. There were 65 warriors and 113 women, boys, and girls, for a total of 178. The Geniocane declared their wish to become Christians, and Larios consoled them, saying that once they had learned their prayers he would baptize them. Fr. Larios, as commissary of the missions, took official charge of his functions in the area. (Portillo 1886: 123)

*[Version B:] They arrived at the place and small stream (**riachuelo**) of San Pablo about 8 leagues (20.8 miles) northward of San Isidro. In the place of abode (**vivenda**) of the Giniacane, and at their request, Bosque gave Fr. Larios the ecclesiastic administration of those Na-*

tives and their area. When the Giniacane asked for baptism Fr. Larios told them that he would visit them often and would teach them to pray [and then they could be baptized]. The Giniocane were counted and were found to have 75 adult males and 113 women, boys, and girls for a total of 188 [shown as 178 in the original text and corrected on the side of the manuscript as 188; the correction was made by another scribe]. (Bosque 1675a)

Comments: The Geniocane were not part of Don Esteban's following and were even at war with them (Portillo 1886: 129). The other Native groups mentioned were the Xoman, Tereodam, Teaname, and Teimamar, who were accompanying Bosque and Larios. These groups were members of the Gueiquesale coalition. The writer of Version B, probably Fr. Larios, did not say that he knew the Geniocane, nor did he baptize their children as he had done with the former groups. The Geniocane had not come to Monclova because they could not risk traveling out of their area, and it appears that Fr. Larios had not visited them prior to this occasion, but he was planning to visit them often. There is a discrepancy in the number of warriors: Bosque's diary shows 65 warriors, while Version B shows 75 warriors. Thus, the ratio of warriors to nonwarriors in the former version is 1 to 1.5, while in the latter it is 1 to 1.7.

The Spanish word *vivenda* could denote a single dwelling. However, there are several documents from this same period and written by friars that employ the same word. This does not mean that the writer of Version B did not use the word to mean a single dwelling, but the frequent use of the word decreases its potential specificity. Unlike Bosque's diary, Version B names the small stream (San Pablo). The writer of Version B appears to have made a mistake about the distance traveled from S. Isidro to the Geniocane *ranchería*.

There is a conspicuous absence of information on questions put to the Geniocane and on the identity of the interpreter. The similarity between the ethnic names Geniocane and Ocane cannot be dismissed.

May 22, 1675, Day 23

There is no entry in the diary for this day.

May 23, 1675, Day 24

At San Jorje, Bosque made an assessment of the situation based on his observations. He acknowledged that there were many groups of Natives who wanted to be Christians and be settled in pueblos, since each day their captains contacted him with that intent. All these groups had their settlements at a great distance from Monclova, and most were enemies who fought and killed each other. He stated that the land was divided into three chains of settlements arranged according to the Native custom. The first one, northward from the town of Monclova and to his left hand [west], obeyed and followed Don Esteban, the Gueiquesale; the one in the middle [north of Monclova] included the groups of the following of Juan de la Cruz, captain of the Bobole; and the one on the right-hand side [to the east of Monclova] included the Catujanos, Tilijaes, Apes, Pachaques, and their following.

*Bosque stated that he did not have military strength to prevent their dissensions and had decided to return to Guadalupe [Monclova] to inform Balcarcel of the situation and to determine the best course of action for the Spaniards. On the way to Monclova, he wanted to count the people of Don Esteban, who had not been accounted for. He told the Geniocanes to remain wherever it was more convenient for them and to avoid conflicts (**para su conservasion y quietud**). (Portillo 1886: 124)*

Comments: Bosque recognized the existence of three chains of settlements, and their respective coalitions under the "leadership" of the Gueiquesale, the Bobole, and the Catujano, Tilijae, Ape, and Pachaque validating the existing coalitions. It is interesting that the latter coalition had a multiple-group "leadership."[28] The location Bosque reported for the Gueiquesale is at odds with statements by members of the Gueiquesale coalition, who stated that they lived in the Edwards Plateau area north and east of Monclova. Bosque noted that the settlements were set according to Native tradition, which implies that the settlement pattern had been seen elsewhere. Bosque also commented on the inability of the Spanish to intervene in the dissension of the groups.

May 24, 1675, Day 25

There is no entry in the diary for this day.

May 25, 1675, Day 26

*Bosque left San Jorje and traveled northward about 14 leagues (36.4 miles). He reached a small stream (arroyo) with many trees between some hills and small mountains with tall projections like nipples (**unas lomas y serritos altos como tetillas**). He took possession of the place, named it San Pablo Ermitano, and had a tall wooden cross erected on the spot. Fr. Buenaventura taught the doctrine to the Native Americans. Bosque ordered the captains of the four groups he had met at San Isidro, the Xoman, Tereodan, Teaname, and Tumamar or Teimamar, to be peaceful in their lands and live without killing each other (**se estubiesen quietos en sus tierras bibiesen bien y sin matarse unos a otros**). Bosque stated that these nations belonged to the following of Don Esteban, and he told them to join with those of their Capitán Grande, Don Esteban. The captains said that they would do accordingly, and would wait for a priest to teach them the doctrine until the time when they would be settled in pueblos. (Portillo 1886: 124–125)*

Comments: San Pablo was probably near the headwaters of the more southerly Dry Devils River, about 4 miles south-southwest of the Texas A&M Agricultural Experimental Station #14, and about 7 miles southeast of the point where the Edwards–Val Verde county line intercepts the south line of Sutton County.[29] This spot was near or at the locality mentioned by the Natives as Yacatsol, because of the mention of small mountains with tall protrusions that looked like nipples. After visiting the Dacate area, Bosque proceeded to Yacatsol. This area was within the lands of the Xoman, Tereodan, Teaname, and Teimamar, because they accompanied Bosque to the place, and he told them to remain peaceful in their lands, and they in turn stated that they would be waiting for a priest to teach them. Bosque, who advised the Geniocane to avoid conflicts, did the same for the Xoman, Tereodan, Teaname, and Teimamar (Day 24). The Geniocane could not travel safely either to the north or to the south (within the broken edge of the Edwards Plateau), having been placed in a vise by Don Esteban's factions. I believe that San Pablo is probably at or near the spot called Yacatsol. *Yacatsol* is a Nahuatl or a Nahuatl-derived word. Molina's dictionary (1977 [1551–1771]: 30) shows that *yacatl* means "nose, or something pointed" (*nariz, o punta de algo*). In 1690, Fray Massanet reported that *yacatsol* meant *narices de piedra* ("stone noses") (Lino Canedo 1968: 8). In 1674, Fr. Manuel (Chapter 1) stated that the Native word *dacate* meant "noses" in Castilian. It appears that *dacate* and *yacatsol* are two words, in different Native languages, that mean the same thing: noses or pointed things. Thus, both words would refer to areas *within* the dissected edge of the Edwards Plateau, the Hill Country. Dacate certainly would be a Bagname, Siano (Sana), and Bobole word.

May 26, 1675, Day 27; May 27, 1675, Day 28; May 28, 1675, Day 29

There are no entries in the diary for these days.

May 29, 1675, Day 30

The party left San Pablo Ermitano and returned to Monclova sometime before this date. On May 29, Bosque arrived at a different spot on the Río San Buenaventura [Rio Grande]. Bosque met there a number of the Bobole [who were there] with their women and children. They were hunting buffalo for their sustenance. They had been there for some time and therefore away from their pueblo. Bosque ordered them to return to San Miguel de Luna and join their captain [Juan de la Cruz] as well as the rest of their people. They did as told. Fr. Larios taught the Christian doctrine to the Natives. (Portillo 1886: 125–126)

Comments: Quite likely Bosque returned to the Rio Grande by the easiest and most direct route from modern Carta Valley, and thence southwest some 8 miles to a point east of the junction of modern U.S. highways 277 and 377. At this point, he turned southward and down Sycamore Creek, and crossed the Rio Grande between Sycamore Creek and Pinto Creek, some 15 miles southeast of modern Del Rio.[30] The majority of the Bobole were hunting somewhere near Sycamore Creek and Pinto Creek; others were with their captain at San Miguel de Luna, and at least twenty Bobole warriors were accompanying the Bosque-Larios party. This constitutes a good example of the daily activities and patterns of dispersion of a single group, and should serve as a reminder that strict association may not be warranted between a given group and a particular area where they may be found at any one time.

May 30, 1675, Day 31; May 31, 1675, Day 32

There are no entries in the diary for these days.

June 1, 1675, Day 33

Bosque left the Rio Grande [either on the 30th or 31st of May], traveled about 20 leagues (52 miles) to the west, and reached a river which the Natives said was called Nueses. Near some springs formed by the river, Bosque found the Bacora and Pinanaca captains. The spot had many walnuts and other kinds of trees. Bosque took legal possession of the spot, placing a high wooden cross on the land. The doctrine was taught to the Natives and an altar was erected in a bower where Fr. Buenaventura said mass. When the mass was over, a small bell was rung and the people recited the creed. Afterward, the people of the Bacora were counted and were found to be 150 people: 62 warriors and 88 women, boys, and girls. Fr. Larios was placed in charge of the ecclesiastic administration of the area (Portillo 1886: 126).

*[Version B:] After having traveled from the other side of the Rio Grande [north bank], and crossing the rivers San Pablo and S. Jorge, Bosque arrived at the river they called the Nueces. He took possession of the area and named it Santa Clara. On that spot Bosque met the Bacora captain with his people and the captain of the Pinanaca. Bosque placed Fr. Larios in charge of the ecclesiastic administration of the area, and to mark the occasion an altar was built. After mass was celebrated and the doctrine taught, the Bacora were counted. There were 62 warriors and 88 women, boys, and girls. The Pinanaca captain stated that his people were away (**retirada**) because of the lack of food and that he would rejoin the people of Don Esteban (Bosque 1675b).*

Comments: Bosque did not mention in the diary entry for this day that he named this spot. The next entry includes the name. Santa Clara de las Nueces (see next entry) was on the northern Los Alamos River, near the village of El Colorado, about 20 miles west-northwest of Zaragoza.[31] The Bacora people were counted, but the Pinanaca were not included in the count, although the presence of the Pinanaca captain was acknowledged. The ratio of warriors to nonwarriors was 1 to 1.4.

Version B of the diary clarifies the issue of the presence of the Pinanaca by stating that only one Pinanaca captain was present at Santa Clara. The Pinanaca and the Bapocora or Bacora were closely associated (Chapter 1).

June 2, 1675, Day 34; June 3, 1675, Day 35; June 4, 1675, Day 36

There are no entries in the diary for these days.

June 5, 1675, Day 37

The party left Santa Clara de las Nueses and traveled about 14 leagues (36.4 miles) to the south and toward the city of Nuestra Señora de Guadalupe [Monclova]. They arrived at a river where they met the Gueiquesale and the Manos Prietas. Bosque took possession of the spot and named it San Diego. After mass was said by Fr. Larios the people were counted and found to number 387 people: 103 warriors and 284 women, boys, and girls. They reported that some of their people were away killing buffalo while others were with Don Esteban in Monclova. Fr. Larios took legal possession of his ecclesiastic duties (Bolton 1916: 306).

Version B of this entry is almost identical, but it specifies that some of the Manos Prietas and the Guiquesal (Gueiquesale) were with their captains killing buffalo (Bosque 1675c).

Comments: San Diego was probably on the Alamos River southeast of Lomas El Oso.[32] It should be noted that there are two rivers named Alamos in the same area; one is named Los Alamos and the other Alamos. Portillo does not include this entry in his transcription; therefore I had to use Bolton's translation (1916: 306). These discrepancies compound the problem of the accuracy of the documents, since some things are missing in Bolton and others in Portillo. The counting of the Gueiquesale and the Manos Prietas did not include those people remaining at Monclova. The ratio of warriors to nonwarriors for the people counted at this spot is 1 to 2.8. However, the Gueiquesale and Manos Prietas who were at Monclova amounted to 305 warriors and 287 women, boys, and girls (Portillo 1886: 157). When the number of people at Monclova is added to the number at San Diego, the total becomes 408 warriors and 571 women, boys, and girls, for a grand total of 979 people.[33] The ratio of warriors to nonwarriors then becomes 1 to 1.4 and reflects the population and bowmen of two groups. If we add to this number the 100 Gueiquesale warriors who were supposed to be traveling with Bosque, the ratio becomes 1 to 1.1. The fact that members of both groups were hunting buffalo on the Rio Grande as of June 5 confirms that buffalo hunting season extended to early June and often overlapped with the onset of the season for gathering tuna (prickly pear) in the area between the Río Sabinas (Mexico) and the Rio Grande.

June 6, 1675, Day 38; June 7, 1675, Day 39; June 8, 1675, Day 40; June 9, 1675, Day 41

There are no entries in the diary for these days.

June 10, 1675, Day 42

*Bosque left Sr. San Diego and traveled about 22 leagues (57.2 miles) southward. He passed the valley of the Río San Antonio de Sabinas and entered an opening between some large mountains (sierras), which the Natives called Los Obayos. They reached a stream (arroyo) which they found unoccupied (**yermo y despoblado**). Bosque took possession, named it San Ambrosio, and erected a tall wooden cross on the spot. Mass was celebrated by Fr. Larios. The ceremony was attended by Don Bernabé, captain of the Contotore. After mass and the preaching of the doctrine, the Contotore were counted and found to have 68 warriors and 130 women, boys, and girls. Fr. Larios took official charge of his ecclesiastic duties. (Portillo 1886: 126–127)*

Version B of this entry states that Bosque placed Fr. Larios in charge of the religious affairs of the people of Captain Don Bernave, Contotore, at the place called San Ambrosio. Most of the information is identical, except that the Obayos Mountain is called Obaios La Grande, and instead of 68 Contotore warriors this version shows 78 warriors (Bosque 1675d).

Comments: San Ambrosio was probably 3 miles west-southwest of the modern town of

Obayos, in the eroded heart of the Sierra Obayos and the Sierra Hermanas.[34] Although Bosque declared the place unoccupied, he found the Contotore there. The notion of *yermo y despoblado* referred to European occupation and not Native American presence (Day 11). The ratios of warriors to nonwarriors are 1 to 1.9 and 1 to 1.7 (Version B).

June 11, 1675, Day 43

There is no entry in the diary for this day.

June 12, 1675, Day 44

Bosque left San Anbrosio [Ambrosio] and traveled about 14 leagues (36.4 miles) toward the city of Monclova. He arrived at a spot that faced the town and was located at the foot of a large sierra on its west side. Bosque stopped at a water source which he found unoccupied. He took possession, placed a tall wooden cross on the spot, and named it San Bartolome. Bosque was visited by Don Salbador, the Bobosarigame captain who was there with some of his people. Don Salbador offered to send for the rest of his people who, out of necessity, were out searching for food. Fr. Larios taught the doctrine to the Natives and the people were counted. There were 42 warriors and 75 boys and girls. This number included the Tetecore people who were also present. Bosque told them to join the others and to be sure that Don Bernabe, Contotore, and Don Esteban, Gueiquesale, kept an eye on the Bobosarigame and the Tetecore (Portillo 1886: 127–128).

Comments: The camp of San Bartolome was located at the southeast end of the Sierra Sacramento.[35] Again Bosque declared a spot unoccupied, even though there were Native Americans present. Don Salbador's statements about the dispersal of his people in search of food reaffirms a pattern of fission-fusion, which I believe to be the norm among peoples who relied on dispersed food resources. Abundance or absence of localized resources enhanced one or the other of these patterns. There were *no women* counted among the Bobosarigame and the Tetecore. It is possible that women were out gathering vegetable resources, but it is unreasonable that there were none at the camp. It is also possible that there were no women present because they had all been captured and taken to Parral in December 1674 (Portillo 1886: 80). The capture of Native women by the Spanish was a continuous problem between the Native groups and the Spanish authorities. The ratio of warriors to nonwarriors is 1 to 1.8.

The Bobosarigame were not among the groups of the following of Don Esteban, but they were said to recognize his authority. The Tetecore were listed among Don Esteban's following in December 1674. The influence of Don Esteban and Don Bernabe over other groups is affirmed by the orders Bosque gave to the Bobosarigame and Tetecore. A great deal of the authority held by some Native individuals resulted from the authority granted to them by the acts of the Spanish. Obviously this authority had to be sanctioned by the members of the groups, but the prestige conferred by the Spanish was not negligible.

June 12, 1675 — Bosque's Report

On arrival Bosque made a report and recommendations to Don Antonio Balcarcel based on his observations and impressions.

*He stated that he had been sent by Balcarcel to meet the Native groups of the following of Don Esteban, who inhabited the Dacate land, its surroundings, and other areas within the district (**las partes de la tierra Dacate sus contornos y las mas de su distrito y comarca**), because the messengers of these nations had informed Balcarcel they wanted to be Christians and settle in pueblos. Bosque stated that he had traveled the land north-south and east-west and realized that it was divided into three major coalitions, or three divisions (**tres sequitos ó parcialidades de jente**), each with a great number of people.*

The most bellicose, but the least numerous, was the following of Don Esteban Gueiquesale, which consisted of all the people who had been counted, except the Yorica, Jumee, Vivit [Bibit], and Geniocane, since those groups belonged to the followings of the Bobole, and the Catujano-Tilijae. These groups had many conflicts among themselves. They killed each other, ate each other, and kidnapped each other's children, as they themselves stated. At the time of the report several groups were at war: the following of Don Esteban was at war with the Geniocane and their allies; the Yorica, Jumee, and Vivit were at war with the Arame and the Ocane and those of their following; and the Bobole were at war with the Yurbipiame.

*The chains of settlements included very many people, and Bosque stated that the Spaniards did not know where the Native territorial boundaries were located, since neither to the north nor to the east did the Spanish possess any information about their limits. Bosque stated that although he had been asked by the Natives to visit their **rancherías** and those of their allies [further north?], because of the reasons mentioned above, he made the decision not to proceed beyond S. Jorje. For the same reasons he wanted to count the people of Don Esteban on his way back to Monclova, to inform Balcarcel of the situation, and to provide him with the intelligence obtained during the trip.*

*He declared that the various nations wanted to be Christians and settle in pueblos, but they wished to get individual economic and spiritual help, and did not want to be placed together in a pueblo because this would result in conflicts. Even the slightest disagreement would result in fights and killings, generating an environment of discord. Bosque thought the best solution would be to create three main pueblos for the three separate coalitions, whereby they would acknowledge each other, but would remain independent. One of the main settlements (**poblasones cabeseras**) would be located in the valley of San Antonio and the Río Sabinas, a vast area that could encompass many settlements; another, near the Baluartes[36] and the Río San Francisco, would be established in a similar manner; and the third would be the one already established in the town of Guadalupe [Monclova].*

Bosque did not think it possible to keep the Native Americans as practicing Christians because one of the followings was far too barbarous [which one?], and the others were not only barbarous but their contacts with the Spaniards, both in Nueva Vizcaya and in part of the Galizia, had been based on robbing and killing for more than twenty years. He also did not believe that the friars could teach the Natives and keep them in one spot, because the Natives were not accustomed to work to survive and would soon return to their Native ways.

Bosque considered it the wrong policy to keep the people in one spot, since it would bring further unrest, and no Spaniards would be willing to settle the land under such an arrangement. It was common knowledge that some settlers had already left and others continued to abandon the area because of the rumors being spread. Bosque also thought that Santa Crus would be the best spot for the placement of military forces because it was located at about 14 leagues (36.4 miles) from the Valley of San Antonio, at about the same distance from the Valley of the Baluartes, and at about 20 leagues (52 miles) from the town of Nuestra Señora de Guadalupe [Monclova]. Thus Santa Crus was located in the very heart of the land where he proposed the establishment of the three main pueblos. He stated that the military forces now available were insufficient for the needs, and that Santa Crus should have no fewer than 70 military men, since the post would be about 60 leagues (156 miles) from Saltillo and about the same distance from the Kingdom of Nuevo León, which were the nearest supply areas.

Apart from all this, Bosque stated that missionaries would also have to be provided because the Native Americans requested them. The groups did not want to share the friars, but wished to be ministered to individually. Besides, the Native groups spoke different languages and were very numerous, and their settlements were located at great distances. For the moment, at least four missionaries were needed for each chain of settlements, and if the King wished to accept their request and place them in pueblos, it would be necessary to provide seed, oxen, and Tlaxcaltecan families to help with the settlement. Bosque stated that this was his advice because of what he had observed and his experience of more than twenty years among the Natives (Portillo 1886: 128–130).

Comments: In 1739, the *Real Academia Española* defined *parcialidad* as "Se toma tambien por el conjunto de muchos que componen una familia ò facción, lo que es común entre los Indios . . . Porque en conquistando cada Provincia luego reducian los Indios à Pueblos y comunidád, y contabanlos por parcialidádes, y à cada diez Indios ponion uno que tuviesse cuenta de ellos" (RAE, vol. 5, 1739: 125). Thus, the notion of *parcialidad* had a particular meaning in colonial settings. It denoted a large group of Natives that could constitute a family or a faction. The dictionary specifies that when the Spaniards conquered a province they placed (*reduced*) the Natives in pueblos and counted them according to their factions or families (*parcialidades*). For every ten Natives the Spaniards appointed one particular Native to be in charge. In a later document (Anonymous 1746), it is stated that the minimum legal number of people to establish a pueblo was ten.

AFTERMATH

1675–1676, COAHUILA AND TEXAS

On June 22, 1675, the settlers and the Native Americans at Monclova finished planting the corn they had sown in May. Twelve *fanegas* (about nineteen bushels) of seed had been given to the Natives for planting (Portillo 1886: 132). In July they planted beans, vegetables, and grapes. On June 30, Balcarcel and Fr. Larios presided over the religious ceremonies at San Miguel de Luna. During the ceremonies the Bobole captain Juan de la Cruz, his lieutenant, and the captain of the Ape were baptized. Juan de la Cruz and his lieutenant took wives in matrimony. At the ceremonies the Commissary of the Missions, Fr. Juan Larios, preached a sermon in the Mexican language. That same day the Spanish counted the people of Don Esteban not previously counted by Bosque (Portillo 1886: 157).

By July 3, 1675, Balcarcel realized the volatility of the situation: there were too many people and too many conflicts at San Miguel de Luna. He ordered the Ape, Bobosarigame, Catujano, and Manos Prietas to leave the pueblo for their own lands. He promised them religious and material support (Portillo 1886: 159). On July 5, Larios traveled to Guadalajara to ask for help for the conversions in Coahuila. He also asked for the legal authorizations and testimonies that confirmed the religious activities of the Franciscans in the settlement and conquest of Coahuila. Larios stated that he had four religious companions and that there were three Native group-coalitions (*parcialidades*). The Natives had no fixed abode because they had no stable food supply; they sustained themselves with roots and wild fruits that they gathered within a 500-league (1,300-mile) range (*circuito de mas de quinientas leguas*) (Larios 1675). Fr. Larios reported that he was in possession of the baptism, marriage, and burial books that pertained to the three *parcialidades*: Boboles, Huiquesales, and Catuxames and all their allies (Larios 1675a).

For quite some time afterward Fr. Larios, and later Fr. Peñasco, continued to request legal testimonies of their work. At one point Balcarcel confirmed that he had seen the church books and that the baptismal records showed that, between January 26, 1674, and July 5, 1675, 455 people had been baptized, and that the other books included various marriages and burials (Balcarsel 1675).

On July 6, 1675, Balcarcel wrote a very eloquent and unusual letter to the Audiencia de Guadalajara.[37] In it he recommended the establishment of several pueblos, made suggestions for their organization, and recognized the shortcomings of San Miguel de Luna, the inadequacy of the resources available, and the failure of promises made to the Natives (Portillo 1886: 161–171).

On October 26, 1675, Balcarcel was visited by Captain Christobal, a Catujano representative of the Ocane, Maquimixe, Mancequan, Papuliquier, Paponaca, Pahaque, Patoloque, Mesquite, Pataquaque, Canoome, Pausale, Pamafeo, Papanaque, Chanoada, Panaque, Tochi, and Michi nations. The Catujano captain estimated the total population of these groups to be over 2,000 people (a minimum average of 118 people per group). Christobal declared that they wished to settle in pueblos and become Christians. Balcarcel told them to return to their lands and stated that he would inform the King of their wishes (Portillo 1886: 175).

On November 17, 1675, Balcarcel was visited by Juan de la Cruz and Don Esteban, who came on behalf of their people and other groups staying at San Miguel de Luna. These Native leaders were preoccupied with the continuous conflicts, the poor conditions in the pueblo, the rumors circulating among their own people, and the conflicts that resulted from the different languages and the actions of manipulative interpreters (Portillo 1886: 176).

On November 20, 1675, Balcarcel stated his intention to visit the surrounding area and assess its problems in an attempt to keep the peace. It is not certain that this trip ever took place. On the same day he counted the people in Monclova and stated that there were 8 Spaniards and 232 Natives. The rest of the people had left to hunt and eat buffalo near the Rio Grande. By the end of 1676, Balcarcel had left Monclova and was living in Saltillo (Portillo 1886: 179).

THREE

A Move to Revolt

GATHERING THREADS

The 1658 Native efforts to establish autonomous pueblos finally brought about the creation of mission-settlements in the vast area north and east of Saltillo designated as Coahuila: the Valleys of the Buffalo and the Rio Grande, as named by Fr. Larios (Chapter 1). The establishment of these settlements would not have been possible without the help of influential civilians like Antonio Balcarcel and the indefatigable work of Fr. Larios and his Franciscan colleagues. Nonetheless, the result of these endeavors fell short of the expectations of both the Natives and the civilian and religious leaders who strove to make them happen.

By the end of 1675 there were perceptible changes in the attitudes of the friars toward the Natives. Fr. Larios, who in 1674 was adamant against the establishment of military presidios in Coahuila, ended up requesting their creation in 1675. He considered that the fear of the army was essential to prevent destruction of the mission-settlements by the Natives like the assault on Mission Santa Rosa. Consequent moves of the mission-settlements closer to Monclova confirm the missionaries' uneasiness and the difficulty of dealing with resupply and protection issues. Fr. Manuel de la Cruz, who was probably the most pragmatic of the friars and who had an uncanny ability to summarize difficult issues in a simple fashion, realized that some mission-settlements were unlikely to succeed. He considered that, in cases such as the mission of San Buenaventura de las Cuatro Cienegas, the religious and monetary investment might prove unwarranted (de la Cruz 1679).

Businessmen like Balcarcel wanted to invest in worthy causes like the salvation of Native souls, but they also had profit ventures in mind. Since the time of Carvajal, Monclova was known to have good mining possibilities, and Balcarcel was not above increasing his revenues both in heaven and on earth. Although little is known about his short sojourn as Alcalde Mayor of Monclova, we know that he experienced stiff opposition from the Saltillo authorities and businessmen and that he may have miscalculated the extent of their determination and influence.

As for the Native groups, their varied ethnic and social backgrounds as well as their agendas made long-term cohesion a difficult, if not impossible, goal. Their acts, if not their words, speak about disillusionment, distrust, and incomprehension of the expectations of the friars and the rules according to which they were supposed to live and behave. In this case, the heuristic gap between Western and Native worldviews encompassed such basic living issues as how to obtain food, and when and how to sustain themselves.

The philosophy behind the practice of making a living by hunting animals and gathering plant foods implies a very precise and sophisticated geographic knowledge of the land, its water sources, and the location and timing of floral resources as well as the behavior of animals. Place and seasonality (space and time) outline a yearly resource map. The hunting and gathering strategy requires that the location of the place of abode be subsidiary to considerations of time and location of resources. The social structure of groups that hunt and gather and that are highly mobile in order to procure resources entails requirements and arrangements very different from those developed by settled folk. The social structure of hunters and gatherers has to stretch and contract like a rubber band to accommodate times of dispersion as well as times of concentration of groups, and to remain effective under very different social and living conditions. The location and allocation of resources demands that groups and individuals maintain a vast network of friendly contacts, that individuals be easily identified while traveling, and that people abide by recognized and expected behavioral rules—i.e., a behavioral baseline (Wade 1999, 2001). The mobility necessary to locate and procure resources (for present or future use) enhances the conveyance of information; if there is one commodity that a hunter and gatherer can carry without hindrance to his or her movements, it is information. The friars considered the mobility of groups an obstacle to their missionary efforts, but they constantly utilized that mobility to receive and transmit information.

Hunters and gatherers extract a living from nature's bounty by manipulating its localized resources; they do not actively control nature. Horticulturists and agriculturists locate themselves in the land to partially control nature. They build houses to tend and to be near their crops. It is the cyclical control of nature that brings economic rewards, and the space and labor requirements demanded by a farmer's philosophy of making a living are very much at odds with those of a gatherer and hunter. The farmer is bound by the land and the expected crop: he shall not stray. It is symptomatic that the Spanish word for "crop field" is *labor*. That concept, and the expectation of labor in farming, explains the Europeans' contradictory comments about how gatherers and hunters procured a living, and their dismissal of the Natives' work as labor.

The settlement project envisioned by the Native groups and the Franciscan friars in 1673, and again in 1674, resulted from two completely different philosophies of how to make a living, the knowledge required to achieve results, the meaning and practice of labor, and what it meant to be settled in social and economic terms. Neither the Spanish nor the Native Americans understood the chasm between their philosophic views of life and their utilization of nature. Both sides held unrealistic expectations of what these pueblos would be like and what it would take to achieve success. The friars thought that a few head of cattle and the planting and expectation of a crop of maize would entice the Native groups to be settled. The Native Americans did not comprehend the extent of the economic and social changes entailed by a move to a settled life, or the fact that making a living by a mixture of horticultural and hunting-and-gathering strategies could not be achieved in a few months. Furthermore, the spokespersons of major Native groups could try to persuade their group members about the advantages of settled life, but they could not impose their will. The structure of their societies and the immediacy of their common decisions found no counterpart in the slow, inefficient, and bureaucratic processes of Spanish decision-making.

Fr. Larios and his companions, who for several years fought to have several pueblos established, provided whatever help they could obtain from benefactors such as Don Antonio Balcarcel. But the supplies were less than adequate, and the friars and the Natives had to contend with the concerted and armed opposition of the Saltillo authorities. Often the Native groups were asked to furnish the friars with buffalo meat and vegetable foods. The letters and reports written by Fr. Larios, Fr. Peñasco, Fr. Buenaventura, and Fr. Manuel de la Cruz provide the best glimpse at the Natives' approach to hunting and gathering, resource utilization, and scheduling.

The picture that emerges is applicable, in general, to a variety of Native groups and shows that they hunted buffalo from late November through late May–early June, immediately north and south of the Rio Grande, probably in two different hunting seasons. Meat was jerked and pelts obtained. During this period, some groups, with populations ranging from one hundred to five hundred, established *rancherías* north of the Rio Grande, even though members of some groups, such as the Bobole, Catujano, Gueiquesale, and Manos Prietas, remained close to the Spanish settlements of Monclova and Saltillo. Other groups, such as the Ape, Bibit, Geniocane, Jumee, and some Yorica, appear to have remained north of the Rio Grande for most of the year, with limited and strategic forays into the southern margin of the Rio Grande. From late April through November most of the groups gathered the tuna of the prickly pear, mescal, berries, and nuts. Fish and lard were used most of the year, but particularly after November when the tuna became scarce. The friars are specific about the abundance of natural resources of which they partook, even though most were not to their liking.

After the mission-settlements were established in Coahuila, the Native groups that frequented those missions used the food resources produced there, such as fowl, cattle, and cereal crops, to add to their yearly schedule of resources. According to the friars, the Natives spent the winter hunting buffalo and deer. Around March they returned to the mission-settlements to profit from the crops produced and stored in the missions. They departed the missions in June when the tuna ripened. From June to September they survived on the tuna and other vegetable resources. Obviously Native groups in different areas benefited from a variety of different resources, but it appears that, for most of the groups, this resource scheduling did not differ in its basic principles.

SETTING THE STAGE

THE NORTHERN FRONTIER OF NEW SPAIN — SIXTEENTH AND SEVENTEENTH CENTURIES

The process of contact between Native communities and the colonizers in northern New Spain can be visualized as the perpetual movement of a pendulum: never at rest, sometimes at extremes, but mostly somewhere between appeasement and revolt.

The Native American groups of northern New Spain did not accept easily the changes that the arrival of the Spaniards brought into their lives. Soon after the Spanish colonizers moved into a specific area, localized revolts flared up like wildfires dotting the northern landscape. As soon as the Spanish put out one rebellious fire, another one erupted somewhere else. These conflicts eroded the Spaniards' resources, but not their resolve, spurred as it was by the lure of silver and souls.

The picture that emerges from Galaviz's (1963, 1967) and Florescano's (1969) summaries of major revolt movements during the sixteenth and seventeenth centuries leaves no doubt that Spanish settlement, missionary activities, mining operations, and other economic ventures brought about indigenous grievances and led to rebellion.

During the sixteenth century the major rebellions track Spanish attempts to colonize indigenous areas. Starting with the province of Panuco (1529–1530) (Galaviz 1963: 144), and ending with Topia and Sinaloa in the 1590s, every decade was marked by one or more major revolt in the various areas of northern New Spain undergoing colonization. During that same century, the Native populations in Saltillo organized at least three major revolts: Guachichile (1575), northern nomadic groups (*chichimecos*) (1582), and Guachichile and Pacho (1586–1589). One hundred years after their first revolt in Saltillo (1575), the Guachichile were said to number but a handful (Chapter 1). Nevertheless, the Guachichile and their allies appear as leading members of revolt movements until 1618–1621 (Florescano 1969: 73).

The seventeenth century started with the rebellions of the Acaxee, Tepehuane, Tarahumare, and Xixime in Sinaloa and Durango and ended with the revolt of the Seri and the Salinero in Sonora. Within the jurisdiction of Nueva Viscaya, which encompassed various modern Mexican states, there were thirty-one major revolts during the seventeenth century, which included the revolts of the Quamoquane and the Cacaxtle in Coahuila (Chapter 1; see also Chapa and Foster 1997: 49, 55–56).

In 1680 the Pueblo groups of New Mexico demonstrated the effectiveness of a cohesive and well-orchestrated revolt. For over a decade the Puebloans managed to hold the Spanish at bay. But, as well organized as some of these revolts were, the lack of a concerted effort by the various Native groups meant that the Spanish were not expelled from occupied Native territories. Instead, the revolts depleted Native resources and led to massive displacements of Native populations. The enslavement of populations, their forced movement to other areas where they had no support networks, and the congregation of large groups in settlements established by the Spanish resulted in long-term social and demographic disruptions.

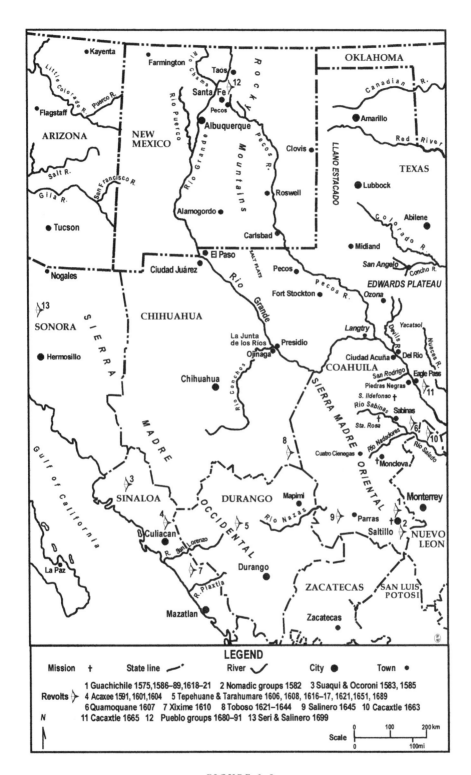

FIGURE 3.1
Major revolts in northern New Spain during the sixteenth and seventeenth centuries.

COAHUILA

1676–1682

On January 24, 1676, the bishop of Guadalajara, Don Manuel, visited the Coahuila mission-settlement. Don Manuel was welcomed by Fr. Larios and five or six Bobole. The bishop inspected the church buildings and paraphernalia and issued directives as to the improvements to be made in the church, the building of the friars' housing, and their conduct toward the Natives and the Spanish population. He ordered the friars to keep records of their missionary activities in books of white paper and to put as much emphasis on teaching the Natives how to grow their food and build their houses as on teaching doctrine.

Don Manuel entreated the Franciscans to learn the Native languages because it was impossible to teach them and administer the sacraments if the two parties could not communicate. He stressed that the friars should get the assistance of ladinos, who were very quick to learn other languages, and who in turn could teach the friars the local languages. The bishop commented that the maternal language of the Natives from the Monclova area was very different from Mexican (Nahuatl) (*que es muy distinta de la de los Mexicanos*) (Banegas 1676).

On January 25 Don Manuel assigned the four missions to the friars. Fr. Estevan Martinez was assigned the mission and province of the Catuxanes. Fr. Dionisio de San Buenaventura was assigned the mission of Quatro Cienegas. Fr. Francisco Peñasco de Lozano was assigned to Santa Rosa, where he would be with Don Estevan Gueiquetzale. Fr. Manuel de la Cruz was assigned the Coahuila mission (Monclova), where he would be with the Bobole and their following (*y sus parciales*) (Banegas 1676).

Fr. Larios was given an impossible assignment: he was told to be the conscience of Nueva Vizcaya. In fact, the bishop of Guadalajara ordered Fr. Larios to contact all the people in Saltillo and other settlements in and around Coahuila who kept Natives to use as slaves (*para servierse de ellos en lugar de esclavos*), to admonish them not to keep Natives as slaves and to free them. Don Manuel stressed that such were the legal commandments of His Majesty, and failure to do so was to be punished with excommunication (Banegas 1676).

After Fr. Larios died in September 1676, Fr. Peñasco continued to request the originals of the documentation that confirmed their work in the area. A series of documents from 1677 and 1681 (CAH 1698) discuss the economic help to be given to the Native Americans and the friars working in the area. By order of the bishop of Guadalajara, 600 *fanegas* (about 948 bushels) of corn plus 200 calves were to be given each year to the Native converts in Coahuila. These supplies had been earmarked for the Guachichile, but their numbers had been so reduced that they no longer needed such abundant food supplies. It appears that this help was being provided, even though final approval was not formalized until February 1679 (Marques de la Laguna 1681a). In April 1677, the documents refer to four coalitions (*parcialidades*) and not three, as was the case during Larios's time.

This agrees with the pueblo distribution mentioned above and the assignment of friars made by the bishop of Guadalajara.

On April 10, 1679, Fr. Manuel de la Cruz wrote to the Father Commissioner a detailed report on the state of the Coahuila missions (de la Cruz 1679). Fr. Manuel was in charge of the four Franciscan missions in Coahuila. What follows is an extensive digest of the report.

The Mission of San Francisco de Coahuila (Monclova) (SFC) was in good condition. It had a church, a baptistery, and a convent with four cells. These flat-roofed buildings were whitewashed and equipped with windows, doors, and keys. Apart from the four cells, the convent included an entry area, a corridor, a kitchen, and a chicken coop. The pueblo had three acequias that provided sufficient water for the pueblo and the fields. The residents had sown wheat and corn and expected a good crop. The mission was equipped with oxen as well as all the tools needed to work the land.

The Natives that lived in the pueblo were the most tractable (*domesticos*) of the barbarous (*barbaros*) groups, and worked harder than the Natives from other missions. Periodically the Native males left to go buffalo hunting, but their women and children remained in the pueblo, which they considered as their own settlement (*poblacion*). The young Native people were very capable: they learned the Christian doctrine, and some assisted at mass. The Natives lived in well-made *jacales* and raised poultry and other animals. There were also six Tlaxcaltecan families, three of which had flat-roofed (*tejado*) houses: the other three families were still building their dwellings. Four Spanish families remained from the earlier settlement and resided at the pueblo. The mission had good lands and sufficient water, but was poor in wood for construction. Fr. Manuel de la Cruz and Fr. Balthazar were in charge of the mission.

The Mission San Bernardino de los Baluartes (later called La Candela) (C), was located 18 leagues (46.8 miles) from Mission San Francisco in Monclova. The terrain between these two missions was level, and east of Monclova there were four water sources along the way. They had built the church and sacristy, which were flat-roofed and whitewashed. The portion of the convent already constructed had two cells, an entry hall, and a corridor. The cells were equipped with windows, doors, and keys. The mission had an acequia that was sufficient for the needs of the pueblo and the crop fields. The water supply was good, and wood could be obtained at a distance of 1 league (2.6 miles). They had oxen and all the tools needed to work the land. They were expecting good crops of wheat and corn.

The Native people who lived in the mission were the most jovial as well as the most peaceful (Catujano, Tilijai, and Milijai). Although they did not work very hard, they were the easiest to "reduce" because of their peaceful behavior. There were also four Tlaxcaltecan families residing in the pueblo, and they had flat-roofed houses. The weather conditions were generally mild. Fr. Estevan Martinez and Fr. Dionisio de San Buenaventura were in charge of the mission.

Mission Santa Rrosa [*sic*] (SRSM2) was located 6 leagues (15.6 miles) from Mission

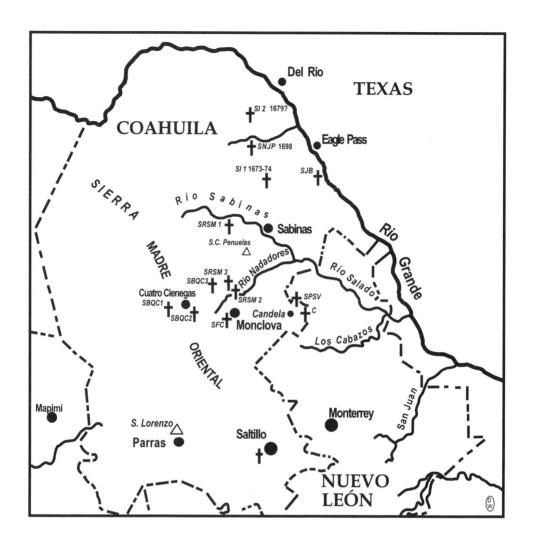

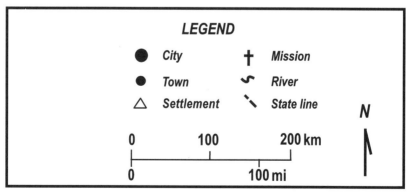

FIGURE 3.2
Map of sixteenth-century Coahuila missions mentioned in the text.

San Francisco in Monclova. The terrain between these missions was level, and there was a water supply northward and midway between the two missions. The mission had an excellent location: the middle of a spacious meadow near the Río Nadadores. This river carried such abundant waters that it could be forded in only a few places. The friars had built a church as good as the one in Monclova, and with better wooden beams. There was a large cell for the friars equipped with door and key. The mission had a good acequia that carried sufficient water for the needs of the pueblo and to irrigate the fields. The lands of the pueblo were exceptionally good for corn and they had planted 8 *fanegas* (12.64 bushels) of wheat and the crop was doing well. The mission had oxen and all the equipment necessary to work the land.

A great many Natives frequented Santa Rrosa, and these were the most intractable in the land. They belonged to the groups that lived in the Valleys of the Buffalo and the Rio Grande. They lived in remote areas eating buffalo in the winter, returning to the mission and leaving again at the time of the prickly-pear tuna, which in the Sabinas area began in June. When they came to the mission they arrived in large groups, ate away all the crops, and shot the oxen with arrows. They destroyed all they could find, broke walls to get to the stored crops, and took the mules or horses (*bestias*). This had occurred the previous year (1678), and such occurrences disheartened the friars. The actions of these Natives incited those of the closest mission (San Francisco at Monclova) to the same rebellious activities. For these reasons the crops and supplies were never sufficient. Fr. Peñasco and Fr. Juan Macias were in charge of this mission.

Mission San Buenaventura de las Quatro Cienegas (SBQC2) was located 14 leagues (36.4 miles) from Mission San Francisco amid very high and rugged mountains. The terrain between the two missions was level and had many water sources. Facing the pueblo and to the east were four swampy lakes of bitter, salty water. The water that supplied the pueblo issued from a gap in the mountains located to the west. The sweet water was taken from some lagoons. Because of the mountainous terrain the weather was harsh with high and continuous cold winds. They had finished erecting the church and baptistery, and these buildings looked quite beautiful, supported with twenty-nine sturdy wood beams. Over the baptistery was located a tower equipped with a bell. The convent had two cells and a sacristy erected with wooden supports. The pines for these supports were brought by the Natives from a mountain located about 3 leagues (7.8 miles) from the pueblo.

The baptistery had a stone cross with pedestal and steps. This cross was carved by a Tlaxcalteco whom Fr. Manuel brought to the mission to teach the Natives and to help Fr. Juan de Leon, who at that time was alone in the mission. At the time of the report, Fr. Juan de Leon was being helped by Fr. Juan Barrero. The Tlaxcaltecan artisan who carved the cross was going to remain in the mission until the design and layout of the pueblo were completed. The mission was in good shape and had an acequia that provided water for the pueblo and the cornfields. They had two teams of oxen and all the tools needed to work the land. The Natives had sown their fields (*milpas*) using shovels and the field of the pueblo (communal?) had been started.

The mission served very many diverse Native groups, among which were some very bad individuals. Because there were so many different groups and they all got together at the time the storehouses were full, they ate everything during their peace gatherings. At such times they danced and made beverages from peyote and from a small bean (*peyote y frejolillo*). Few cared to work, and all were interested in consuming the calves and the corn. Once the food supplies ran out they departed: some to the mountains, others to Parral, and others to Parras. As Fr. Manuel noted, those who went to Parral were "the poor and unfortunate ones who would pain in the mines" (de la Cruz 1679). In less than three months the poor friars were left without supplies, without Natives, and often without seed to plant the next crop.

In 1762 Fr. Alonso Muñoz (1762) wrote a lengthy report to the Franciscan Commissary General. Although the report was written long after the period considered in this chapter, its contents require that it be included in this narrative. The report confirms much of what Fr. Manuel de la Cruz stated in 1679 but adds important information, including the various moves each mission underwent.

The Mission San Francisco de Coahuila (Monclova) (SFC) was located northward of the church established by the friars between 1673 and 1679. To the south was located the pueblo of San Miguel de Luna. The mission-settlement of San Francisco had been established with twenty Tlaxcaltecan families who came from San Estevan del Saltillo to teach the new converts how to build their houses and work the land. According to this report Fr. Larios and his companions decided to establish the other mission-settlements due to the natural enmities among the various ethnic groups. The mission was founded primarily for the Obaya and the Bobole, and later for the Toboso.

The Mission San Bernardino de la Candela (C) was located 22 leagues (57.2 miles) from Coahuila (Monclova), and it had been established for the Catuxane, Milixai, and Tilixai.

The Mission of San Buenaventura de los Colorados (Quatro Cienegas—SBQC1) was located 20 leagues (52 miles) west of Coahuila (Monclova) at Quatro Sienegas (Cuatro Cienegas). It was established for the Cabeza (Cabesa), Contotore, and Bausarigame. The mission remained in that locality for a few years, but it was moved to the place of the Contotore (Puesto de los Contotores), 14 leagues (36.4 miles) from Coahuila (Monclova) and 6 leagues (15.6 miles) east of Quatro Sienegas (SBQC2). This move occurred before 1679.

The Mission of Quatro Sienegas (San Buenaventura) remained in this new locality until the conflicts that pitted the Bausarigame against the Cabesa and the Contotore reached their zenith. One night these groups became involved in a pitched battle and some (Cabesa and Contotore) hid in the friars' cells. Because the friars defended the Cabesa and the Contotore during the fight, Fr. Ygnacio Telles was wounded in the arm and Fr. Bartholome de Cardenas would have been killed except for the intervention of an elderly female (Cabesa or Contotore). The Bausarigame ran from the pueblo, but the Contotore and the Cabesa caught up with them. In an open field the three groups fought a fierce battle that lasted from sunrise to sunset. The Contotore were decimated (*se consumio la nacion de los Contotores*), and only a few Cabesa survived. After the battle the remaining Cabesa, together with their "leaders," Don Pedrotes and Don Santiago, left for Parras, where their descendants were still living in 1746.

The Mission of Quatro Sienegas (San Buenaventura) remained abandoned until 1691 when Fr. Martin Ponce traveled to the interior (*tierra adentro*) and reduced and brought to the mission the Colorado and the Toca. The mission was reestablished in the Rio Nadadores Valley 9 or 10 leagues (23.4 to 26 miles) from Monclova (SBQC3). It was at this time that the mission became known as San Buenaventura de los Colorados. The mission remained in that locale for several years. Later it was moved again to the place called San Joseph, about 5 leagues (13 miles) from Coahuila (Monclova), where it remained until 1746 (SBQC4).

Mission Santa Rosa de Nadadores (SRSM1) was first established for the Quetzal (Gueiquesale) and Manos Prietas. It was then located at the foot of a very high mountain about 40 leagues (104 miles) to the northwest (actually northeast) of Coahuila (Monclova). It remained in this location only a short while because of the many groups that frequently raided it. The mission was moved to the Río Nadadores prior to 1679: it was at this time that it became known as Santa Rosa de Nadadores (SRSM2). While in the Valley of the Río Nadadores, the mission was moved twice. In 1693, the mission was destroyed by the Toboso and moved once more, with the few people who still remained in it, to a spot about 6 to 7 leagues (15.6 to 18.2 miles) from Monclova (SRSM3). The mission retained its earlier name under the care of Fr. Buenaventura Boniel (or Boriel).

During this period there were several rebellions and desertions. At one time Fr. Balthazar Pacheco would have been burned alive except for the intervention of a young Quetzal (Gueiquesale) male. On another occasion Fr. Juan Yerben traveled inland for six months and managed to bring the Natives back to the mission. At another time Fr. Christoval Mexia spent sixty-one days in the interior looking for the Natives, but he managed to bring them back to the mission, where they remained in 1762.

Mission San Phelipe de Santiago de Valladares (SPSV), as the mission was known in 1736, was originally established by Fr. Estevan Martinez, one of the friars who worked with Fr. Juan Larios. The writer states that Fr. Estevan set up San Phelipe 2 leagues (5.2 miles) distant from Mission San Bernardino de la Candela (C). This mission was established for the Acaphe and Chantaphe whom Fr. Estevan brought from the most remote points of Sierra de Leones. Fr. Estevan wanted to congregate the Acaphe and the Chantaphe with the Catujano, Milixai, and Tilixai, but the ethnic enmities among these groups ruined his plans. Because he did not have a friar to reside at San Phelipe, Fr. Estevan was forced to keep San Phelipe as a *visita* of Mission Candela. However, the Natives were not pleased with the arrangement and slowly abandoned the mission. Later, some other natives, who had been *encomendados* in Nuevo León, approached the friars and asked to be placed in San Phelipe. The friars used that mission as a way station when traveling to the Rio Grande and Texas. In time, the mission was entrusted to the clergy (Ordinario), but it remained without a priest for one or two years. In 1691 Bishop Galindo reestablished the mission, this time under the name of San Phelipe de Santiago de Valladares (Phelipe after His Majesty the King, and Valladares after the Viceroy). As a result of the report of Rábago y Therán, the mission was closed in 1746 (Chapter 6).

The friar also related the history of Mission Ssmo Nombre de Jesus (SNJP), initially located 60 leagues[1] (156 miles) north of Coahuila (Monclova) near the river called San Yldephonso (SI1?). This mission was first established by Fr. Peñasco (1673–1674) with twenty Quetzale (Gueiquesale) families and four Tlaxcaltecan families. After two years these Natives left the mission because of the constant enemy raids. Later, Fr. Augustin Carrera reestablished the mission and managed to keep it functioning for a period of four years (SI2?), but enemy attacks once more led to its abandonment.

In 1698, Fr. Manuel Borrego and Fr. Bartholome Adame traveled to the interior with two Spanish soldiers and some Natives. While on this trip they were fortunate to encounter the large nation of the Xijame, who were fleeing from the troubles raised by the Coyame, the Tripas Blancas, and the Gavilane. The Xixame (Xijame) were quick to join the friars, and together they settled in the mission, which by then was located 10 leagues (26 miles) closer to Coahuila (Monclova) than the previous mission: it was at this time that the mission became known as SSmo Nombre de Jesus de los Peyotes (SNJP).

Meanwhile, in August 1681, Fr. Peñasco (Real Cedula 1681) again requested the legal documentation the Franciscans had been asking for since 1675. He also requested the books of baptism, marriage, and burial. Just as Fr. Larios had done in 1675, Fr. Peñasco asked the Viceroy Marqués de la Laguna to establish a presidio in the area to be manned by fifty soldiers and a corporal. These soldiers were to be hired from among the settlers in the province.

In 1681, the King and the Viceroy appointed Fernando del Bosque Alcalde Mayor and Capitan de Guerra of the New Settlements and Conversions of the Natives of Coahuila. He was to be put in charge of a company of twenty-five soldiers. In a statement to the Viceroy, Bosque wrote that the Toboso were the most troublesome group, asked for families to settle the land, and made several requests for military supplies. Bosque also mentioned the fear and preoccupation that the New Mexico Native revolt of August 1680 was causing among the military and the settlers (Marques de la Laguna 1681). In his royal appointment, Bosque was given authority to allot lands and grant water rights to new settlers (*la faculdad para que repartam tierras, aguas, solares, y huertas a las familias*) (Marques de la Laguna 1681; Real Cedula 1681). On April 17, 1682, Don José de Bracamonte was appointed war captain of the province of Coahuila.

REFLECTIONS

The pattern of revolt movements tracks Spanish settlement and economic pursuits in northern New Spain and probably also reflects the pattern of removal of rebellious Native populations to other regions. Mission-settlements provided refuge from immediate conflict, bought time, and often served as bases of operations to plan the next revolt.

Various documents covering almost a century of missionary work in northeast Coahuila and the Rio Grande show that the mission-settlements were plagued with problems. Even if Native groups had been prepared and willing to remain in the mission-
settlements and had labored to make them flourish, the Spanish appetite for the best and
most profitable lands fated the mission-settlements to an ever-diminishing role.

FOUR

The Mendoza-Lopez Expedition, 1683–1684

THE ARCHIVAL DOCUMENTS

The translation of the diary of the expedition of Maestro del Campo Juan Dominguez de Mendoza and Fr. Nicolas Lopez was first published by Eugene Bolton in 1916. Bolton did not include the complete diary of the expedition's return trip. Bolton's translation (1916: 343) terminates at the point where the Spaniards reached the road they had taken on the outbound journey. Bolton's translation was based on the diary that appears in a series of documents compiled in *Provincias Internas,* vol. 37. The *Itinerario* can be found in *Expediente 4, fojas* 69–82, and it is followed by a series of documents related to the expedition. One of these documents is the diary of the trip from La Junta de los Ríos to El Paso. This version of the diary is available in typescript at the Center for American History (Mendoza 1684). It was copied by D. Pedro Ladron de Guebara at El Passo [*sic*] on October 7, 1684. This version is said to correspond to the original, which remained in the archives of El Paso, and to have been corrected in the presence of two witnesses, which may indicate that this copy was "castigated" (see Introduction). Guebara was Governor Cruzate's secretary. The typescript was produced in Mexico on September 17, 1909, by, or under the orders of, Justino Rubio. However, the microfilm version of *Provincias Internas,* vol. 37, available at the Benson Latin American Collection (hereafter called BLAC), does not include Mendoza's diary.

There are at least two more copies of the diary, which appear in *Archivo General de la Nación* (AGN); *Historia,* vol. 298, frames 371–399 (Mendoza 1684a); and *Historia,* vol. 299, frames 173–188 (Mendoza 1684b). Both versions state that they are copies from the original that exists in the Viceroyal oldest documents. Bolton (1916: 318) mentioned the set of documents in *Historia,* vol. 298. Neither version includes the scribe's name or the date of the copy, nor are they the original documents. Both *Historia* volumes are available in microfilm at the BLAC.

There are some discrepancies among these three versions of the diary, principally the number and spelling of names of Native groups that Mendoza included in the diary. The diary version of *Provincias Internas,* vol. 37 (CAH), presents eleven groups in the first list, while the versions from *Historia,* vols. 298 and 299, present nineteen group names in the first list. All versions present thirty-six group names in the second list. Bolton's translation (1916: 339) presents nineteen groups in the first list, which means that, unless he had a different copy than the one housed at CAH, he used the lists that appeared in *Historia*.

In 1999, I found another version of Mendoza's travel diary at the University of New Mexico. This copy (Mendoza 1684c) is the typewritten translation of a document that France Scholes apparently obtained at the Biblioteca Nacional de Madrid and is included in the France V. Scholes Collection at the Center for Southwest Research (see References). When the contents of this version were scrutinized it was immediately apparent that this version (hereafter called Version M) was very different from all the other travel diaries. The differences are so substantial that they affect previous interpretations, including my own (Wade 1998). Thus, pertinent information and divergences of Version M from the version translated here (hereafter called Version L) will be included and discussed at the end of each diary entry. In the translation of the travel diary I have used the copy that appears in *Historia*, vol. 298, because this version (Version L) is closer to the version translated and published by Bolton (1916).

Bolton (1916) preceded the translation of the Mendoza-Lopez expedition with some short historical comments. Charles Wilson Hackett (1934: 329–353) translated Pichardo's *Treatise on the Limits of Louisiana and Texas* and commented on the material used by Pichardo, which included a discussion of Mendoza's trip, and identified some of the sources used. J. W. Williams (1962: 111–133) traced Mendoza's route, using Bolton's translation. In 1969, Seymour V. Connor (1–29) retraced and commented on Mendoza's route. Connor used the version of the diary in *Províncias Internas,* vol. 37, but had some parts of the journal retranslated.[1] None of these researchers fully mapped the Mendoza-Lopez expedition route or included the return trip from La Junta to El Paso.

SETTING THE STAGE

The Spanish expedition of Juan Dominguez de Mendoza and Fr. Nicolas Lopez to the territory later known as Texas took place in 1683–1684. The expeditionary party left El Paso del Río del Norte in December 1683, traveled east to the lands of the Jumano in west and west-central Texas, and returned to El Paso in July 1684. As was the case with the Bosque-Larios *entrada,* knowledge of the events that preceded the Mendoza-Lopez expedition is essential in order to comprehend the motives that led to the expedition, as well as some of the events that took place during and after the trip. The route traveled by the expedition provides information on the location of Native groups, environment, and resources, and also places in context events that took place long before the expedition.

The Pueblo Revolt of 1680 forced the New Mexico Spanish population and some Native groups to flee and take refuge, temporarily, at El Paso del Río del Norte. This temporary refuge camp evolved into a town, changing the character of the small settlement that existed prior to the arrival of the refugees. In 1683 the conditions at El Paso continued to be dire. Short of food, clothing, and military supplies, the Spanish had been abandoning the town, with or without permission.

The church and military officials at El Paso made repeated requests for economic help and for the reconquest of New Mexico, but their petitions elicited a lukewarm, if not a negative, response. The continuous threat of the rebellious Native populations in New Mexico, the frequent Apache raids, and the eruption of rebellious nuclei all along the northern Spanish territories and along the Rio Grande kept the citizenry on edge. Fear of the Native populations and lack of food and clothing fostered very low morale. The situation was so bad that the friars celebrated Sunday mass at night because the people were embarrassed to be seen in rags in daylight (La Bastida 1684).

The 1680 Pueblo Revolt materialized the worst nightmare of the colonial settler, but it also disrupted long-term and complex relations of friendship, dependency, and enmity, which often congealed into trade issues. The century of European presence in New Mexico had fostered symbiotic and mutualistic relationships among the various Native groups and the Europeans, with some measure of mutual benefit. Trade in crops, manufactured goods, and slaves had developed into a considerably profitable business. While it is clear what commercial benefits the Europeans derived, it is not always as clear how the Native Americans profited. But profit they did, because at the time of the Mendoza-Lopez expedition both Native Americans and Spaniards were deeply interested in reestablishing trade ties.

During 1683, both New Mexico governors, Antonio Otermín and his replacement, Domingo Petris de Cruzate, were visited by delegations of Native Americans led by Juan Sabeata, a Jumano. These Natives wanted to reestablish trade ties with the Spaniards and to request the help of the Spaniards against their common enemy, the Apache. The request of the Jumano and other Native groups played into the hands of Governor Cruzate. Cruzate, a newcomer to the area, faced the concerted discontent of powerful Spanish families, such as the Mendozas, who had suffered heavy personal losses with the Pueblo Revolt and deeply resented the inertia of the Crown regarding New Mexico. Cruzate feared the unrest of these influential people, especially in view of the economic and military problems being experienced by the community. Thus, when an opportunity arose to get rid of Mendoza for a good period of time, Governor Cruzate was happy to do so.

The expedition provided Governor Cruzate with another bonus. He had been requesting weapons and ammunition from the Viceroy without success (Cruzate 1683). The Viceroy made it clear that Cruzate was engaged in a defensive war against the Apache and did not need more supplies. If Cruzate became engaged in a new discovery, the request would be treated differently. The expedition to the Jumano lands provided the perfect excuse to request weapons and ammunition, while also creating the possibility for personal glory.

Fr. Nicolas Lopez was a man of action. Since his arrival he had worked incessantly to improve the conditions at El Paso, both for the Spanish and the Native communities. His continual requests for help from the ecclesiastic and military authorities were responsible for some of the relief given to those communities. He considered the location at El

Paso del Rio inadequate for settlement and continued scouting for a more appropriate location. While working with the Jumano, he not only learned the language, but developed a written vocabulary for it. Fr. Lopez's interest in the expedition was twofold: the anticipated conversions and the potential for promoting a new area for settlement. The Jumano invitation to travel to their lands, establish pueblos, and minister to their people fulfilled his ambitions.

Juan Dominguez de Mendoza needed to get away from El Paso and his legal problems. He too was interested in finding another area for settlement where he could recover his losses. Now in his fifties, he had spent all his adult life soldiering for the King in New Mexico. He had lost most of his wealth and was disillusioned with the Crown and the feeble prospects for the reconquest of New Mexico. In 1681 and 1683, two legal charges had been brought against him, the first for disobedience and the other for profiteering. He had little left to lose, and was sufficiently interested in the trip to the Jumano to partly cover the cost of the expedition (Madrid et al. 1684).

In December 1683, Governor Cruzate ordered the expedition to the Jumano lands in the east. He placed edicts calling for volunteers, and those who wanted to participate were asked to outfit themselves (Cruzate 1683c). The explicit purposes of the expedition were to consider the possibilities for settlement, minister to the groups who were asking for baptism, and help the Jumano and their allies against the Apache. Maestro de Campo Juan Dominguez de Mendoza was to be accompanied by seventeen Spaniards and by the Franciscans Fr. Nicolas Lopez, Fr. Juan Zavaleta, and Fr. Acevedo. This was certainly a very small military force with which to fight the Apache.

According to Version L, which I assume to have been written by Fr. Lopez or Fr. Sabaleta, Juan Sabeata and Mendoza had such strong disagreements during the trip that Mendoza accused Sabeata of lying and cheating, and expelled him. What really happened is not clear; what is clear is that the Spaniards never fought the Apache, even when the Apache attacked them. The Spanish were supposed to meet a large number of Native groups who belonged to the Jumano coalition, but for most of them no meeting ever took place because Mendoza's small military force could not face the Apache attacks.

The diary version I assume to have been written by Mendoza (Version M) accuses Sabeata of being a liar and a cheat, but downplays his activities and clearly indicates that Sabeata was not expelled. Unlike all other versions, this version refers to the problems Mendoza experienced with his own Spanish troops, which led Mendoza to sentence two of his compatriots to death. Only the intervention of the friars spared the lives of the accused. This version of the trip includes events that challenge the interpretations made from the analysis of the other diary versions. The interpretive dilemma caused by the discrepancies between versions L and M can stand as a case study in the difficulty and fragility of the interpretation of historical events and the need for continuing research.

Nevertheless, on balance, the Jumano coalition had very little to show for its efforts. Sabeata and his allies did supply pelts and food, since both Spaniards and Natives hunted large numbers of buffalo. If the Apache were to have been made aware of an alliance between Spaniards and the Jumano coalition, this did not happen. When attacked by the

Apache and the Salinero, the Spanish returned home. Sabeata lost face: the old Jumano friendship with the Spaniards was not translated into a profitable military alliance. Mendoza and Fr. Lopez did look over the country in great detail and found it suitable for settlement. Later, both men traveled to Mexico City to plead their case for settlement in the area of the Edwards Plateau, but the Crown was not swayed. The exploration of Texas was postponed.

PAST EVENTS

1583–1683

The thread that ties the Mendoza-Lopez expedition to the past runs through several decades. In 1629, Father Juan Salas traveled eastward over 100 leagues (260 miles) from New Mexico to the lands of a group called the Jumano. Fr. Salas, who had been in New Mexico since 1616 (Scholes and Bloom 1945: 58), had previous contacts with the Jumano, who had requested the help and presence of friars. Fr. Alonso de Benavides, New Mexico custodian (1625–1629) and Salas's superior, postponed missionary work among the Jumano because he was short of friars for the work among the puebloans.

In 1629, Benavides was replaced as custodian by Fr. Esteban Perea, who brought along a new group of friars to relieve the shortage of missionary workers (Scholes and Bloom 1945: 58). On July 22, 1629, a fifty-member Jumano delegation visited the friars at San Antonio de Isleta (Old Isleta, below the present city of Albuquerque), requesting baptism and a visit from the friars (Fernandez Duro 1882: 57). Fr. Benavides reported that at the time of this visit there was a drought on the plains: the water sources used by the Jumano had dried up, and the large buffalo herds they relied on for their sustenance had moved away. A Jumano shaman insisted that the group should move to look for food (Ayer et al. 1965: 59). Between 1630 and 1632, Fr. Salas was appointed prelate of New Mexico (Scholes 1936: 283). In 1632, Fr. Salas visited the Jumano again, accompanied by Fr. Diego Ortega and a group of soldiers (Fernandez Duro 1882: 57). This time they traveled 200 leagues (520 miles) southeast from Santa Fé to reach the Jumano lands on a river called Nueces.[2] Fr. Salas returned to Santa Fé, and Fr. Ortega, probably with some soldiers, stayed in the area for six more months (Fernandez Duro 1882: 57). In his religious zeal to document the triumph of good over evil, Fr. Benavides may have provided the clue to the southward movement of these Jumano groups. The drought conditions and the movement of the buffalo herds may have forced some Jumano to move to the Río Nueces (the Concho River near San Angelo, hereafter called Concho River), where Fr. Salas visited them in 1632.

In 1583 the Espejo-Luxán party encountered Jumano groups near the modern town of Pecos in western Texas (Chapter 1). These Jumano, who were hunting buffalo near the modern town of Pecos and just upstream from the junction of Toyah Creek and the Pecos River, were familiar with the course of the Pecos River to its point of entry into the Rio Grande. It appears that the hunting range of the Jumano groups extended at least from the area around Toyah Creek, Texas (1583), to Carlsbad, New Mexico (1629), and

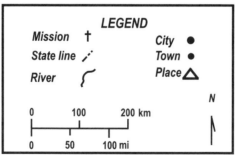

FIGURE 4.1
Map showing important places mentioned in the text.

farther east to the drainage of the Concho River (1632). It is also likely that Castaño de Sosa's party (1590) passed through some of the area traveled by Mendoza in 1684.[3]

In New Mexico the decades of the 1630s and 1640s were characterized by continual conflict between members of the Church and the Crown, and little time was left for conducting expeditionary and missionary work.[4] In 1641, when Governor Juan Flores de Sierra y Valdez replaced Governor Rosas, tensions were temporarily relaxed, and in 1650, Sergeant Major (or Capitan) Diego del Castillo and Captain Hernan Martin visited the Jumano on the Concho River (Fernandez Duro 1882: 57–58; Sabeata 1683a). They departed from Santa Fé and traveled southeast 200 leagues (520 miles). They obviously traveled the same route taken by Fr. Salas on his 1632 trip to the Jumano. After reaching the Concho River, the Martin-Castillo group traveled further to a body of water they called Río de las Perlas (Fernandez Duro 1882: 57–58).

While in the area, some members of the expedition traveled 50 leagues (130 miles) further in an east-southeast direction through the lands of the Cuitoa, Excanxaque, and Ayjado, reaching the western confines of the lands of the Tejas (Caddo). The Spaniards decided not to enter the Tejas territory because it was very vast and populous, and the Spaniards were not sure of their welcome. Aware of the Spanish presence, the leader of the Tejas sent one of his captains to visit Diego del Castillo. The Spaniards remained in the area six months. During their stay they collected samples of freshwater pearls, which later were sent to Viceroy Alva de Liste (Fernandez Duro 1882: 58). Interest in these pearls led in part to the next expedition, which took place four years later. The visit of Diego del Castillo to the Jumano lands was later confirmed by Juan Sabeata (1683a).

In 1654, Sergeant Major Diego de Guadalajara, with a group of thirty soldiers and about two hundred Christian Native Americans, traveled again to the Jumano lands on the Concho River. This trip probably took place before Easter, because Christoval de Anaya (1663), who was defending himself against the charge of heresy, testified that he had fulfilled the Catholic duty of annual confession while on a trip to the east with twenty-nine other soldiers. According to Anaya (1663), they had gone to discover new lands and had traveled east about 300 leagues (780 miles) through the lands of infidel, but friendly, Natives. On this trip, which took nine months, they found some pearls. At the end of the trip they entered enemy lands and engaged in battle with those enemies (Anaya 1663).

Among the soldiers who went with Guadalajara was a young Juan Dominguez Mendoza (Fernandez Duro 1882: 58). When the Spaniards wanted to proceed on their journey, the Jumano informed them that there was a conflict that involved the Cuitoa, Excanxaque, and Ayjado.[5] Guadalajara remained on the Concho with the Jumano, but sent Captain Andres Lopéz with twelve soldiers to the lands 30 leagues (78 miles) eastward. After traveling this distance, Captain Lopéz reached a *ranchería* of the Cuitoa. The Spaniards engaged the Cuitoa in battle, captured two hundred prisoners, and got two hundred bundles of deer, elk, and buffalo hides. During the battle, the Spaniards were told that the Excanxaque were on their way to help the Cuitoa against the Spaniards (Fernandez Duro 1882: 58).

At the time of Mendoza's legal appointment as General Maestro de Campo (Miranda 1671), as Mendoza stated in a deposition he gave in 1683 (Fernandez Duro 1882: 58), he had participated in the battle against the Cuitoa. This means that Mendoza traveled east of the Concho River and knew some of the terrain he would cover in 1684. After Captain Lopéz rejoined the Guadalajara group, they returned to Santa Fé. Although it is not noted that the Guadalajara party collected pearls, Anaya's testimony indicates that some pearls (*algunas perlas*) were gathered. It is possible that the conflict with the Cuitoa prevented access to and collection of more pearls, but the booty of slaves and pelts obtained in battle was considerable. The Spaniards may have made these trips to the Concho River area in order to exchange iron tools and horses for pelts and buffalo meat, which means that these trips would have been scheduled around local trade fairs. The prolonged Spanish presence in the Concho River area of Texas at this early date raises important questions about acculturation and the introduction of material cultural items in the area.

Trade continued between the Spaniards and the Jumano between 1654 and 1683. Sabeata himself confirmed these visits (Sabeata 1683). There are, however, clear indications that major changes were occurring in the areas of the Concho and Colorado rivers, east of the Rio Grande, and among the pueblos north of the El Paso area.

In 1654 the Cuitoa, Excanjaque, and Ayjado were present in the area south and east of the Concho River drainage, but in 1684 these groups were not mentioned as being in the area, nor were they listed by Mendoza among the groups he was to meet. Between 1669 and 1676, the New Mexico pueblos of Jumana, Abo, Tabira, Chilili, Quaray, Tajique, and Senecú were abandoned because of Apache raids in the Salines and Manzano areas (Ayer et al. 1965: 220, 227, 275; Gerald 1974: 138). In April 1675, Fernando del Bosque and Fr. Juan Larios left Monclova for the north side of the Rio Grande. In the months prior to the expedition many Native groups expressed serious interest in the settlement proposals of Balcarcel. It is possible that these groups were aware of Apache raids in the north and feared the incursion of refugee populations who were fleeing the Apache.

On August 10, 1680, the Upper Rio Grande pueblo groups rebelled against the Spanish, overthrowing colonial rule. It is noteworthy that neither the Piro nor the Jumano participated in the revolt; the Piro were not invited and the Jumano were not involved (Ayer et al. 1965: 273). In October there were threats of a revolt at El Paso (Hughes 1914: 334). The conditions at El Paso were very difficult, and the poverty was extreme for both the Spaniards and the Natives who had fled with them. Bad crops, attempts at revolt, and lack of help from the Viceroy fostered conditions of internal and external strife for the colony. In January 1682, the Apaches carried off two hundred horses and mules from El Paso, depleting the already meager resources (Hughes 1914: 335). The drought continued in 1682, and an epidemic affected the Native population. In August 1683, Don Domingo Petris de Cruzate was appointed governor. Fr. Nicolas Lopez, who would participate in the Mendoza expedition to the east, arrived the same year.

During the ensuing years several short and unsuccessful attempts were made to reconquer New Mexico. Meanwhile, the economic conditions at El Paso did not improve.

Continual requests for help were made to the Viceroy, but they went unheeded until 1686. Juan Dominguez de Mendoza, Pedro Duran y Chaves, and various members of their extended families were accused of profiteering from the poor economic conditions at El Paso. On September 26, 1683, Cruzate wrote to the Viceroy requesting authority not to proceed against Mendoza and Chaves in order to maintain peace and quiet in the province during such difficult times (Cruzati 1683a; 1685). The New Mexico Spanish families were tightly knit. The familial connections through marriage and *compadre*[6] relationships meant that each individual was related to everybody else. In fact, Pedro Chaves was Mendoza's father-in-law. The Junta followed the opinion of the Fiscal and approved Cruzate's line of action (Marques de la Laguna 1684).

On August 11, 1683, one day after the third anniversary of the Pueblo Revolt, a group of twelve Jumano captains from several *rancherías* visited Governor Antonio de Otermín at El Paso. Among the members of this delegation was Juan Sabeata, a Jumano captain who probably acted as spokesman for the group.[7] The declaration made by the Jumano delegation pointed out that the Spaniards had maintained relations of friendship and trade with the Jumano since the time of New Mexico. These interchanges were conducted in such security that Spaniards traveled every year to the Jumano lands and *rancherías,* in groups as small as six. When the Jumano heard of the events in New Mexico, they wanted to find out if, as the Apache reported, the Spanish were finished in the area. The purpose of the Jumano visit was to ask the Spaniards for help against their common enemy, the Apache. Otermín, who was hard pressed for food supplies and ammunition, hinted at his economic difficulties and told the Jumano to return in three months, to discuss these matters with the governor who was about to replace him (Sabeata 1683). The Jumano, keenly aware of the economic difficulties at El Paso, offered to supply the Spaniards with foodstuffs in exchange for help against the Apache, and agreed to return to discuss the matter with the new governor. This was not the first time the Jumano had come to see Otermín; a Jumano captain had previously visited Otermín to make certain that the rumors of the Spaniards' demise had been greatly exaggerated (Cruzati 1683b).

On October 20, 1683, Juan Sabeata came to see Governor Cruzate. As spokesman for a delegation of six Native captains he presented a proposal to the Spaniards. The Jumano and their allies were requesting (1) friars to minister to the groups, especially those that were Christians; (2) Spanish families to settle in their lands; and (3) military help against the Apache. In exchange for this help the Native coalition would supply the Spaniards with foodstuffs and pelts. The Jumano were concerned with the proximity of an Apache *ranchería* to their lands and were making this request based on their very old friendship with the Spaniards (Sabeata 1683a).

Cruzate questioned Sabeata extensively, and Sabeata included in his answers some of the information he wished to impart to the Spaniards, including a summarized list of friendly nations with whom the Jumano had alliances and trade relationships (Sabeata 1683a). Because of the importance of the statements made by these Natives, the texts of both declarations are fully translated (Appendix). There is, however, some information conveyed by these documents that needs to be analyzed at this point.

Sabeata stated that the Jumano had been waiting for ministers since the time (1650) when Diego del Castillo had visited their lands. At that time, Castillo met with a lieutenant of the leader of the Tejas (Sabeata 1683a). Sabeata's statements confirmed Castillo's trip to the Jumano lands on the Concho River and his contact with the Tejas, as well as demonstrating that Sabeata was aware of these encounters, either because he had already been born or because he had been told about the events that had taken place.

Apart from offering supplies in exchange for help, Sabeata enticed the priests by mentioning several miraculous events relating to a cross that fell from the sky.[8] This cross, a copy of which Sabeata had tattooed or painted on his hands, was made of wood and painted with different colors. The cross was kept in the Jumano lands, and the Spaniards could see it at the time of their visit.

During the interview Sabeata provided distances, translated into travel time between several key places. This was an efficient way of relating time to distance covered, because it took into account difficulty of terrain, mode of transportation, and effort spent. He stated that (1) it took about eight days to travel between El Paso and La Junta de los Ríos; (2) he lived at La Junta de los Ríos; and (3) between where he lived and the lands where *other people* of the Jumano nation lived there were about six days of travel—three days to where the buffalo herds began and three more days to where the *rancherías* on the Río Nueces (Concho) were located (or where they started). In the previous declaration of August 11, Sabeata, or whoever the Jumano spokesman had been, stated that in the river called Nueces (Concho) there were shells that contained small grains that the Spaniards called pearls, leaving no doubt that the Río Nueces (Concho) and the river where the pearls were found were one and the same.[9] As for the distance from La Junta de los Ríos to the Kingdom of the Tejas, Sabeata stated that it took about fifteen to twenty days, taking the longest road (Sabeata 1683a).

The Jumano request for help against the Apache, along with their stated wish for Spanish settlers and friars, was the perfect solution to several of Cruzate's pressing problems. First, it gave him an excuse to remove from El Paso several people who were creating internal strife, the most important being Juan Dominguez de Mendoza. It put the Chaves and the Mendoza families at arm's length, defusing a potentially dangerous situation, especially for a newly arrived governor. Second, it provided the excuse to ask for further military supplies. Third, it pleased the friars, whose aid was essential in order to convince the Viceroy of the pressing economic needs at El Paso (Gomez et al. 1684; Lopez 1684). Fourth, it offered the possibility of obtaining, at little cost, pelts and meat that the colonists desperately needed. Fifth, it provided a potential new area for settlement if the reconquest of New Mexico proved impossible (Lopez 1686). The fact that the Mendoza family provided some of the funds for the expedition made it all the more attractive. Finally, it might keep the Apache occupied away from El Paso.

The Jumano and their allies were interested in creating an effective barrier against the Apache who were encroaching on their lands. At this time there were no Spaniards north and east of El Paso. All Spanish settlements were to the west and south. The primary adversaries of the Spaniards were the Pueblo groups of New Mexico, the groups along the

FIGURE 4.2
*Drawing of Sabeata's cross as it appears in **AGN, Provincias Internas,** vol. 35, frame 79.*
Courtesy Benson Latin American Center, University of Texas at Austin.

Rio Grande and the Río Conchos (Mexico), those westward at Parral, Casas Grandes, and Sonora, and lastly the Apache. There was an Apache presence in these conflicts to be sure, and they may have been one of the catalysts for the revolt, but they were not the force behind the revolutionary movement.

The Apaches had not moved south; since the beginning of continuous historical documentation the Apache, in their various appellations, had wrapped around the Upper Rio Grande pueblos and hunted on the eastern plains (Ayer et al. 1965: 39–42, 53–57). They had been poised on the northwest and north-central edges of the territory that we now call Texas since at least the time of Fr. Alonso de Benavides, and almost certainly well before that (Ayer et al. 1965: 39–42, 53–57). They were not moving south; they were already there. I am not arguing that they did not travel south to hunt, to trade, to fight, or to steal; nor do I wish to state that no southward movement had occurred, especially after the 1680 Pueblo Revolt. But there were no major, permanent Apache moves into Texas en masse: not by 1684, at least.

THE EXPEDITIONARY ORDERS

The expeditionary orders recorded by Mendoza in his travel diary (*derrotero*) state that he was to proceed eastward and discover the East and the Kingdom of the Tejas because of the request made by Don Juan Sabeata, a Native American of the Jumano nation, and other captains of his nation.[10] This request for spiritual and temporal support had been made to Governor Cruzate and to Fr. Nicolas Lopez. Mendoza stated that Cruzate entrusted him with the execution of the trip in view of the benefits to the Crown. Mendoza (1684) added that he prepared a narrative of the events that took place during the expedition to comply with the orders and instructions received, and to make sure that all was done according to the rules.

Mendoza's declaration to the Viceroy (Mendoza et al. 1684b) does not mention how many Spaniards or Natives traveled with him. Cruzate said that he sent a group of soldiers with a corporal and that they were all volunteers (Cruzate 1683c; Cruzati 1684). In Fernandez Duro's discussion of Peñalosa and his alleged trip to the Kingdom of Quivira (1882: 49), Mendoza is quoted as saying that he traveled with twenty men. The list compiled matches that number if one includes the three friars who traveled with Mendoza. The list includes:

1. Maestro de Campo Juan Domingues de Mendoza—Cabo y Caudillo
2. Sergeant Major Diego Lucero de Godoy (f)
3. Sergeant Baltasar Domingues de Mendoza (f)
4. Captain Hernando Martin Serrano—interpreter for the Jumano language (ef)
5. Captain Felipe Romero (f)
6. Captain Ygnacio Baca
7. Diego Barela, chief of squad
8. Diego de Luna, ensign
9. Antonio Solis, ensign
10. Nicolas Lucero (f)
11. Miguel Luxan (ef)
12. Melchor de Archuleta (ef)
13. Francisco de Archuleta (ef)
14. Felipe Montoya (ef)

15. Antonio Gomes (ef)
16. Juan Dominguez the Younger (f)
17. Anttonio Jorge (ef)
18. Fray Nicolas Lopez
19. Fray Juan de Sabaleta (or Zavaleta)
20. Fr. Antonio de Acevedo

The men identified with (*f*) following their names were close family members of Juan Dominguez de Mendoza. Those identified with (*ef*) were members of Mendoza's extended family, mostly related through marriage. Baltasar Domingues de Mendoza and Juan Dominguez the Younger were Juan Dominguez de Mendoza's children (Chavéz 1954: 4, 6, 15, 16, 18–19, 24–27, 78, 97).

THE TRIP

In an effort to retain the ambiguities of the original Spanish texts and the idiosyncrasies of the original writers, I have not attempted to produce a text that is pleasing or grammatically correct in English. Although the text is not rendered in the first person singular, but as reported by an outside observer, the contents of the diary are completely and faithfully rendered.

All comments in parentheses appear in the original document (Version L). Equivalency of measurements and Spanish words from the original are also given in parentheses. All comments in square brackets are my interpolations. Discrepancies in spelling appear in the original copy I used (e.g., *habrevadero* versus *abrevadero*). Following each diary entry is a commentary that includes my interpretation of each camping location and comments relative to the various diary versions. Quotes from Version M are referenced in the text as T., followed by the page number of the transcript on file at the Center for Southwest Research, University of New Mexico, Albuquerque.

TRAVEL LOG

December 15, 1683: departed Real de S. Lorenzo and arrived at San Bartolome. Day 1.

*Mendoza and his group of soldiers left El Real de San Lorenzo, which was distant from La Conversion de los Mansos and the Paso del Río del Norte about 12 leagues (31.2 miles). They traveled south more or less 5 leagues (13 miles), from San Lorenzo to the place where Thome Domingues de Mendoza had lived. Mendoza was traveling along the south bank of the Rio Grande. The spot had an adobe house and a good watering place (**habrebadero**). The low-lying plain provided good pasture and plenty of wood. The writer named this place S. Bartolome and a cross was erected on the spot.*

Comments: San Bartolome was probably near the modern village of Reforma, Mexico.[11] El Paso del Río del Norte was then located at the modern city of Ciudad Juárez,

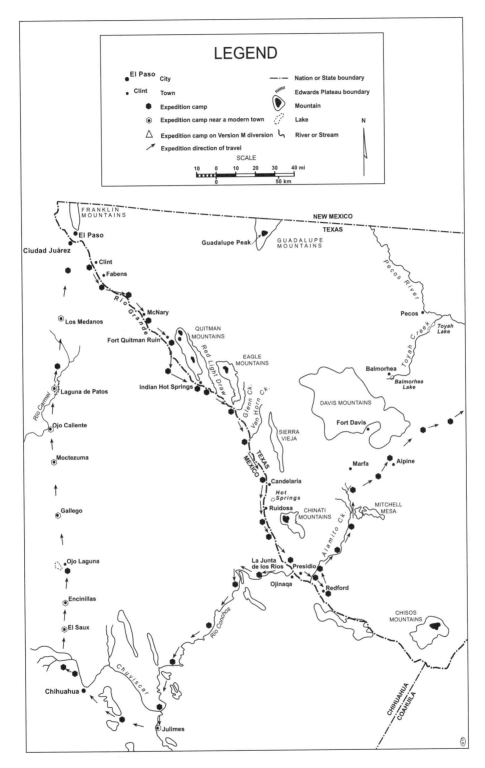

FIGURE 4.3

Route of the 1683–1684 expedition of Fr. Nicolas Lopez and Juan Dominguez de Mendoza (west).

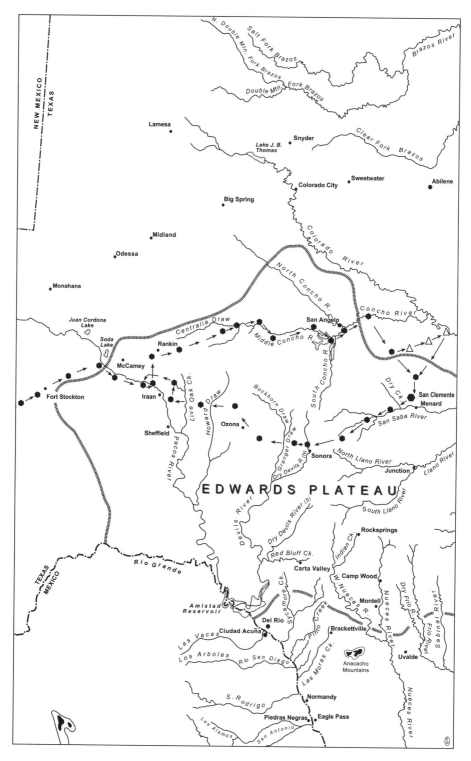

FIGURE 4.4

Route of the 1683–1684 expedition of Fr. Nicolas Lopez and Juan Dominguez de Mendoza (east).

Mexico (Bolton 1916: 320). In 1916, Bolton stated (321) that San Bartolome was the house of Juan Dominguez Mendoza's father. Mendoza's father, who died in 1656 (Chavéz 1954: 24), was named Tome Domingues. Mendoza was the family name of Juan Dominguez's mother (Elena de la Cruz, alias Elena Ramírez de Mendoza). This was the house (former house) of Thome Domingues Mendoza, Juan Dominguez's elder brother. The home Mendoza visited on his return trip, on the road from Chihuahua to El Paso, was a house owned by his brother Thome. Generally, all diary entries were signed by Juan Dominguez de Mendoza, Diego Lucero de Godoy, Baltasar Dominguez de Mendoza, and Hernando Martin Serrano, except on Day 19 of the expedition and on Day 159, the last day the signature of Baltasar Mendoza appears in the diary. Version L states that on December 15, 1683, Mendoza and a group of soldiers left El Real de San Lorenzo for La Junta de los Ríos, where Mendoza joined Fr. Nicolas Lopez and Fr. Juan Sabaleta, who were to travel with the expedition. Version M states that all the friars departed San Lorenzo with Mendoza and that Sabeata guided the expedition, but that, at San Bartolome, the friars and Sabeata left Mendoza's party and proceeded to La Junta de los Ríos (T., p. 1). Version M probably is correct, since no mass was celebrated until December 31 (Day 17). Due to the similarity of the versions during this part of the expedition, it is apparent that one of the diarists (Fr. Lopez) used the other's (Mendoza's) travel log. Since I have not seen the Spanish original of Version M, it is difficult to evaluate the extent of the differences. Nevertheless, quite clearly this part of the diary was written by Mendoza, because it is quite unlikely that the friars and Sabeata followed exactly the same route.

December 16, 1683: departed San Bartolome and arrived Santissima Trenidad. Day 2.

The party traveled southward to a place they named Santissima Trenidad, distant about 7 leagues (18.2 miles) from San Bartolome. They stopped on a hill (loma), where there was a rancheria of the Suma. Mendoza placed a cross on that hill. In front of the hill, facing north, there was a large cottonwood (alamo) near which ran the Rio Grande. Below the cottonwood was the watering place for the horse herd. There was no other suitable place for the herd [to drink] because the river narrowed there. They crossed the river with haste.

Comments: Santissima Trenidad was on the north side of the Rio Grande, probably about 7 miles northwest of the present village of Fort Hancock.[12] Bolton's translation (1916: 321) says that the cross placed atop the hill faced north. The grammatical subject of the sentence is not clear. I interpret the phrase as referring to the hill and the description as given from the point of view of a man's position standing on top of the hill. Mendoza's party did not stay at the Suma *rancheria* but crossed the river to the north bank on the 16th to spend the night. On the return trip from La Junta de los Ríos to El Paso, Mendoza stated that one of the reasons he took the road from Chihuahua to El Paso was that if he went up the Rio Grande he would have to cross it four times, and these crossings were difficult because the river was running high. This would have been one of the crossings. Version M states that at this spot the river ran through a narrow canyon. This version seldom mentions the erection of crosses (which is included in the other versions), gives less detailed information about each camping stop, and often does not include the full name given to each campsite.

December 17, 1683: departed La Santissima Trenidad and arrived at Nuestra Señora del Pilar de Saragosa. Day 3.

The party traveled southward to a place they named Nuestra Señora del Pilar de Saragosa, about 8 leagues (20.8 miles) from La Santissima Trenidad. At this place they found a populous **ranchería** *of the Suma. On the way, between La Santissima Trenidad and N.S. del Pilar de Saragosa, they encountered several other Suma* **rancherías.** *The writer described the Suma as poor folk who sustained themselves with mescal, which they prepared by boiling (***que son palmas cocidas***). All the people in the* **rancherías** *asked for help against their common enemy, the Apache. They stated that they were willing to become Christians, which in reality many of them already were. They had been reduced and lived in settlements. They said that the Apache did not leave them alone in their lands (***no los dejan en las tierras***). Mendoza stated that, since they were asking for help, after their fashion, he offered to help them when he returned. He placed a cross on top of a hill.*

Comments: N.S. del Pilar de Saragosa was probably on the north side and near the Rio Grande, some 3 miles southeast of the present village of McNary.[13] Bolton's translation (1916: 322) says that the Apache did not allow the Suma in their lands. That translation does not make sense, since Mendoza said that they were settled and reduced. Probably the remark "que los dichos apaches [*sic*] no les dejan en las tierras" means that the Apache were harassing them in their lands. Also, Mendoza stated that the Arcos Tuertos (Day 42) were in all respects like the Suma, which could mean that just like the Jumano, Suma groups lived in two distinct geographic areas: the Rio Grande and east of the Concho River in Texas.[14] Mendoza stated that he would offer the Suma all the help he could when he returned, which implies that he planned all along to come to La Junta on his return trip. When Mendoza returned to La Junta, the Suma were in revolt. Version M states that "the Suma alleged they were Christians even though they were living among infidels; others, [declared] that they desired to become [Christians]" (T., p. 2).

December 18, 1683: departed N.S. del Pilar de Saragosa and arrived at N.S. de la Limpia Consepcion. Day 4.

*The party traveled southward about 8 leagues (20.8 miles) from N.S. del Pilar de Saragosa to a place they named Nuestra Señora de la Limpia Consepcion. The place had as geographical features a deep arroyo, which, at the point where it joined the Rio Grande, formed a stony riverbed like a beach. This was the watering place (***habrebadero***). This spot [or nook] had good pastures and timber. Mendoza placed a cross on top of a hill.*

Comments: N.S. de la Limpia Consepcion was very likely about 3 miles southeast of what is now the ruins of historic Fort Quitman, near the mouth of one of the many steep arroyos that arise on the southwestern slopes of the Quitman Mountains and that empty into the north side of the Rio Grande.[15] The original document says that the arroyo emptied into the Rio Grande, forming a *playal de piedra* (singular)—a stony beach, or a riverbed made of large cobbles or boulders that could produce the appearance of a continuous stone bed. However, if the word *piedra* were written in the plural, indicating the presence of small cobbles or pebbles, that would describe a different appearance of the riverbed. The word *habrebadero* or *abrevadero* means "el sitio ò lugar donde hai agua, y acostumbra el ganado ir à beber" (RAE 1726: 19). Version M names the camp La Purisima Consepcion, and also mentions the erection of a cross at this spot.

December 19, 1683: departed N.S. de la Limpia Consepcion and arrived at N.S. de la Soledad. Day 5.

*The party traveled southward to a place they named Nuestra Señora de la Soledad, about 8 leagues (20.8 miles) distant from N.S. de la Limpia Consepcion. N.S. de la Soledad was more or less 3 leagues (7.8 miles) from the south bank of the Rio Grande. Between N.S. de la Soledad and N.S. de la Limpia Consepcion were three Suma **rancherías**. On this side [west] there was a mountain range (sierra) from which issued an arroyo of good water. This arroyo, which flowed into the Rio Grande, had enough water to supply any army. The arroyo had a very good grove of cottonwoods (**alamos**). The spot had very good pastures and plenty of timber. Mendoza placed a cross on top of a hill.*

Comments: N.S. de la Soledad was probably about 7 miles southwest of the Rio Grande on the Arroyo de los Frailes and near the present village of Los Frailes.[16] Before this date Mendoza crossed the Rio Grande again to the west side (south bank), although the diary does not provide that information. This would have been his second river crossing. Version M states that they left the river, traveled 8 leagues, and found the arroyo, which was located by traveling "from west to east about 3 leagues away from the river, which we had left to the south of us" (T., p. 2).

December 20, 1683: departed N.S. de la Soledad and arrived at N.S. del Transito. Day 6.

*The party traveled southward and reached a spot they named Nuestra Señora del Transito, about 8 leagues (20.8 miles) distant from N.S. de la Soledad. The place was on the Rio Grande. A range of hills framed or defined the pastureland, with abundant low-lying pastures and plenty of wood. In some areas the land was rough (**doblada**). Between [the two named places or the range of hills?] there was a hot spring that made the river [actually the water of the spring ran into the Rio Grande, since the spring did not make the Rio Grande]. The water source (**habrevadero**) was good. The land was intractable. There were some **rancherías** of settled people. Mendoza had a cross placed on top of a hill.*

Comments: Nuestra Señora del Transito was almost certainly located at the southern end of the Quitman Mountains and downriver from the point where the waters from

Indian Hot Springs entered the Rio Grande.[17] The grammar and construction of the text are not easy to follow. Some sentences may have more than one meaning. In such cases, I have noted the questionable meanings. In the cases mentioned above, a range of hills does not make (*hace*) pastureland, nor does the hot spring make (*hace*) the Rio Grande. Version M states that they "traveled 4 leagues over broken country as far as the hot spring. From here we traveled another 4 leagues until we reached the Río del Norte again and halted" (T., p. 2). This version includes fewer topographic and environmental details, but states that the *rancherías* that were found belonged to the non-Christian Suma.

December 21, 1683: departed N.S. del Transito and arrived at N.S. del Buen Suseso. Day 7.

Mendoza and his party traveled about 4 leagues (10.4 miles) from N.S. del Transito to Nues-tra Señora del Buen Suseso. This spot had good pastureland and timber. It was located near the canyon (caxa) made by the Rio Grande at the point one leaves the trail, turns west, and immediately after turns east. The party stopped for the night at this spot [the double bend of the river] because the land ahead of them was too rough to be traveled by night. The follow-ing day they were to travel over rough terrain overgrown with mesquite and catclaw. This rough terrain was passable. The writer stated that they did not travel further that day because they did not want to travel in the dark. Soon after crossing this area they were faced with a very steep cuesta. The east side of this cuesta was precipitous and covered with lechuguilla that extended almost to the Rio Grande. At the bend of the Rio Grande Mendoza had a cross placed atop a hill. In the ground covered that day, they saw three rancherías inhabited by the Suma.

Comments: Nuestra Señora del Buen Suseso was probably on the south side of the Rio Grande, 3 to 4 miles west of the mouth of Red Light Draw.[18] Version M does not in-clude any details, but the diary entry for the following day (December 22) includes most of the topographic and environmental information included in this entry. However, the *cuesta* is not mentioned, and the text implies that it is the path that extends and leads to the river and not the lechuguilla that grew almost to the river's edge (T., p. 3).

December 22, 1683: departed N.S. del Buen Suseso and arrived at N.S. del Rosario. Day 8.

The party traveled about 8 leagues (20.8 miles) from N.S. del Buen Suseso to a place they named Nuestra Señora del Rosario. They crossed the rough land described in the previous entry. They reached the banks of the Rio Grande, where they found some rancherías of the Suma. The place had very good low-lying pasturelands, timber, and a good watering place (habrevadero). Mendoza placed a cross on top of a hill.

Comments: The camp of Nuestra Señora del Rosario was quite likely located at the southern end of the Eagle Mountains, upstream from the mouth of Green River, slightly north of where Jeff Davis County intersects the Rio Grande.[19] From the beginning of the expedition, Mendoza's party had been winding down the course of the Rio Grande in a southerly direction, skirting the difficult terrain as much as possible and camping near the river. After leaving El Real de S. Lorenzo, Mendoza encountered, at an absolute minimum, fourteen Suma *rancherías*. The first one was located at Santissima Trenidad, 31.2 miles south of San Lorenzo. He specifically mentions eight *rancherías* between Santissima Trenidad and N.S. del Rosario. In three instances he says he encountered some or several *rancherías*. In these three cases it may be assumed that he referred to no fewer than two *rancherías* (and very likely more). When he reached N.S. del Rosario he had covered 114.4 miles and encountered at least fourteen *rancherías*, which provides a possible average distance between settlements of 8.8 miles. Between N.S. de la Limpia Consepcion and N.S. de la Soledad (20.8 miles), Mendoza found three Suma *rancherías*, which can provide a possible average distance between settlements of 10.4 miles. Of course, these ranges would be affected by the terrain, environment, and cultural choice of locations. After leaving N.S. del Rosario, Mendoza did not mention any more Suma *rancherías;* nor did he mention any crops being grown by the Suma.

December 23, 1683: departed N.S. del Rosario and arrived at N.S. de Regla. Day 9.

[*Note:* The diary entry for this day states that the party left a place they called Nuestra Señora de Regla. Since the diary does not mention their arrival at this place, they must have arrived on December 23 and departed on the 24th. According to Version L, Mendoza is a day behind in his diary entries. To avoid confusion I have corrected the dates and have continued to include the date of arrival and the date of departure for all stopovers.]

Day 9.

*Mendoza traveled to a place they named Nuestra Señora de Regla distant from N.S. del Rosario about 8 leagues (20.8 miles). The place had as important landmarks a very beautiful meadow and a chain of hills very close to the mountain range (sierra). To the north there was a cotton-wood grove (**bosque**); the Rio Grande was sandwiched between this cottonwood grove and a long valley on the other side [north] of the river. The water source (**abrevadero**) was good. Mendoza had a cross placed on top of a hill (**esta loma que mira al norte**), which faced north and was located south of the river.*

Comments: Nustra Señora de Regla was likely located on the west side of the Rio Grande about 1 mile north of the mouth of Van Horn Creek.[20] The grammatical construction of this entry makes the meaning of the sentences unclear. The writer said that Mendoza placed a cross on this hill as if the writer was on the hill describing what he saw. Version M states: "[O]n the 23rd we went on, and after traveling 8 leagues we halted. Here the river runs through a beautiful plain and there is a good watering place" (T., p. 3).

December 24, 1683: departed N.S. de Regla and arrived
at N. Señora de Belen. Day 10.

*The party left Nuestra Señora de Regla and traveled 8 leagues (20.8 miles) to a place they named Nuestra Señora de Belen. The writer named the place N.S. de Belen because of a narrow pass (**portillo**) high on the mountain range. The pass was about half a league (1.3 miles) from N.S. de Belen. The narrow pass looked like a window opening. The place had as landmarks a range of hills and woods (**bosque**) shaped like the letter O. In the center of the O there was a stretch of low-lying meadows through the middle of which the river ran. The water source (**abrebadero**) was good. Mendoza had a cross placed on a hill on the north side.*

Comments: The camp of Nuestra Señora de Belen was probably located on the south side of the Rio Grande and about 8 miles north and upriver from Candelaria.[21]

As this was the Christmas season, the allusions connecting geographical features with the birth of Jesus are understandable and interesting. The narrow pass and the opening that resembled a window connote the difficult trip of Mary and Joseph to the grotto, and the area shaped like the letter *O* recalls the cult of the Virgin of the *O,* which is the pregnant and birthing Mary. These references show a rather religious individual who attributed religious meaning to natural occurrences. I have previously noted these details (Wade 1998: 165) and attributed them to Mendoza's religious nature. However, textual details such as these would appear to indicate that Version L was penned by one or more of the friars. But according to Version M (Day 1), the friars were not traveling with Mendoza. This statement is reinforced by the fact that no masses were celebrated until the 15th day of the trip. Still, it is bothersome that, for instance, Version M simply states: "[O]n the 24th, after going 8 leagues, we reached a place which we named Nuestra Señora de Belen because of a great rock on the summit of a nearby sierra which forms a kind of portico with its window. Today, 8 leagues. The watering place is good" (T., p. 3).

December 25, 1683: departed N.S. de Belen and arrived at N.S. del Populo. Day 11.

*The party traveled 8 leagues (20.8 miles) to a place they named Nuestra Señora del Populo. The place had as landmarks a large, tall rock (**peñasco**), separated from the mountain range (**sierra**), and with spurs on its sides. The long axis of the rock ran north-south. This large rock resembled a church and it was located on the north bank of the Rio Grande. Mendoza was on the New Mexico side of the river [south bank], and the place where they camped was south of the rock's southern point. Behind the campsite there was a large grove of cottonwoods and other trees. On the south side the river forked; on the island formed by the fork of the river there were pasturelands and a hill, atop which Mendoza placed a cross.*

Comments: Nuestra Señora del Populo was probably located 4 miles north of Ruidosa, near the mouth of the La Chiva arroyo on the west side of the Rio Grande.[22] The description of the landmarks is, once again, less than clear. The writer said that he was on the south bank and that he was located at 12 o'clock. His camp thus had to be south of the rock. At this time Mendoza did not consider the north bank of the Rio Grande as part of New Mexico territory. On his return trip to El Paso he wrote an official declaration to take legal possession of the north bank of the Rio Grande for Spain and the jurisdiction of New Mexico (Mendoza et al. 1684a). Version M includes fewer details. It states that they traveled along the course of the Rio Grande and halted on a plain that they named N.S. del Populo. This version does state that they were on the south side of the river.

December 26, 1683: departed N.S. del Populo and arrived at N.S. de Atocha. Day 12.

*The party left Nuestra Señora del Populo and traveled about 3 leagues (7.8 miles) to reach a place they called Nuestra Señora de Atocha. They cut the trip short because they lost some horses. The place where they stopped was surrounded and shaded by hills; on the west side there was the mountain range (sierra) and on the south side there was a narrow pass [an entry, an opening] through which the Rio Grande flowed. The chain of hills was covered with prickly pear, which the writer thought would provide good fruit. The water sources (**abrevaderos**) were all along the stony riverbed. There were good pasturelands, abundant timber, and all other necessary things [for a camp].*

Comments: Nuestra Señora de Atocha was probably west of the Rio Grande and about 3 miles southwest of Ruidosa, Texas.[23] Version M includes fewer topographic and environmental details.

December 27, 1683: departed N.S. de Atocha and arrived at N.S. de los Remedios. Day 13.

*The party left N.S. de Atocha and traveled about 7 leagues (18.2 miles) to a place they called Nuestra Señora de los Remedios. On the north side [of their path?], [there was] a high mountain range (sierra) located next to a hill (**loma**) that served as a landmark. The path went down that hill. Before reaching the spot where they camped they passed a dry creek (**arroyo seco**). At this spot the Rio Grande flowed eastward and the low-lying meadows, on both sides of the river, were also oriented eastward. There were abundant pastures and timber, and the water source (**habrevadero**) was good. Mendoza had a cross placed on top of a hill.*

Comments: Nuestra Señora de los Remedios seems to have been on the north side of the Rio Grande, 14 miles south of Ruidosa.[24] Version M includes the same basic information, but with fewer details.

December 28, 1683: departed N.S. de los Remedios and arrived at N.S. de Guadalupe. Day 14.

The party left N.S. de los Remedios and traveled about 7 leagues (18.2 miles) to a place they called Nuestra Señora de Guadalupe. From their camping site they could see two mountains; the one on the north side was about 3 leagues (7.8 miles) away, and the other one, which faced the Rio Grande on one side, was about a quarter of a league (0.65 miles) distant. On each side of the Rio Grande there was a grove of cottonwoods. The area was thick with cane *and the water source (**abrevadero**) was good. Mendoza had a cross placed on the top of a hill immediately next to the path. He signed his name on the cross.*

Comments: The camp of Nuestra Señora de Guadalupe was quite likely located on the north side of the Rio Grande, 7 miles northwest of Presidio, Texas.[25] Mendoza did not report any *rancherías* between N.S. del Rosario and N.S. de Guadalupe (106.6 miles). Version M states that there were two mountains nearby and to the north and that Mendoza placed a cross on a height.

December 29, 1683: departed N.S. de Guadalupe and arrived at La Nabidad en las Cruces. Day 15.

*The party left N.S. de Guadalupe and arrived at a place they named La Nabidad en las Cruces because of the many crosses they saw in the Julime **rancherías** on both sides of the Rio Grande. The Julime were versed in the Mexican language, and all of them sowed wheat and corn. Mendoza joined Fr. Nicolas Lopez the custodian and ordinary judge, Fr. Juan de Sabaleta commissary of the Holy Office, and Fr. Antonio de Acebedo. In general, all the Julime asked for baptism, and more than one hundred people were baptized at this time. The lowlying lands (**begas**) of the Rio Grande were spacious and good, and the area had abundant pasturelands and timber. The weather was good.*

Comments: The *ranchería* of La Nabidad en las Cruces was near modern Ojinaga, Mexico.[26] Mendoza did not give the distance covered from N.S. de Guadalupe to La Nabidad en las Cruces. In October 1683, a group of Native Americans, probably including Sabeata, requested missionaries for the *rancherías* of the Jumano and the Julime in the Río Conchos and Rio Grande areas. They had built at least two churches and a house to serve as a residence for the friars (Mendoza et al. 1684b). According to Version M, the friars departed El Paso with Mendoza to work among the La Junta Natives (Day 1). The text indicates that there were several *rancherías* in the area and on both sides of the Rio Grande. La Nabidad en las Cruces means "Christmas amid the Crosses," a poetic name for a camp. The use of the symbol of the cross by the Julime, the Jumano, the Gediondo, and many others is intriguing. Sabeata's declarations about the cross and its supernatural powers may explain the widespread use of the Christian symbol among some Native communities.

The writer of Version L never actually states that they were at La Junta at this time. However, Mendoza's Certifications and Declaration (Mendoza et al. 1684; 1684a; 1684b), as well as Version M, make it clear that they were at La Junta on the inbound and outbound legs of the trip. Version M reports that "we reached the junction of the Río del Norte and the Conchos" (T., p. 4). This version also states that Fr. Acevedo "remained in this place called La Junta de los Ríos, which we named La Navidad en las Cruces because of the [crosses] which these Indians had already erected on both banks of the Río del Norte, to instruct and minister to them" (T., p. 4). Version M states that they remained in this spot one day.

December 30, 1683: Mendoza remained at Nabidad en las Cruces. Day 16.

December 31, 1683: departed La Nabidad en las Cruces and arrived at El Apostol Santiago. Day 17.

The party left La Nabidad en las Cruces and traveled about 7 leagues (18.2 miles) to a place they called El Apostol Santiago. They arrived there New Year's Day. Fr. Nicolas Lopez and Fr. Juan de Sabaleta were now traveling with the group. These ministers said mass, and Mendoza had a cross placed atop a hill. The terrain they covered was passable, but in some cases very rocky. The place where they camped had, as a landmark, a stream (arroyo) that flowed north-south. There was abundant pasture, some green and some dry.

Comments: El Apostol Santiago was probably upstream on Alamito Creek about 9 miles northeast of its confluence with the Rio Grande.[27] Although the diary does not say so, Fr. Lopez was accompanied by his personal Jumano servant (Santo 1684). The group included more Native Americans, but we are not told until much later that the Spaniards were actually accompanied by some Native groups. In most cases, we do not know when or where these Native groups joined the party. It is very likely that some Piro had been with Mendoza since the start of the trip, and, according to Version M, the party included some Jumano. Version M refers to this place as Santiago, the name given to the arroyo.

January 1, 1684: departed El Apostol Santiago and arrived at Nuestro Padre San Francisco. Day 18.

The party left El Apostol Santiago and traveled about 7 leagues (18.2 miles) to a place they named Nuestro Padre San Francisco. The spot had as landmark a hot water spring that flowed from the north to the east [literally north-southeast]. This spring originated in a high spot and provided good water. The pasturelands were good and the land was open, level, and with little timber. Because of this lack of wood Mendoza did not erect a cross.

Comments: Nuestro Padre San Francisco was probably on or near Alamito Creek close to Casa Piedra.[28] Version M states that the friars celebrated mass before departure.

January 2, 1684: departed N. Padre San Francisco and arrived at San Nicolas. Day 19.

*The party left N. Padre San Francisco and traveled about 7 leagues (18.2 miles) to a place they named San Nicolas. Their camp was at the extremity of a mesa that extended to the north. The watering place was a beautiful reservoir (**algibe** or **alxibe**) fed by rainwater. Around the reservoir there were several kinds of trees, including ash (**fresno**). The passageways [the cracks, **esladeros**] between the rocks made two steep crags [like walls] on the sides. It was very shaded. Near the reservoir, and in the cavities made by the crags, there was a great quantity of maidenhair ferns (**culantrillo**) and very beautiful grapevines. Mendoza had a cross placed atop and near the edge of one of the steep crags. On the west side there was a beautiful plain with good pasture of grass (**grama**). The friars celebrated mass. The writer stated that they* *had been traveling northward. Phellipe Romero, Ygnacio Baca, and Anttonio Jorje signed this diary entry.*

Comments: The camp of San Nicolas was quite likely located on Alamito Creek about 4 miles north of the town of Plata.[29] The writer uses the word *aljibe* instead of *abrebadero* to describe the rain-fed water source. This is significant because an *aljibe* is a cistern, a man-made reservoir constructed of stone. Mendoza may not be implying that this is a man-made reservoir, but he wanted to connote the difference in the water sources; this one was lined with rock like a cistern. It is also suggestive that there are three other signatories to this diary entry. These names do not appear before this date in the signature list that closes each entry of the diary. However, the names do appear after this date. It is possible to speculate that these men joined the party at this spot, in which case their meeting would have been prearranged. Version M provides essentially the same information. The translator of this version translated *grama* as couch-grass.

January 3, 1684: departed San Nicolas and arrived at Nuestro Padre San Anttonio. Day 20.

*The party left San Nicolas and traveled about 7 leagues (18.2 miles) to Nuestro Padre San Anttonio. The camp was in the middle of some hills and the water source (**algibe**) was located amid those hills. The water reservoir was enclosed by bare rock and was sufficient for any horse herd. The access to the water reservoir was through an arroyo that flowed westward. The flat land had plenty of oak trees (**encinos**), and there were junipers (**sabinos**) on the heights. All the land was flat. Somewhere in the middle of the land traveled (**distrito**), between San Nicolas and N. Padre San Anttonio, there were some small pools of brackish water. Around these pools there was a lot of white and yellow mesquite. Amid the undergrowth there was a little spring (**pozuelo**) of fresh, sweet water, with easy access. The writer found this spring so unusual, and its appearance so unexpected, that he described it in detail. Mendoza had a cross placed atop some rocks next to the little water source. Mass was celebrated on this spot.*

Comments: Nuestro Padre San Anttonio was probably located about 9 miles south of Marfa, Texas, and on the northwest edge of Mitchell Mesa.[30] The writer referred to the water source as an *algibe*. This water reservoir was also enclosed in rock. Version M states that the pools of brackish water were encountered 3.5 leagues (9.1 miles) after departure from San Nicolas. This version states also that the "rest of the terrain of this day's journey is salinitrous" (T., p. 5).

January 4, 1684: departed N. Padre San Anttonio and arrived at San Lorenso. Day 21.

*They left N. Padre San Anttonio and traveled about 4 leagues (10.4 miles) to a place they named San Lorenso. They named this place San Lorenso because of the fire that occurred during the night and spread to very near the camp. They managed to avoid disaster by cutting a clearing around the campground. The land they traversed was in some parts rocky with knolls (**questasillas**), and in other areas it was plain with no rocks. The camping spot was at the foot* *of a small hill (**serro**) on the east side; on the north side issued a small stream (**riachuelo**) that flowed northward. This stream carried sufficient water for any horse herd. The pastures were good, but timber was scarce; the available wood came from widespread [or distant] oak trees. They did not place a cross because there was no wood to make one.*

Comments: San Lorenso was quite probably near the railroad siding of Paisano.[31] The fact that Mendoza did not erect a cross indicates that the oak trees were too far away to be used. The use of the diminutive *cuestasilla* (small *cuesta*) indicates the recorder's perception of size. Such relative terms are difficult to assess. Version M states that they were following the same trail and describes the small stream north of the campground as a spring. This version includes fewer topographic details and does not describe how they put out the fire.

January 5, 1684: departed San Lorenzo and arrived at Parage de los Santos Reys. Day 22.

*The party left San Lorenso and traveled about 5 leagues (13 miles) to reach Parage de los Santos Reys, which was so named because it was the eve of the day of the Magi. Two masses were celebrated at this spot. From S. Lorenso they traveled west of north. They strayed from the path they were following half a league before reaching this place and entered a **cañada**, a valley with good pasture. There were mountains on both sides of the valley and a dry arroyo with many nut trees (**nogales**). They continued northward and upstream along the arroyo and found that it carried good water. Mendoza had a cross placed on this spot.*

Comments: Parage de los Santos Reys was probably on a northwest tributary of Paisano Creek and near its junction with Alpine Creek.[32] As King's Day is an important Christian holiday, two masses were celebrated. One mass, a solemn one, was probably sung. Version M states that after "leaving the trail about half a league to our right, we took a wide valley with good land and pasturage. After going 5 leagues we halted by an arroyo, which runs through it. It has no permanent water but holds it in some pools" (T., p. 6).

January 6, 1684: departed Parage de los Santos Reys and arrived at San Pedro de Alcantara. Day 23.

*They left Parage de los Santos Reys and traveled about 6 leagues (15.6 miles) to a place they called San Pedro de Alcantara. The party remained at this spot the following day. They were detained because the Jumano and other Native Americans who were traveling with the Spanish did not have any food and requested a delay to hunt. The Natives organized a surround (**dar un serco**) to catch deer and other animals to assuage the need that the whole party was experiencing. This place was in a beautiful plain that extended eastward; on the north side there were some hills denuded of trees. From the slope of one of those hills (**seros**) issued a beautiful spring surrounded by this fine black soil. There was little timber at this place; because of this Mendoza did not erect a cross. Mass was celebrated on this spot.*

Comments: San Pedro de Alcantara was quite likely near Paisano Creek, about 4 miles southwest of the Pecos County line.[33] This is the first time the writer clearly states that the Jumano and other groups were traveling with them. It is not possible to know what groups were traveling with Mendoza at this time because he provided that list much later in the trip (May 1, 1684). According to Version L, the names of the groups (*naciones*) that may have been traveling with Mendoza, apart from the Jumano, were the Ororosos, the Beitonijures, the Achubales, the Cujalos, the Toremes, the Gediondos, the Siacuchas, the Suajos, the Isuchos, the Cujacos, the Caulas, the Hinehis, the Ylames, the Cunquebacos, the Quitacas, the Quicuchabes, Los que Hasen arcos, and the Hanasines. In the list Mendoza includes Los que Hasen arcos ("Those Who Make Bows") and the Gediondos. The Gediondos joined the party later and "Those Who Make Bows," which may be the Arcos Fuertes ("Strong Bows" in *Provincias Internas,* vol. 37; Arcos Tuertos or "Twisted Bows" in *Historia,* vols. 298 and 299), also joined Mendoza later. Even if "Los que Hasen arcos" and the Arcos Tuertos are the same group, the list, nineteen groups in total, still contains a higher number of groups than Version L. Version M shows yet a different list of groups, stating: "In addition to the Indians who accompanied us and belonged to the following nations: the Jumanas, the Orasos, the Beitonojanes, Chubates, Cujacos, Taremes, Hediondos, Siacuchas, Suajos, Isuchos, Caucas, Chinchis, Llames, Cunchucos, Quitacas, and Cuicuchubes; in addition to these, I say, we were expecting various other nations, who, through their ambassadors, had promised to come to meet us" (T., p. 13). This list does include sixteen groups, the number stated by the writer of Version L (Day 93), even though that version, as translated and published, includes nineteen groups. Apart from the different spellings of several groups, Version M does not include the Cujalo (repeated?), "Los que Hasen arcos," or the Hanasines.

Historical references to the cultural practice of hunting by means of a surround are rare. The Jumano and other groups accompanying Mendoza engaged in a surround to hunt. Some of the deer pelts obtained in the hunt may have been the pelts offered to Mendoza later in the trip (Day 36). If this is the case, it took about twenty-eight days to prepare the pelts to make *gamusas,* and at least seventeen deer were caught in the surround. Version M includes fewer topographic and environmental details, but the information is basically the same.

January 7, 1684: remained at San Pedro de Alcantara. Day 24.

January 8, 1684: departed San Pedro de Alcantara and arrived at San Bernardino de Sena. Day 25.

The party left S. Pedro de Alcantara and traveled about 8 leagues (20.8 miles) to a place they named San Bernardino de Sena. They traversed level country and stopped in an area where they had neither water nor wood.

Comments: San Bernardino de Sena was probably along the Atcheson, Topeka, and Santa Fé Railroad (ATSF), 5 miles northeast of Chancellor Siding.[34]

January 9, 1684: departed San Bernardino de Sena and arrived at San Francisco Xaviel. Day 26.

Mendoza left S. Bernardino de Sena and traveled about 4 leagues (10.4 miles) to a place they named San Francisco Xaviel. This camping site was located on a plain, but there was no water. The writer stated that it looked like the water source was about 3 leagues (7.8 miles) further away.

Comments: San Francisco Xaviel was located about 6 miles southwest of Fort Stockton.[35] Version M states that they found water 4 leagues (10.4 miles) after departure and made camp. The stop was "on a plain with good pasturage and mesquite wood. Toward the west there were three little hills and toward the north, a cliff from which a spring of alkaline, though potable water arises" (T., pp. 6–7). This version condenses some of the information given in Version L for the diary entries of January 9 and 10. It seems that Version M presents the correct sequence of events. However, this discrepancy supports the argument for two diaries written by different people who recorded the daily information on different days (see next entry). Also, it could be that, in some instances, the traveling party was divided in two groups and one group traveled ahead of the other, which would lead to descriptive overlaps and discrepancies in camping time and travel time (see Day 33).

January 10, 1684: departed San Francisco Xaviel and arrived at San Juan del Rio. Day 27.

*The party left S. Francisco Xaviel and traveled about 4 leagues (10.4 miles) to reach a place they named San Juan del Rio. [It seems that for all, or at least part, of those 4 leagues they traveled through a waterless plain, as we learned in the previous entry.] The place had three small hills (**serillos**) on the west side, and to the north a cliff from which issued a spring of alkaline but drinkable water. The pastures were good and there was plenty of mesquite wood. Here they saw the first tracks of buffalo. Although they searched for the animals, none was found. Mendoza did not erect a cross because there was no suitable wood to build one. Two masses were celebrated on this spot.*

Comments: San Juan del Rio was about 5 miles northeast of Comanche Spring and Fort Stockton, Texas.[36] The writer considered mesquite wood unsuitable for making a cross, possibly because it could not be hewed straight; therefore the other crosses must not have been made of mesquite. Version M describes in this entry the campground of San Juan del Rio and the events that took place there. Again, the descriptions and events of January 10 and 11 are included in this entry (T., p. 7). This version clarifies a problem that exists with the other versions: it states that they remained one day at San Juan del Rio. Version L states that Mendoza's party left San Juan del Rio on both the 11th and the 12th (see Day 26).

January 11, 1684: remained at San Juan del Rio. Day 28.

*The party remained at San Juan del Rio. The place was on a beautiful plain framed by four tall mesas. From the small mesa on the north side issued a spring, and within about three harquebus shots another five beautiful springs issued. Within the distance of half a league (1.3 miles) a very beautiful river was formed [by these springs]. This river had no trees of any kind, only aquatic plants (**camalotes** or **camalotales**). The water of the river was very clear, although a little alkaline. There was abundant fish. In this place they killed three buffalo bulls (**toros**) to relieve the great need of the whole camp. Mass was said, but a cross was not erected because there was no suitable wood to fashion one, even though there was plenty of mesquite.*

Comments: This is the first time they saw and killed buffalo. These were bulls on the fringes of the herd located near the westward limits of the buffalo range in this area and at this time. Don Juan Sabeata stated that the Jumano lands started six traveling days from La Junta de los Ríos, and that it took three days to reach the area where the buffalo herds began, and three more days to where the Jumano lands commenced. It had taken Mendoza ten to eleven days to reach the buffalo herds from La Junta. That is nearly four-fold the traveling time mentioned by Sabeata. If this ratio is used, they would enter the borders of the Jumano lands February 1 or 2, allowing for stopovers, which they did.

January 12, 1684: departed San Juan del Rio and arrived at San Anselmo. Day 29.

*The party left San Juan del Rio and traveled about 5 leagues (13 miles) to a place they named San Anselmo. Midway between San Juan and San Anselmo they came across a beautiful spring that flowed to the north. Toward the east ran a chain of mesas (**meseria**), which was on their right hand as they traveled. The road was level and without rocks. There were abundant pastures and mesquite wood, as well as other woods. Mass was celebrated, but Mendoza did not erect a cross because there was no proper wood to make one.*

Comments: San Anselmo was probably near the ATSF railroad and Baldridge Siding.[37] Although the writer says that there was other timber besides mesquite, no cross was erected. Version M states that the beautiful spring was found 2.5 leagues (6.5 miles) after departure. The campground was on a "waterless plain, which has a range of mesas toward the east" (T., p. 7).

January 13, 1684: departed San Anselmo and arrived at San Christoval. Day 30.

The party left S. Anselmo and traveled about 6 leagues (15.6 miles) to San Christoval on the Río Salado [Pecos River]. The writer described the Salado as the river that flowed through New Mexico with a southeastward course. The Salado carried as much water as the Río del Norte [Rio Grande], although its water was muddy, somewhat alkaline, but drinkable. There were no trees of any kind, but there was abundant mesquite and good pasture. Mass was celebrated. They did not erect a cross because there was no appropriate wood to make one.

Comments: San Christoval was approximately 2 miles upstream on the Pecos River from the modern town of Girvin, Texas.[38] It is interesting that the writer stated that there were no trees, but abundant mesquite wood. Either the writer did not consider mesquite trees to be proper trees, or, more likely, he was referring to mesquite bushes. Version M states that the Pecos runs north to east. According to the transcriber and translator of this version, the document has a note written on the margin that states the following: "This river must be the Pecos joined to the Salado" (T., p. 7). Since I have not seen the Spanish original, it is unclear who added this note and when.

January 14, 1684: remained at San Christoval. Day 31.

*The spot at which they camped on the Río Salado [Pecos] faced a small mesa (**meseria**) separated from other mesas. During this stopover they hunted and killed six buffalo bulls (**toros**) to supply the traveling party. They also discovered a large saline. The saline did not have water but had abundant salt. The salt grains were white and of good quality. The saline was located on the other side [east] of the Salado River; it was located about 1 league (2.6 miles) between a high hill (**loma**) and a mesa located further eastward [i.e., 1 league from a high hill and between that hill and a mesa]. All these features were to the east of the river. The writer described again the landmarks that characterized the camp at San Christoval. He stated that on the west side, in his direction, there was a small mesa separated from the other [mesas], and facing this small mesa there was a saline [modern Soda Lake]. Mass was celebrated.*

Comments: Salt was an important trade resource for Native Americans, and with the arrival of the Europeans it acquired double importance as a condiment, and also as an important element in mining operations (Chapter 5). Version M includes the same basic information, but with less detail. The information provided by Version M is always clearer and better organized, if we are to judge from the translation available.

January 15, 1684: departed San Christoval and arrived at Santo Domingo Soriano de la Noche Buena. Day 32.

The party left San Christoval and traveled about 3 leagues (7.8 miles) to a place they named Santo Domingo Soriano de la Noche Buena. The writer explained that they gave this name to their camping spot because the night was very warm, and about midnight it started to rain as if it was summer, but Santo Domingo saw fit to stop the rain, which was a great blessing because all his companions did not have tents.

Comments: Santo Domingo Soriano de la Noche Buena was probably on the Pecos River, due south from the common corner of the Texas counties of Upton (southwest corner) and Crane (southeast corner).[39] Version M states that they were following the same river. According to the diary some individuals (the friars?) carried tents. Once more the description and events that took place on January 15 and 16 are condensed in this diary entry. This version does not mention the rainstorm but states that the weather was fair. Version M refers to this camp simply as Santo Domingo Soriano.

January 16, 1684: departed S. Domingo Soriano de la Noche Buena and arrived at San Juan de Dios. Day 33.

*The party left S. Domingo Soriano and traveled about 6 leagues (15.6 miles) to a place they named San Juan de Dios. The river water at San Juan was better [clearer and less alkaline]. On the west there was a large mesa that had the appearance of a chain of hills; on the east side, about 4 leagues (10.4 miles) on the other side of the river [east], there was a small mountain range (**sierrarilla**) and from it extended another long mesa. Above this long mesa rose another small mesa that commanded a great view. They did not place a cross because there was no suitable wood to make one. Two masses were celebrated at this place.*

Comments: San Juan de Dios must have been on the Pecos River about halfway between Texas highways 349 and 305.[40] San Juan de Dios was the place they reached on their return journey and from which they turned southward on the way to La Junta de los Ríos. As noted above, Version M includes in this entry the information provided by Version L for the entries of January 15 and 16 (see Day 26). It also states that they were traveling along the margins of the Pecos River.

January 17, 1684: departed San Juan de Dios and arrived at San Ygnacio de Loyola. Day 34.

*The party left San Juan de Dios and traveled about 1 league (2.6 miles) to a place they named San Ygnacio de Loyola. [This distance is given on the diary entry for January 24.] They stopped 1 league (2.6 miles) away from a **ranchería** of a Native group called the Jediondos [Gediondos or Hediondos]. The party did not enter the **ranchería** because the pastures were burned near the **ranchería**. The land they traversed was level, and the pasturelands along the banks of the Salado River appeared to be good. The captains of the Jediondo and other people came out of the **ranchería** to welcome Mendoza with great demonstrations of happiness. These captains were on horseback and the other people were on foot. They were carrying a heavy wooden cross, very well made, and painted red and yellow. The cross was about 2.5 varas (6 feet 11 inches) long and fastened with a nail, which they call **taxamanil**. The cross appeared to have been made some time ago. They also carried a flag made of white taffeta that was slightly less than 1.5 varas (4 feet) long. In the middle of the flag there were two successive crosses of blue taffeta; these were very well made. When they saw Mendoza and his party, the Jediondos fired several harquebus shots and Juan Sabeata answered, firing a shot from a harquebus barrel, with a fuse, because it did not have a lock.[41] Mendoza ordered the salute returned with two shots. Once the two groups joined, Mendoza ordered the soldiers not to dismount; only the friars dismounted. Fr. Nicolas Lopez and Fr. Juan de Sabaleta, on their knees and with great devotion, kissed the cross. Mendoza and his companions also kissed the cross, but did so without dismounting. The Natives kissed the frocks of the friars, and both groups proceeded toward the **ranchería**. The river crossing was next to the **ranchería**. They crossed the river to the east side and entered the **ranchería** where they were welcomed by the majority of the women and children with shouts and expressions of joy. The women and children kissed the frocks of the* *friars. The various captains and other people had prepared, within their village, several huts of reed (***xacales de tule***) for the visitors. Mendoza, using reasonable excuses, did not accept the invitation to stay in the village because he was fearful of the troubles that could arise from such intimacy. He set up camp on a rise, according to the custom of war. The camp was separated from the ***ranchería***. The ***ranchería*** was located at the foot of a great rock (***peñol***) that sheltered the Gediondo from their enemies, the Apache. Mendoza remained at San Ygnacio, waiting for information about a large ambush that was to be made on the Native Americans to steal their horses.*

Comments: San Ygnacio de Loyola was evidently down the Pecos River about 2.6 miles, east-southeast of San Juan de Dios.[42] The Gediondo or Hediondo ("Stinking Ones") probably were given that name because the sulfur-rich water they used and drank gave them a particular odor. Some soldiers that traveled through the area in 1775 called the water *hedionda* because of its sulfur (*azufre*) smell (B. Rodríguez 1775). The *ranchería* of the Gediondo was on the east side of the Pecos River immediately after the place where the party crossed the river. It appears that some Gediondo had horses, but most did not. However, since the Apache were supposed to attack the *ranchería* to steal their horses, they must have had a few more horses than the Native captains rode on when they came to meet the Spaniards. The Gediondo had some harquebuses with which they fired a salute. Sabeata had a damaged harquebus, which he had modified in order to be able to fire it. This diary entry shows the presence of horses and guns and, in the case of Sabeata, a not inconsiderable knowledge of European weapons.

The Natives were carrying a well-made wooden cross painted yellow and red. This was the same cross that Sabeata had described to governors Otermín and Cruzate when he visited El Paso in 1683. Sabeata mentioned (Appendix) that the cross had been used in more than one battle. The Gediondo also carried a flag of white taffeta with two crosses of blue taffeta. Taffeta is a rather fine fabric that would be uncommon to find on the colonial frontier, especially in an area not visited by Europeans. The blue crosses were either embroidered or appliquéd. It should be emphasized how this reception was choreographed by the Natives. Mendoza did not dismount to kiss the cross, but the friars did. Note that Mendoza felt that dismounting was dangerous and would diminish the status of the soldiers, while the status of the friars would not be affected by such an act.

When the whole party arrived at the *ranchería* they were welcomed by the women and children who had remained in the *ranchería*. The Gediondo had prepared huts made of reed to lodge their European guests. The word *tule* (reed) is a loanword from Nahuatl, *tolin* (Silver and Miller 1997: 261). This hospitality practice seems to be part of a behavioral baseline accepted and honored by groups with diverse socioeconomic systems (Wade 2001). Mendoza did not accept the lodging, but he was well enough aware of the consequences of refusing Native hospitality to explain his refusal with appropriate excuses. Mendoza set up his camp away from the *ranchería,* following war rules. This procedure reflects prudence and Mendoza's vast experience as a military commander, even as it highlights his distrust of the people who, for the moment, were his hosts and partners. The writer stated that the Native *ranchería* was located in such a manner as to afford them protection from the Apache. This statement is difficult to interpret: either the Apache were very close to the *ranchería* or the rock was rather substantial. Either way, it would have been dangerous for the Spanish to camp so close to the Apache. Also, it is significant that Version M does not comment on the large rock (*peñol*).

Version M states that, in the Hediondo *ranchería,* there were "Jumanas and some Indians belonging to other nations" (T., p. 8). The taffeta banner is said to have measured less than a vara long. This version also states: "Don Juan Sabeata came forth leading them, for he had arrived before us" (T., p. 8). This indicates that, on occasion, Mendoza's party traveled in two distinct groups. In the same entry it is stated that they remained with the Hediondo for seven days to regain strength and obtain food. During their stay they killed twenty-seven buffalo. The writer states that he "found the Indians docile and affectionate. They were expecting an incursion by the Apaches, and all the captains of this ranchería, Hutacas or Hediondos, as well as Jumanas, begged me to attack the aforesaid Apaches" (T., p. 9). The writer reports that the Native Americans offered him deerskins (Day 36) to make leather jackets, but he does not indicate how these were distributed among the soldiers, or whether more skins would be delivered later.

The next paragraph included in Version M is completely unique to this version, and, because its contents are so important, they will be included as they appear in the translation. The document reads:

> Several soldiers and squadron leaders, who had been clamoring to return from the time we were at La Junta de los Rios, rebelled against the commander. They caused some disturbances among the other citizens and great consternation on the part of these Indians. The discord became so serious that two of the malcontents put their hands to their swords with the intention of wounding their commander and made it necessary for him to defend himself. Therefore he proceeded against them according to the usage of war and sentenced them to be shot. But the father vice-custodian and his companion, seeing that this might result in general aversion toward Christianity on the part of all these infidels, as a result of the behaviour [of the Christians] [brackets in the original translation] who were there, appealed in behalf of the criminals, and their lives were granted to them. Some days later they fled with seven other citizens and a number of Indians and reached El Paso much sooner than the others. So it is recorded in the journal itself, folios 13 to 45 [T., pp. 9–10].

The information contained in this diary entry raises many questions, most of which cannot be answered with the available evidence. First, this and subsequent entries clearly indicate that Mendoza had far more serious troubles with his compatriots than with Sabeata or the Apache. Mendoza was a seasoned military man: he would not court-martial and sentence to death two fellow soldiers unless there was no other solution. Besides, Mendoza was leading such a small military contingent that the loss of any soldier would be significant. The diary states that, a few days later, the malcontents together with seven other citizens and several Natives left for El Paso. This means that the diary entry was either written ex post facto or was amended at a later date. Also, since Mendoza was supposed to have been accompanied by seventeen men-at-arms, this meant that he was left with eight!

As for the identity of the malcontents, we can explore two clues. First, the writer states that they were soldiers and squadron leaders. In August 1685, Cruzate sent a letter to the Viceroy in which he stated that "the story of the holy cross turned out to be false. From this it must be inferred that all the rest contained in the journal is probably the same" (Cruzate 1685a). This letter was hand-carried by Captain Diego de Luna, who accompanied Mendoza to the Jumano. The letter is very unflattering to Mendoza and even to Fr. Lopez, who had advocated that the New Mexico governorship be given to Mendoza. Whatever had happened since late 1683, in 1685 there was no love lost between Mendoza and Cruzate. Cruzate, who stated that he had privately interviewed the soldiers who had participated in the journey, sent Diego de Luna to give the Viceroy an oral report: he would do so only if he trusted Diego de Luna. Thus, it would appear that Diego de Luna might be one of the malcontents. However, on February 2 (Day 50), the Apache stole nine animals, one of which, a donkey or a mule, belonged to Diego de Luna. This seems to indicate that Diego de Luna was not one of the malcontents who deserted Mendoza.

The other clue that can be explored consists of the names of those who received deerskins to make *gamusas* (Day 36) and those who did not. From the list of individuals who are known to have been among the group, the only ones who did not receive deerskins were: Juan Dominguez de Mendoza, Diego Lucero de Godoy, Diego Barela, Diego de Luna, and Anttonio Jorge. Of the whole list, only Anttonio Jorge had the rank of soldier. Godoy is supposed to have signed all diary entries in Version L, and only inspection of the original of Version M would confirm whether the same holds true for this version. Barela got his toe bitten by a snake (Day 93), and Diego de Luna had his mule or donkey stolen (Day 50). These three individuals appear on Day 138 as the officials who agreed with Mendoza's decision to return to El Paso. From this list, the only one who could be implicated in the mutiny was the soldier Anttonio Jorge. Thus, from these clues we do not know the identity of the deserters.

The other pertinent issues are why these men were so eager to leave for El Paso and why none of these events appears in the other versions of the diary. Although several scenarios can be proposed, the available evidence does not substantiate any of them.

January 18, 1684: remained at San Ygnacio de Loyola. Day 35.

January 19, 1684: remained at San Ygnacio de Loyola. Day 36.

*The party remained at San Ygnacio by request of the Jumano and other groups (**naciones**), and also because Mendoza was outfitting the soldiers with weapons and other supplies for war. On this day all the captains of the different nations joined with Juan Sabeata and informed Mendoza that they wanted to talk to him. For his part, Mendoza ordered all the chiefs of squad and soldiers of rank to assemble and be present at this meeting. At the gathering Sabeata and all the other Native American captains, in unison, asked Mendoza, for the love of God,* *to make war on their common enemy, the Apache. They emphasized that the Apache were also enemies of the Spaniards. Mendoza stated that Sabeata and the other captains pointed out to him that it was not wise to leave them behind because of the troubles that could occur, or because of the great damage they could inflict on the Apache if they were together (**por los muchos danos que se podia conseguir**). Mendoza declared that, since this was true and they made their request in earnest, he agreed to fight the Apache. Sabeata and the other captains were very pleased.*

Comments: Once they reached the Gediondo *ranchería,* the Spaniards prepared themselves for war, choosing a strategic camping spot and outfitting the soldiers for battle, presumably because of the ambush the Apache were to make on the horse herd. Given Sabeata's statements about an Apache *ranchería* near the Jumano lands, this spot indicates the perceived southward limits of Apache presence in this area. The writer made the curious statement that Mendoza had agreed to take along the groups of Native Americans because of the problems that could occur, or because of the great damage that might be done (to whom?). The ambiguity of the text makes it unclear whether the writer is hinting at the problems experienced by Mendoza with his own soldiers or at the possible problems with the Apache. The latter scenario appears to be the more logical. The writer also stated that Mendoza agreed to fight the Apache, which is interesting, since the main purpose of the trip was to jointly fight the Apache. Version M does not mention any preparations for war. Given the events reported in Version M, it is perplexing that Mendoza would agree to fight the Apache while facing dissension among the Spanish.

January 20, 1684: remained at San Ygnacio de Loyola. Day 37.

*The party remained at San Ygnacio. Don Juan Sabeata came to see Mendoza and offered him seventeen prepared deerskins (**gamusas**) in order that some men might be armed [outfitted for battle]. Sabeata promised to bring more **gamusas** for those who did not get them. Mendoza divided the skins among those who needed the most. Captain Hernando Martin Serrano got three, Nicolas Lucero two, Miguel Luxan two, Melchor de Archuleta two, Felipe Montoya two, Captain Felipe Romero one, Captain Ygnacio Baca one, Alferez Anttonio Solis one, Sergeant Baltazar Domingues one, Juan Domingues the Younger one, and Anttonio Gomes one. Mass was celebrated every day, and on Saturday two masses were said to the Holy Virgin. One of masses was sung. On Sunday two masses were celebrated. During the seven days they remained at San Ygnacio they killed twenty-seven buffalo.*

Comments: The gift of prepared deerskins was part of the commitment Juan Sabeata and the captains of the other groups made to the Spaniards in return for their visit and their help against the Apache. The deerskins were used either for clothing or possibly as *cueras,* the breastplates used by soldiers. The skins may have been obtained from the animals killed on Day 23. It is important to note the ritualized form taken by the Native requests for help. A meeting was held, a formal request made and accepted: the following day Sabeata delivered a gift or first payment. Although Sabeata stated that other gifts would be made, no mention of later gifts is reported. It may be that lack of performance by the Spaniards negated the promise of other gifts. The gift of seventeen *gamusas* appears to confirm the composition of the Spanish party: Mendoza, seventeen soldiers, and two friars (Day 1).

It is impossible to estimate how many Natives were in the traveling party, especially later in the trip, when the number of buffalo killed may have reflected concerns other than subsistence. I cannot tell how much of the meat obtained was used for the people in the Gediondo *ranchería*. In an effort to evaluate the relationship between the number of buffalo killed and the number of people traveling with Mendoza, I have prepared some estimates, which should be taken as an exploratory exercise of relative relevance. In seven days they killed 27 buffalo, a daily average of 3.86. John Ewers gives 400 pounds of usable meat as a reasonable estimate for an average buffalo (Ewers 1985: 550). That would result in 1,544 pounds of meat per day if most of the animal was used. Ewers (1985: 168) also provides a conservative average daily consumption rate of three pounds of meat per person. This average daily consumption was provided by Native American Blackfoot informers. Using these average numbers, 515 is the maximum number of people who could be adequately fed with the buffalo killed (for additional information, see Day 162).

Version M does not include any of the details concerning the distribution of deerskins, nor does it provide details about the formal request made by the Native Americans, but it does give the basic information about that request. Between January 17 and January 23 there is only one entry in Version M: that of January 17.

January 21, 1684, Day 38; January 22, 1684, Day 39; January 23, 1684, Day 40. They remained at San Ygnacio de Loyola.

January 24, 1684: departed S. Ygnacio de Loyola and arrived at La Conbercion de San Pablo. Day 41.

The party left San Ygnacio de Loyola and traveled about 5 leagues (13 miles) to a place they named La Conbercion de San Pablo. They traversed a plain where the grass was burned. For this reason Mendoza pitched camp in a high spot with good pasture. They spent the night at San Pablo without water. They killed some game at this place. Sabeata informed Mendoza that his spies were following the tracks of the Apache horses. Two masses were celebrated at this place.

Comments: La Conbercion de San Pablo was probably near the intersection of modern highways 349 and 67, west of the Texas town of Rankin and near Five Mile Creek.[43] The writer does not specify how many animals were killed. Sabeata's spies were tracking the movements of the Apache. No other spies seem to have been involved in the gathering of information. This is the second time that the diarist mentions the burning of grasses. According to Joutel (1998: 172, 174, 176, 185), the burning of dry grass stimulated new growth and attracted the buffalo herds. High spots, however, were not burned, and there was good pasture at those locations. Version M reports that "Juan Sabeata and other captains were going in pursuit of the Apache, who were carrying off the horse herd. Trail toward the east" (T., p. 10). The other diary versions do not indicate that Mendoza went eastward.

January 25, 1684: departed La Conbercion de San Pablo and arrived at San Honofre. Day 42.

The party left La Conbercion de San Pablo and traveled about 5 leagues (13 miles) to a place they named San Honofre. On the way from San Pablo to San Honofre they killed five buffalo. They crossed a plain, but the pasture was burned. The land was level and there was plenty of wood. At the camp of San Honofre they were gratified to find abundant game, pasture, and timber. The camp was on a low spot on a plain. There was a spring of good, soft water. They arrived at San Honofre on the 25th, and remained at this place for two days to rest the horses. During their stay they killed thirty-four buffalo. Mendoza's party was joined by the Native American group called the Arcos Tuertos or Arcos Fuertes ["Twisted Bows" or "Strong Bows"].[44] This group resembled the Suma in all aspects, including their attire. Mass was celebrated every day, but a cross was not erected for lack of appropriate timber.

Comments: San Honofre or Onofre is best located about 4 miles east of Flatrock along the ATSF railroad.[45] Mendoza had covered about 13 miles of prairie land that was, at least in part, burned. The burned area was between the *rancherías* of the Gediondos and the Arcos Tuertos. This is probably no coincidence and reflects manipulation of the environment by Native Americans to control and direct the location of buffalo herds, as stated by Joutel (1998: 172). I assume that, at this time, this was the homeland of the Arcos Tuertos, who joined Mendoza at this point. Version M includes the same basic information, but it does not mention the burning of the grasses. This version also calls the Native group Arcos Tuertos.

January 26, 1684, Day 43; January 27, 1684, Day 44: they remained at San Honofre.

January 28, 1684: departed San Honofre and arrived at San Marcos. Day 45.

*The party left San Honofre and traveled about 10 leagues (26 miles) to a place they named San Marcos. They gave this name to the camp because on their arrival a buffalo bull (**toro**) was caught inside the area of the camp and killed. The spot had abundant pastures and timber. A spring issued from a high spot. A cross was erected because there was appropriate wood to build one. Mass was celebrated.*

Comments: San Marcos was probably located on a small tributary of Centralia Draw and 5 miles east of Texas Highway 33.[46] The writer seldom mentions that they caught male buffalo (*toros*). He does so at the beginning of the trip, at the end of the trip at San Juan de Dios, and in this instance, where a single male was caught within the camp. Buffalo cow meat is supposed to have been preferred to bull meat (Roe 1970: 118). Version M states that they traveled 3 leagues (7.8 miles), not 10 leagues (26 miles), as do the other versions. The loss of horses, which is part of the next day's entry in Version L, is included in this entry in Version M. According to this version they remained at San Marcos January 29 and 30 (see Day 26).

January 29, 1684: remained at San Marcos. Day 46.

The party remained at San Marcos because they lost some horses. Counting the first buffalo bull, they killed a total of thirty-one buffalo. Another mass was celebrated.

January 30, 1684: departed San Marcos and arrived at San Joseph. Day 47.

The party left San Marcos and traveled at least 4 leagues (10.4 miles) to a place they named San Joseph. The site was on a gorge (barranco) that had a good pool of water, as well as plenty of timber and pasture. Mass was celebrated and a cross erected. The writer stated that they stayed at San Joseph one more day because of the good pasture.

Comments: San Joseph is probably located at Centralia Draw near its junction with South Mustang Draw on the headwaters of the Middle Concho River.[47] According to Version L they remained at San Joseph one more day, January 31; according to Version M they remained two days at San Marcos (January 29 and 30) and two days at San Joseph (January 31 and February 1). Version M states that on February 1 they departed San Joseph and traveled 6 leagues (15.6 miles) to Nuestra Señora de la Candelaria (T., p. 11).

January 31, 1684: remained at San Joseph. Day 48.

February 1, 1684: departed San Joseph and arrived at Nuestra Señora de la Candelaria. Day 49.

The party left San Joseph and traveled about 6 leagues (15.6 miles) to a place they named Nuestra Señora de la Candelaria. The writer stated that he spent February 2 at this spot because it was the day of N.S. de la Candelaria, and he had agreed to celebrate the feast. Fr. Nicolas Lopez celebrated a high mass [sung], while Fr. Juan Sabaleta celebrated a second normal mass (resada). They camped at the point where they reached the Río Nueces. The site was very pleasant and had abundant pastures, timber, and fish. They caught and ate some catfish. The source of the river was in some springs, and the river flowed eastward. A cross was placed on the spot.

Comments: Nuestra Señora de la Candelaria was located on the Middle Concho about 6 miles below the junction of Kiowa Creek and Mustang Draw.[48] This is the point where Mendoza first reached the river mentioned in his expeditionary orders, the Río Nueces (Concho). The party was now able to supplement its diet with fish. The feast of the Virgin of Candelaria is celebrated on February 2. According to Sabeata's traveling time estimates, adjusted to the Spaniards' travel and accounting for stopovers, the Spaniards had entered Jumano lands. These would be the lands of the Jumano proper, and not of their allies and neighbors to the west, the Arcos Tuertos and the Gediondos. Version M also states that they had reached the Río Nueces (Concho), but condenses the entries for February 1, 2, and 5 (see February 2).

February 2, 1684: departed Nuestra Señora de la Candelaria late in the day, and arrived at El Arcangel San Migel. Day 50.

*They departed N.S. de la Candelaria after the religious festivities. They traveled about 3 leagues (7.8 miles) to a place they named El Arcanjel San Migel. They remained there two and one half days to rest the horses that were worn out and thin. In this place there was a river carrying abundant water. The writer stated that he did not know the source of this river because it came from beneath the earth and issued from amid some rocks (**penas**). Mendoza placed a cross atop the rocky mouth from where the river water issued. This spot was called the Place Where the Dogs Live (**donde viven los perros**), because a great quantity of dogs of all colors came out of the water. These dogs were the same size as other dogs and of the same species (**especie**), although raised in the water. The writer was told they were more fierce [than normal dogs], tearing up people as well as buffalo cows and bulls that came to drink right to the spring mouth. The writer, who found this very peculiar, stated that he saw buffalo bones [of cows and bulls], as well as the excrement and tracks of the dogs. The river flowed eastward with good and crystalline water and joined the river of the shells (Río de las Conchas). This river [Río Nueces] also had many shells, and a great variety of fish. The oaks were very tall and so thick that one could fashion carts and even larger things from their trunks. There was a great variety of plants. The turkeys [or prairie chickens] made tremendous noise at dawn. The meadows were large and fertile, and in the groves (**bosques**) there were many vine shoots, springs, and plenty of prickly-pear plants. At this spot they saw their first pecans (**nogales**); the river bottoms were full of pecan groves. The whole party collected many nuts, which were very welcome because they had been subsisting only on meat. The writer stated that this description applied to both river margins. The water sources (**habrevaderos**) for cattle and buffalo were so close to the roads (**caminos**) that it was not possible to engage in a surround (**juntarlos**) to hunt buffalo. While at this place, they were continually under the threat of a storm, but the weather held until the very last night, when the storm finally broke. During their stay the Apache stole nine animals: eight horses and a mule or a donkey (**bestias**). Seven of the animals belonged to the Jumano and the other two belonged to the Spaniards: one to Mendoza [a horse] and the other to Alferes Diego de Luna [a donkey or a mule]. The writer said that this occurred because the animals [of the Spaniards] had been mistakenly mixed with those of the Natives. They could not follow the Apache because of the great advance [elapsed time and lead in distance] they had. Each day they celebrated two masses.*

Comments: El Arcangel San Migel was probably on the Middle Concho just below the junction with Wallace Draw.[49] According to all versions except Version M, this locale was called the Place Where the Dogs Live. The writer was told that these were fierce dogs that attacked people and buffalo. He saw the bones of buffalo supposedly killed by those doglike animals, but he did not see the dogs. He did see their footprints and their excrement. Version M states only that "water dogs (so they call them around here) of various colors and of the same species and size as tame dogs, breed here, and although they are bred in water, these Indians [*sic*] say that they are so fierce that when the bison come down to drink they attack and bite them" (T., p. 11). Regarding the noisy birds, it appears that prairie chickens make much more noise than turkeys (T. Campbell, personal communication).

The writer stated that the Río Nueces, which joined the River of Shells, also had shells, but he did not mention having looked for or gathered pearls. Because of the writer's statement on January 5, when he saw nuts (*nogales*), it appears that the nuts seen and gathered at this spot were different from those seen on January 5. Thus, I assume that these nuts were pecans. The word *nogales* is used in both instances, but *nogales* is a generic word for nuts, and the Spaniards did not have a specific word for pecans. Version M adds that the pecans were still lying on the ground. Sabeata mentioned that many of his Native allies and friends gathered pecans in the area (Appendix). The party wanted to make a surround to kill buffalo, but the distribution and location of the water sources where the animals drank did not provide the conditions needed for that hunting method.

While Version M states that Sabeata went in pursuit of the Apache who had taken some horses, the writer of Version L simply mentions that the Apache stole some horses. During the two and a half days that the party remained at Arcangel San Migel, the Apache stole nine animals; seven of these animals belonged to the Jumano. To date, these were the only two reported unfriendly actions of the Apache. The theft of these horses may indicate that at least seven captains of the Jumano were accompanying the expedition, since captains usually had horses, and twelve captains of different Jumano *rancherías* visited Governor Otermín at El Paso.

The only animals stolen from the Spaniards were taken because they had been unwittingly mixed with the animals belonging to the Natives. It appears that Mendoza maintained the practice of setting camp away from the Native camping grounds and that the horses were also kept separate. This Spanish practice should be kept in mind when doing intensive archaeological surveys or excavations. It is also clear to me that the Apache had no intention, at this point, of provoking the Spaniards or engaging in a military confrontation. If indeed the Apache stole those animals, they were stealing horses from Natives, not from Spaniards. The writer said that they could not give pursuit because of the great time and distance advantages of the Apache, although Version M states that Sabeata pursued the perpetrators. Mendoza's attitude appears to have been part of a pattern of avoidance that continued as the trip proceeded. Still, the evidence provided by Version M (Day 34) makes it clear that Mendoza did not have the manpower to fight the Apache. According to Version M they departed El Arcangel San Migel on the 6th and not on the 5th.

February 3, 1684, Day 51; February 4, 1684, Day 52: they remained at El Arcangel San Migel.

February 5, 1684: departed El Arcangel San Migel and arrived at Señor San Diego. Day 53.

*Mendoza left El Arcangel San Migel and traveled about 6 leagues (15.6 miles) to a place they named Señor San Diego. The writer stated that they remained at this spot four days because they were awaiting news from the spies who had been dispatched. When the spies returned to camp, they reported that they had found an Apache **rancheria** nearby. Mendoza sent a second group of spies to verify the information. The first news proved to be false, although not totally; tracks were found, but they were old. On the way to Señor San Diego the Spaniards and the Native Americans killed about sixty buffalo, probably more and not less, by means of a surround. While they were camped at San Diego they killed forty-three buffalo. The camping place of San Diego was on a clearing (**plassa**) framed by large groves of lofty pecan and oak trees. There was a great quantity of turkeys and other kinds of game. The water source was a beautiful river that flowed eastward.*

Comments: El Señor San Diego very likely was located on the Middle Concho about 11 miles west-southwest of the city limits of San Angelo, Texas, and about 4 miles north of Highway 67.[50] The spies brought news of an Apache *rancheria* nearby, which means that the Apache (one *rancheria*) were present north and west of San Angelo. Quite possibly this *rancheria* was the same one Sabeata mentioned when he came to see Governor Cruzate at El Paso in October 1683 (Sabeata 1683a). Mendoza dispatched a second group of spies to verify the information: they reported that the evidence was old. Mendoza was prudent, but also playing for time. If the Apache had stolen the horses (Day 50), they knew the location of the Spaniards and could have moved on to avoid confrontation. I am convinced that neither the Spaniards nor the Apache were interested in facing each other, and the Apache were favoring Mendoza's plan. Between El Arcangel San Migel and San Diego the writer said they killed more than sixty buffalo. Since they were on the move, it is likely that only choice parts were consumed and some surplus transported. While at San Diego they killed forty-three buffalo by means of a surround.

Note. The writers of all versions stated that they remained at Señor San Diego four days and that they left the place on February 11. These dates do not fit the dates reported: they must have remained five days at San Diego. According to Version M they departed San Miguel (spelled that way in Version M), traveled 6 leagues, and reached a little river where they made camp. They departed San Diego on the 11th after spending four days waiting for the spies who had been sent to gather information on the Apache *rancheria* (T., p. 12).

February 6, 1684, Day 54. February 7, 1684, Day 55. February 8, 1684, Day 56.
February 9, 1684, Day 57. February 10, 1684, Day 58: they remained
at Señor San Diego.

February 11, 1684: departed Señor San Diego. February 12, 1684: arrived
at El Angel de Guarda. Days 59 and 60.

The party left Señor San Diego and traveled about 4 leagues (10.4 miles) to a place they named El Angel de Guarda. They did not reach their destination on the 11th because halfway through the trip they were caught by a powerful thunderstorm, and also because of the various messages received from the spies who claimed that the Apache were nearby and that it was better to stop. The writer stated that these reports from the spies were suspicious and resulted from the guile and sinister manipulations of Juan Sabeata, who had not been telling the truth in everything he had said. The stopover and the camp at El Angel de Guarda were both on the banks of a river that joined the principal branch [of the river], which they called the River of Pearls. The water was good and there was an abundance of nuts and other resources, such as turkeys,[51] camotes, buffalo, and many other kinds of animals. The river had abundant fish, such as catfish, boquinete,[52] and matalote, as well as many shells. There were many kinds of birds and very pleasant songbirds. They killed more than eighty buffalo. Mass was said every day.

Comments: Quite possibly El Angel de Guarda was at the junction of the Middle and South Concho rivers, near Lake Nasworthy Dam.[53] This was the place specified in Governor Cruzate's orders as the objective of the trip. When Mendoza arrived at Señor San Pedro (Day 70), he stated he had reached his destination 8 leagues (20.8 miles) before, which confirms that he reached his destination at El Angel de Guarda. The writer said that the spies continued to insist that the Apache were close by. He did not believe the information and attributed these reports to the falsehoods and manipulative behavior of Juan Sabeata. It is likely that Sabeata was indeed manipulating the information to cause a confrontation with the Apache. The defeat of the Apache was the main reason why he had gone to the trouble of organizing the coalition with all the other Native groups, and also why he guided the Spaniards and supplied them with food and other resources. Sabeata invested a lot of time and effort in order to establish the Native coalition and prepare for this trip; he wanted to deal a crucial blow to the Apache, or at least make the Apache aware of the alliance between the members of the coalition and the Spaniards. Mendoza thwarted Sabeata's goals. All the evidence points to Mendoza's determination to avoid a confrontation with the Apache. According to Version L they remained seven days at Angel de Guarda (February 12 through February 18). During this time they killed more than eighty buffalo.

The word *camotes* has been translated as "sweet potatoes" (Bolton 1916: 336; Silver and Miller 1997: 259). *Camote* is a loanword from Nahuatl, *camotli,* which means "*batata, rayz comestible*" (Molina 1977 [1551–1771]: 12). It is unclear whether the roots mentioned by the writer were those of what we call today "sweet potatoes." It is best to assume the writer was simply referring to some sort of edible tuber.

Version M states that El Santo Angel de la Guarda was "on the shore of another river which joins the principal one called the Río de las Nueces, or [Río] de las Perlas" (T., p. 12). This version also reports that they remained at this campground ten days and not seven as the other versions state. If one follows the dates reported in Version M, they left Angel de la Guarda on February 21 (see below).

February 13, 1684, Day 61. February 14, 1684, Day 62. February 15, 1684, Day 63. February 16, 1684, Day 64. February 17, 1684, Day 65. February 18, 1684, Day 66: they remained at El Angel de Guarda.

February 19, 1684: departed El Angel de Guarda and arrived at San Bissente Ferrer. Day 67.

They left El Angel de Guarda and traveled about 3 leagues (7.8 miles) to a place they named San Bissente Ferrer. On this day, the writer states that Mendoza left El Angel de Guarda, and that he expelled or sent away (despache) Juan Sabeata and the Jumano spies because of the frauds they had committed. The expelled Jumano were accompanied by two Piro Natives who had been traveling with Mendoza. Mendoza's party arrived at San Bissente Ferrer and remained there three days to rest the horse herd. The camp was on the same river along which they had been traveling. Both margins of the river were very fertile. There were good meadows, an abundance of nut-bearing trees and other kinds of trees, and good pastures. There were many wild grapes, and great variety of game on the wing and turkeys. The river had a great quantity of fish. They killed eleven buffalo to supply the camp. Mass was celebrated every day.

Comments: San Bissente Ferrer must have been near the junction of the North Concho and the South Concho in the city of San Angelo.[54] At San Bissente Ferrer, the writer of Version L states that Mendoza expelled Juan Sabeata and his Jumano spies (see below). The text is not clear as to whether Mendoza also expelled the Piros or they left of their own accord. It is significant that Mendoza expelled Sabeata after he reached the spot where he had been in 1654 as a member of the Guadalajara expedition. The clear indication is that Mendoza no longer needed Sabeata; he had become more of a handicap than an asset. It is also noteworthy that, with the exception of Mendoza, it appears that no other Spaniard knew their intended final destination, because only Mendoza had been there before. The party killed eleven buffalo to feed the people in the camp.

Version M states that the Mendoza party left El Angel de la Guarda for San Vicente on February 21. The entry that corresponds to the campsite of San Vicente (spelling in Version M) does not include any of the information provided in the other versions (T., p. 13). Version M also does not report the expulsion of Sabeata or that of the Piro Natives. If Version M is to be believed, the assumptions made above regarding Mendoza's behavior toward Sabeata are invalid. However, the absence of information regarding Sabeata's expulsion raises the issue of who wished to blame Sabeata for the troubles experienced during the trip, and why.

**February 20, 1684, Day 68; February 21, 1684, Day 69: they remained
at San Bissente Ferrer.**

**February 22, 1684: departed San Bissente Ferrer and arrived
at Río del Señor San Pedro. Day 70.**

*The party left San Bissente Ferrer and traveled 5 leagues (13 miles) to a place they named Río
del Señor San Pedro. The writer stated that this was the principal river they called River of the
Pearls, or by another name, River of the Nuts, even though all these rivers had nuts. This was
also the river mentioned in the discovery orders that Mendoza was given by Governor Don
Domingo Jironza de Cruzate. Governor Cruzate's orders were thus fulfilled. They now were
downriver about 8 leagues (20.8 miles) from where Don Diego de Guadalajara had arrived.
The area had luxuriant plant life, just like the other places where they had been, but it had
more water because at this spot several rivers joined. They killed seven buffalo.*

Comments: Río del Señor San Pedro was probably on the Main Concho River about
3 miles west of Highway 692 and about 4 miles southwest of the town of Miles, Texas.[55]
The writer stated clearly that he was at the junction of several rivers that were all part of
one river, the River of the Pearls, which was also called the River of the Nuts. The writer
considered the drainage of the Concho (with its three branches) to be one river. This
was also the river that was reached by Diego de Guadalajara in 1654, when Mendoza had
been a member of that expedition. The Concho was the Río Nueces and the heart of
Jumano lands. Version M states that they had reached the River of the Nuts "into which
all the others except the Salado empty. Although there is an abundance of pecan trees on
the banks of the others and shells in some of them, this alone is the one that is called the
Río de las Nueces, or [Río] de las Perlas, and now by the new name of San Pedro" (T.,
p. 13). Otherwise the basic information contained in the two diary versions is identical.

February 23, 1684, Day 71: remained at Río del Señor San Pedro.

**February 24, 1684: departed Río del Señor San Pedro and arrived
at San Pablo. Day 72.**

*The party left the Río del Señor San Pedro and traveled about 6 leagues (15.6 miles) to a place
they named San Pablo, where they stayed for two days. They pitched camp on a spot that did
not have permanent water. The water source consisted of rainwater. They killed about twenty
buffalo. Mass was celebrated every day and twice on feast days.*

Comments: San Pablo was west of the town of Vick on the Tom Green County and
Concho County line near Highway 306.[56] Version M states that they remained at this
spot because of the bad weather (T., p. 13).

February 25, 1684, Day 73; February 26, 1684, Day 74: they remained at San Pablo.

February 27, 1684: departed San Pablo and arrived at San Isidro Labrador. Day 75.

The party left San Pablo and traveled about 8 leagues (20.8 miles) to a place they named San Isidro Labrador. They remained at San Isidro Labrador from February 27, 1684, to March 15, 1684, or sixteen days, excluding March 15, the day of departure. [This makes March 15 Day 92 of the trip.] The place at which they camped was on the headwaters of a beautiful river. It was enclosed in a valley that had rocky mesas (mesas de piedra) on both sides. The road was level with abundant pastures, woods (bosques), and many turkeys. There were also many pecan trees. They killed more than two hundred buffalo. Mass was celebrated every day.

Comments: Quite likely San Isidro Labrador was in Concho County near the head-waters of Brady Creek and about 3 miles south of the town of Eden.[57] It is unclear why Mendoza continued on his trip. On February 12, he reached his assigned destination. According to Version L, Mendoza expelled Sabeata, and no statement is made about who was leading the remaining Native Americans. Also, Mendoza was supposed to meet a large number of Native groups. On the other hand, Mendoza needed to set up camp to be able to engage in extensive buffalo hunting. He and the Natives needed time and facilities to process the large quantities of buffalo meat and pelts. As for the Native groups he was expecting, it is reasonable to assume that they were either to visit him here or later at San Clemente. At San Isidro Labrador they killed two hundred buffalo. The writer of Version L stated that they left San Isidro Labrador on March 15 and arrived at Río del Glorioso San Clemente on March 16. This is probably a mistake in the recording of dates, since it is not likely that they traveled all night and did not pitch camp, or that it took them so long to cover 5 leagues (13 miles). Clearly, the discrepancies in dates and distances result from the facts reported in Version M and the effort to accommodate them.

Version M presents very different information. The diary entry for March 27 states that they

continued toward the east as far as another place which we named San Sebastián, and halted there, having traveled 3 leagues (7.8 miles). On the 28th we traveled 5 leagues (13 miles) in the same direction. We received information from the Jumanas Indian spies, who were going in advance, that the Apaches were on the road, and we halted at a watering place of rainwater which we named Los Desamparados. 5 leagues.

Here our greatest difficulties occurred, for several of our malcontents declared themselves. The two mentioned above had been sentenced to death; and, their lives having been granted them at the instance of the reverend fathers, they fled, taking with them a number of the best horses and many of the friendly infidels who had come with us. This resulted in such ill feeling among those who remained that the Reverend Fathers Fray Nicolás López and Fray Juan de Zavaleta, had great difficulty in pacifying them, since they now consider false all they had heard from their reverences about evangelical doctrine and all that I had told them about the royal service and protection. So bad a storm came up that for ten days we could not travel nor did we see the sun. As a result the horses grew thin and several horses died. Because most of the latter belonged to the friendly infidels, their ill feeling increased.

On the 9th day of the month of March we left this place called Los Desamparados and after traveling 5 leagues (13 miles) we reached a beautiful river abounding in shells. There are many pecans and other trees on its banks. We named it San Roque. 5 leagues. We remained here until the 14th.

On the 14th we went on, over flat country abounding in pasturage, trees, and turkeys or wild hens. After traveling 8 leagues (20.8 miles) we reached the source of another river which we named San Isidro Labrador. There are many pecan trees here. In the preceding place about 200 bison were killed. 8 leagues.

Comments: Version M states that they left S. Pablo February 27 and traveled east to San Sebastian (7.8 miles). San Sebastian was about 6 miles east of the town of Vick and 12.5 miles north of the town of Eden.[58] On the 28th they proceeded to Los Desamparados (13 miles), where they remained until March 9. Los Desamparados was about 10 miles north-northeast of Eden and 5 miles south-southwest of the town of Millersview.[59]

This version states that they followed the Jumano spies, while Version L reports that the spies were expelled on February 19 (Day 67). Version M also reports that the Spanish soldiers who had previously rebelled now deserted and took with them not only many friendly Natives, but also some of the best horses. At Los Desamparados they were caught by very bad weather that prevented them from traveling for ten days. The time spent by Mendoza in his excursion to the east corresponds to the period of sixteen days spent by the remainder of the group at San Isidro. The writer states that the Natives were very despondent because they lost many horses due to the weather and lack of pasture. It appears that, as early as 1684, Native groups in Texas had many more horses than has been assumed. On March 9 they departed Los Desamparados and traveled to San Roque (13 miles). San Roque was almost certainly on the Colorado River, 9 miles southeast of its confluence with the Concho River and near the mouth of Mustang Creek.[60] On March 14 they departed San Roque and arrived at S. Isidro Labrador (20.8 miles). On March 16 they left S. Isidro and arrived at San Clemente (13 miles). Version M states:

On the 16th we set out from San Isidro, traveled 5 leagues (13 miles) and halted on the bank of another river which we named San Clemente. In this region it has no shells whatsoever, but six days' journey farther down, according to what I heard, it produces estremely [*sic*] large ones, in many of which there are pearls. It flows toward the east, and on both banks there are pecan trees in abundance, wild grapes, blackberries, and plums. In this region there is also an abundance of game birds, bears, deer, a few pronghorn antelope, and a great many herds of bison. 5 leagues.

In addition to the Indians who accompanied us and belonged to the following nations: the Jumanas, the Orasos, the Beitonojanes, Chubates, Cujacos, Taremes, Hediondos, Siacuchas, Suajos, Isuchos, Caucas, Chinchis, Llames, Cunchucos, Quitacas, and Cuicuchubes; in addition to these, I say, we were expecting various other nations, who, through their ambassadors, had promised to come to meet us. Therefore we remained on this Rio de San Clemente from the 16th day of March until the first day of May. On a height near the camp we built a fortified tower of adobe with two rooms. In one of them mass was said every day and the offices of Holy Week were celebrated with all possible decorum, to the wonderment of the infidels who were with us. During all this time, the Christians and pagans of the army together killed 4,300 large head of bison, not counting many which were left for lost in the field and a larger number of calves which were caught and which are not included in the aforesaid number. The nations whom we were expecting could not come: and they all belonged to the Tejas, with these names: Huicaciques, Ayelis, Aguidas, Amichienes, Tujujos, Amomas, Manaques, Durjaquitas, Chuncotes, Anchimos, Colabrotes, Unojitas, Chinsas, Quaysabas, Payubunas, Pahuachianes and others [T., pp. 13–16].

Much of what followed is the same information presented in the other versions. After declaring his intention to begin the journey home, the writer of Version M stated that he dispatched to their lands all those Natives who would not accompany the Spanish. The writer commented that "only Juan Sabeata remained behind with a few families of all those who had accompanied us to here, because he feared that he would be punished for his misconduct, and impelled by this same fear, he approached some of these nations to conspire with him to take our lives, according to what they themselves assured us, but they behaved with fidelity toward us" (T., p. 16).

Version M includes stops, campgrounds, and events that do not appear in the other versions. The campgrounds of San Sebastian, Los Desamparados, and San Roque do not appear in Version L, nor does this version mention the continual conflicts between Mendoza and his compatriots and the problems that resulted from their departure. Version M describes the "baluarte" built at San Clemente as a fortified adobe tower, and gives the number of buffalo killed as 4,300, not 4,030 (transposition of digits?).

The Native groups who were to visit Mendoza are all said to belong to the Tejas (Caddoan), and the list includes sixteen groups instead of the thirty-five named in Version L. Allowing for possible synonymy, the groups not named in Version M are the Flechas chiquitas (or reniquitas), the Bobidas, the Injames, the Dijus, the Acanis, the Humez, the Bibis, the Conchumuchas, the Teandas, the Pojues, the Papanes, the Puchas, the Isconis, the Pagaiames, the Sabas, the Bajuneros, the Novraches, the Pulchas, the Detobitis, the Puchames, and the Oranchos. The Juamas could be the Amomas, but the Amichienes, Manaques, and Durjaquitas present in Version M are not included in the other lists (see below).

March 15, 1684: departed San Isidro Labrador. Day 92. March 16, 1684: arrived at Río del Glorioso San Clemente. Day 93.

The party left San Isidro Labrador and traveled about 5 leagues (13 miles) to a place they called Río del Glorioso San Clemente. They remained at this stop from March 16 to May 1, or 46 days. [May 1, the day of departure, was the 138th day of the trip.] They camped at a spot where the *Río de San Clemente* flowed eastward. The banks of the river were very fertile with abundant plant life, nuts, grapes, mulberries, and groves of plum trees. In the area of the river where their camp was located there were no shells, but Mendoza learned that downriver, about six traveling days, there was a great quantity of very large shells that had pearls. There was abundant game, turkeys, and a great variety of animals, such as bear, deer, and antelope.[61] The number of these animals was not comparable to that of the buffalo. The buffalo were so many that only God could attempt to count them. The Spaniards and Native Americans killed 4,030 buffalo. This number referred only to adult buffalo that were actually killed and brought into the camp; those carcasses from which only pelts were taken were left in the fields and were not counted, and neither were the calves that were brought into the camp. The number of the animals they killed and did not count was very large. The writer stated that they were detained at San Clemente because they were awaiting the arrival of people from forty-eight nations. The writer added that this number did not include those who were traveling with the party, whose number was sixteen, nor did it include many other nations that, through their ambassadors, he was expecting and whose names, although peculiar, he included. The names of the nations that were traveling with his party were the following: First of all the Jumana nation; the Ororosos, the Beitonijures, the Achubales, the Cujalos, the Toremes, the Gediondos, the Siacuchas, the Suajos, the Isuchos, the Cujacos, the Caulas, the Hinehis, the Ylames, the Cunquebacos, the Quitacas, the Quicuchabes, Los que hacen arcos, the Hanacines. [Although the writer stated that the nations traveling with Mendoza were sixteen, he provided nineteen names.] The names of the nations Mendoza was waiting for were as follows: The people of the Río de los Tejas, who had sent a message informing that they would come, the Huicasique, the Aielis, the Aguidas, the Flechas chiquitas (or reniquitas), the Echancotes, the Anchimos, the Bobidas, the Injames, the Dijus, the Colabrotes, the Unofitas, the Juamas, the Yoyehis, the Acanis, the Humez, the Bibis, the Conchumuchas, the Teandas, the Hinsas, the Pojues, the Quisabas, the Paiabunas, the Papanes, the Puchas, the Puguahianes, the Isconis, the Tojumas, the Pagaiames, the Sabas, the Bajuneros, the Novraches, the Pulchas, the Detobitis (or de Tobites), the Puchames, and the Oranchos. The writer stated that the names included in the last list were the nations Mendoza could not wait for. However, these nations were assured of the Spaniards' friendship, and Mendoza made an agreement with the nations that were traveling with him and their ambassadors to return in about one year. During their stay at San Clemente, Mendoza ordered a bastion (**baluarte**) built. This bastion had two parts or rooms (**piessas**): the lower one served as a church (**hermita**), and the other part or room (**piessa**) served as protection from enemies. The bastion was built on a high spot and provided great protection to the camp and to the horse herd. Mass was said every day in the room that served as church. All the celebrations of Holy Week, most of them sung, were attended by many Christian Natives who were among the heathen. All the Natives who were with the Spaniards asked for baptism. The writer reported an accident suffered by Alferez Diego Barela. This soldier was bitten on his little toe by a venomous water snake. In the time that it took to recite four credos the poison took over his body (**le subio el beneno**) and he was in such pain that they all thought he would soon die. Fortunately Fr. Nicolas Lopez carried with him an herb (**contrayerba**) that served as antidote for all types of poison, and the *friar, with his own hands, cured the bitten toe [lanced the toe?] and made the patient drink the herbal concoction. Soon after Diego Barela expelled a great quantity of a black substance like coal and God spared his life.*

Comments: I believe the Río del Glorioso San Clemente was the San Sabá River and that San Clemente was near the modern town of Menard.[62] This is the spot where Mendoza's party spent the longest period of time. The Río de San Clemente did not have shells. Mendoza was told that six days' travel downriver there were very large shells that had pearls. The writer of Version L does not say if he traveled downriver to get those shells while he was at San Clemente. Version L states that Mendoza found some shells before arriving at San Clemente, but it does not mention that he gathered freshwater pearls. However, Mendoza must have traveled downriver to get pearls, because Cruzate stated that they had brought samples of pearls and acorns (*bellotas*), and Fr. Lopez delivered some to the Viceroy (Cruzati 1684a). The number of names of Native groups provided is thirty-six (see Appendix), not forty-eight, as the writer of Version L states. The total number of names provided is fifty-five. The list of groups traveling with Mendoza does not include the Arcos Tuertos or Arcos Fuertes, but we know that they joined the traveling party. Version L states that the people of the River of the Tejas did not come, but sent an ambassador to Mendoza. Version M, however, states that the "Huicaciques, Ayelis, Aguidas, Amichienes, Tujujos, Amomas, Manaques, Durjaquitas, Chuncotes, Anchimos, Colabrotes, Unojitas, Chinsas, Quaysabas, Payubunas, Pahuachianes and others" (T., pp. 13–16), all belonged to the Tejas (sphere of influence?).

Version L reports that they erected a building that Mendoza called a *bastion*. The *Diccionario de la lengua Castellana* defines *baluarte* as "termino de fortificación. Es un cuerpo pentágono, que puesto en los ángulos de la Piaza sale avançado hácia la campaña para defender el muro. Son de diferentes modos y fíguras, Metaphoricamente se toma por qualquiera cosa que defiende, guarda y conserva à otra" (RAE 1726: 540). *Bastion* is said to be a French loanword and to mean the same as *baluarte* (RAE 1726: 571). Thus, a *baluarte* or *bastion* meant, metaphorically, any type of defensive enclosure, and if we credit Version L, Mendoza's building should not be interpreted as having a particular shape. Version M, however, states that the edifice was constructed of adobe and had a tower. From an archaeological point of view there should be, at least, some substantial postholes, since, from the description, the building was two-storied. Under the room that served as church there should be burials, since several children and adults died while they were at San Clemente and were buried there (Lopez 1685; Mendoza et al. 1684b).

At San Clemente they killed well over 4,030 buffalo (see Day 162). The accident suffered by Diego Barela provides some cultural details worthy of mention. First, the writer used a traditional Catholic prayer, the *credo* (creed), to time how long it took the poison to overtake the patient. One creed takes about one minute and fifteen seconds to recite. I found another document (Bustamante 1723) in which the creed was used to time the crossing of a river (see also Karttunen and Lockhart 1976: 75). Luckily for Barela, Fr. Lopez carried a survival kit that was effective. When I first read this diary entry I was disturbed because the writer described in great detail the accident Barela suffered, but said little about the troubles with the Apache and the Salinero. After finding Version M, the text makes sense: the incident involved Fr. Lopez (or Fr. Zavaleta), who, I believe, wrote Version L.

In a declaration made after the trip, Mendoza (1684b) stated that he was left with ten men at this time, while the friars, accompanied by some soldiers (seven or eight), had gone to preach. The declaration makes no sense unless Mendoza's original traveling party included about ten more people. Due to the loss of rebellious Spanish soldiers, Mendoza had eight soldiers left. If he provided Fr. Lopez with an escort of seven or eight men, Mendoza was left either alone or with one soldier! Fr. Lopez (Gomez et al. 1684; Lopez 1686), on the other hand, reported that he traveled inland guided by the Jumano, having been as close as 25 leagues (65 miles) to the lands of the Tejas. In a letter to the Viceroy, Alonso de León[63] (Lino Canedo 1968: 156) mentioned that, while at San Francisco de los Tejas, he met a ladino Native named Tomás, who was from Coahuila. Tomás said he had entered the land with some soldiers and the custodian of New Mexico at El Paso. Tomás accompanied them to a mountain range (sierra) that, according to Alonso de León, was located about 12 leagues (31.2 miles) above the Paso del Río Hondo. It is unlikely that Alonso de León meant the Río Hondo in Medina County. According to Tomás, the friar and the soldiers wanted to go to the Tejas, but they did not dare go beyond that mountain range; thus they sent him to locate the settlement of the Tejas. Tomás went from *ranchería* to *ranchería* and finally found the Tejas. He had been with the Tejas for over one year (Lino Canedo 1968: 156). It appears that Tomás traveled with the Mendoza-Lopez expedition and guided Fr. Lopez to near the San Roque campground (Day 75). According to Version L, when the Mendoza-Lopez party left San Clemente, several groups also departed, heading either south or southeast (Day 138). These groups were under the leadership of a Native who was Christian and spoke Mexican and Castilian. It is possible that this individual was Tomás. This same individual may have been the one who met Terán de los Rios and Massanet in 1692 (Lino Canedo 1968: 243–244), and the one who absconded with the papers Sabeata was bringing to Governor Pardiñas (Chapter 5). Version M, on the other hand, does state that all the Natives departed for their own lands, except for Sabeata, who remained in the area with some families.

May 1, 1684: departed El Río del Glorioso San Clemente and arrived at San Atanacio. Day 138.

*On the day of his departure from San Clemente, the writer states that Mendoza made several important statements. He explained that it had been agreed by the friars and all the soldiers of rank, such as Sergeant Major Diego Lucero de Godoy, Squadron Leader Captain Hernando Martin Serrano, Alferez Diego de Luna, and Alferez Diego Barela, that they should leave this place and return home. They considered it better to depart because they could not face the war their common enemies, the Apache, were making on them from the north. The Apache had made three incursions (**abances**) on their camp by night and by day. On the night of*

April 30, they had been attacked and a soldier was wounded by three arrows. The Apache had caused other damage.[64] *From the west, the pirate (corsarios) Natives of the Kingdom of La Vizcaya, whom they [the people of Nueva Vizcaya?] called Salineros, also attacked (abanses) their camp three times at night. The Salineros had killed two friendly Gediondo who had gone out to hunt and had fallen asleep in the field. The writer stated that Mendoza was short of manpower and ammunition and he thought it would be better to return home and inform Governor Cruzate of what had occurred in order that the governor might decide on the best course of action. These were the reasons that prevented Mendoza from waiting for the nations that were supposed to come and meet him. When they left camp, some nations departed to their lands with the Native who was their leader. He was Christian and proficient in the Mexican and Castilian languages. Mendoza's party departed, accompanied by the nations that were traveling with them. Their Native traveling companions amounted to just a few families. The writer stated that Juan Sabeata, fearful of the troubles he had caused, fled. Sabeata struck a deal with some nations to kill the Spanish, but became aware that those nations had faithfully informed the Spaniards of the plot. The writer continued by saying that, considering the evil deeds of Juan Sabeata, who was to know if those same nations had not killed him already, since he had lost his reputation with those nations and was in disagreement with them. The writer reported that Mendoza named Captain Hernando Martin Serrano interpreter for the Jumano language, and that on their return trip [inbound leg], they were taking a different route than the one they had followed on arrival [outbound leg]. They departed El Río del Glorioso San Clemente and traveled about 4 leagues (10.4 miles) to a place they named San Atanasio because it was the Saint's feast day. The camp was on the same river [San Clemente], and it had basically the same plants, animals, and abundance of fish. On arrival they killed four buffalo. Mass was celebrated.*

Comments: San Atanacio must have been on the San Sabá River southwest of Clear Creek Lake and about 8 miles northeast of Fort McKavett.[65] During the forty-six days spent at San Clemente, the writer of Version L stated that they suffered three incursions from the Apache, made both at night and by day, and in one of those a soldier was wounded. He reported no details about these affairs, but the soldier, whose name we do not learn, was well enough to travel the following day. The writer also reported three attacks by the Salineros and the killing of two friendly Gediondo.

I believe that Mendoza never had any intention of fighting the Apache, and that Sabeata probably realized this early on during the trip. Both versions of the diary report problems with Sabeata, but while Version L emphasizes Sabeata's evil deeds as the underlying reason for the mishaps, Version M deemphasizes Sabeata's role in the problems and stresses the mutiny of Mendoza's Spanish soldiers. The writer of Version L muddies the water by stating that Sabeata fled on account of his evil deeds. Early on, the writer stated that Mendoza expelled Sabeata, and predicted his demise at the hands of other groups with which he was in disagreement. Sabeata was not killed, and continued to enjoy a position of prestige. In 1689, Sabeata reappeared in the historical record when he informed Governor Pardiñas of the presence of the French among the Tejas (Chapter 5).

Mendoza named Captain Martin Serrano interpreter for the Jumano language because Sabeata was no longer traveling with the party. This means either that there were Jumano still traveling with Mendoza or that some of the groups traveling with him spoke the Jumano language. We know that the Gediondo were still traveling with Mendoza. I suggest that the Gediondo were a Jumano group and spoke the Jumano language.

When the Spanish left San Clemente some of the nations traveling with them also left for their lands. Bolton (1916: 340) suggests that these nations took a southerly direction. They certainly did not go west, and it is unlikely they went north. They could have gone east, or, more precisely, southeast. They were accompanied by a ladino who spoke Castilian (Tomás?). Mendoza stated that he was accompanied by just a few families of Natives. They killed four buffalo. Version M does not include any of the information reported in this diary entry. There is no mention of a Native "leader" who departed with the groups of his following, of the Apache attacks, or of the injured soldier.

May 2, 1684: departed San Atanacio and arrived at Santa Crus. Day 139.

The party left San Atanacio and traveled 3 leagues (7.8 miles) to a place they named Santa Crus. The night of their arrival they were expecting an attack, but their fears were unfounded. They remained at this spot on May 3, because it was the feast day of the Holy Cross. A solemn mass and a normal mass were celebrated. They killed thirty buffalo.

Comments: Santa Crus was located upstream on the San Sabá River very near Fort McKavett.[66] Version M states that they were traveling south and west. The writer of this version states that they received information that led them to believe they would be attacked. The Spaniards were now more vulnerable because they had fewer Natives with them and were traversing new terrain for Mendoza. It seems, however, that the Apache were close by.

May 3, 1684: remained at Santa Crus. Day 140.

May 4, 1684: departed Santa Crus and arrived at San Agustin. Day 141.

The party left Santa Crus and traveled about 6 leagues (15.6 miles) to a place they named San Agustin. The writer said that they chose this name because they camped in the valley of a river that flowed westward and had many pine trees. The area had many mulberries, plums, and pond ferns. They killed 120 buffalo. Mass was said every day.

Comments: San Agustin can be placed on a west-flowing tributary of North Llano Draw, 16 miles southwest of Fort McKavett on State Highway 864.[67] The writer of Version L chose to name this place after San Agustin because the saint received his revelation in a beautiful garden, with which the writer must have associated the appearance of the place. Version M names this campground San Agustin de las Cuevas. The river flowed west, but there is *no mention of pine trees.*

May 5, 1684, Day 142; May 6, 1684, Day 143: they remained at San Agustin.

May 7, 1684: departed San Agustin and arrived at La Hasencion del Señor. Day 144.

Mendoza departed San Agustin and traveled an unknown distance to a place they named La Hasencion del Señor. The place was on a beautiful river that flowed eastward. There were abundant pecan trees (nogales), grapes, and mulberries. They remained four days at this spot, waiting for some spies who had gone to explore the terrain. They killed 255 buffalo.

Comments: La Hasencion del Señor was probably on an east-flowing tributary of the Dry Devils River, about 2 miles north of the town of Sonora.[68] The writer does not provide the distance covered this day. Also, we do not know who were the spies that Mendoza was now using. They killed 255 buffalo. Version M classifies this stream as a little river, and the writer states that they remained four days waiting for "some men who had gone to explore the country" (T., p. 17).

May 8, 1684, Day 145; May 9, 1684, Day 146; May 10, 1684, Day 147:
they remained at La Hasencion del Señor.

May 11, 1684: departed La Hasencion del Señor and arrived at San Lazaro. Day 148.

The 11th of May was the feast day of the Ascension of the Lord. Before they departed on their journey a solemn mass [sung] and a normal mass were celebrated. They departed La Hasencion del Señor and traveled about 5 leagues (13 miles) to a place they named San Lazaro. Midway between La Hasencion del Señor and San Lazaro they encountered the headwaters of the river on which they had camped at La Hasencion. The land they traveled over was rough and had many wooded hills (montes), even though it was passable. The only water available was rainwater. They killed three buffalo. Mass was celebrated.

Comments: San Lazaro seems to have been on a southwest-flowing tributary to Granger Draw where it intersects Highway 290, about 8 miles west-northwest of Sonora.[69] Version M reports that they camped at some pools (bateques) of rainwater.

May 12, 1684: remained at San Lazaro. Day 149.

May 13, 1684: departed San Lazaro. Day 150.

May 14, 1684, Day 151; May 15, 1684, Day 152; May 16, 1684, Day 153;
May 17, 1684, Day 154.

Stopovers between San Lazaro and Nuestra Señora de la Piedad to search for a lost man.

May 18, 1684: arrived at Nuestra Señora de la Piedad. Day 155.

The party left San Lazaro and traveled about 14 leagues (36.4 miles) to a place they named Nuestra Señora de la Piedad. Between San Lazaro and N.S. de la Piedad, the party made four stopovers because a young man by the name of Francisco de Archuleta got lost while he *was out hunting (**matar carne**). They traveled six days searching, but could not find him. Fr. Nicolas Lopez sang a special mass to Saint Anthony in order that the saint would guide the young man and bring him safely to the camp. With this same intention they named the place after N.S. de la Piedad to intercede with the Virgin for his return. Mass was said every day. During the stopovers, they killed over 150 buffalo. All the water sources they used were rain-fed. The land was wooded (**monteriça**), had good pastures, and overall [was] very pleasant.*

Comments: Nuestra Señora de la Piedad was probably located on the headwaters of a south-flowing tributary to Granger Draw, about 3 miles south of Highway 290 and 10 miles east of Highway 163, 11 miles southeast of Ozona.[70] This is the longest mileage recorded for the trip, because it reflects the four days spent searching for Francisco de Archuleta. A special mass was said to Saint Anthony because he is the patron saint of lost things (and people). In Version M this entry corresponds to May 13. The writer reports that a young man "got lost while following bison" (T., p. 17). The writer also reports that the country "is mountainous and broken" (T., p. 17). The other information provided in this version is the same as in Version L.

May 18, 1684: they remained at N.S. de la Piedad. Day 155.

May 19, 1684: departed N.S. de la Piedad and arrived at El Hespiritu Santo. Day 156.

*The party departed N.S. de la Piedad and traveled 8 leagues (20.8 miles) to a place they named El Hespiritu Santo. On the date the diarist wrote this entry the young man who was lost had not been found. The writer stated that since they had left San Clemente, they had been traveling a different route from the one taken on the inbound journey. When they started on the return trip, they had turned to their right hand [westward] and followed a route almost due west. The land they traversed was level and traversable. The water source was not permanent, but rain-fed. They killed twenty buffalo. The writer noted that the luxuriance of the plant life diminished as they traveled westward. The fields were covered with good pasture and some chaparral. There were wild grapes in the dry streams (**arroyos secos**). A solemn mass was sung by Fr. Nicolas, while Fr. Sabaleta said a normal one.*

Comments: El Hespiritu Santo may have been on a southeast-flowing tributary to Junction Draw, about 12 miles north-northwest of Ozona.[71] The writer confirmed that they had been traveling due west using a route different from the one used enroute to San Clemente. He pointed out the vegetation cline that is still visible when one moves westward from east-central Texas. The decrease in luxuriance, translated in abundance, variety, and size, primarily reflected, as it does today, the decrease in rainfall and increase in evapotranspiration. Version M provides almost no environmental or topographic information.

May 20, 1684: remained at El Hespiritu Santo. Day 157.

May 21, 1684: departed El Hespiritu Santo and arrived at San Geronimo. Day 158.

The party left El Hespiritu Santo and traveled about 7 leagues (18.2 miles) to a place they named S. Geronimo, where the terrain was much like that of the previous stop and where the water source was also rainfed. They killed six buffalo. Mass was celebrated.

Comments: Quite likely S. Geronimo was near the headwaters of an east-flowing tributary to Howard Draw, about 2 miles south of U.S. Highway 190.[72] The three versions of the diary (see Archival Sources) show different mileage; the versions in *Historia* show 7 leagues (18.2 miles), while the version in *Províncias Internas* and Version M show 5 leagues (13 miles). Version M simply notes the distance traveled and the name of the campground.

May 22, 1684: departed S. Geronimo and arrived at San Pantaleon. Day 159.

The party departed S. Geronimo and traveled an unrecorded distance to reach a place on the Río Salado [Pecos], which they named San Pantaleon. They reached the river at sunset well downstream from the place they had reached on their outbound journey, which was at the site they called San Ygnacio de Loyola [Day 34]. They were very happy when they arrived because they came upon the tracks of Francisco de Archuleta, the young man who had been lost. They celebrated mass. The Xediondo [Gediondo] group, who had been traveling with them, left without asking permission or informing Mendoza of their departure. They [Spaniards and Gediondos?] killed three buffalo.

Comments: San Pantaleon must have been located on the escarpment, just south of Highway 190, overlooking the Pecos valley and the modern town of Iraan.[73] The Gediondo left without informing Mendoza, which implies that Native groups normally asked permission and informed the Spanish commander of their moves. The fact that the Gediondo did not do so indicates they realized how little they had gained from this enterprise. This is the last diary entry that bears the signature of Baltasar Domingues. It is possible that Mendoza's son left the expeditionary party, but the writer does not mention it. Version M states that "from the place called San Ignacio to here we have been taken another route, always leaving to our right the one we took on the outward journey. The one we have been following now is toward the west, with a slight inclination toward the south" (T., p. 18).

May 23, 1684: departed San Pantaleon and arrived at Corpus Christi. Day 160.

*The party left San Pantaleon on the Río Salado and traveled about 5 leagues (13 miles) to a place they named Corpus Christi. They reached a beautiful river of very good water and fertile pastures that looked like barley (**cebada**). Fr. Lopez sang the mass of the Holy Sacrament (Corpus Christi) to pray for rain, which had been lacking. God took pity on them and it rained. They killed two buffalo bulls (**toros**).*

Comments: Corpus Christi was probably located on a southwest-flowing tributary to Live Oak Creek, 8 miles north of U.S. Highway 190.[74] This was actually the first feast of Corpus Christi celebrated within modern Texas territory. Once again they reached the fringes of the buffalo herd. It is noteworthy that there were bulls in the area in January and May. This could mean that the structure and range of the herd did not change much between January and May 1684. Version M reports that the river was "formed by two springs, from each one of which a great amount of good water gushes. It flows from north to south and joins the Salado within a short distance. There are great meadows with abundant pasturage, and its groves are of willows and tangles of rockrose" (T., p. 18). This is one of the rare occasions when the environmental information supplied by Version M is more detailed than that provided by the other versions.

May 24, 1684: remained at Corpus Christi. Day 161.

May 25, 1684: departed Corpus Christi and arrived at Santo Thomas de Villanueba. Day 162.

*The party left Corpus Christi and traveled about 10 leagues (26 miles) to a place on the Río Salado [Pecos], which they named Santo Thomas de Villanueba. They crossed the Salado at this spot, found the road they had taken on their outbound trip, and followed it to San Juan de Dios. They killed only one buffalo bull (**toro**). Mass was celebrated.*

Comments: Santo Thomas de Villanueba was quite probably located on the Pecos River at the mouth of Five Mile Creek, about 2 miles east-northeast of San Juan de Dios.[75] On their outbound trip Mendoza first encountered buffalo tracks between San Francisco Xavier and San Juan del Rio (Day 27). They killed their first buffalo the following day at San Juan del Rio (Day 28). Now, on their return trip, they recorded their last killing of buffalo on the Pecos somewhere between Corpus Christi and San Juan de Dios. San Juan de Dios is about 62.4 miles east of San Juan del Rio. I cannot say that they did not kill more buffalo on their return to La Junta, but it is possible that the spring-summer buffalo range, at this time and in this area, shifted eastward 62.4 miles, since they apparently had seen only a few buffalo bulls between San Pantaleon and San Juan de Dios. Version M reports that after traveling 10 leagues they "again reached the Río Salado and took the road of our outward journey at the place called San Juan de Dios. We halted at another place which we named Santo Tomás de Villanueva" (T., p. 19). According to this version they found Francisco de Archuleta, the lost youth, at this spot (Day 159).

Relative to the numbers of buffalo killed and the relationship between the number of people traveling with Mendoza and the quantity of animals hunted (Day 37), it should be noted that from January 25 through March 14 the estimates produced for the number of people who could be fed on the quantities of buffalo killed varied widely, from 467 to 1,667. However, if one takes the total number of buffalo killed during this forty-nine-day period, the computation suggests a party of 1,336 people who could have been supplied with meat. On the other hand, during the forty-six days at San Clemente the buffalo kills easily would have fed more than 11,700 people.

From May 1, when they left San Clemente, to May 26, when they reached the Pecos River on the return trip, the number of buffalo killed could have fed more than 3,000 people. It seems certain that many more buffalo were killed than were needed for sustenance during the forty-six days at San Clemente, and particularly after they left that camp to return home, when the traveling party was reduced to a few Spaniards and some families of Native Americans.

I strongly believe that Mendoza and the other people in his party were hunting not only for daily sustenance, but also to obtain jerked meat and pelts to take back to El Paso. Mendoza was accused earlier of profiteering from the misery of the people at El Paso (Cruzati 1683a). Actually, the decision by the Viceroy not to formalize the charges against Mendoza (and his father-in-law, Pedro Duran y Chaves) was not rendered until October 1684.

On his trip back to El Paso, Mendoza stopped at the hacienda of his father-in-law, Pedro Duran y Chaves, and at the house of his brother. These visits are perfectly reasonable, but they could also be very expedient. The stopovers provided perfect places to obtain information about his legal status and to unload goods before reaching El Paso. Some of these goods would have been taken to El Paso. I have no way to prove these assumptions, but I believe this is what happened.

Note. This is the end of the *derrotero* of the Mendoza-Lopez expedition as it was published by Bolton (1916: 320–343). Many scholars who have looked at Mendoza's route have used Bolton's translation or some modified version thereof. J. Charles Kelley (1986) mentioned Mendoza's visit to La Junta de los Ríos and his route up the Mexican Conchos River as far as Julimes, but, as far as I could determine, did not publish the material referring to Mendoza's return to El Paso. Version M includes one more diary entry.

May 26, 1684: departed Santo Tomás de Villanueva (Day 163), and arrived at La Junta de los Ríos on June 6. Day 173.

On the 26th of May we went on, leaving the road of our outward journey for another route which they told me was shorter, and within eleven days we reached La Junta where the Río del Norte and the Conchos join. I am not setting these stopping places down individually because it is rough land, with little water, and almost impassable. On the sixth day of June we reached La Junta where the aforesaid Río del Norte and Conchos join. And in order that it may be of record, I signed it as head and commander of this detachment, together with my corroborating witnesses, on June 6th, 1684. Juan Domínguez de Mendoza, Diego Lucero de Godoy, Hernando M[artin Serrano] [T., p. 19].

The last entry recorded in Version M clarifies the problems that existed regarding Mendoza's return trip. In this version the writer states that they did not return to El Paso by the same route they had taken on his outbound journey, gives the reasons for taking such a route, and reports when they arrived at La Junta de los Ríos.

On June 12, Mendoza wrote an official declaration, *Certificacion Primera*[76] (Mendoza et al. 1684), addressed to Governor Cruzate. This declaration certified that seven Native groups at La Junta had given obedience to the King of Spain, and requested six more friars to minister to them. Congregated in this place were more than five hundred Native Americans. On June 13, Mendoza made a second declaration, *Certificacion Segunda* (Mendoza et al. 1684a). This declaration, written at the New Conversations of La Junta de los Ríos on the north side of the Rio Grande (not the Concho), was to ascertain whether anybody had previously taken official possession of this area for Spain. The Natives in the area were questioned and stated that they had been visited by the Franciscans Fr. Garcia de San Francisco and Fr. Juan Sumesta, but that neither friar had remained in the area. Mendoza took official possession of the area for New Mexico, naming four Natives as captains of their groups and giving them staffs as symbols of authority.

Version M includes both official declarations made by Mendoza. At the end of the declarations Mendoza reported:

> The reverend fathers preachers Fray Juan de Savaleta and Fray Antonio de Acevedo remained here to administer these conversions, and I, with the reverend father vice-custodian and the rest of the party, left for El Paso on the fourteenth day of June by way of the Río de Conchos, the Sacramento, Tabaloapa, Encinillas, etc., and I arrived on the eighteenth day of July of 1684. [In the margin: "From la Junta de los Ríos to the pueblo of El Paso, 100 leagues (260 miles) by the Río del Norte. From the same to Tabaloapa, 42 leagues (109 miles)"] [T., p. 21].

This diary entry is followed by a note placed in brackets and apparently included by France V. Scholes that states: "The Escalante version ends at this point" (T., p. 21). Scholes included in his translation the portion of the diary from La Junta to El Paso, which is part of the text in *Províncias Internas,* vol. 37, included in my dissertation (Wade 1998) and which follows. My translation differs in some minor details from Scholes's.

According to Version L, on June 14, 1684, Mendoza left La Junta de los Ríos to return to El Paso del Norte. The writer explained that he and his party decided to take the Conchos (Mexico) route because (1) the route up the Rio Grande traversed some rough land and many narrow spots; (2) the river was running high; (3) they would have to ford the river at least four times and the crossings were dangerous, particularly at the time; (4) the whole area was in rebellion, especially the Suma, and Mendoza had received information that the rebellious groups were waiting to attack them; and (5) he was too short of soldiers to be able to engage in war. Mendoza's route back to El Paso followed the preferred road from Chihuahua to El Paso. To the best of my knowledge, the translation of the document that follows was not published in full before 1998.

June 14, 1684.

Mendoza left la Junta de los Ríos following the course of the Río Conchos in the direction of the Río del Sacramento. They traveled about 8 leagues (20.8 miles) to a spot that they named Santa Catalina. At this place they found many non-Christian Native Americans.

Comments: Santa Catalina was located on the Río Conchos near the present village of El Mezquite.[77]

June 15, 1684?

Mendoza departed Santa Catalina and traveled about 8 leagues (20.8 miles) to a place they named Santa Polonia. At Santa Polonia there was a very large **ranchería.** *On their way, they stopped at the foot of a mountain and crossed, for the third time, the Río Conchos [Mexico]. He named this crossing Santa Juana de la Cruz. They crossed at the* **ranchería** *and the distance from Santa Juana or Santa Polonia to Santa Catalina was the same: 8 leagues.*

Comments: Santa Polonia[78] was located near the present town of Cuchillo Parado.

During this part of the trip, Mendoza often did not provide dates for his stopovers. The first date provided after June 14 is June 21, 1684 (see June 21).

June 16, 1684?

They departed Santa Polonia and traveled about 11 leagues (28.6 miles) to a place they named Santa Teresa. On the way they crossed the Río Conchos twice and reached several **rancherías** *that were located in close proximity. Mendoza named the area where the* **rancherías** *were located Santa Teresa.*

Comments: Santa Teresa[79] was located near Urrutia.

June 17, 1684?

The party left Santa Teresa and traveled about 12 leagues (31.2 miles) and reached a place he named Santa Brigida. They traveled from sunset to sundown. They stopped in a valley where there was a spring.

Comments: Santa Brigida[80] was on the Río Conchos (Mexico), about 4 miles downriver from its junction with the Arroyo Grande.

June 18, 1684?

The party left Santa Brigida and traveled about 14 leagues (36.4 miles) and reached a place they named Santa Monica. They traveled all day without water and reached the junction of the Río Conchos with the Río del Sacramento. This was the last time they crossed the Río Conchos. Counting this crossing they had been across the river 13 times.

Comments: Santa Monica[81] was located in the place named Chuviscar.

June 19, 1684?

The party left Santa Monica and traveled an unknown distance to the pueblo of Santo Anttonio de Julimes. This was a pueblo of Christian Native Americans well versed in the Mexican language. The Spanish were very well received by the Julime and Mendoza stayed in their pueblo four days to rest the horses. The Julime pueblo had an adobe church. The writer stated that they left the pueblo June 21st.

Comments: Since the writer seldom provided dates in this diary, I allowed one day for each travel entry. If the writer is correct, the dates provided do not fit. It is possible that Mendoza incorporated more than one travel log entry in one day, but the distances traveled are considerable. To avoid confusion, I will keep the few dates the writer provided. Thus, even though he stated that he remained four days at S. Anttonio de Julimes, I will place his departure on June 21.

Santo Anttonio de Julimes[82] was near the modern town of Julimes.

June 21, 1684.

The party left S. Anttonio de Julimes and traveled 6 leagues (15.6 miles) to a place called El Tule. There was a spring at El Tule.

Comments: El Tule[83] was located near modern U.S. Highway 45, near the eastern end of the pass between Sierra Santo Domingo and Sierra El Ojito.

June 22, 1684.

The party left El Tule and traveled about 14 leagues (36.4 miles) to the Hacienda de Tabalaopa. They traveled without water.

Comments: The Hacienda de Tabalaopa[84] was about 8 miles north-northwest of Chihuahua.

June 23, 1684.

The party left the Hacienda de Tabalaopa and traveled about 3 leagues (7.8 miles) to the house of Sergeant Major Don Pedro Duran y Chabes. They remained there eight days to rest the horses. The writer stated that they left on July 2.

Comments: The house of Pedro Duran y Chabes was about 4 miles due south of the Villa of El Ojito.[85]

July 2, 1684.

Mendoza left the house of Pedro Duran y Chabes and traveled about 8 leagues (20.8 miles) to a place called Los Sauses, and the house of Maestro de Campo Thome Dominguez de Mendoza, his brother. They remained at his brother's house six days, resting the horses and getting supplies. They left July 8.

Comments: Los Sauces was at El Saúz.[86]

July 8, 1684.

Mendoza left Los Sauses and traveled about 6 leagues (15.6 miles) to a place called Las Ensinillas.

Comments: Las Ensinillas[87] was at the modern village of Encinillas.

July 9, 1684.

Mendoza left Las Ensinillas and traveled about 6 leagues (15.6 miles) to a place called El Ojuelo. They remained at this spot one day.

Comments: El Ojuelo was near the village of Ojo Laguna.[88]

July 11, 1684.

The party left El Ojuelo and traveled about 7 leagues (18.2 miles) and arrived at a place called Gallego.

Comments: Gallego[89] was located about 2 miles south of the modern village of the same name.

July 12, 1684.

The party left Gallego and traveled about 10 leagues (26 miles) to the place called Portesuelo.

Comments: Portesuelo was located near the modern village of Moctezuma.[90]

July 13, 1684.

The party left Portesuelo and traveled about 6 leagues (15.6 miles) to Ojo Caliente.

Comments: Ojo Caliente[91] was at the modern village of the same name.

July 14, 1684.

The party left Ojo Caliente and traveled about 8 leagues (20.8 miles) to the place of Los Patos.

Comments: Los Patos was located near the southern end of the modern lake named Laguna de Patos.[92]

July 15, 1684.

The party left Los Patos and traveled an unknown distance to La Ranchería, where they joined and escorted the mail wagons. Halfway through their journey that day they saw the tracks of many cattle the enemy had driven toward the Rio Grande.

Comments: La Ranchería was located 3 miles north of the modern village named Ojo del Lucero.[93]

July 16, 1684.

The party left La Ranchería and traveled about 9 leagues (23.4 miles) to a place called Los Medanos.

Comments: Los Medanos[94] was located at the modern village of the same name.

July 17, 1684.

The party left Los Medanos and traveled about 9 leagues (23.4 miles) to the Presidio. Mendoza stated that on the following day, July 18, 1684, with the grace of God, they would arrive at El Paso del Río del Norte and Conbercion de los Mansos.

AFTERMATH

The revolt of the Manso, Jano, and Suma continued till the end of 1685. In July 1684, Fr. Nicolas Lopez sent his Jumano servant to arrange peace talks with the Manso (Santo 1684). This initiative did not work, and Cruzate executed several Native rebel leaders. On August 16, 1684, Cruzate sent a large punitive expedition against the Apache, but the Spanish could not locate them. On September 19, 1684, the Franciscan friars met at El Paso and wrote a petition to leave the area because of the poor conditions at El Paso and the lack of help from the Spanish authorities. Fr. Lopez was chosen to deliver the petition (Gomez et al. 1684; Lopez 1684). The muster rolls taken at El Paso on November 11, 1684, showed the extreme poverty of the people in the community (Valle 1684). Between June 1685 and the end of that year, Fr. Lopez and the citizenry of El Paso wrote several petitions to the Viceroy asking permission to leave El Paso (Gomez et al. 1684; Lopez 1685). The requests were denied (La Bastida 1686).

In 1686, Fr. Lopez and Juan Dominguez Mendoza went to Mexico City to plead their case before the Viceroy. They wanted to settle in Texas in the Edwards Plateau area where they had been. In his petition Fr. Lopez asked for two hundred soldiers (or convicts) to settle the area. Mendoza stated that he and his group had lived well off the products of the land. Fr. Lopez mentioned the friendship of seventy-five Native groups, some of which were located in New Mexico and others in the lands that extended to the Mississippi. Sixty-six of these groups were from the interior and nine were the friendly and Christianized groups of La Junta de los Ríos. Fr. Lopez mentioned the immense abundance of buffalo in the areas they visited during their trip to the Jumano lands. He stated that he knew the Jumano language, preached in that language, and had made an extensive vocabulary of that language. He also said that another friar working with him also knew the Jumano language. According to Fr. Lopez, seventy-five groups had asked for help against the Apache. He argued that if the support from the Natives was used properly and expediently, the Spanish could prevent the advance of the Apache and the increased influence of the French. Such a plan would prove much less onerous than if action was postponed. Both Fr. Lopez and Mendoza delivered the pearls they collected and a map of the area to the Viceroy (Lopez 1686; Mendoza et al. 1684b). After the matter had been reviewed, the Fiscal issued a negative opinion and the Viceroy refused the various requests (La Bastida 1686a; Marques de la Laguna 1686).

In 1686, the Jumano visited the Tejas in East Texas. They stated that they had been at war with the Spaniards and that some of the Tejas groups had been their allies (Kelly 1955: 985). In the fall of 1688, the Jumano reappeared among the Spaniards at La Junta de los Ríos.

REFLECTIONS

The 1683–1684 expedition of Maestro de Campo Juan Dominguez de Mendoza and Fr. Nicolas Lopez to the territory known today as Texas resulted from the request of Juan Sabeata, a Jumano captain. Sabeata was the spokesperson for a large coalition of Native groups interested in curtailing the movement of Apache groups into their lands and in reactivating trade networks that existed before the Pueblo Revolt of 1680.

The proposal made by Sabeata and his allies offered food supplies and pelts in exchange for help against the Apache, and requested that the Spaniards consider settling in their lands on the Concho River drainage in Texas. Unknown to Sabeata, his request provided several individuals with a plausible reason for pursuing their private objectives under the guise of helping the Natives and while engaging in the discovery of new lands. This was obviously a ruse, since the area where Mendoza was going had been visited frequently by the Spaniards from New Mexico since 1632.

After the Pueblo Revolt, the Spanish communities from New Mexico took refuge in El Paso, where extreme economic distress led to desertions, profiteering, and internal strife. Short of food, clothing, and ammunition, the citizenry would have abandoned the area except for the threat of military and civil prosecution. Both the church and the civil authorities were eager to find another area for settlement.

Fr. Lopez, like Fr. Salas, made the Jumano the center of his missionary efforts. He believed the Jumano territory would prove to be an area for settlement that the Crown might be inclined to approve. Governor Domingo Cruzate, short of military supplies, pressured by a stressed and disgruntled population, and harassed by Apache robberies, did not want to add to his troubles the threat represented by the influence of powerful New Mexico families such as the Mendozas.

Juan Mendoza, Cruzate's highest-ranking military commander and by far the most experienced, had a criminal lawsuit pending against him for profiteering from the poor economic conditions at El Paso. It is not hard to understand that Cruzate saw this journey as an opportunity to relieve the tensions at El Paso and obtain food and pelts at almost no cost. This "discovery" allowed Cruzate to request military supplies that were intensely needed. In sum, all the protagonists had good reasons to welcome Sabeata's proposal, but their reasons had little to do with the priorities of the Native Americans.

Sabeata and his allies, on the other hand, baited their request for help against the Apache by offering food and pelts for clothing, which they knew the Spaniards needed desperately, and by reporting the miracles performed by a cross that had descended from the sky and that they kept in their territory.

From the start, the projected trip was pregnant with conflict. The military group that traveled with Mendoza was too small. Sabeata must have guessed Mendoza's intentions early on, but commitments had been made and the project had to run its course. The trip was uneventful until they reached the Pecos, where the Gediondo, a group of the Jumano, were awaiting the Spaniards. The Jumano and their allies choreographed an elaborate reception to welcome their guests. With a few gun salutes the Native captains brought forth the miraculous cross. Well made of wood with a nail fastening its arms, the cross was too real to be heavenly. Later Fr. Lopez would say that the reported miracles were just a ruse to attract the friars.

The Jumano and their allies formally requested help against the Apache, and the following day Sabeata delivered seventeen prepared deerskins to Mendoza: a first installment had been made. The Spaniards benefited from Native hospitality, ate the deer and buffalo hunted on Native lands, and saw the miraculous cross. The Native coalition lived up to its side of the bargain.

Rumors of Apache enemies close to their route never materialized, and the clues to the possibility of Apache presence were dismissed by the Spaniards as unfounded or as malicious rumors disseminated by Sabeata. During the trip a few horses were stolen, presumably by the Apache. Of the nine horses stolen, seven belonged to the Jumano. It is conceivable that the Jumano were trying to force Mendoza into engaging the Apache. If so, the attempt failed.

But Mendoza's problems were with his brethren. At the Gediondo *ranchería,* two soldiers rebelled and took up arms against Mendoza. He sentenced them to death. The friars intervened and the soldiers were pardoned. Later, at Los Desamparados, the two rebels deserted, taking with them several other Spaniards and many Native Americans. The departure of these Natives raises questions about the nature of the quarrel between Mendoza and the rebellious soldiers.

The expeditionary orders commanded Mendoza to help the Jumano coalition against the Apache, to contact many Native groups, in particular the Tejas, and to survey the territory. With the exception of the territorial survey, none of the objectives was achieved. Version L implies that the reason for the failure to fulfill these orders resided in the problems caused by Sabeata and the Apache.

Version M, on the other hand, implies that the rebellion of Spanish soldiers was the reason for noncompliance with some of the orders. The discrepancies in the reporting of the events during the expedition cannot be explained by the documentary evidence available. It seems logical that Mendoza wrote Version M, because the rebellion reported in it affected his military reputation and justified his actions. If Version L, or at least part of it, was written by the friars, the reasons for this version and its sanitized contents are speculative. Nevertheless, if the friars traveled ahead of Mendoza to La Junta de los Ríos, they had to copy Mendoza's diary from El Paso to La Junta, since the friars and Mendoza did not travel together. On the other hand, if the friars were with Mendoza, as he says they were, at the campgrounds of San Sebastian, San Roque, and Los Desamparados, why are those entries excluded from Version L? At the Gediondo *ranchería,* Mendoza reported on the soldiers' mutiny and commented on events that happened many days later. Thus, both versions, or parts of them, were written ex post facto.

During the journey to the Concho River drainage, Mendoza was supposed to have been accompanied by nineteen (or sixteen) Native groups, but he mentioned the location of only three, including the Jumano. He provided no information on the remaining groups. At San Clemente the Spanish and the Natives killed more than four thousand buffalo, not counting calves and a large number of animals from which only skins were removed. Mendoza also collected a sample of freshwater pearls, which were later delivered to the Viceroy. Sometime during the period spent at San Isidro or San Clemente, Fr. Lopez took a trip with the intention of contacting the Tejas. He was accompanied by some soldiers, some Jumano, and a Native from Coahuila by the name of Tomás. According to Tomás, the Spanish were fearful of the Tejas's reception and did not travel very far, nor did they get very close to Tejas territory. According to Fr. Lopez, however, he was as close as 25 leagues (65 miles) from Tejas territory.

At San Clemente, Mendoza was expected to meet with forty-eight Native groups (in addition to those who were accompanying the expedition). He provided the names of thirty-six groups and stated that he could wait no longer for them because of the Apache attacks. He gave no other information about these groups, except to say that many of them had sent their ambassadors to him and that he promised them to return in one year. Among the groups he was expecting were the Tejas, who were members of Sabeata's coalition and who sent ambassadors saying that they would visit Mendoza (Appendix). One wonders why Fr. Lopez took the trip to the Tejas and, having done so, did not enter their territory. Mendoza's party left the San Sabá area and returned home to El Paso by way of La Junta, taking the modern Chihuahua road. He reached El Paso July 18, 1684. He had been gone seven months. Soon after Mendoza's arrival the criminal charges against him were dismissed.

Between 1684 and 1686 Fr. Lopez and Mendoza traveled to Mexico City to present a series of petitions to the Viceroy to obtain permission from the Crown to settle in the Edwards Plateau. Their requests were repeatedly denied. In his expositions to the Viceroy, Fr. Lopez did not comment on the Apache, but focused on the goodwill expressed by all the friendly Native groups and the conversions accomplished. Oddly, Fr. Lopez seems to have maintained good relations with the Jumano, because in a petition made by all the friars at El Paso describing the extreme hardships experienced by the community, the friars recommended that Fr. Lopez travel to Mexico City with the Jumano because they had faithfully guided him to the Tejas.

For Sabeata and his allies the trip was a resounding disaster, or so it seems. They invested time and resources to put a coalition together and to deal a blow to the Apache, or at least to convince the Apache of an alliance between their groups and the Spaniards. Not only did this not occur, it is likely that the opposite message was conveyed.

How much this fiasco damaged Sabeata's reputation is unknown, but his prominence as a spokesman for Native groups continued into the 1690s.

Quite likely, the Apache had no interest in seriously attacking the Spaniards. The Apache learned not only that the Spaniards would not go to battle for the Jumano coalition, but also that they likely would not care if the Apache made a concerted move onto Jumano lands.

As for the Spanish, it seems reasonably clear what they wanted out of this expedition: a place to settle, conversions, food and clothing, and some pearls to entice the Crown to approve the settlement. They got some of what they wanted, but despite their intensive efforts, the Crown denied their request for settlement on the Edwards Plateau. If these requests had been approved, the history of settlement in Texas might have been very different.

FIVE

A New Frontier:

TIERRA ADENTRO, TIERRA AFUERA

SETTING THE STAGE

In the late seventeenth century the Crown of Spain considered the territory east of the Rio Grande and west of Florida as part of its colonial domain: there was no rush or incentive to explore or colonize it. North of the Rio Grande was the unknown—the magnet for zealous and courageous churchmen and soldiers who systematically narrowed the gap between the unknown, *tierra adentro,* and the known, *tierra afuera.*[1]

There are two guiding perspectives on the motivations that led to the exploration of the modern territory of Texas. The first concerns the political and strategic reasons that led the Crown to order the official expeditions to the east. The second relates to the intentions and agendas of individuals who pushed the frontier eastward.

These two perspectives result in two temporal research approaches that consider the unfolding of history from a long-term point of view and from the point of view of the serendipitous event (Braudel 1996: 20–21; Hunt 1986). The history of the long term is the Crown of Spain's (and the French Crown's) view of the events. The Crown benefited from its command of history and its ownership of archival holdings. Events such as the rumors of the presence of Jean Gery north of the Rio Grande, the embarrassing spying episode of Count Peñalosa, and La Salle's trip to the Gulf Coast were placed in the larger context of European colonial history. From the Crown's perspective, be it Spanish or French, Gery's phantom presence had relevance only as an element defining the conjuncture, whose overall pattern was recognized as the concerted threat (or effort, depending on the point of view taken) by the French to extend their domain to Texas.

The second perspective (history of the event) is represented by the acts of single individuals in the field of action who, because of their personal agendas, introduced slight variations in the Crown's master plan, and in so doing reshaped the history that might have happened. Although there are many people whose individual actions combined to affect the history of the modern territory of Texas, a few had a particularly active and influential role. This chapter looks at some of these individuals who, probably unwittingly, shaped the events that resulted in the next sequence of moves to colonize modern Texas. The timelime of events (long-term and event) presented in this chapter reflects a composite of these two perspectives, but emphasizes the influence of single individuals, such as Juan Sabeata, Alonso de León, Le Sieur de la Salle, Diego Ramón, Louis de Saint-Denis, and others.

In the late 1680s, the Spanish Crown was forced to adopt a defensive posture in its colonial policy due to dynastic and political problems at the heart of the Empire. Most of the practical decisions that affected the colonial possessions originated in political decisions made in the courts of Europe. The Hapsburg War between France and Spain, which began in 1688, finally came to an end in 1697 with a series of treaties among France, the United Provinces (primarily modern Holland), England, and Spain. Among other issues, these treaties established the rights of succession of the Hapsburgs and the Bourbons to the thrones of France and Spain. Charles II, who was King of Spain in 1683, died on October 2, 1700. According to the treaties that ended the Hapsburg War, the Crown of Spain was to revert to Joseph of Bavaria, but he had died on February 6, 1699. This event led Charles II, on his deathbed, to designate Philippe D'Anjou as his sole successor and thus join the crowns of France and Spain. The stage was set for the War of Succession (1702–1714) between Spain and France. At the end of the conflict Philippe D'Anjou became Philippe V of Spain.

These decades (1688–1714) of overt European conflict, especially between France and Spain, produced sympathetic skirmishes in the provinces of New Spain. That the Native American groups of New Mexico and northernmost modern Mexico chose the last decades of the seventeenth century to rebel against their colonizers was perhaps fortuitous, but it resulted in further unease among Spanish officials and strained their resources to the limit. In the feverish positioning for power and territories, the actions of the French in Mississippi, Louisiana, and Texas became particularly significant. Definition of boundaries and potential territorial claims, based on de facto possession through settlement, constituted a threat to both crowns.

In August 1683, Juan Sabeata informed New Mexico Governor Antonio Otermín that white folk with red hair and blue eyes had been trading with the Tejas groups (Caddo) and their friends. These "Spaniards," as Sabeata called them, came to the Tejas in wooden houses that walked on water (Sabeata 1683). The significance of this information appears to have been lost on Otermín, preoccupied as he was with the problems of the loss of New Mexico. This failure in the Spanish intelligence network proved costly to the Spanish and gave the French a few more years to pursue their colonization program. This oversight plus the lack of interest shown by the Crown in the Texas settlement proposed by Fr. Lopez and Dominguez Mendoza delayed the colonization of Texas. New Mexico turned its eyes northward to Santa Fé and the reconquest. Later, Governor Pardiñas of Nueva Vizcaya tried to score points by capturing Jean Gery, but it was too late: the Kingdom of Nuevo León, in the person of Captain Alonso de León, had secured the coveted Frenchman.

The first known land expedition into modern Texas, resulting from the concerns about the French presence in Texas, was entrusted to Alonso de León, son of the explorer by the same name. Before the expedition got under way, a Pelon Native reported that the

Pajarito and Blanco Native groups had seen white men on the Rio Grande (Weddle 1991: 46). On June 27, 1686, Alonso de León left Candereyta and traveled to the mouth of the Rio Grande via present-day Matamoros. Unable to obtain any news or detect any evidence of a settlement of white people, Alonso de León returned home (Weddle 1991: 46). The second attempt to locate the French took place in March 1687, when Alonso de León skirted the southernmost Texas coast, probably as far as modern Kingsville, but he returned without evidence of the French presence. Two other Spanish land expeditions from Florida attempted to locate the French settlement without success (Weddle 1991: 49–50). News of the French interest in the lands west of Florida also resulted in several very thorough coastal explorations of the Gulf of Mexico. These voyages found evidence of the French presence, but failed to locate the reported French settlement.

Alonso de León was named governor of Coahuila at the request of the bishop of Guadalajara, Don Juan de Santiago León Garavito, and he took charge of the province in October 1687 (Portillo 1984: 145). According to Portillo, when Alonso de León arrived, the city of Nuestra Señora de Guadalupe (Monclova) was in ruins and there were two pueblos, one inhabited by Tlaxcaltecan Natives and another by other Natives. Portillo's statement is difficult to understand, since most of the archival documentation of the late 1670s (e.g., de la Cruz 1679) and the early 1690s (CAH 1692) indicates continued presence of the military, church officials, and missions. As had been requested by Fr. Peñasco and Fernando del Bosque, a presidio was established in Coahuila: the Presidio de San Francisco, near the mission of the same name. Alonso de León was placed in charge of twenty-five soldiers, the same number given to Fernando del Bosque in 1681 (Portillo 1984: 148).

In 1687–1688, Alonso de León faced widespread Native unrest. Under the general leadership of Don Pedrote, at least twenty Native groups were involved in hit-and-run attacks that spanned Coahuila, Nuevo León, and Nueva Vizcaya. The coalition of Don Pedrote had the cooperation of many mission Natives as well as several other groups, including the Toboso. These groups concentrated on attacking convoys and merchants along supply routes (Portillo 1984: 150).

In January 1688, Alonso de León attempted a peace agreement with Don Pedrote and his coalition. Alonso de León followed the advice and information given to him by one Juan de la Cruz, a faithful Native to whom one should listen (*indio fiel y que se le debe dar crédito*) (Portillo 1984: 157). Alonso de León's efforts were only partly successful. In April 1688, Alonso de León feared a general Native uprising and tried to enlist the help of officials from other provinces of New Spain. He asked Don Agustin de la Cruz, a Tlaxcalteco, to find Native warriors willing to fight the rebellious groups. Don Agustin crossed the Rio Grande and brought news of the Frenchman who lived with several Native groups. On May 18, 1688, Alonso de León left Coahuila to capture the Frenchman, Jean Gery.

In November 1688, the governor of Nueva Vizcaya informed the King that trustworthy Native Americans had informed him there were foreigners in the Tejas territory. This letter was hand-delivered to the King on August 16, 1689 (Hackett 1926: 228–233). The informers referred to these individuals as white men or Spaniards. It is clear that the officials at Nueva Vizcaya and those in Nuevo León were engaged in simultaneous attempts to acquire information about the French. To find the French would be a feather in anyone's cap, and Alonso de León got the feather, probably because of Fr. Massanet's information.[2] On March 23, 1689, Alonso de León left Monclova for central Texas and Matagorda Bay. He was to look for the French settlement in Texas.

Diego Ramón, a frontier veteran who was present at the establishment of the first mission settlements in Coahuila and had been working with Alonso de León since at least December 1687, accompanied him in the search for the French colony. When Alonso de León died in 1691, he was replaced by Captain Diego Ramón (Portillo 1984: 150, 185).

The various Spanish attempts to gather information about the French provide a useful timeline of events. This timeline places events that occurred in various areas of northern New Spain in chronological order, provides a broader perspective, and allows the connections between events to be perceived. The following timeline is certainly not exhaustive, and the archival information included has been selected to emphasize events that led to the colonization of Texas and to stress points related to the groups connected with the Edwards Plateau.

TIMELINE

1683

August and October

Juan Sabeata, a Jumano, informed the New Mexico governors Antonio de Otermín and Domingo Cruzate that "Spaniards" had arrived at the lands of the Tejas and traded with the Tejas and several other nations. Among many other pieces of information was Sabeata's statement that the Tejas raised and maintained large herds of horses.

1685

January

La Salle and his contingent arrived at Matagorda Bay.

1687

March

La Salle was killed in the Tejas territory.

May

The people at the French settlement near modern Garcitas Creek on the Texas coast were still alive.

? 1687

Fr. Augustin Colima was asked, by Cibolo and Jumano Natives, to send a letter to the "Spaniards" who visited the Tejas.[3] The friar told these Natives to get a letter from those "Spaniards" in east Texas and to bring it to him (Hackett 1926: 240–241).

1688

March–April

Alonso de León asked Agustin de la Cruz, a Tlaxcalteco, to find some Native warriors who would help fight the rebellious groups. Agustin crossed the Rio Grande and found a very large *ranchería* headed by Jean Gery. Gery stated that he had sent messages to Alonso de León to come visit him. Gery provided Agustin, and later León, with six Native guides to conduct them to and from the *ranchería*. Fr. Damian Massanet stated, with acrimony, that as early as 1687 he had informed Alonso de León of the rumors circulating among the Natives about the French presence (Lino Canedo 1968: 17; Portillo 1984: 174).

May 30

Alonso de León traveled 62 leagues (164.3 miles) from Monclova, crossed the Rio Grande, and arrested Jean Gery. About 350 Native people were at the *ranchería,* and some 500 were away hunting buffalo (Portillo 1984: 176–178, 182–184).

June 6

Alonso de León returned to Monclova with Jean Gery.

June 7

Gery was interrogated at Monclova by Alonso de León and by the governor of Nuevo León, Fernández de la Ventosa (Portillo 1984: 179–182).

June 12 and 16 and July 20

Jean Gery was interrogated by the Viceroy in Mexico City.

July 16

Diego de León, an Ervipiame, declared in Coahuila to Alonso de León that the Ervipiame, the Tejas, the French, and possibly the Jumano had attacked the Apache and destroyed them all. Obviously Diego de León was talking about a particular Apache *ranchería* (or *rancherías*), and not all Apache. The Jumano were with the Ervipiame at the *ranchería* where Diego de León acquired this information. He also stated that the Tejas were now friends with the Ervipiame (Portillo 1984: 184).

November 2

General Juan Retana was sent by Governor Pardiñas to La Junta de los Ríos, and then to the Río del Norte, to get a French prisoner and to travel north of the Rio Grande until he found the settlement of the Frenchmen (Hackett 1926: 249–257).

November 15

General Retana left on the trip.

November 18

Fr. Colima reported that the friars were leaving the area of La Junta de los Ríos because of a Suma rebellion. The friars and the Natives who were leaving La Junta reported that Native couriers mentioned the presence of foreigners in Tejas territory (Hackett 1926: 245–246).

November 21

Don Nicolas, a Cibolo lieutenant from La Junta de los Ríos, testified before Retana that some friendly Cibolos on the Rio Grande traded with the couriers from Don Nicolas the Cibolo (note: Don Nicolas the Cibolo lieutenant and Don Nicolas the Cibolo were two different men). Don Nicolas the Cibolo notified the Natives at La Junta that he would arrive with his people and that he was bringing a "Spaniard" who had been separated from others who were near the Tejas. Don Nicolas the Cibolo was bringing letters from the "Spaniards" near the Tejas to the friars on the Rio Grande. Don Nicolas the lieutenant had heard Cibolo Natives say that the "Spanish" in east Texas traded axes and clothing for horses and traveled in and out of the area.

November 21

Don Juan de Salaises, who came with Don Nicolas the lieutenant, stated that the "Spanish" individual whom Don Nicolas the Cibolo was bringing had cut his hair after the Native fashion, shaved his beard, and had a damaged weapon that the foreigner said he could repair. Salaises stated that these Cibolo came from the east (of La Junta de los Ríos). Salvador, another Native who accompanied Don Nicolas the lieutenant, confirmed the presence of foreigners, the information about trade, and the physical appearance of the "Spaniard." He stated that the "Spaniard" had fled from others who wanted to kill him. Salvador reported that the "Spaniard" had helped them in an attack against the Michi. The Michi were not allied with the Cibolo. Don Nicolas the lieutenant, Don Juan de Salaises, and Salvador had come from north of La Junta (Hackett 1926: 234–238).

November 22

Pedro and Alonso, two Native couriers, were sent by General Retana to tell the Cibolo who might be at the Rio Grande to send messages to their captain, Don Nicolas the Cibolo, in order that he might bring the letters and the "Spaniard" to Retana at the Rio Grande. Retana declared he was going on a punitive campaign upriver (Hackett 1926: 238–239).

November 23

Fr. Colima testified that, on September 5, five Cibolo came to La Junta and reported that the "moor" had one harquebus, a helmet, and body armor. He helped the group he was living with in an attack against the Michi. In this attack half of the Michi were destroyed. Later, other Cibolo stated that the foreign people slept in wooden houses. These houses were on the water and one of the houses had sunk. The foreigners traded clothing for horses and crops (Hackett 1926: 240–242).

November 23

Fr. Joachin de Hinojosa confirmed the testimony of Fr. Colima. He added that the Natives also traded red dirt (hematite) to the Frenchmen in return for axes and other things. The "moor" lived with a group near the Tejas (Hackett 1926: 242–243).

November 25

Retana stated that the French were trading with the groups from the north and the east, including the Cibolo and the Tejas (Hackett 1926: 244–245).

Winter 1688

Sometime in the winter of 1688, the people at the French settlement on Garcitas Creek were massacred.

Before proceeding with the timeline, there are several issues to be addressed. First, all these contacts took place *well after* Alonso de León's expedition crossed the Rio Grande to fetch Jean Gery. Because of the descriptions of the "moor's" appearance, it is clear that some of the information provided by the Natives referred to Gery, while other information referred to the Frenchmen at Garcitas Creek, and possibly one or more people staying with or near the Tejas in east Texas. Second, Alonso de León was invited and guided to Gery's *ranchería*: he knew exactly where he was going.

The descriptions of Gery's appearance agree with the descriptions made by Fr. Massanet and Alonso de León (Lino Canedo 1968: 9, 75; Portillo 1984: 175). It is difficult to explain who was the Spaniard that Don Nicolas the Cibolo said he was bringing, unless one accepts that the description fits Jean Gery. On the other hand, a Pacpul Native by

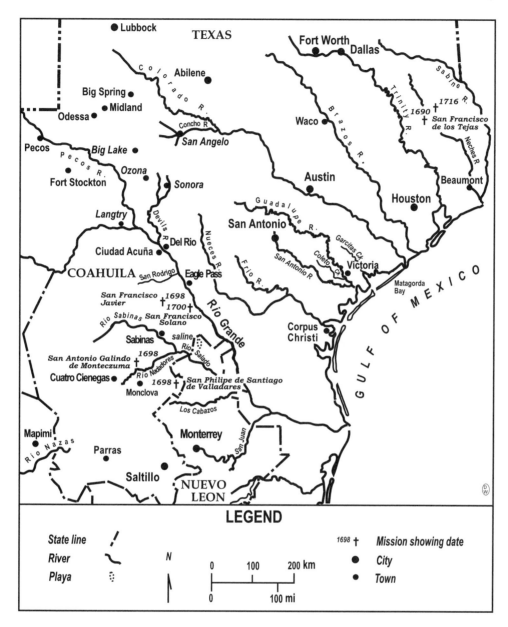

FIGURE 5.1
Map showing important places mentioned in the text—seventeenth century.

the name of Juan or Juanillo informed Fr. Massanet, prior to the expedition of Alonso de León, that he (Juan) had gone to Yacatsol (Chapter 2), had seen Jean Gery, and had moved him to another *ranchería* (Lino Canedo 1968: 8–10). Thus, Jean Gery had been earlier at Yacatsol in the Edwards Plateau, and had been moved once (maybe twice) to another *ranchería* before arriving at the *ranchería* where he was apprehended by Alonso de León. This move occurred before Alonso de León's expedition. These events took place before the Cibolo reported any of this information to Governor Pardiñas. By that time, Gery had already been arrested and interrogated in Mexico City.

There is yet another angle to this issue. Among the groups listed by Jean Gery as belonging to his following was the Jumano (Lino Canedo 1968: 8). This information was confirmed by Alonso de León, who encountered them on the south side of the Rio Grande in 1689. According to Jean Gery's deposition, he had been in the area since 1685 (Portillo 1984: 180). This means that the Jumano had known about Gery for some time and probably participated in some of the battles in which Gery and his groups were said to have been involved. A case in point is the battle against the Michi in which the Cibolo, who were very close allies of the Jumano, had been involved (see above). It is significant that the Jumano never mentioned Gery's presence to the Spaniards. All the information provided by the Cibolo was given to the Spaniards after Gery was arrested by Alonso de León. Jean Gery may have become a liability by this time, and his Native friends wanted to dispose of him in a friendly manner, but one that won them favor with the Spaniards. On the other hand, Gery may have wanted to return to his own people for reasons that may, or may not, be related to La Salle's demise.

The Cibolo confirmed that the French traded axes, clothing, and red dirt (hematite) to the Tejas (Caddo) and other Native groups in exchange for horses and foodstuffs. The Natives showed little interest in European weapons, even though there were Natives who had a sophisticated knowledge of them (Chapter 4). The lack of interest in weapons is confirmed by the spoils taken by the Natives from the French at Matagorda Bay: clothing and books. It is noteworthy that gatherers and hunters, who wore a minimum of body coverage, would be so taken with clothing, or body decoration in the form of clothing. On the other hand, the taking of these items testified to a group's victory.

1689

March 3

While at the Pecos River Retana reported to Governor Pardiñas that he had met Don Juan Sabeata four days' travel from La Junta de los Ríos. Retana stated that Sabeata was the principal chief of the Cibolo and the Jumano (*Capataz principal de las naciones zivola y Jumana*). Sabeata informed Retana that the French on the coast had all been killed; only four or five foreigners remained among the Tejas. Sabeata brought with him papers and a ship drawn on parchment. These papers were wrapped in a lacy neck cloth (Hackett 1926: 257–259).

March 23

General Alonso de León left Monclova for Matagorda Bay accompanied by one hundred men. He was to look for the French settlement in Texas (Lino Canedo 1968: 89–116; West 1905: 199–224).

March 30

Governor Pardiñas ordered Retana to send Sabeata and his companions to Parral. Pardiñas told Retana to supply these Natives with provisions and horses (Hackett 1926: 258–259).

April 10

Sabeata testified before Pardiñas at Parral. Sabeata declared that he and others had been attending the fairs with many people, including those downriver from (below?) the Tejas (*a sus ferias Con las naciones del Rio abajo texas*). He stated that the "moors" had been killed, and as proof he brought the drawing of a ship and pages of books (Hackett 1926: 260–262).

The choice of proofs is significant. The ship was the wooden house on water where the foreigners stayed. One should note the selection of a drawing and abstract symbols (printed words) among groups for whom pictographic symbols were a mode of communication. They chose what they perceived as having the power to communicate information and constitute evidence.

April 11

The following day Sabeata continued his testimony. He stated that he had received a message from Retana in November 1689, when he was on the Rio Grande, asking him (Sabeata) to find some bowmen and await Retana. Sabeata waited for many days, but since Retana did not come, Sabeata went to the trade fairs. Sabeata mentioned that he had gone to get Captain Miguel (a Cibolo), who lived in a *ranchería* on the north side of the Rio Grande and downstream from La Junta (probably near Langtry). Sabeata stated that Miguel's *ranchería* was seven days' travel from La Junta de los Ríos. The Spanish interpreted this distance as being between 60 and 70 leagues (about 10 leagues' travel a day).[4] Referring to his trip from the Tejas, Sabeata said that once he obtained proof of the demise of the French, he headed back to La Junta. On the way back Sabeata spent the night at a *ranchería* with a Native named Don Tomás (Chapter 4), who also spoke Castilian and was from Coahuila. Tomás took from Sabeata most of the papers he was bringing as proof of the French demise. Sabeata stated that he was over fifty years old, which means he was born between 1630 and 1639 (Hackett 1926: 260–267).

April 11

Miguel, captain of the Cibolos, Christian and baptized by Fr. Agustin Colima, testified before Governor Pardiñas at Parral. He confirmed Sabeata's testimony. He added that near his *ranchería* there were large herds of buffalo, over the killing of which the Cibolo waged wars with the groups from upriver. They had obtained the first news about the killing of the Frenchmen in a small *ranchería* of the Tejas, and after this stop they proceeded to the main *rancherías* of the Tejas, where the French survivors were staying. Miguel said that it was about eight days' travel from La Junta de los Ríos to the Tejas, if one took the most direct route. He stated that there were no problems traveling to the Tejas, but once the rains started it was difficult to travel in and out of the area because of the flooded rivers and swamps. If one were caught by the rains, one could only return in the winter (Hackett 1926: 268–272).

April 11

Cuis Benive (or Cuisbimue), a gentile[5] Cibolo, testified before Governor Pardiñas. Cuis Benive lived in a different Cibolo *ranchería* from the one in which Miguel lived. He confirmed the information given by Sabeata and Miguel. He added that the Frenchmen were killed by the Natives of the mountain (*por los yndios de la sierra*). Cuis Benive had traveled to the *rancherías* of those who had killed the Frenchmen; they were located in a mountain (sierra) where Cuis Benive had been before. In this area they spoke only one language. Cuis Benive and another Native had also traveled to the coast to confirm the death of the French. He stated that, when the Cibolo traveled to the trade fairs, they left their *rancherías* at the time when trees put on new leaves, and returned when the leaves began to fall in order to avoid the rains and flooded rivers. Cuis Benive stated that there were twelve days of travel between La Junta de los Ríos and the *rancherías* of the Tejas where the French were. To get there in twelve days, one had to travel from sunrise to sunset (Hackett 1926: 272–276).

April 11

Muygisofac (or Muygitofac), a gentile Cibolo, testified before Governor Pardiñas. He lived in a *ranchería* where every year they had wars with other Natives over the killing of buffalo. The buffalo herds were, at certain times of the year, between the Rio Grande and the Nueces River. Since the modern Nueces River had not yet been named, Muygysofac was referring to a river where one could find nuts. It could be the modern Nueces River in southwest Texas or the modern Concho River in west central Texas, which was known since at least the 1650s as the Nueces River. Muygisofac confirmed the testimonies of the previous Natives and added that the Frenchmen were killed by the Natives of the mountain range together with those of the coast. Muygisofac said that it took about ten days to travel from La Junta de los Ríos to the Tejas. He stated that on the way to the Tejas there was a very large river. At certain times of the year there were herds of buffalo near this river so large that they covered the plains. When the pasturelands were poor, the animals moved to where there was good pasture (Hackett 1926: 276–280).

April 12

Governor Pardiñas ordered Retana to return to Parral, since it appeared that the French had been killed, and it was the wrong time of the year to travel to the Tejas (too late?). He sent this order by Sabeata and offered Sabeata and his companions clothing and supplies in appreciation of their services (Hackett 1926: 280–282).

April 22

Alonso de León reached Espiritu Santo Bay (Matagorda Bay).

May 13

Alonso de León returned to Coahuila from Texas.

Twenty days before Alonso de León left Monclova for Texas, Juan Sabeata had already informed Juan Retana of the destruction of the French settlement. This was probably not accidental. Cuis Benive stated that Sabeata wanted them to reach La Junta with all speed to relay the news to the governor of Nueva Vizcaya. Sabeata must have known of Alonso de León's expedition and wanted to reap the benefit of scooping the news. Sabeata left for the trade fairs in east-central Texas around December 1688, and in March 1689, he was at the Pecos River to relay the news about the Frenchmen to the Spanish at Parral. These trade fairs were attended by many groups, among which were groups from the Rio Grande, the Edwards Plateau, central Texas, and east Texas. Since the Cibolo and the Jumano stated that they left the Rio Grande in early spring and returned in the fall, the trade fairs should have taken place during the spring–early summer period, coinciding with the spring buffalo-hunting season. However, the schedules provided by Sabeata and the Cibolo appear to indicate that the fairs took place in late winter–early spring[6] (January through March or April).

The Cibolo volunteered the information that they lived in an area of the Lower Rio Grande (some on the north bank), where they had yearly battles over the killing of buffalo. The conflicts were with peoples upriver from their *rancherías*. These statements reaffirm the information given by several groups in 1675 about the conflicts resulting from resource acquisition, and show the continuation of a pattern relating to the use-rights to natural resources. This was particularly true for a resource on the hoof, like the buffalo, which because of its multiple uses was of special economic relevance for Native Americans. Muygisofac commented on the seasonality and behavior of the buffalo, stating that at a certain time of the year there were large herds on the Guadalupe (or the Colorado), and that the buffalo herds moved according to the condition of the pasturelands.

On his 1689 trip to Texas, Alonso de León was accompanied by Jean Gery, the Frenchman captured the previous year. Gery was taken as guide and interpreter. On the south bank of the Rio Grande, Alonso de León met several of the Native groups friendly to Gery. The Spanish butchered five head of cattle for a feast with the Natives, which indicates that no buffalo were available. From there, Alonso de León saw no Natives until he had traveled 182 miles and reached the Guadalupe River (April 14); here the Spanish met the first Natives and saw and killed the first buffalo (Lino Canedo 1968: 91).

1690

In 1690, Alonso de León traveled once again to La Bahía de Espiritu Santo (Matagorda Bay) and to eastern Texas. Alonso de León was ordered to make a more complete reconnaissance of the bay, verify whether some Frenchmen remained in the area (as the reports indicated), and establish religious missions within Tejas territory. He was accompanied by three Franciscan friars: Fr. Damian Massanet, born in Majorca; Fr. Miguel de Fontcuberta; and Fr. Francisco de Jesus Maria, also called Francisco Casañas. Fr. Casañas was a Catalan (Lino Canedo 1968: 19). Before crossing the Rio Grande (April 3, 4, and 5), Alonso de León encountered several of the Native groups friendly to Jean Gery that they had met the previous year. The Spanish also hunted buffalo on the south bank of the Rio Grande. From that point onward until they crossed the Guadalupe River, where my survey left them, they saw no buffalo and very few Natives. Fr. Massanet was struck with the absence of Natives and commented on the fact (Lino Canedo 1968: 34).

March 26

Alonso de León left Monclova for Texas.

May–June

Mission San Francisco de los Tejas was established.

July 15

Alonso de León returned to Monclova.

1691

The expedition of Terán de los Rios (Hatcher 1932: 10–67; Lino Canedo 1968: 171–258) to Texas was meant to reinforce the Spanish military and religious presence in east Texas. While the country was surveyed and the French presence assessed, the friars raised the religious standard with the establishment of eight missions. In the short term, very little was achieved by this expensive endeavor. The lasting historical legacy of this expedition lies in the data obtained about the environment and the Native groups in Texas.

Before crossing the Rio Grande, Terán de los Rios met several of the groups friendly to Jean Gery (May 27) and saw large herds of buffalo. From the Rio Grande onward they saw large herds almost every day. They also encountered a good number of Native groups. Terán de los Rios was traveling northward of the route taken by Alonso de León, especially after crossing the Frio River. This might be a contributing factor to the presence of more buffalo. It seems, however, that the main reason was the time of the year: Terán de los Rios crossed the Rio Grande heading east to Texas at about the time most expeditions returned home to Monclova.

The presence of buffalo is a clear reason for the presence of multiple groups of Native

Americans, and possibly the northerly route contributed to the frequency of encounters. The presence of Spanish settlements in east Texas, together with the resolution of the problem of the French settlement on the coast, eased fears among the Natives of Spanish retaliation for the massacre at Matagorda. It is well to remember that the Native Americans saw the French and Spaniards as white-skinned peoples and therefore as the same. It may have taken a while before they made sense of the enmities between these two groups. I suspect that the "deliverance" of Jean Gery to the Spaniards was part of this effort. After all, they referred to Jean Gery as a Spaniard.

The frictions between the Tejas (Caddo) and the Spanish living in Caddo country opened possibilities for other groups to benefit from Spanish friendship and trade possibilities. On June 17, 18, and 19, Terán de los Rios met, near the Guadalupe River, several groups with their captains. These groups lived in west and central Texas. Among the captains present were Juan Sabeata, governor of the Cibolo and Jumano, and Don Nicolás (also called Tomás), captain of the Catqueza. Both captains tried to talk Terán de los Rios and Fr. Massanet into staying with their groups and not going to east Texas. While Sabeata was subtle in his invitation and said nothing detrimental to the Tejas, Captain Nicolás (Tomás) was overt about the problems between the Tejas and the Spanish, and his statements were true, as Terán de los Rios would later verify. Sabeata's subtlety was understandable, given the long-standing Jumano friendship with the Tejas (Lino Canedo 1968: 177–180, 240–243). The meeting of these groups with Terán de los Rios and Fr. Massanet was not fortuitous. Their elaborate displays were reminiscent of the performances put on by the Jumano and the Gediondo on the Pecos when Mendoza visited them in 1684 (Chapter 4). Fr. Massanet and Terán de los Rios misread, in part, their intentions. This was, on the part of the Jumano, probably a last attempt to befriend the Spaniards in Texas. The events of 1693 make this clear.

February 22

Diego de Vargas Ponce de León took possession as governor of El Paso.

May 16

Domingo Terán de los Rios left Monclova.

1692

March 24

Domingo Terán de los Rios left the Texas coast. The remaining Spanish troops traveled overland to Monclova under the direction of Captain Francisco Martinez.

April 7

Governor Vargas of New Mexico, at El Paso, reported the discovery of thirteen salines in the Salt Flats west of Guadalupe Peak on the modern New Mexico–Texas state border.

The report stated the absolute need for salt supplies, especially after the destruction of the saline they previously had used on the north bank of the Rio Grande. The saline disappeared due to a change in the course of that river. He mentioned that various attempts had been made to locate the Apache salines. The Spanish were elated because they had located the Apache water sources, food sources, and hideouts (*aguages, enboscadas, cazaderos y comederos*). The Spanish had found a short and easy route to the Pecos to be used whenever they went on campaigns (Vargas 1692).

May–July

Fr. Antonio Baga, commissary of the Franciscan missions in Coahuila, was having serious problems due to conflicts among his friars, some civilians, the military, and some Natives. The intimacy between the friars and the Natives and between the friars and some females led to widespread rumors of misconduct by the Franciscans in charge of the Coahuila missions. Military men and civilians explored the power of these rumors and events to undermine the sway of the religious over the Natives. Although it is clear that the conduct of some of the friars was reproachable, at the heart of the confrontations was the control over Native labor. The problems reached such a threshold that Fr. Baga ordered all the friars under his purview not to leave the area of their missions without written permission, on pain of excommunication. The documentation makes it clear that these problems were already occurring during the decade of the 1680s (Baga 1692; Baga et al. 1692). The Franciscans were also involved in a power struggle with Padre Xptoval Boca Negra, Cura of Monclova. The controversy focused on who had the authority to minister to the Natives who worked for the Spaniards as domestics and as laborers (*laborios*) in the farms or mines (Baga et al. 1692a; Boca Negra 1692). This conflict was about control over Native labor and about the revenues supplied by the Crown for its Native wards. Fr. Baga charged that civilians and military personnel purchased non-Christian Natives from other Natives in order to use them as laborers (Baga et al. 1692a). In turn, Padre Boca Negra charged that it could be proved that some friars also kept Natives as captives for labor. In this power struggle and epistolary war, Captain Diego Ramón, governor of Coahuila, acted as mediator, even though he was seen as siding with Fr. Baga, if not with the Franciscan friars (Ramón 1692).

August 14

Diego Ramón made two campaigns against the Toboso. Ramón was helped by the Gueiquetzale, enemies of the Toboso (Ramón 1692a).

September 13

Governor Diego de Vargas entered Santa Fé, and the Natives in the area yielded power without resistance.

1693

January

Gregorio Salinas Varona was appointed governor of Monclova. At the outset of his term in office, Salinas Varona apparently offended Fr. Baga, who, after counsel with his Franciscan brethren, officially requested the removal of Salinas Varona as governor (Baga et al. 1693).

May 6

Captain Diego Ramón informed the Viceroy that he had found two salines: one about 30 to 50 leagues (78 to 130 miles) east of Monclova between the Río Sabinas and the Rio Grande, and another on the north side of the Rio Grande. In the area of the first saline he encountered four hundred Chantiaco and Pachialla Natives. These groups were also said to be the Chantuac, Pachiliado, and Ochapaqualiro. The Viceroy agreed that great profit could be obtained if the Crown explored the salines, or, alternatively, rented them for exploration. In either case, exploration could not begin unless the Natives were removed from the area. The Viceroy approved Diego Ramón's plan, and two hundred Native families were removed to Mission La Caldera (Candela) near Monclova (Vilar 1695). The saline east of Monclova was probably located east of the modern Mexican town of Progreso.

May

Gregorio de Salinas Varona's trip to east Texas (Lino Canedo 1968: 277–307) was basically a resupply mission to the Spanish. There had been reports from Native Americans about the problems the friars were experiencing in east Texas. Salinas Varona encountered a fair number of Native groups,[7] but he did not mention hunting buffalo, except on the day after crossing the Rio Grande (May 11). The herd was so large that it completely disrupted their march. Salinas Varona did not mention hunting buffalo until he reached the Guadalupe River, where this survey leaves the Spanish party. After crossing the Rio Grande, Salinas Varona learned from the Pacuase (Pacuache) that the Jumano and the Toboso were waiting to attack the Spanish. Indeed, Salinas found a large and well-armed group of Jumano between the San Antonio and Guadalupe rivers, possibly near Coleto Creek: the Jumano did not attack, but neither were they friendly.

May 3

Salinas Varona left Monclova.

July 17

Salinas Varona returned to Monclova.

June–July

In June and July, General Retana gathered about 400 Chiso families at La Junta de los Ríos after more than 300 people were killed in several campaigns. The campaigns against the Chichitame, Satapoyogliglas, Guasapoyogliglas, and Osatayogliglas were accomplished with the help of two other Chiso groups, the Batayogliglas and the Zuniyogliglas, who previously had been reduced. The latter two groups were moved to the S. Francisco Pueblo, near the Presidio de S. Francisco de los Conchos. The population numbers provided for these groups were 130 families (or 148 families), for a total of 2,500 people[8] (Hackett 1926: 325–328, 345–359, 398; Lizenciado Brial 1702).

July

Sergeant Major Juan Bautista Escorza from Presidio El Pasaje reported on Native groups and on the military situation. Escorza noted that a widespread epidemic had killed many Natives, especially leaders of groups (Manzaneque ca. 1693).

September

Report of Maestro de Campo Joseph Francisco de Marín to Viceroy Conde de Galvé (Hackett 1926: 387–408).

1696

The reconquest of New Mexico was considered to be complete.

1698

July–October

In July some Alazapa Natives, who had been working in Monterrey, came to Coahuila to request placement in a pueblo with the Espiagilo, Apinami, Exmalquio, and Cenizo. The Alazapa had ties of friendship with these groups and had joined them (*coligado*). Don Francisco Cuerbo y Valdez gathered these groups on the newly named Valle de Candamo, 26 miles northward from Monclova. Their mission was located near some salines. Cuerbo y Valdez sent the Viceroy a sample of the salt extracted from the salines. These groups were placed in the mission of S. Antonio Galindo de Monteczuma, reestablished on October 28, 1698 (Cuerbo y Valdez 1698).

The mention by Native Americans of the process of aggregation (*coligado*) of different ethnic groups shows that the process was a viable solution for Native groups if the circumstances so required. In this case, as in 1658 and in 1673–1675, Native groups were proposing to settle, but they were choosing their companions. Although their acts were obviously dictated by historical circumstances, they were still making the choice of whom to live with.

October–November

The Acafe, who were moved from Mission Santiago to Mission S. Bernardino de la Candela by Salinas de Varona, governor of Coahuila, requested permission to move back to Santiago because they could not live at Candela. Seven other groups wanted to join the Acafe at Santiago: the Quejamo, Ocane, Molia, Canoa, Patalo, Chantague, and Patacal. In November, 220 people, including adults and children, were relocated in the valley of Santiago in the Mission S. Phelipe de Valladares (Cuerbo y Valdez 1698a).

November–December

In November the Chantaf and other aggregated groups requested a pueblo near a large spring 50 or 40 leagues (130 or 104 miles) northward from Monclova, between the river called both Alamo and Sabinas and the Rio Grande. On December 13, 1698, the Mission of Nombre de Jesus y Valle de S. Bartholome was established for the Chantafe, Pacoo, and Paiaguas. Ninety-five people, including adults and children, gathered at the mission (Cuerbo y Valdez 1698b; Ramón 1698).

1699

November 1698–January 1699

In late November, Diego Ramón undertook a punitive expedition against the Toboso. The Ervipiame accompanied Diego Ramón on this campaign. Since Ramón was going to unknown territory (*tierra adentro*), the friars asked him to bring back Natives who might want to gather in a pueblo. When Ramón returned from the expedition, he established a pueblo for the Ervipiame 40 leagues (104 miles) northwest of Monclova, halfway between the Río Sabinas and the Rio Grande. More than two hundred Ervipiame gathered at what became Mission San Francisco Javier y Valle de San Xpristobal. Official possession was given to the Natives on January 5, 1699 (Cuervo y Valdez 1699).

1698–1699

Diego Ramón, acting governor of Coahuila, wrote a fifty-one-page report (Ramón 1699–1700) complaining about the behavior of the Franciscan friars in charge of the Coahuila missions. The scathing report accused the friars and the Franciscan commissary, Fr. Portoles, of all types of misdeeds, from sexual misconduct to abuse of power, misuse of resources, violence, and name-calling, most of it directed at the Natives. Ramón also complained bitterly about the friars' disrespect for his gubernatorial authority. He was particularly resentful that the friars did not assist his sister, Maria Ramón, on her deathbed. Maria Ramón died July 5, 1699: although invited, no friar attended her funeral. At the end of this report, Diego Ramón indicated his intention to establish a settlement in the Valley of Santiago, the area where Mission San Bernardino de la Candela and Mission San Philipe de Valladares were located. The friars became rather upset when they learned of Ramón's plans, particularly because Ramón already had several Spanish settlers ready to move to the area. The friars wrote a rebuttal to Ramón's accusations (Illegible 1700). In this letter, they respond to some of the accusations leveled against them, blaming Ramón and his acolytes (including Francisco Cuerbo) for much of the violence. The friars declared that they were so fearful of the conduct of the governor and the military that they had filed declarations against Ramón in Saltillo and not in Monclova. The friars stated that Diego Ramón had ordered all settlers not to provide the friars with any help, food, or lodging: the penalty for disobedience would be flogging. According to the friars, the real reason for Ramón's complaints was the governor's economic self-interest.

June 24

Fr. Francisco Hidalgo and other friars reestablished the mission and pueblo of San Juan Bautista y Valle de Santo Domingo for the Chaguane, Pachale, Mescale, and Xarame. One hundred and fifty people, including adults and children, gathered in the new frontier pueblo (Cuerbo y Valdez 1699a).

December 16

Captain Diego Ramón, commander of the Presidio de San Juan Bautista on the Rio Grande, was authorized to go *tierra adentro* to the north and northeast to ascertain if there were any Native groups that wanted to enter a mission. Ramón was accompanied by Fr. Antonio de San Buenaventura, Fr. Francisco Hidalgo, and twenty men. On March 1, 1700, Diego Ramón and the friars founded a mission for the Xarame, Papanac, Paiaguan, and Siguan. These groups had been gathered during Ramón's expedition north of the Rio Grande. The mission, named S. Francisco Solano, was located in the Valle de la Zircunzizion, 2 to 3 leagues (5.2 to 7.8 miles) from the banks of the Rio Grande (Cuerbo y Valdez 1699b; Cuerbo y Valdez 1700; Ramón 1700).

REFLECTIONS

The last two decades of the seventeenth century saw the emergence of the French threat in New Spain in the form of La Salle's colony, as well as its disappearance through a historical conjuncture and without Spanish intervention. The Spaniards too might have said that God was on their side. But in trying to retrieve the few French persons left in the aftermath of the massacre at Matagorda Bay and satisfy the missionary zeal of the Franciscans, the Spanish found the French wedged in east Texas. The genie was out of the bottle, and the Spaniards continued to feel, sometimes more acutely than others, the malaise of the French presence.

The conversion efforts in east Texas, in which the Franciscans were fully invested, were aborted by 1693 with the retreat of the friars. The Natives of the most promising area for reduction and colonization rejected the Spanish. It must have been devastating for the friars that the least "barbarian" of the groups in Texas forced them to leave. After all, these were the only people the Spanish had met in Texas who made pottery, grew abundant crops, and slept in beds. Although the Spanish never again truly occupied Caddo country, a close relationship with the Caddo continued. This relationship was mostly based on trade and was often maintained against Spain's best interests.

After the east Texas debacle, the Spanish shifted focus to the Rio Grande, where a presidio and three missions were established: the Presidio de San Juan Bautista and the missions of San Juan Bautista, San Francisco Solano, and San Bernardo. After dislodging the Franciscans of the province of Xalisco from eastern Coahuila and Texas, their brethren of Queretero were forced to round up Natives to keep alive the missions on the Rio Grande.

For the Native Americans, the four major expeditions that entered Texas after 1689 showed the vulnerability of their territories to Spanish expansion. It is inconceivable that the Native populations did not fully evaluate the results of the European occupation of their territories and did not wish to preserve some areas from such control. If nothing else, the Pueblo Revolt in New Mexico and the revolts along the northern frontier of New Spain exemplify this vital concern. This was a colonial setup in which both the colonizer and the colonized became trapped in "must/need" situations. The colonizer must fight the Natives because their attacks jeopardize the very reason for being a colonizer, but he needs the Natives to labor and open up the country for him. The colonized must fight the occupier because the land, its resources, and its people are at stake, but he needs the products the colonizer provides. This economic entanglement becomes a matter of life and death.

It is not easy to document the change of Native attitudes in Texas because the colonizing process had just begun. However, the Jumano welcomed Terán de los Rios in 1691 in a very friendly manner. Fr. Massanet, who traveled with the expedition, had to dissuade Juan Sabeata from the idea that the friars should travel to his lands to set up a mission instead of going to east Texas (Lino Canedo 1968: 243–244). By the time Salinas Varona entered Texas (1693), he was warned that the Jumano (and others) were waiting to kill and rob the Spanish (Lino Canedo 1968: 281).

Several factors may have been at work in the Native change of attitude toward the Spaniards. The pathogens that affected the east Texas groups also affected other groups that came in contact with Spaniards. The Caddo certainly established a cause-and-effect relationship between the presence of Spaniards and the diseases that were killing them. Over a century and a half earlier, the coastal peoples had connected the presence of Cabeza de Vaca and his companions with the onset of disease that devastated their *rancherías*. In 1690 Fr. Casanas reported that he eased Caddo fears by arguing that Fr. Fontcuberta and a soldier had also died (Lino Canedo 1968: 60). It is doubtful that the argument really worked; a mortality ratio of 2:300 would be hard to rationalize.

Another factor that may have influenced Native attitudes was the recent, but short-lived, military successes against the Apache. In July 1688, Diego de León, an Ervipiame, informed Alonso de León that the Ervipiame, the Tejas, the French, and possibly the Jumano had attacked the Apache (Portillo 1984: 184). In June 1691, when Terán de los

Rios met a series of Native groups near the Guadalupe River, most of the Natives were on horseback and had small riding saddles with stirrups. When asked by Fr. Massanet where they had obtained the saddles, they replied that they had taken them from the Apache in war. Among these groups were the Jumano (Lino Canedo 1968: 241).

Quite possibly these two events are connected, but even if they are not, it is clear that, at this time, the Native groups in Texas, with the help of the French, were checking the Apache southward movement. In 1683, the Jumano, the Tejas, and many others requested Spanish help against the Apache. The Spanish did not deliver. These events notwithstanding, the Jumano and the Catqueza were still interested in a Spanish presence in their areas. I think these groups were hedging their bets and minimizing the control of the Tejas over their people. On the other hand, they were well aware of the problems that existed at this time between the Spanish and the Caddo (Lino Canedo 1968: 243–244). Why not profit from the tension?

I do not wish to gloss over a situation that is exceedingly complex, but a few other factors merit consideration. Most, if not all, of the information the Spanish obtained about the French, and certainly about Native groups, was provided by Natives. The archival documents show that, at this time and in this area, most of the information came from ladinos at missions, as well as from the Cibolo and Jumano. The value of the trade in information was translated in appointments to positions of leadership, gifts, safe-conduct papers, trust, and prestige—and, most important of all, further information (Hackett 1926: 284; Lino Canedo 1968: 156, 178, 183, 243; Portillo 1984: 159–160, 173, 184). Then as now, information was power. To what extent the travels of the Spanish through Texas diminished the value and power of these traders in information is hard to measure, but important to consider.

Spanish settlements meant resource centers of European goods with periodic need of resupply. If horses (and other goods) could be snatched from Spanish military convoys by any Native group in east or central Texas, the advantage of the groups closer to the Spanish settlements in the west decreased. Besides, if the Natives in Texas feared the Apache would begin raiding further south to intercept the expeditionary and supply convoys in order to acquire horses, they were probably correct.

Last but not least, there is the problem of the buffalo. The events during the Bosque-Larios expedition (1675), as well as the testimonies of the Cibolo in 1689, show a serious preoccupation with, and conflicts arising from, buffalo hunting rights. In 1689, the Cibolo were asked many questions concerning different matters, but they were not asked about buffalo; yet they volunteered the information. The presence of buffalo herds in an area controlled by group X guaranteed that group's survival (all other things being equal), but also ensured that other groups needed to maintain friendly relations with group X. The diminution of buffalo numbers within a given area had crucial social implications: friends who needed access to buffalo hunting grounds might be denied such access, be unable to enter into alliances, and thus become enemies. To patrol resource areas might be too onerous for groups in terms of time, resources, and manpower. A corollary to these comments is that, before the late 1600s and early 1700s, it might have been

easier to travel northward to hunt buffalo when the herds did not come further southward (i.e., onto and south of the Edwards Plateau). The presence of northern groups such
as the Apache, Pawnee, Ute, and Comanche, among many others, may have curtailed
such options (French 1851: 68–69, 72–74).

No European could know better than the Native Americans what affected buffalo
ranging patterns. The transmission of information by oral means would have given Native
Americans a record of past events, particularly those connected with their most important food resources. Oral history is obviously not easy to document, but Juan Sabeata's
confirmation in 1683 of the trip of Diego de Castillo in 1650 (Chapter 4), as well as the
reports received by the Espejo-Luxán expedition about Cabeza de Vaca and his companions, are cases in point (Hammond and Rey 1929: 62–63).

There are several recorded instances of buffalo affecting the traveling of Spanish military columns enroute to central and east Texas (Lino Canedo 1968: 173, 177, 179, 181,
186, 187, 188, 189, 281–282). Did the Native Americans fear the buffalo would change
migration patterns because of these disruptions and the presence of large numbers of
horses and cattle? Spanish expeditions traveled through buffalo hunting grounds during
the peak hunting season. Cuis Benive, a Cibolo, remarked to the Spaniards that buffalo
changed their range according to the quality of the pasture. In 1685–1687, Joutel (1998:
83, 139, 142, 172, 174) made similar observations. The results of hunting, as well as cattle
and sheep ranching by the Spaniards in northern Mexico, did not bode well for the future
of buffalo herds in Texas. All of this, coupled with pressure from other groups moving
from the north and from the west, must have worried the peoples who lived within Texas
territory.

To play my own devil's advocate, I should mention that the expedition of Terán de
los Rios (1691–1692) recorded very large herds of buffalo from the Rio Grande to east of
the Colorado River. Herds of three thousand, four thousand, and more were recorded
during this expedition. That was not the case with Alonso de León's expeditions of 1689
and 1690. There is a major difference between León's expeditions and that of Terán de
los Rios; while Alonso de León crossed the Rio Grande in the first days of April, Terán
de los Rios crossed it in early June. In the case of Alonso de León it was too early for the
herds to have made their way south of the Edwards Plateau. The expedition of Salinas
Varona (1693) is essentially mute on the point because he crossed the Rio Grande in mid-
May and crossed it again on his return trip in mid-July. Alonso de León (1690), Terán
de los Rios (1691–1692), and Salinas Varona saw large numbers of buffalo near the Rio
Grande, on both the south and the north banks.

I propose that the bulk of the buffalo herds that came southward through the Llano
Estacado continued southeastward and entered the northwest area of the Edwards Plateau, near the headwaters of the Concho River system. At this point, one migration route
(east fork) would go eastward, following the Concho to the Colorado River and skirting
the rugged edge of the Edwards Plateau to the east, southeast, and south. The westward
route (west fork) followed from the Llano Estacado through level terrain to reach the
area west of the Nueces River and east of the Devils River. The westward route followed

a path from the towns of Big Lake, Ozona, and Sonora to the Rio Grande and the Rio Grande Plains. This buffalo corridor (west fork) would have been very important to the groups encountered by the Bosque-Larios expedition as well as to those, such as the Cibolo, that hunted in the area in the 1680s and 1690s.

The information from Joutel, however, complicates the issue further. Joutel, and other members of the French colony on the coast, saw abundant buffalo between February 1685 and the first days of November (Margry 1879: 128, 131, 136, 157–158, 183, 192). In his diary, Joutel was not referring to the immediate area around Garcitas Creek, but to the region overall ("comme il avoit bien huit ou dix jours que l'on ne voyoit point de bœufs dans ce canton") (Margry 1879: 192). Later, Joutel stated that they had been without buffalo for quite a while, but he remarked that he saw herds of five to six thousand animals in the last days of November 1685 (Margry 1879: 192, 195).

Between December 1685 and May 1686, Joutel and his companions reported seeing fewer buffalo, but attributed this fact to the manipulation by the Natives of the herd's movements (Margry 1879: 200, 209–210, 214, 233, 240–243, 245). Between May and August 1686, the references to buffalo hunting are scarce. It appears that the animals were in the area, but they were not as abundant. Joutel stated that the people in the colony burned the grass to encourage new growth and attract the animals (Margry 1879: 233, 252). In January 1687, La Salle and some of his people left for the Cenis (Tejas). While traveling northward they encountered buffalo almost every day until they reached the outskirts of the villages of the Cenis in mid-March 1687 (Margry 1879: 259, 261–274, 287, 293, 303, 310–312, 319).

The crucial issues may be either that buffalo were more prevalent year-round in the east and east-central regions of Texas than in the west and west-central regions, or that, if the herds came to the end of the south plains, there would be plenty of buffalo, but if they did not, there would be none. This might have been what worried the Native Americans.

In July 1693, Bautista Escorza, stationed at Presidio El Pasaje, made some important remarks about the changes occurring in the area (Hackett 1926: 319–325). He stated that the familiar enemies, like the Toboso, constituted, by that time, a very small number of the rebels, but the rebellious groups were being reinforced by groups from Coahuila and the Rio Grande. These groups from northern Coahuila (between Santa Rosa and the Rio Grande) were at peace in Coahuila, but were raiding further west and south. Alonso de León had noted the same pattern in 1688 (Portillo 1984: 158–159). Escorza noted that the rebels were attacking out of necessity. They had no buffalo to sustain themselves and were forced to steal cattle and horses from the Spanish. For Escorza the depletion of the buffalo herds in the lower Rio Grande was owing to the Natives. Escorza continued by stating that "formerly the local indians were so numerous that they had no need to enlist the help of other indians from the interior: on the contrary, the local indians prevented those from other areas to enter their territory." In 1693, however, "when they have been consumed by time and war until there are but few of them left, not only do they not prevent the strange indians from coming in, but rather they solicit them and invite them, subordinating themselves to them" (Hackett 1926: 319–325).

This assessment of the situation shows not only the problems with the buffalo as a resource, and the effects of disease and war, but also a change in coalitions out of necessity, as well as a change of war tactics vis-à-vis the Spaniards. Members of Native coalitions made sure that they obtained some measure of peace by making peace agreements with the Spaniards at their home bases. This allowed them to raid in other jurisdictions with relative impunity and return home to safety. Native traditional mobility patterns were used to enhance the pattern of hit-and-run warfare. This type of guerrilla warfare capitalized on the Spanish problems with performing joint military operations, the poor dissemination of military intelligence between different jurisdictions, and the unwillingness of military officials to stray far from their home bases.

The Spanish military felt the impact of this change in tactics (Hackett 1926: 429). In February 1693, Maestro de Campo Joseph Francisco de Marín was charged by the Viceroy Count of Galvé to review the military situation in Nueva Vizcaya and other areas of the northern frontier. What transpires from Marín's report, and its digest by the Fiscal in 1698 (Hackett 1926: 365–457), is the preoccupation with comprehending the dynamics of the Native groups in Nueva Vizcaya and Coahuila and the attempts to establish a conservative fiscal policy, to reorganize and reapportion military resources, and to make a concerted effort to protect the roadways and mineral wealth. Marín suggested that the Natives not be allowed to select the sites where they wanted to live because they chose locations away from the presidios, and from there, in peace, they were able to commit their hostilities (Hackett 1926: 435). Marín provided lists of Native groups from Durango to Texas. These lists are very important in order to make sense of other lists of Native group names from the same period.

The discovery of various saline deposits in southeastern New Mexico, Coahuila, and Texas in the 1690s brought about the forced displacement of some groups and likely contributed to the movement of others. The economic importance of salt in the mining industry, as a condiment, and in the preservation of foods cannot be over-stressed. The documents state that various groups were willing to leave areas where salines were located in order that Spaniards could explore the salines. The evidence that salt was a commodity traded among Native Americans leaves no doubt that this resource would have been important to them, and therefore their willingness to leave the area is rather questionable.

To summarize, in the last decades of the seventeenth century the French presence north of the Rio Grande forced the Spaniards into the exploration of what would become Texas territory. Throughout this period, and in this area, the majority of the information dictating Spanish policy was supplied by the Native groups, of which the most visible were the Cibolo, the Jumano, and the Tejas. What information the Spanish gathered through their diplomatic sources and their spies in Europe they obtained because they had been alerted by reports supplied by Native Americans.

With the expansion of settlements in northernmost Mexico, efforts were made by both Natives and Spaniards to congregate groups in settlements or mission-settlements. When the relocation moves were initiated by Native groups, they were dictated by conditions that imperiled Native survival, such as loss of population, disease, warfare, and displacements. Aggregation with groups with kin ties or similar traditions may have been the best of a set of undesirable options. In all likelihood it was an option exercised at times before European colonization. When the movement of Natives into settlements was initiated by the Spanish, it was driven by the need to explore certain areas and resources and to facilitate the control and management of Native populations. This is, after all, the quintessential colonial tactic of pushing the border troubles outward. The region beyond the Rio Grande was to be dealt with in the ensuing decades.

SIX

Hard Choices:

THE APACHE, THE SPANIARD, AND THE LOCAL NATIVE GROUPS, 1700–1755

SETTING THE STAGE

At the close of the seventeenth century some major changes had taken place in the Spanish perception of the wilderness territory referred to, ironically, by a Native word said to mean "friends." *Tejas* was the word used by some Native peoples to proclaim their nonaggressive attitude when faced with the European explorers (Lino Canedo 1968: 53). Spanish interest in the Texas territory was brought about in part by the French presence on the Texas coast and among the Caddo. That presence forced Spain into a defensive posture. The interaction between the French and the eastern groups, particularly the Caddo, contributed to the definition of a boundary that would later take the legal form of the province of Texas or New Philippines.

The Spanish understood and lived by hierarchical social structures: from their perspective, the Tejas (Caddoan groups) provided a person in authority with whom they could talk, the Xinesí. Massanet's letter to Don Carlos de Siguenza y Gongora illustrates the Spanish view. When three Native Tejas were to visit Coahuila, the Xinesí asked Massanet to take care of his relatives and not let anybody give them orders or make them work. Massanet commented that such recommendations clearly showed that among the Tejas there were noblemen and ordinary people, and that the classes were treated differently ("de donde se ve que entre ellos hay nobleza y se distinguen los nobles de la gente ordinaria") (Lino Canedo 1968: 31). The implication is clear: all the other groups in Texas were ordinary people, with headless social structures (in Western terms) and nobody to talk to in authority.

In the European theater, the Crowns of Spain and France were temporarily joined with Philip V, and an uneasy truce prevailed. A series of events, reports, rumors, individual fears, and desires for profit created a historic conjuncture that again focused attention on Texas and its people. The precarious peace between France and Spain, and the problems of succession, led the two colonial powers to maneuver behind the scenes to guarantee an advantageous position upon the death of Carlos II of Spain. Pierre Le Moyne d'Iberville's trip (1699) to the Gulf of Mexico, the Mississippi, and Louisiana raised, once more, the specter of the French in the Spanish psyche.

Pierre d'Iberville's return to the Mississippi in 1700 brought to the stage Captain Louis Juchereau de Saint-Denis. Before leaving for France on May 28, 1700, Iberville ordered Saint-Denis to go west and "penetrate as far as possible, seeking information on the mines and Spanish settlements of New Mexico, the overland trails and navigable streams, and the availability of building materials and cultivable land" (Weddle 1991: 178). According to Weddle, Saint-Denis made two unsuccessful attempts to fulfill these orders, but on his third try (1701) he reached the Red River and the Kadohadacho (Weddle 1991: 178). The news of these French forays raised the fears of Spanish officials and echoed a responsive note among the Franciscan friars, who, despite the failures of 1688–1693 among the Tejas, continued to dream of harvesting souls from Texas soil. The statements of Diego de Léon, an Ervipiame, confirm that the French had penetrated into modern Texas territory before June 1688 and were affecting the balance of power between the Apache and their enemies.

Confirmation of these events seems to appear in the report La Salle received in east central Texas. In mid-February 1687, La Salle met a group called Teao, who mentioned that the Chouman, Teao, and Cenys (Tejas) wanted to join together and make war against a great nation that they called Ayano and Cannohatinno. The Ayano and (or) Cannohatinno were at war with the Spanish and stole horses from them whenever they could set an ambush ("pour marcher en guerre contre une grande nation qu'ils appeloient Ayano et Cannohatinno lesquels font la guerre aux Espagnols et leur dérobent des cheveaux, lorsqu'ils en peuvent surprendre quelque troupe") (Margry 1879: 299). They also said that some "Spaniards" were coming to the Cenis to join them in this battle. When these "Spaniards" learned of La Salle's impending arrival, they decided to postpone their plans.

Joutel, who was quite a reliable witness, acknowledged that all this interchange took place by means of signs, and he was not sure if they understood correctly all that was being conveyed (Margry 1879: 299). If there is a connection between these events, it is possible that the Frenchmen who helped the Tejas and the other groups against the Apache were actually the three (or more) men who left La Salle's group earlier in the enterprise (Margry 1879: 300). The identity of these French individuals is not essential for this discussion. What is important is the presence of the French in the area and their intervention, together with the Tejas, against the Apache.

The French threat to Spain's colonial dominions was real, but the roots of the conflict were continental, not colonial, as the solution would be. The effects of the conflict on the daily lives of colonists were not particularly relevant, and rarely life-threatening, but its effects on Native American populations were considerable and double-edged. While Native populations benefited on occasion from the rivalry between the two European powers, they also were used by those nations in their power plays against each other.

The appearance of the Apache groups, south of the New Mexico colonial territory and into Texas and northern Coahuila, had a great and lasting impact on the lives of Spaniards and an even greater impact on the lives of the Native groups living in the latter territories. The bellicose attitude of Apache groups was a problem rooted in the colonizing efforts of various European nations. As in all other colonial situations, when the problems became unbearable the colonizer could return home; the colonized had no other home.

In July 1690, in a letter to the Viceroy, Alonso de León stated that the Tejas were continually at war with the Apache, who were to the west of the Tejas (Lino Canedo 1968: 156). In September of the same year, Fr. Massanet wrote to the Viceroy and stated that the Apache were enemies of the Tejas. They were located to the west of the Tejas, and because they could reach the direct west-east route from the Colorado River to the Tejas territory, they made that route unsafe (Lino Canedo 1968: 161). In 1691, Fr. Francisco Casañas, stationed in the east Texas missions, wrote a report about the Tejas. In this report (*La Relación*), he placed the Apache, or Sadammo, west of the Tejas. According to Fr. Casañas the Apache were also called Caaucozi or Maní and were enemies of the Tejas and their allies (Lino Canedo 1968: 53–54).

Fr. Casañas gave four different names for the Apache (Apache, Sadammo, Caaucozi, and Maní). If he understood the four names to refer to the same group and not four divisions of the same group, as is possible in the early period of Spanish contact with the eastern Apache, what he actually provided were the Tejas names for divisions of the Apache. Almost assuredly the Tejas knew well the history of the Apache and had very specific names for their divisions, while our knowledge is based on what the Spaniards knew, and that was precious little, especially between the 1700s and the 1730s.

As soon as the Spanish settled on the San Antonio River, Apache groups began to harass the settlement. The first explicit warnings were given to Aguayo in 1721. Apart from taking horses from the Spaniards, the Apache stuck arrow shafts in the ground near the presidio. These arrow shafts had red pieces of cloth attached to them like small flags. The interpreter said that those signified a declaration of war (Aguayo 1721; 1725). From that time onward the Apache became the dreaded nemesis of Spanish settlements in Texas. It is often assumed that the Lipan Apache were the group responsible for the problems that afflicted San Antonio de Béjar in the early decades of the 1700s. Actually, we have no proof that such was the case. Contrary to common belief, and as far as I could determine from the archival records, the Lipan name does not appear in the records before December 1732.

The problem of the identity of the Lipan, where they came from, and when they became the focal group in the Apache-Spanish relations in Texas is yet to be solved. Schroeder (1974), who did extensive research on the Apache, stated that the first mention of the "Lipan or Kiowa Apache may have been the Canecy and/or the Conexeros of the last half of the 1600s in the Texas Panhandle" (Schroeder 1974: 114). He stated that "the Canecy Apaches of post-1660, may have been one and the same as the Conexero Apaches, who in the 1690's lived to the east of the Cipayan Apaches on the Canadian River" (Schroeder 1974: 113).

This connection between Canecy and Lipan is based on the Caddoan name for the Apache, which was Kansti, Gentsi, and Cancey (three versions of the same name, or three divisions of the group?). This name "usually was applied to the Lipan, and also to the Kiowa Apache" (Schroeder 1974: 114). On the other hand, Schroeder stated that the first reference to the Kiowa Apache probably occurred in the mid-1700s (1749–1752). At this time they would have been called the A, the Ae, or the Aes (Schroeder 1974: 384). Schroeder also stated that, in 1695, the Chipaynes were mentioned for the first time when they reported to Governor Vargas an attack on the Conexero by some white men from the east (Schroeder 1974: 326). The Chipaynes were the "Lipan Apaches who were located on the Canadian River, probably below present Conchas Dam" (Schroeder 1974: 288). In 1715, the Spanish from New Mexico led a campaign against the Chipaynes or Cipayno and found their *ranchería* on the Canadian River, which the Natives called Rio Colorado (Schroeder 1974: 325–326). Schroeder assumes the identification of the Canadian River with the Colorado. Although Schroeder's work provides information and clues, his arguments are in this case circular, and offer no primary archival documents to confirm the identity of the Lipan or their appearance in the historical record.

While retracing most of the archival research done by William Dunn (1911), who wrote extensively on the Apache, I found the first documents in which the name Ypandi appears. The records of the campaign of Nicolás Flores (Baldes 1724) do not discriminate among Apache groups. On December 9, 1732, Governor Bustillo y Zevallos with a force of one hundred men attacked a Native *ranchería,* killing more than two hundred Natives and capturing about thirty women and children. This *ranchería* had Natives of four nations: Apaches, Ypandi ("a quien nosotros llamamos Pelones"), Yxandi, and Chenti.

In 1784, Texas governor Domingo Cabello wrote a historical sketch on the Apache (Dunn 1911: 220). He stated that the Apache lived along the Río del Fierro (the Iron River, probably the Wichita River, which runs through Wichita Falls) until 1723, at which time they were defeated by the Comanche during a nine-day battle and had to flee their lands. The Apache then moved to the region between the upper Colorado and Brazos Rivers, about 120 leagues (320 miles) from the province of Texas (Dunn 1911: 220). This would place the Apache northwest of Abilene, Texas, below the escarpment of the Llano Estacado.

Pursuant to the same principles stated before (Chapter 5), what follows is a timeline that presents a chronology of events while highlighting the actions of particular individuals.

TIMELINE

1700

March

On March 1, 1700, Mission San Francisco Solano was established on the Rio Grande. Between May and December 1700, a series of letters shows that the missions in the area were doing very poorly as a result of disease, strife, lack of food, poor military protection, and, particularly, the absence of Natives. In May the friars informed the governor that they would have to abandon the missions if they did not get help (Olibares 1700).

December 13

Fr. Olibares informed his superior, Fr. Felipe Galindo, that the group of Don Thomas, together with the Ervipiame, had killed two soldiers from Coahuila, and that these Natives were planning to attack the missions. The Sijame from a *ranchería* connected with the mission of Peyotes fought the Ervipiame, killing nine of their sixteen warriors. On this date the friars were alone at the mission because they had no food to offer the Natives (Olibares 1700a).

1701

April 24

In a letter to the Father Provincial (Franciscan Xalisco province), Fr. Lucas de Llerena (1701) reported that Fr. Olivares of the Cretaro [*sic*] brothers announced the establishment of two Queretaro missions on the Rio Grande. A rumor was circulating that the Viceroy had ordered that the supplies in the Crown's storehouses be shared with the missions on the Rio Grande. Fr. Llerena was very distressed because the existing supplies were already too meager to assist the four Coahuila missions. He stated that the Natives were very upset and asked that the order be rescinded. Fr. Llerena (1701) stressed that Xalisco had four missions with many Natives, while the Queretaro brothers had only two, with few residents. The friar feared that without supplies the Natives would abandon the missions and return to the woods, from which they would soon attack.

1707

February–March

In February the new governor of Coahuila, Don Martin de Alarcón, ordered Captain Diego Ramón to travel to the Colorado River (San Marcos River) to punish the enemy. In March, Diego Ramón left on this trip, accompanied by Fr. Isidro de Espinosa and 150 soldiers and local citizens. Diego Ramón gathered more than 100 Natives, of which 26 were from enemy groups. Near Cotulla, Texas, Diego de Ramón found a fifteen-hut *ranchería,* which he said was called Ranchería Grande. The huts were covered with skins from mares.[1] Before reaching the *ranchería* the soldiers were attacked by 26 warriors armed with bows, arrows, and shields. Some of the members of Ranchería Grande were ladinos who spoke Mexican and hurled insults at the Spanish. Ramón's party saw no buffalo and had to eat fish and turkey (Leon 1700; Olibares 1700a; Ramon 1707). This expedition to the north bank of the Nueces River was clearly a trip to hunt and gather Natives for the missions.

March 9

Diego Ramón and the friars left for the Nueces River.

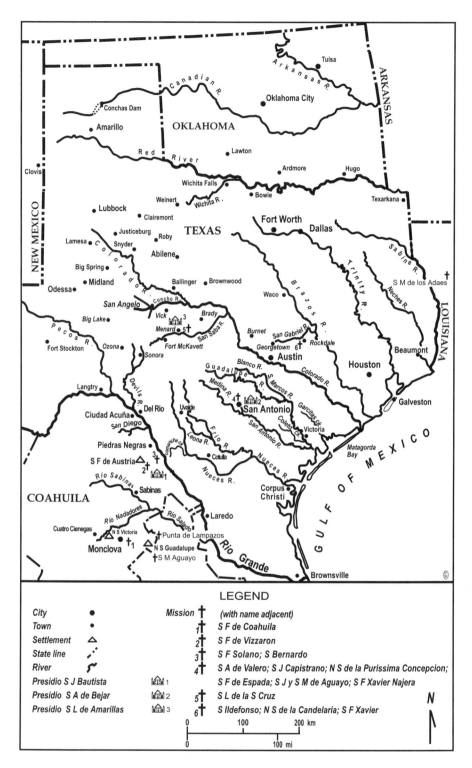

FIGURE 6.1

Map showing important places mentioned in the text—eighteenth century.

April 3

Diego Ramón and the friars returned to Mission San Juan Bautista.

1709

April

The short reconnaissance expedition commanded by Captain Pedro Aguirre was motivated by the rumor that the Tejas had moved from the Trinity-Neches area to the Colorado River and was spearheaded by Fr. Isidro de Espinosa and Fr. Antonio de Olivares (Tous 1930: 3–14). This expedition reflected a continuing effort on the part of the Franciscans (particularly Frs. Espinosa and Hidalgo) to missionize the Tejas despite the latter's prior refusal.

On their journey the Spanish met a Pacuasian group that was hunting rodents between the Comanche Creek and the Nueces River. Near the Leona River they met another Pacuasian party accompanied by two Xarame. They encountered Pampoa near the Medina River on their inbound and outbound trips. They met the Payaya near San Antonio, and near the San Pedro Springs they saw a party composed of about five hundred Chaularame, Siupan, and Sijame. Four individuals from the latter groups were used as guides. Some Sana were also used as guides and scouts. After reaching the Colorado River they were visited by forty members of the Yojuan, Simomo, and Tusonibi, accompanied by a Captain Cantona, who acted as their spokesman. Together they put on a performance similar to the one witnessed by the Mendoza-Lopez expedition (Chapter 4) and the one witnessed by Terán de los Rios and Fr. Massanet in 1691 (Chapter 5). Although this performance took place east of the Guadalupe River, the geographic threshold maintained in this work, it is included here for its cultural significance.

The Spanish did not encounter buffalo until they reached the Colorado River (April 19).

April 5

Captain Aguirre and the friars left the Rio Grande.

April 28

Captain Aguirre and the friars returned to the Rio Grande.

1711

January 11

Fr. Francisco Hidalgo wrote a letter to the governor of Louisiana, asking if it would be feasible to establish missions among the Tejas (Weddle 1991: 191).

1713

? Date

Fr. Hidalgo wrote a letter to the French in Louisiana (Shelby 1924: 196; also see the entry for 1715). Fr. Hidalgo continued to try to return to Tejas territory.

1714

Saint-Denis, three other Europeans, and about twenty-five Tejas were attacked by people of the Texas coast on the west side of the Colorado River. They were traveling westward from the Tejas to the Rio Grande (Saint-Denis 1715).

July

Saint-Denis reached Mission S. Juan Bautista on the Rio Grande.

1715

February 1

Lamothe Cadillac confirmed having finally received Fr. Hidalgo's letter. This letter was delivered to Bienville two years earlier by a Native (Cadillac 1715).

1716

The 1716 expedition to Texas was ordered by the Viceroy Conde de Linares to reestablish political and religious ties with the Tejas. The Spanish were accompanied by Louis de Saint-Denis. Seven religious (including Frs. Espinosa and Hidalgo) and Domingo Ramón (son of Diego Ramón) were to determine the best places to establish a mission or missions closer to the Rio Grande, possibly near the San Antonio River. During the trip to the Tejas they saw very few Natives and almost no buffalo. They killed five animals near Brushy Creek (Foik 1933: 3–23; Tous 1930: 4–24). They encountered some Natives near Comanche Creek, and near the Frio River they saw three Paragua *rancherías*. After crossing the Frio they meet a Mesquite Native who informed the Spanish of a large Native gathering near the Colorado River.

April 26

Domingo Ramón, Saint-Denis, and eight friars left the Rio Grande for the Tejas.

June

Domingo Ramón and his group arrived at the Tejas. Four Spanish missions and one presidio were established in Tejas territory.

1717

In 1717, Saint-Denis, Diego Ramón, and others returned to the Rio Grande from the Tejas with French merchandise to be sold within Spanish territory. This amounted to smuggling, because it was illegal to sell French goods within Spanish territory without prior approval and the payment of duties to the Crown. However, the friars welcomed Saint-Denis's influence and help with the Tejas groups, and the Ramón family as well as merchants in the Rio Grande, Coahuila, and Nuevo León were deeply interested in the profits that smuggling could bring (Weddle 1991: 197–200).

March 17

Saint-Denis, Diego Ramón, and others left the Tejas. Derbanne and the mule trains with goods lagged behind.

April 8

Derbanne's mule train headed for the Rio Grande with French goods. En route, the party was attacked by sixty mounted Apache west of the Colorado. The Apache stole twenty-three mules and kidnapped a mulatto woman who was part of the convoy (French 1851: 48; Margry 1888: 206; Salinas Varona 1717).

April

Saint-Denis and his group arrived at S. Juan Bautista on the Rio Grande.

November 4

Fr. Hidalgo wrote a letter in which he acknowledged having written two letters, at different times, to the French. One of these letters reached the French (Hidalgo 1716).

1718–1719

February

New Orleans was founded.

The expedition of Governor Martín de Alarcón to Texas was undertaken to determine the best place to establish a mission and a presidio on the San Antonio River. Alarcón was also to resupply the east Texas missions and to investigate Matagorda Bay. The expedition saw very few Natives between the Rio Grande and the Guadalupe River. Only the Pacuache were mentioned. They did not encounter any buffalo until they reached the Colorado River (September 19). The expedition used a Muruame and a Payaya as guides (Hoffman 1935: 43–89; Hoffman 1938: 312–323).

April 9

Governor Martín Alarcón crossed the Rio Grande on the way to central east Texas.

April 25

The Alarcón expedition reached the San Antonio River.

May

San Antonio de Béjar was founded.

November 28

The Alarcón expedition left east Texas for the Rio Grande.

1719

Six missions and one presidio were established in east Texas, while one mission and one presidio were established in San Antonio.

January 9

War was declared between France and Spain.

May 14

The French attacked the fortress of Santa Maria de Galvé (Pensacola, Florida).

June

The French attacked S. Miguel de los Adaes. The Spaniards in east Texas abandoned the area and sought refuge in San Antonio.

1720–1722

The Aguayo expedition to Texas was a show of force by the Spanish to put to rest the French ambitions in the central east Texas territory and to show the Natives, in unequivocal terms, the power and friendship of the Spaniards (Buckley 1911: 1–65; Forrestal 1935: 3–68; Santos 1981). The expedition was a very elaborate affair that brought into Texas large amounts of cattle, horses, and goods in general. The wide distribution of gifts to the Natives and the expensive and showy clothing given to Native spokespersons demonstrate a concerted effort to win the sympathies of Native groups from the French and to guarantee stability in the area. The Marqués de Aguayo very wisely clothed this overwhelming display of power and wealth with empowering ceremonies for the leaders, gift giving, protection, and promises of help in the wars against their enemies. The latter offer was particularly important for the Tejas groups, who were engaged in serious wars with the Chickasaw (French 1851: 68).

During 1721–1722, several convoys with large amounts of merchandise traveled between the Rio Grande, San Antonio, and east Texas. The traffic had never been so heavy. The disruption that such traffic of people and animals caused in the area is not known.

At the Rio Grande crossing, Aguayo was helped by *indios nadadores*. These individuals were either Natives who could swim or, more likely, Natives from the Nadadores area, who certainly could swim (Forrestal 1935: 4; Santos 1981: 25, 59n). Between the Rio Grande and the Guadalupe River, on the inbound (1721) and outbound (1722) legs of the trip, the party did not mention encountering any Native groups, nor did they see any buffalo. They did see deer and a great deal of small game. In San Antonio, Aguayo was visited by fifty Natives from the Ranchería Grande, who were accompanied by Juan Rodríguez, El Cuilón. The Spaniards saw many Natives in the area of San Antonio, but gave no information about them.

The Marqués was concerned about salt supplies. He was told about salt deposits west of San Antonio (?), and to the north near the Tejas country. He pursued both prospects with great diligence. In April 1721, he obtained a sample of salt from the salines west of San Antonio. The Natives had gathered the salt in January and had kept the sample since. From the Tejas salt deposits, located 15 leagues (39 miles) from the presidio, Aguayo obtained twenty-five mule-loads of salt (Forrestal 1935: 16, 55–56; Santos 1981: 31–32, 70).

Aguayo was also interested in establishing contact with the Apache. The soldiers had orders to be friendly and establish peace if and when they encountered any Apache. On the trip from San Antonio to east Texas, Aguayo left crosses along the way as a sign of the Spanish presence. The Apache, like the Spaniards, interpreted the cross as a sign of peace (Forrestal 1935: 19, 21, 24, 29, 43; Santos 1981: 34, 36, 39, 58). Not one Apache was encountered.

November 1720

Mules and other supplies were sent to San Antonio as part of the Aguayo expedition.

December 20, 1720

Aguayo and part of the entourage reached the Rio Grande.

1721

February 2

Sana couriers informed the Aguayo party at the Rio Grande of a large Native gathering taking place 30 leagues (78 miles) from San Antonio. The invitation was made by the French, who were to gather there with the Native groups. The couriers were sent by the Spanish commander in San Antonio to deliver the message (Forrestal 1935: 9).

February

After receiving the news of this meeting, Aguayo sent Lieutenant General Fernando Almazán with more than one hundred men to protect San Antonio (Forrestal 1935: 9).

? February

A Sana came to San Antonio to inform Juan Rodríguez that the Natives of Ranchería Grande and others had gone to meet with the French. The meeting was being held between the two branches of the Brazos de Dios above the Texas Road. The Natives at the meeting had many muskets and horses (Forrestal 1935: 10).

February 25

Juan Rodríguez returned from a fact-finding trip to San Antonio. He was sent by Captain García, who was stationed at San Antonio, to determine the location of the French and Native gathering. Juan Rodríguez had gone as far as Brazos de Dios, but had not been able to find his people of the Ranchería Grande (Forrestal 1935: 10).

March 23

The Marqués de Aguayo completed the crossing of the Rio Grande.

April 4

The Marqués arrived in San Antonio.

April 18

Captain Domingo Ramón, who was part of the Aguayo expedition, reported taking possession of Espiritu Santo Bay (Forrestal 1935: 17).

October 5

Truce between France and Spain.

November

Completion of the Presidio Nuestra Señora del Pilar de los Adaes.

1722

March 10

Mission S. Francisco Xavier de Najera was established.

May 25

The Aguayo expedition returned to Monclova from Texas.

In 1722–1723, there were several Apache attacks near San Antonio de Béjar and along the corridor between the Rio Grande and San Antonio. These raids were aimed principally at stealing horses and other goods from the Spanish. In August 1723, after some horses were stolen and a Spaniard killed, Captain Nicolás Flores led a punitive expedition of thirty men against the Apache. Flores traveled five days north from San Antonio and reached some hills (Almazan 1724a; Baldes 1724). Thirty-one days later, after covering 130 leagues (338 miles), he encountered an Apache *ranchería* with 200 warriors and an undetermined number of Apache. On September 24, the Spaniards engaged the Apache in a six-hour battle, killing thirty-four Apache, including their "leader," and capturing twenty women and children. The Spaniards also took a great deal of booty, including 120 horses and mules, saddles, bridles, knives, and spears. They returned to San Antonio in nineteen days by way of the modern San Gabriel River (Almazan 1724b; Baldes 1724a).

The trip northward took longer than necessary because the Spaniards were trying to locate the *ranchería* and avoid detection (Dunn 1911: 207–208). It is likely that the Apache *ranchería* was a bit over 100 leagues (260 miles) north of San Antonio and that the battle took place near Brownwood (Pecan Bayou). If Captain Flores traveled more to the northwest, the battle could have taken place in the San Sabá area.[2]

After the battle, peace negotiations were established through an Apache woman captive, who was given a horse and sent to her people. It can be assumed that the woman peacemaker did not return to the place where the battle was fought, since its occupants would not have remained there. She returned twenty-two days later accompanied by a spokesman and others. She should have reached her destination in no more than eleven days' travel. The male "leader" came to ascertain whether the Spanish peace offer was genuine. He offered Captain Flores a gold-tipped cane and declared that the Apache would hold council with the other five "leaders" to discuss the peace proposal (Aguayo 1725a; Almazan 1724b).

Reports from other sources indicated that these peace negotiations were a ploy to gain time and obtain the release of the Apache captured in battle. Thirty Apache arrived at Béjar in late December. Their spokesman reported that four of the "leaders" were interested in a peace agreement, but the fifth was not. The Apache asked for the release of their people, and the friars wanted to comply in order to gain their trust and goodwill. Captain Flores, however, did not consent. The tensions that developed between church and military continued, and ultimately resulted in the temporary removal from Béjar of Captain Flores (Blas 1724; Gonzales 1724).

The policy of using captives as hostages to force the Apache into peace agreements was suggested by the Marqués de Aguayo, and it became the standard in dealing with the Apache (Dunn 1911: 213–216). Enslaving Apache provided a labor force for the settlers, who could not use the mission Natives, but could enslave hostile Natives captured in military engagements. This policy would brand the Spanish-Apache relations forever.

1724–1725

Apache depredations continued throughout 1724 and 1725. In at least two cases in which Spaniards were killed, the Spanish authorities did not know whether the Apache were responsible for the attacks. Furthermore, when the attackers were designated as Apache, no specific Apache group was named in the attacks (Almazan 1724, 1724a; Baldes 1724; F. Menchaca 1724). The evidence from 1723 shows that there were five Apache groups under different "leaders" involved in attacks in Texas. These "leaders" consulted and recognized the authority of a Capitán Grande, without whose permission no expedition was undertaken, although the five "leaders" had a voice in decisions to make peace with the Spaniards in Texas (Dunn 1911: 216–217, 220, 221–222). No names were provided for these five groups and *no mention of the Lipan* was made at this time.

During 1723–1724, there were isolated attacks by the Apache against other Native groups that resulted in some deaths. Intimidation, thievery, and personal grievances seemed to have been the reasons for these attacks. There are, however, two known exceptions to this pattern: a major attack on the Sana that took place before January 1726, and another attack on the Pacuache at about the same time. The attack on the Sana drove them from their *rancherías,* but despite this, they did not enter a mission (Sevillano 1726). Early in January 1726, the Apache made a second attack on the Pacuache near the Nueces River. According to Fr. Sevillano, the Pacuache asked to join a mission for fear of the Apache (Sevillano 1726). Between 1725 and 1730, the Apache committed almost no warring acts that attracted the attention of the Spaniards. This lull in their warring activities against the Spaniards might have been due to increased engagements against other Native groups in Texas in order to consolidate Apache territorial control over the area. A similar pattern of Apache warfare appears to have occurred in the pueblos along the Rio Grande in New Mexico. A systematic study of their attacks may shed light on Apache military strategies.

1727

Late in 1727, Brigadier General Pedro de Rivera y Villalón began an inspection of the military facilities in Coahuila and Texas. He was to reassess the capabilities of the Spanish military and make recommendations for improving the location, organization, and particular needs of each military unit. The Brigadier was also to create maps and provide information about the environment and populations. Rivera provided little information relevant to the current study of Native Americans. He mentioned a Native pueblo near San Antonio where the Mesquite, Payaya, and Aguastaya groups were living, and he encountered buffalo in mid-August on the San Marcos River and on the Blanco Creek.

July 24

Brigadier Pedro de Rivera left Monclova for Texas.

August 1

The party reached the Presidio San Juan Bautista.

August 16

The party arrived at San Antonio de Béjar.

December 18

Brigadier Pedro de Rivera returned to San Juan Bautista on the Rio Grande.

1731

The abandoned missions of east Texas were moved to San Antonio. They became: Mission San Juan Capistrano, Mission Nuestra Señora de la Puríssima Concepción, and Mission San Francisco de la Espada.

March 9

Ten Canary Islands families arrived in San Antonio de Béjar to establish the Villa de San Fernando de Béjar.

1732

On December 9, Governor Bustillo y Zevallos, with a force of one hundred men, attacked a Native *ranchería,* killing more than two hundred people and capturing thirty women and children. This *ranchería* had Natives of four nations: Apaches; Ypandi, whom the Spaniards called Pelones (*a quien nosotros llamamos Pelones*); Yxandi; and Chenti (Bustillo y Zevallos 1732; Perez et al. 1732). According to declarations of the captive Native women, this was a small *ranchería* that included warriors of all the other *rancherías* and was composed of about four hundred tents and about eight hundred warriors ("ramos de las otras rancherías principales de sus naciones cuios ramos se componen de 400 tiendas de campaña y 800 indios de armas") (Bustillo y Zevallos 1732). In a real sense, this was a military contingent to wage war against the Spanish that was composed of warriors (two hundred warriors from each group?) from the different divisions of Apache.

The Spaniards learned that the Yxandi and Chenti (Almazan 1733) had joined the Apache and Ypandi to attack them ("se les juntan las nasiones llamadas Yxandi y Chenti tan numerosas como qualquiera de las otras"). The Apache women captured earlier stated that in the *ranchería* that was attacked[3] there were no Jumano, but that the Jumano were a very large (*numerossissima*) nation. They also stated that the largest *ranchería* was northward of the one attacked, that it was located about 140 leagues (364 miles) from the Presidio de Béjar, and that it was occupied only by the Ypandi (alias Pelones). The tents of this *ranchería,* which were not widely separated (*que no estaban retiradas unas de otras*), covered an area of about 4 leagues (10.4 miles) (Bustillo y Zevallos 1733). This information was confirmed by friendly Natives from the missions, including a Native named Asencio who saw the big *ranchería*[4] (Bustillo y Zevallos 1733; Perez et al. 1732).

The Spaniards' victory and rejoicing were well tempered by what they saw and the superior expertise of the warriors they encountered ("pues solo vendolos se podra creer el regime y compostura con que pelean") (Almazan 1733). The difference from Native attacks perpetrated before this time, and the prospect of the battles to come, led all the people in Béjar to request immediate action or they would remove their families to the Rio Grande (Perez et al. 1733).

In 1756, there was a series of inquiries to determine whether San Sabá was under the jurisdiction of Texas or of Coahuila. It was repeatedly stated that the jurisdiction of Coahuila extended to the Medina River 6 leagues (15.6 miles) south of San Antonio, and that the 1732 campaign against the Apache had taken place on the San Sabá River (Cepeda 1756; Morain 1756; Santa Cruz 1756).

The Lipan have always been considered as the focal point in the Spanish-Native relations after the 1700s. Their presence and influence before the 1730s, however, are not borne out by the archival records or by the type of warfare experienced by the Spanish. Furthermore, the other groups involved in this coalition, such as Apache, Yxandi, Chenti, and Jumano, were not, on the testimony of Apache Native women, either small in numbers or dependent on the Lipan.

If indeed the Apache (*sensu lato*) fought a decisive battle with the Comanche in 1723 (this chapter), which displaced the Apache from their former lands, one wonders what kind of military capabilities the Apache had before the battle with the Comanche, and what it took to defeat the Apache. This was the year of the first major Spanish campaigns made from San Antonio against the Apache. If the six-hour battle in which the Spanish engaged the Apache in September 1723 was fought immediately before or after the nine-hour battle pitched between the Apache and Comanche, the losses and devastation caused by either confrontation would have cropped the Apache military. The human and military losses from both conflicts would be sufficient to force the Apache into hiding to heal their wounds, literally and figuratively.

The appearance of the Lipan in the archival records in December 1732, after a lull in the Apache (as an all-inclusive term) warfare activity, as well as the qualitative and quantitative difference in organization, group membership, warfare tactics, and weaponry, implies that these groups jointly reassessed their situation vis-à-vis the Spaniards and probably other groups, such as the Comanche. They may have spent those months of perceived inactivity restructuring, making new alliances, accumulating and improving their weaponry, and likely aggregating smaller group units who could no longer make claims by force on their own.

It may be recalled that in 1683–1684 the Jumano were in the Concho River (Texas) area, slightly north and west of the San Sabá region, and that the Apache, their bitter enemies, had established a *ranchería* north of them, which greatly perturbed the Jumano. In 1731, the Jumano were still there, but in coalition with the Lipan (and others), and the Apache were now powerfully and forcefully entrenched in the area. It is clear that the Jumano had entered into a coalition with their former enemies, the Apache. It is not so clear whether the Jumano had become guests in their own home or were full-fledged members of a coalition of five groups: Apache, Ypandi (alias Pelones), Ysanti, Chenti, and Jumano.

The captured Apache women declared that all these nations were numerous and that there were several other *rancherías*. They stated that the Ypandi *ranchería* was the largest and had no admixture of groups, and that the Jumano were a very large group that joined the Apache to make war on the Spaniards ("se incorpora con la de los Apaches para venir a darnos guerra") (Bustillo y Zevallos 1732). The women also added, and the actions of their compatriots confirmed it, that the decisions over war and peace hinged on the Capitán Grande (Bustillo y Zevallos 1732). This evidence leads to the conclusion that the Jumano had followed the old adage: if you can't beat them, join them. The Jumano, however, had not become Jumano Apache, in the sense of having lost their group identity or having been absorbed by the Apache. It may have been advantageous for both groups to join forces.

When we encountered the Jumano in Coahuila in 1673, they were entering a coalition with the Bobole, the Gueiquesale, and others; when we encountered them through their spokesman, Juan Sabeata, in 1683, they were members of a coalition of thirty-six groups; and in 1731 they had become members of an Apache coalition. Not much had changed in the process except that this time the Jumano were allied with their former enemies. Times had changed.

While efforts to establish peace with these groups were under way, two more soldiers were killed by a group of Apache near the Presidio de Béjar. The disfigurement and mutilation of the bodies angered and horrified the Spaniards (Dunn 1911: 237). The ensuing panic brought about an increase in the garrison at Béjar and the appointment of Joseph de Urrutia as captain of the presidio (Perez et al. 1733).

Joseph de Urrutia entered Texas with Terán de los Rios in 1691. While on that expedition he suffered an accident (or so he reported) on the return trip and spent seven years among the Catujano, Too, Yeme, and one other nation. He stated that he remained in the *ranchería* of Captain Catujana for seven years, learned several Native languages, and participated in attacks against the Apache with other nations, including the Pelones[5] and the Jumane (Jumano). He expressed his surprise at the fact that the Jumano were now friendly with the Apache, since, at the time of his stay among the Natives (1691–1698, a time when Juan Sabeata was still the Jumano spokesperson), they had been enemies. He stated that, although it had been some time ago and some captains of the *rancherías* had very likely been killed in the interim, there would still be some older Natives whose opinions would carry considerable weight ("no obstante el largo que se ha passado y que en el precisamente habran muerto algunos capitanes de sus rancherías y no dejado de

quedar algunos que aunque viejos los yndios acen mucho aprecio de sus dictamenes")
(Thoribio Urrutia 1733). Urrutia's statement indicates that older Jumano warriors would
not easily accept the friendship with the Apache, and that such a switch in alliances may
have brought about considerable generational rifts among the Jumano. It also confirms
that the Jumano were not allied with the Apache before 1698.

1733–1739

Urrutia's appointment was based largely on the knowledge and experience he had acquired with the Natives, but whatever those capabilities were, they were not effectively
used to deal with the Apache and other groups threatening the Spanish settlements in
Coahuila, along the Rio Grande, and in San Antonio. The pattern of small raids against
supply convoys, horse herds, and mission Natives continued until the winter of 1739,
when Captain Urrutia finally undertook a punitive campaign against the Apache. According to Fr. Santa Ana, the campaign was little more than a slave-hunting expedition.
Testimony given in 1756 showed that Urrutia had attacked the Apache on the San Sabá
River (Dunn 1911: 250).

1740–1743

At his death, Joseph Urrutia was replaced by his son Thoribio Urrutia. In November
1741, Thoribio was visited by Cuero de Coyote, an Ypandi captain, who expressed the
wish to settle on the margins of the Guadalupe River about 25 leagues (65 miles) from
San Antonio. He stated that his people needed protection from some Natives, whom
they believed to be the Tejas, who were attacking them with firearms (T. Urrutia 1741). In
1742, Thoribio requested permission to conduct several punitive campaigns against the
Apache. One of the reasons used to convince his superiors of the value of these campaigns
was the existence of mineral deposits in the San Sabá area (Dunn 1911: 251–251).

1743

In 1743, Fr. Benito Fernandez de Santa Ana proposed the establishment of missions for
the Apache in their own lands. Fr. Santa Ana commented that the Apache were under
increased pressure from the Comanche. The Pelones (Ypandi) had been displaced from
their lands by the Comanche in a very fierce battle (the battle reported earlier or another one?). Fr. Santa Ana pointed to the potential wealth that could be obtained from
exploring the rich minerals said to exist in Apache territory (Dunn 1911: 255).

1745

In May 1745, Fr. Santa Ana wrote to the Viceroy, reaffirming the convenience of the opportunity to establish missions for the Apache. He stated that the Ypandi had only 166
warriors and the Natagé 100. He suggested the location of presidios on the Pedernales,
Salado, and Colorado rivers (Dunn 1911: 250). In April 1745, Thoribio Urrutia made a

punitive expedition against the Apache. About 80 leagues (208 miles) north and east of San Antonio the Spaniards found a *ranchería* with Ypandi and Natagé individuals. Most warriors were out hunting, and the Spanish had little trouble in capturing women and children (Dunn 1911: 251). This campaign, which later was said to have been in the San Sabá area, was little more than another slave-hunting expedition. The Ypandi and Natagé retaliated by attacking the Presidio de San Antonio on June 30. At this time the Ypandi "chief" was a Natagé, and it is clear that both groups were allied. This attack was unusual in that it involved 350 individuals, and included women and children.

In October, the "chief" of the Ypandi requested a mission and a presidio, or a mission without a presidio, for his people. It appears that this was not his first request for a mission (Dunn 1911: 255, 266). The Natagé were consistently against the notion of settling in a mission; such reluctance apparently resulted from their negative experiences in New Mexico. This request by a Lipan "chief" may indicate that the two groups held different positions on the best course of action, and may have parted company.

1746

In January 1746, the wife of an Apache "chief" visited Fr. Santa Ana with a request for missions. Three days later a Native girl from the Ranchería Grande, who had been captured by the Apache, was sent to the friars in San Antonio to request a mission and a presidio. The girl stated that the Natagé were opposed to this plan (Dunn 1911: 251–253). Also in January, four captains of the Yojuane, Deadoze, Mayeye, and Ranchería Grande came to Mission Valero to ask that missions be established for them in their lands between the presidios of San Antonio and Los Adaes (Guemes y Horcasistas 1747a; Valcarcel 1755).

In September the Coahuila governor, Don Pedro Rábago y Therán, inspected the missions and military installations in Coahuila. The territory of Coahuila was defined as beginning about 250 leagues (650 miles) north of the Viceroyal Court in Mexico and extending for another 114 leagues (296.4 miles) to the limits of the Rio Medina, where the province of Nuevas Philipinas, or Texas, started ("la que comienza como a docientas y cinquenta leguas al Norte de esta Corte de Mexico, y se alarga por otras ciento y catorze hasta el Rio de Medina en que remata dicha Provincia de Nueva Estremadura, ô Cohaguila y que sigue nuestra ultima Provincia de Nuevas Philipinas ô Tejas") (Rábago y Therán 1746). According to this report, there were nine missions in Coahuila: seven under the jurisdiction of Guadalajara (Xalisco Province) and two under the jurisdiction of the Queretaro brothers. The latter two were the missions of San Juan Bautista and San Bernardo, located on the banks of the Rio Grande.

The report provides important demographic information and details on the settlements and development in the area around the Rio Grande and between the town of Monclova and the Rio Grande. Mission S. N. de Jesus de Peyotes had 66 Natives, Mission Vissaron had 213 Natives (106 couples) of various groups, Mission San Bernardo had 363 Natives, and Mission San Juan Bautista had 507 (or 511) Natives, of whom 146 were new Pampoa converts. There were some Tilijae (13?), but most of the other Natives had fled to the hills. Therán requested a campaign to retrieve those Natives.

The Presidio de San Juan Bautista on the Rio Grande had thirty-two soldiers, and another thirty settlers lived under the protection of the presidio, most of them in *xacales*. The living conditions near the presidio were described as very poor: the settlers had no gardens and no proper housing. The lack of lands to cultivate was attributed to the fact that the missions held the best lands, leaving nothing for the Spanish settlers. There were some exceptions, and their ranches were located at distances of 4, 6, and 8 leagues (respectively 10.4, 15.6, and 20.8 miles) from the Presidio de San Juan Bautista. Rábago y Therán stressed the problems with Native attacks and proposed a concerted campaign to root out the problem. There had been attempts to settle the fertile lands of the San Rodrigo and San Diego rivers. The settlers were willing to outfit themselves and participate in campaigns against the Natives, provided they were given the spoils obtained in battle as well as the children of rebellious groups captured during the campaigns. The opinion of the Real Audiencia was favorable to Therán's proposals, and the Viceroy approved the request (Guemes y Horcasitas 1747).

Westward, between the Presidio de San Juan Bautista and the town of Monclova, there were some small, isolated settlements with about 22 people, most of them armed. Mission San Philipe Valladares had 52 Natives; Mission San Bernardino de la Candela had 65 Natives, and at the nearby Tlaxcaltecan pueblo of Nuestra Señora de Guadalupe there were 207 persons representing 43 Tlaxcaltecan families. There were several important haciendas, ranches, and farms around the area. The pueblo of Nueva Tlaxcala had 223 people representing 49 families, and the Mission of San Miguel de Aguayo had 113 Natives. Mission Santa Rosa de Nadadores had only 7 Natives, while the nearby Tlaxcaltecan pueblo of N. Señora de la Victoria had 147 people. At that time some 146 Natives, who had fled Mission Dolores de Punta de Lampazos, had been placed at the pueblo of N.S. de la Victoria. The Viceroy ordered that they be remanded to Punta de Lampazos. Mission San Buenaventura had 34 Native people, but only 11 warriors.

Don Pedro reported that there were about 1,636 Natives in the nine missions and 577 Tlaxcaltecans. He requested that the nine missions be consolidated into five: Santiago de Valladares and San Bernardino de la Candela were to be incorporated, as were Santa Rosa de Nadadores and San Buenaventura. The Fiscal and the Viceroy concurred with the program and welcomed the savings to the Crown. Don Pedro was ordered by the Viceroy to beseech the local settlers to develop their lands, while the military and the church were ordered to give all possible assistance to the settlers for that purpose (Guemes y Horcasitas 1747; see also Chapter 3).

1746–1749

In 1746, the process to establish the San Xavier missions near modern Rockdale got under way, but it was not until late 1748 or early 1749 that the missions were established. During the intervening three years the Native groups congregated in the area at various times, expecting the missions to be built. The delays and controversies that surrounded the foundation of the missions gave the enterprise a rocky start. As soon as they were established, Apache groups began harassing the residents (Thoribio Urrutia 1747). One of the founders of these missions was Fr. Alonso Giraldo de Terreros, who became the central figure in the project to found the Apache mission at San Sabá. The missions at Rockdale were eventually reestablished for the Apache in the San Sabá and Nueces Rivers.

May 7, 1748

Founding of N. Señora de los Dolores del Río San Xavier.

1749

Missions S. Ildefonso and Candelaria established on the San Gabriel River.

In 1748 and 1749, at least three other punitive expeditions were made against the Apache. The last one took place in March 1749. The *ranchería* attacked had about four hundred people, but most warriors were out hunting on the Guadalupe River, and the Spaniards easily captured thirty men, ninety women, and forty-seven children. After these last punitive campaigns, Apache groups requested the establishment of missions (Auditor 1750; Dolores 1749). Also in 1749, some Apache groups suffered a smallpox epidemic, which added much to their distress (Santa Ana 1750).

In April, a new round of peace initiatives began. In August, four "chiefs" (two Ypandi and two Natagé), plus one hundred people from each group, declared peace. On August 19, after most of the captives were released, a big feast with elaborate ceremonies was prepared and a peace treaty was signed. Everybody at San Antonio agreed that this time, peace would last (Dunn 1911: 260–262).

1751

A military presidio was established on the San Gabriel River.

1752

The San Xavier Mission on the San Gabriel River was abandoned by the Natives.

1753

In July, Fr. Miguel de Aranda reported to his superior, Fr. Mariano de los Dolores, on a trip he made to the Apache lands to see if they were suitable for missions. He traveled without a military escort to the San Sabá River area, where he visited one Apache *ranchería* with about fifty-eight people and their captain. He was well received by the Apache and was told that most people were to the north hunting buffalo, while others were toward the Rio Grande (Aranda 1753). On August 5, Spaniards from San Antonio began exploring the mines at San Sabá: they were guided by the Apache. No valuable ore was discovered, but prospecting continued (Patten 1970: 228).

1755

On January 12, Thoribio Urrutia reported that, from 1749 to 1755, the Spanish had no troubles with the Apache. On most occasions when cattle or horses were stolen, it was sufficient to inform the Apache captains and the animals were promptly returned ("savidores que han sido los capitanes, las mas han debuelto") (Thoribio Urrutia 1755). This happened not only at San Antonio, but also at San Juan Bautista on the Rio Grande. During this period the Apache had been asking for a mission, and they wanted Spaniards to settle in their lands.

On January 25, Don Pedro de Rábago y Therán inspected the Apache lands to make a decision about their request for missions. On the return trip to Béjar, he found an Apache *ranchería* with 467 people, headed by Captain Chiquito, who was going to San Sabá. The *ranchería* was located at a spring whose waters ran westward. Therán told them the reason for his trip, and they agreed to gather at the missions. At the Puerto Viejo, 8 leagues (20.8 miles) north of San Antonio, Therán found another Apache *ranchería* with more than a hundred people, headed by Captain Pintas. Captain Pintas said that they had been waiting for Don Pedro's return and expressed his desire to have a mission in their lands. Captain Pintas (or Pintos) mentioned that ten other Apache captains, with large groups of people, also were interested in joining the missions. These other groups were, at that moment, gathered at the headwaters of the Río Florido (*cabezeras de el Rio florido*) (Rábago y Therán 1755).

On January 31, Therán informed the Viceroy about his trip and stated that the Río Florido (Concho) was 30 leagues (78 miles) northwest of the San Sabá River. He said that the groups mentioned by Captain Pintas, who were living on the headwaters of the Concho River, were at the boundary of the large Comanche nation to prevent their movement into Apache lands. Therán commented that the Apache were divided into many groups with a variety of names, but all were the same nation and spoke the same language (Rábago y Therán 1755a).

October 1

In a report about the missions on the San Gabriel River it was stated that Mission San Ildefonso was deserted and Mission San Xavier had one friar ministering to 70 people, mostly Ervipiame and Mayeye. The 127 Coco who had been at Mission Candelaria had left without motive or warning (Andreu 1755).

REFLECTIONS

The Spanish settlement in Texas in the 1700s resulted from the logical expansion of the frontier and from the presence of the French in east Texas and Louisiana. Colonial policy was a result and an extension of European continental policy. What is often lost in the analysis of the confrontation between the European powers and the colonial expression of their policies in New Spain is that the Spanish knew about the French presence in Texas because of the information provided by Native Americans. It is obvious that the Native information system, from which the Spaniards benefited, had been in operation long before the arrival of Europeans. These information networks became enhanced with the presence of the foreigners, but they were not a consequence of their arrival.

The power plays between France and Spain, which culminated in the ostentatious displays of the Marqués de Aguayo, asserted Spanish might, but made the Spanish conspicuous. While other Native groups profited from and were impressed by Spanish largesse, the Apache stuck arrow shafts with red flags in the soil of San Antonio as a declaration of war. This act, among many others, drew the battle lines between Apache groups and Spaniards. It also put on notice, if any was needed, other Native groups: either they were with the Apache or they were against them.

The Apache were the determinant factor that rearranged the human landscape in Texas in the 1700s. The presence of Apache groups forced the Spaniards into a permanent state of alert, slowly eroding their resources and resistance. The Apache also brought into the fold of the mission system many groups who would have preferred not to choose between two evils. The bureaucratic lag that always afflicted empires prevented the church from fully capitalizing on this mixed blessing. The debacle of the San Xavier missions is a good example of this process. The groups interested in entering those missions got weary of waiting. By the time the missions were actually operating, the conditions that made entrance into them desirable no longer existed. Too little, too late.

There were temporary Native pockets of resistance, to be sure. Some groups sought shelter under the Caddoan umbrella, while others sought protection in numbers, such as the groups in the Ranchería Grande. But they had to make many cultural compromises, and their survival was wrestled from cultural impoverishment. On the other hand, the Apache groups made too many enemies and too few friends. Those enemies, pressed by changing conditions in the northern plains, followed the Apache into Texas territory. This circumstance forced the Apache into an unwanted and uneasy peace with the Spaniards. It was again the choice of the lesser evil.

Apache groups, particularly the Lipan after the 1730s, effectively remodeled the Native demographics in Texas. There is little doubt that such was the case. But there is an insidious danger in this assessment. The historical visibility of Apache groups and the Spanish preoccupation with them so overshadows the pedestrian presence of other Native groups that, by the 1760s, one can barely discern their existence. They were in the missions or in the fold of other Native groups whose status and numbers afforded protection.

As for the Apache groups, it took concerted military action and a change in perspective and policies to curb their influence. These changes stemmed from the Marqués de Rubi's actions and the military campaigns that issued from his recommendations, chiefly the Spanish policy that advocated destruction by proxy. The Spanish adopted and fostered a policy of mutual Native destruction: the Comanche and the northern groups would be the agents of Apache annihilation, and in the process would destroy themselves.

SEVEN

The Price of Peace:

FRIENDS, FOES, AND FRONTIERS

SETTING THE STAGE

Since the establishment of the settlements and missions at San Antonio the Spaniards had been at odds with the Apache. In the first two decades of the 1700s, the Spanish showed their incomprehension of the Apache social and political intricacies by using the all-inclusive term *Apache*. During the military campaigns of the 1720s against Apache groups, the Spaniards acquired little information about the nation that would preoccupy them for decades to come.

In the campaigns of the 1730s, the Spanish began to distinguish particular Apache groups, such as the Ypandi, Natagé, Ysandi, and Chenti, but because they continued to mix Apache group names with European descriptive appellations, the confusion continued (and still continues). Until the mid-1700s, Apache groups did not approach the Spaniards to ask for peace: it was almost always the Spaniards who made the first move, by sending captives, mostly women, to begin the negotiating process.

Finally, in the 1740s Apache groups, out of need, requested and accepted Spanish military protection. Pinched by the Ute and Comanche from the north and west, and the Pawnee, Caddo, Wichita, and others from the north and east, they undertook a southward creep as their sole solution. The presence and trade in guns and horses initiated and fostered by the English, French, and Spanish changed the rules of engagement and diminished the advantage of the Apache vis-à-vis the northern groups. Skill and experience were no longer enough: to win, one had to acquire horses and guns.

The campaigns of the 1730s taught the Spaniards that these Apache groups and their allies, like the Jumano, were a superior military foe. They were determined, informed, organized, and well armed, and their war tactics stunned the Spaniards. But the Apache did not use firearms (Almazan 1733), which forced them to wage battles that balanced their unwillingness to sustain heavy losses with their desire for clear-cut victories. The defensive weapons the Apache had developed, such as leather breastplates and horse body armor, were effective against traditional Native weapons, but were found lacking against bullets. More than once the Spanish commented that only with firearms could they defeat the Apache. The horse was treated as a weapon and as a warrior, in the sense that the animal was carefully shielded from injury. On the other hand, the relative superiority of the northern groups and the Comanche resided in their ownership of and skill with firearms. For the Spaniards, that was the danger of the future.

After the peace agreement with the Spanish in 1749, some Apache groups in Texas and Coahuila initiated talks to establish missions. In September 1749, a party of Apache came to San Antonio to ask for a mission in that town. That request was unacceptable, since most other Native populations viewed the Apache as their most formidable foe. The friars proposed a plan to settle the Apache on the Guadalupe River, or, alternatively, to move the San Antonio presidio to the Pedernales River. By September 1750 both plans had been disapproved. Only much later would firm plans be made and resources appropriated for the establishment of Apache missions.

None of the Apache missions was successful, because for the Apache, missions were temporary and expedient solutions to a problem. The Apache were not fickle; they were politicians. They played the game that was proposed to them to their best advantage.

THE APACHE MISSION OF SAN LORENZO IN COAHUILA

In 1750, an Apache "chief" by the name of Pastellano visited S. Juan Bautista on the Rio Grande to ask for a mission. In 1754, Fr. Alonzo Giraldo de Terreros was the president for the missions of the Rio Grande and the minister at S. Juan Bautista. In June 1754, the Natagé, Síbola, and Tucubante captains, with about nine hundred of their people, asked Fr. Terreros for a mission. At the time, these groups were camped on both sides of the Rio Grande. The site chosen for the mission, and approved by the Apache, was 18 leagues (46.8 miles) west of the Presidio de S. Juan Bautista and 2 leagues (5.2 miles) from the town of S. Fernando de Austria. On December 21, 1754, two thousand Apache Natives held a council and took formal possession of the Pueblo de San Lorenzo. Fr. Terreros supervised the construction of the buildings and acequia, and by early March 1754, fifty-two Apache were residing in the area. By late March the number had increased to eighty-three. Three Apache captains were among the earliest residents: El Gordo, El de Godo, and Bigotes (Dunn 1912: 198–199). The number of Apache present at the possession ceremonies, versus the number that remained at the mission, should have constituted a warning to the friars.

When things were running smoothly, Fr. Terreros left the mission in charge of Fr. Martin García, who was well acquainted with Apache groups. Fr. García commented that these Natives were the same he had encountered at San Antonio, where he had been since 1749. In June 1755, Fr. Felix Gutierrez Varona was assigned to the mission (Dunn 1912: 199–200). The growing displeasure of the Natives with the mission became apparent, and on October 4, they burned the mission buildings and left, never to return.

The abandonment of missions by Native groups is often attributed to their fickleness; their self-interest; their wish for gifts, food, and temporary protection from their conflicts with other groups; and certainly their wish to return to their "evil ways." That is the understandable rhetoric of the manuscripts of the time, but it is also the view of several scholars who researched this material. No doubt some such motives were behind the requests for missions, but such requests were almost always acted upon several years after the initial request. Native peoples got tired of waiting, and the particular circumstances or consensus that existed at any one point among members of a group often had ceased to exist by the time the mission was founded. The decision-making processes of the Spanish colonial bureaucracy could not be fathomed by Native peoples and were not even understood by the Spanish settlers.

It also appears that, for the Apache, asking for a mission was simply asking for refuge and did not entail their acceptance of a set of rules and a mode of living that implied permanence. When the circumstances that prompted the request changed, or if the demands on their freedom were too stringent, they voted with their feet. They did the same among their own groups; why should it be any different with the friars?

THE APACHE MISSION OF SANTA CRUZ DE SAN SABÁ AND THE PRESIDIO SAN LUIS DE LAS AMARILLAS

The abandonment of the missions of San Xavier at Rockdale (Chapter 6) made the presidio established in the area a considerable and unnecessary expense. On February 27, 1756, the Junta General met in Mexico City to decide on the establishment of missions for the Apache and on what to do about the soldiers stationed at San Xavier. The Junta decided that a mission should be established for the Apache in the San Sabá area. The military garrison of San Xavier would be transferred to that area and increased to one hundred men (Dunn 1914: 385). The missionaries assigned to San Xavier would move to San Sabá, and the Natives remaining at the San Xavier missions were to be distributed among the missions of San Antonio. The site of San Sabá was explicitly chosen because it was thought that Apache groups would adapt better if they were living in a territory they considered their own. Also, their presence would check the southward movement of the northern groups and act as a buffer to San Antonio. But there were other factors at work, the principal one being the lure of the potential mineral wealth of the area called Los Almagres (Dunn 1914: 386–387).

In November 1755, Captain Rábago y Therán ordered Lieutenant Bernardo de Miranda y Flores to inspect the area called Los Almagres for its mineral potential. On February 17, 1756, Miranda left San Antonio for the Almagre region west of San Sabá. He returned on March 10. Miranda collected soil samples to be assayed by Manuel Aldaco, a mining expert. Aldaco declared the sample too small for a reliable evaluation, but he was not impressed by the results of the assay (Patten 1970: 230). Nevertheless, he contacted Don Pedro Romero de Terreros, a very wealthy man, owner of the mines at Pachuca and Real del Monte, and cousin of Fr. Alonso Giraldo de Terreros, who was then president of the Texas missions and founder of the short-lived Apache mission in Coahuila.

Don Pedro de Terreros offered to bear the cost of the establishment of missions for the Apache for a period of three years. His conditions were simple: the missions were to be located in the territory north of the Rio Grande, where the Apache lived; his cousin was

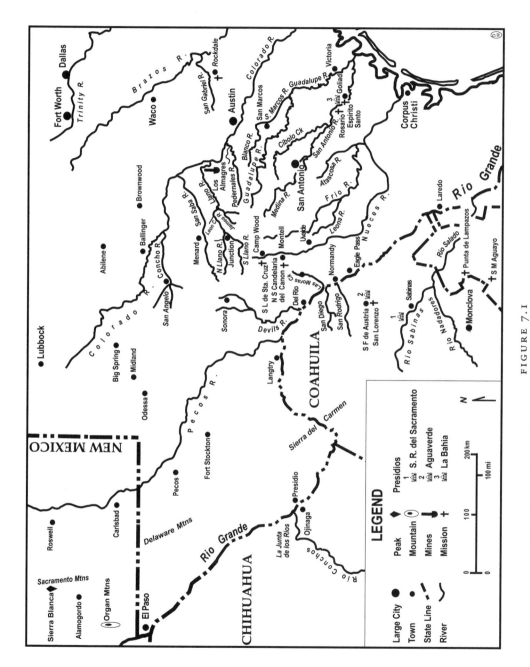

FIGURE 7.1

Map showing the Apache missions and other important places mentioned in the text.

to be in charge of the missions; and the missionaries were to be drawn from the College of Santa Cruz de Queretero and from the College of San Fernando in Mexico City. On August 24, the Junta revised its plans, accepting the gift of Don Pedro Terreros (Dunn 1911: 387; Patten 1970: 231). Whether or not such a generous gift was motivated by the potential gain to Don Pedro de Terreros, it did facilitate both the establishment of the mission for the Apache and the exploration of the mineral region of Los Almagres.

In September 1756, Don Diego Ortiz de Parrilla, who had been appointed commander of the Presidio de las Amarillas, received instructions for the founding of both the mission and the presidio. However, late in 1755, Captain Rábago had removed the garrison of San Xavier presidio to the San Marcos River without asking permission (Dunn 1914: 388–389). There is no good explanation for this move, except for the possibility that mining prospectors in the Llano area needed military protection. The San Marcos post was much closer to Los Almagres and could provide speedier relief for miners than could San Antonio.

On September 4, 1756, Fr. Terreros received his official appointment. The other religious appointees were Fr. Joachin de Baños and Fr. Diego Ximenes from the College of Santa Cruz de Queretero, and Fr. Joseph Santiesteban and Fr. Juan Andres from the College of S. Fernando. Nine Tlaxcaltecan families moved from Saltillo to help with the establishment of the Apache mission. Early in 1757, messengers were dispatched to the Apache to invite them to meet the priests who would be working with them. In February or March, two Lipan chiefs responded to the summons. They said that the Natagé, Mescalero, Pelones, Come Nopales, and Come Caballos were not able to come because they were too far away, but they promised to assemble at San Sabá (Dunn 1914: 391).

Meanwhile, serious conflicts had developed among the friars, and between the friars and the military. These conflicts delayed the establishment of the mission and almost blocked the whole project. Captain Parrilla, who had serious misgivings about the project, continued to postpone his move to San Sabá. One of the reasons alleged for this delay was the winter weather. In March 1757, Parrilla moved cattle, supplies, troops, priests, and the Tlaxcaltecan families to the San Marcos River. It is unclear why he did so, or what kind of facilities they possessed at this post to accommodate such a large group of people and animals. In April 1757, Captain Parrilla started the move to San Sabá, but instead of proceeding from San Marcos to the Colorado and then to San Sabá, he came back to San Antonio. From there he went to San Sabá, but left many of the supplies at the San Marcos post. Parrilla continued to harbor serious doubts about the project and wanted to hedge his bets. Fr. Terreros and Fr. Santissima Trenidad, however, were sure that the delays and unnecessary moves were designed to waste the money of Don Pedro de Terreros (Dunn 1914: 395–396; Hindes et al. 1995: 82–83).

On April 18, 1757, they arrived at the San Sabá location near the modern town of Menard, but work on the missions and presidio did not start until midsummer (Hindes et al. 1995: 82). The missions were to be placed on the south bank of the San Sabá River, while the presidio was to be located on the north bank. It was decided to postpone the building of the second mission until the Apache had begun to congregate. In May, Captain Parrilla had the rest of the supplies brought from San Marcos. By late summer the friars were ready to receive the Apache groups. But no Natives were in sight.

Fr. Varela, stationed at San Antonio, was told to contact the Apache and to convince them to congregate at San Sabá. In May, Fr. Varela went to San Marcos and learned that an Apache woman had reported that the Tejas had attacked her group on the Colorado River (Dunn 1914: 398). This was buffalo hunting season, and it is likely that the attack occurred over buffalo hunting rights and disputed boundaries. The evidence shows that at least some Apache groups advertised their friendly relationship with the Spaniards by having Spanish soldiers accompany them on buffalo hunts.

At about the same time, the Lipan "chief" El Chico visited San Antonio and promised Fr. Mariano de los Dolores to assemble at San Sabá. Word was sent to other groups for the same purpose, and in June the Lipan began to arrive at San Sabá from the south. During the summer months, three thousand Apache gathered near the mission with a great number of horses and mules (Dunn 1914: 398). Wooed by the missionaries with gifts and food, they stayed for a short while, but made it clear they were on their buffalo hunt and were going on a campaign against their northern enemies. Afterward, some of them declared that they were willing to return to San Sabá. While the Lipan "chief" El Chico and others were inclined to return, "Chief" Casablanca insisted on waging a campaign against the Comanche and the Tejas to avenge the attack they recently had made against an Apache group on the Colorado. It is possible that "Chief" Casablanca was a Natagé, or belonged to a group connected with the Natagé, since the Natagé were always opposed to mission life.

The Apache asked the Spanish soldiers to accompany them on the buffalo hunt, and the Spanish complied (Dunn 1914: 399). This was a clear miscalculation on the part of the Spanish, who should have realized that all the enemies of the Apache, including the Tejas, would understand this as an affront. Not only would the soldiers be perceived as protecting the Apache against their enemies (who in some cases were friends of the Spanish), but it also amounted to a declaration of friendship between Spanish and Apache. Such a symbolic act, after the recent attack by the Tejas on the Apache, had to elicit a negative response. At issue is the assumption of the Spaniards that they could be friends with everyone regardless of Native internal enmities, as well as the political arrogance of making new alliances without informing former allies, especially when the new alliances were made with their bitter enemies. Such behavior would not be tolerated in any political or military setting; why would it be countenanced by Native Americans?

About one month after the military abandoned the post at San Marcos, on June 30, 1757, Parrilla wrote to the Viceroy expressing his doubts about the San Sabá project and asking to move the presidio to the Llano River (Chanas River). He proposed to move the full garrison of one hundred men to the Llano to provide protection for the mines at Los Almagres (Dunn 1914: 399–340). That move would have left the friars without military protection. This is one of the reasons I assume that the military post on the San Marcos was manned primarily in order to protect the prospectors. The Viceroy, however, did not accept Captain Parrilla's proposal.

In July, the Lipan "chief" El Chico arrived at the San Sabá mission loaded with buffalo meat, but the group continued its journey southward. The Queretero friars harbored no illusions about the prospects for the mission. The first to leave was Fr. Varela, soon followed by Fr. Baños and Fr. Ximenes. Three friars remained at San Sabá: Fr. Alonzo Terreros, Fr. Santiesteban, and Fr. Santisima Trenidad.

During the fall and winter of 1757, Apache groups visited the mission, but they did not stay. The presidio had a large population of military and civilians (three to four hundred people), but the mission had only the friars and a few servants. There were reports that the Comanche were on the warpath, and Apache spies let it be known that the Norteños were assembling for a move on San Sabá. It was said that the force being gathered was large and that Apache groups did not trust the protection of the Spaniards. These reasons led the Apache to move southward (Dunn 1914: 402). At this time, the appellative *Norteños* designated an unknown number of groups from the north.

In January 1758, Fr. Santisima Trenidad left San Sabá on church business and Fr. Miguel de Molina arrived from the College of San Fernando. On March 2, 1758, a raid was made on the horse herd. Sixty-two horses were stolen. The soldiers gave pursuit without success and returned to report that there were Natives all over the countryside. On March 9, six prospectors were attacked on the Pedernales: three soldiers, two servants, and Don Joseph de Guzman, who later would deliver to Parrilla ore samples for testing in Monclova (Nathan and Simpson 1959: 51, 58–59, 145). All these individuals managed to escape safely to the presidio. This is the other reason why I believe the San Marcos post to have been important for individuals mining in the area. The mention of this attack leaves no doubt that whatever the assay results demonstrated, the lure of the mineral potential of the region continued to attract the Spanish.

Parrilla tried several times to convince the friars to seek refuge in the presidio, but they refused. After sunrise on the morning of March 16, 1758, a large body of Native Americans attacked the mission of San Sabá and the Presidio de las Amarillas. The attack and the siege lasted all through the day and night, and the attackers set fire to the mission, destroying it. Ten people were killed in the attack, including Fr. Terreros and Fr. Santisima Trenidad. The presidial compound suffered little damage.

The attack at San Sabá has been described elsewhere in great detail (see, e.g., Dunn 1914; Gilmore 1967; Nathan and Simpson 1959; Tunnell and Newcomb 1969). There is little that can be added to the description of the sequence of events. My intention is to focus on some of the occurrences and see what can be learned about the Native groups involved in the event.

The first point to be made is that there was ample warning prior to the attack. The raid on the horse herd and the attack on the prospectors gave two weeks' notice to the Spaniards at San Sabá. The officers and friars at San Sabá were experienced men who had an obligation to read the symbolic messages delivered to them, and not to expose themselves and others to danger by disregarding the warnings of Native Americans. I suggest that the Native groups involved in the attack expected the Spaniards to react to the warnings. Their failure to do so may have been interpreted as a challenge, an act of arrogance.

The reports say that, not being able to enter the mission compound, the Natives, in broken Spanish, said they were coming as friends. They were very well armed, displaying unmistakable war paint and attire, and had been discharging their firearms and attacking people outside the compound. It is incomprehensible that their acts would have been interpreted as friendly. Corporal Asencio Cadena peered through the boards of the stockade and saw several people he recognized as Tejas, Vidae, Tancague, and members of other northern groups he had been associated with. Other reports say that there were also Comanche and Yojuane, as well as other groups from east Texas. Among the leaders present and identified were a Comanche dressed in a French uniform and a Tejas captain. These were the same men later described as terrifying in their battle array, wielding firearms, sabers, and spears. And yet Cadena told Fr. Terreros that the Natives meant no harm. Apart from their battle attire and hostile acts, this was a group of an estimated 1,500 to 2,000 people. Of these, about a thousand had firearms.

Once the friars and others were out in the open, the Natives opened the gate and crowded the patio. At first the Natives greeted the friars in a friendly manner, and the friars distributed gifts to them. The Natives proceeded to raid the compound by taking food, clothing, and horses. This raid appears to have had two purposes: to locate any Apache and to plunder. A Tejas leader asked Fr. Terreros for horses. When he was told the mission did not have any more than those already taken, the Tejas asked for a letter in order that he could go to the presidio to get horses. Amid this confusion Fr. Terreros had a conversation with other Tejas Natives about their country. The Tejas assured him they did not wish to harm the Spaniards and were only looking for the Apache who had killed some of their people. This statement confirms that sometime in June or July the Apache groups who had been at San Sabá, particularly Casablanca and El Chico (Natagé and Lipan), had attacked the Tejas who were friends of the Spaniards. Since the Spaniards were shielding the Apache, and even escorting them to the buffalo hunt, what were the Tejas to make of the situation?

When the Tejas leader returned, saying he had not been able to enter the presidio and three of his warriors had been fired upon by the soldiers, Fr. Terreros offered to accompany him to the presidio to gain admittance. When Fr. Terreros got ready to leave, he could not find the Tejas leader. With more than 1,500 armed warriors of different groups outside the gates, the friar rode, unaccompanied by any of the leaders of the attacking group, toward the gate of the stockade to exit. It seems extremely likely that the warriors on the outside were not aware of the reason for the friar's departure; when they saw that he was leaving with a soldier, a shot was fired and the friar was killed. This act unleashed the violent acts that followed and probably made them inevitable.

If the reports are correct, the injured party was the Tejas. To put together the war party the Tejas had made a commitment to battle, which was plainly stated in their attire and weaponry. Even if the Tejas had been willing to depart empty-handed, it is unlikely that their allies would have been. They were unable to capture either Apache or horses, but their investment in the enterprise needed a satisfactory and warlike outcome. The mission, the symbolic refuge of the Apache, was destroyed, and two friars paid for their foolhardy zeal with their lives.

If one goes through the various letters and depositions about the attack, it is noticeable that the first reports of the occurrence, before any official depositions were made, attributed the attack to the Comanche or the Apache (Nathan and Simpson 1959: 15, 19). The testimonies from the witnesses of the attack show, without exception, that the Tejas, Comanche, Tanague, Vidae, Yojuane, and others were the groups responsible for the attack (Nathan and Simpson 1959: 44, 47, 54, 59, 66, 69, 74, 85, 128). Although the Tejas are continually mentioned in the record as participants in the attack, not a word is said about punishing them. Later, when the Lipan were attacked at the missions of San Lorenzo and Candelaria on the Nueces River, the Tejas were said to be involved, but again the Spanish did not comment on their involvement. It appears that the one group (taken as a collective) that the Spanish did not wish to antagonize was the Tejas, and the Tejas knew it.

There was no perfidy in the attack. The intentions of the Native Americans were clearly displayed: they were attacking the allies of their enemy, the Apache. Furthermore, the Apache had advertised their friendship with the Spaniards by way of the buffalo hunts, and the Spaniards had consented, by commission, to that advertisement. I do not wish to make light of a very serious and unfortunate incident, but the acts of the Spaniards, as well intentioned as they might have been, were completely contrary to the canons of war. The soldiers and the friars at the mission let the attackers in; they did not use force to enter. These were warriors, not choirboys. It is easy to see how the trust of the friars was misperceived as less than astute behavior, or worse yet, as a dare. Quite possibly the outcome of this event would have been the same whether the friars had let the warring Natives into the compound or not. The attack was meant to deliver a message, and it did. Seven years later a Taguaya "chief" stated that he "was unwilling to remain at peace with the Spaniards at San Sabá because they aided his mortal enemies, the Apaches" (Dunn 1914: 413).

During the battle and afterward, help was slow in coming, and that which came was ineffective or too late. Although the Spanish authorities and the friars planned to rebuild and maintain the mission at San Sabá, the Apache could not be convinced to settle in the area. The mission was abandoned and never reoccupied. The Presidio de las Amarillas remained in the area even though Captain Parrilla continued to suggest that it should be moved to the Llano River to protect prospectors in the area (Allen 1939: 55; Nathan and Simpson 1959: 144–150).

After the attack the Crown made inquiries to determine the extent of the French involvement in the San Sabá affair and the provenance of the weaponry used by the attackers. Testimony revealed that, in the 1750s, the Spaniards had been continuously engaged in heavy trading with the French, the Tejas groups, and various northern nations. This trade included considerable amounts of weapons, gunpowder, bullets, and knives, as well as buffalo pelts, *gamusas,* horses, and lard, which both the citizenry and the friars obtained from the Natives (Chirinos 1761; Maldonado 1761; Navarrete 1762; Ybañes 1761).

THE SPANISH PUNITIVE EXPEDITION
TO THE RED RIVER

After the San Sabá attack, Spanish authorities had to reestablish the credibility and the supremacy of the colonial military power. On June 27, 1758, the Junta de Guerra y Hacienda decided that a campaign should be made to punish the northern groups. The practical details of the campaign were to be decided by a Junta that would meet at San Antonio (Allen 1939: 56–57).

The Lipan "chief" El Chico visited San Antonio and stated that he and his people wanted to enter a mission, but they would not do so until the Comanche had been punished. The Lipan wanted to profit from the conflict among Spaniards, Comanche, and northern groups and use the opportunity to inflict some damage on the Comanche. Meanwhile the Yojuane attacked the Apache, and in December 1758, the Comanche also attacked the Apache, killing twenty-one. The Apache who survived the attack reported that the Comanche were heading for San Sabá, as in fact they were, but the Comanche did not attack the Spaniards, though they stole some horses (Allen 1939: 58).

In January 1759, Fr. Calahorra, stationed in east Texas, informed Texas governor Barrios that the Tejas were preparing to join some other groups to attack San Sabá and San Antonio. During the same month the Junta met in San Antonio to make preparations for the expedition against the northern groups. It was decided that the groups to be punished were the Tonkawa, Tawakoni, Yscani, and Taovayo. The Comanche were not to be attacked because they lived much further north and the intelligence available did not provide their location. The information about the groups to be attacked was provided by the Legumbres and the Mayeye, who hunted buffalo in the same lands (Allen 1939: 61).

On March 13, 1759, a group of Natives raided the horse herd at San Sabá. All twenty soldiers guarding the herd were killed, and all the animals were stolen. Every soldier had bullet wounds. Not a single arrow was found in the corpses. It is noteworthy that this attack killed twice as many people as the earlier attack at San Sabá mission. These attackers, if they were the northern groups or their allies, left clear indications of their strength and capabilities. No one was allowed to survive to give notice of the attack, which was the normal Native procedure. This fact alone should have conveyed an ominous message to the Spaniards. It appears that the northern groups were aware of the forthcoming attack and left their calling card in the form of the raid on the horse herd and the killing of the soldiers. The exclusive use of bullets was a declaration of might and equality of resources.

After many consultations it became apparent that the military force could not be assembled before June. This force, which was to be composed of 500 men, was a far cry from what Parrilla wanted. There were supposed to be 139 presidio soldiers, 241 militiamen, 30 Tlaxcaltecan Natives, 90 mission Natives, and 134 Apache. The actual force that departed San Antonio for the campaign consisted of 435 men (Allen 1939: 60). This was an ill-prepared and less-than-willing group of fighters, a fact recognized by the commanders before the expedition was undertaken. The intelligence gathered was ignored. According to Fr. Zedano, various northern groups had gathered in a fortified village north of the Brazos River. Their camp had a stockade surrounded by a fosse, which prevented easy access to the village and thus any surprise attack. Intelligence reports indicated that French traders had helped the Natives in the construction of fortifications (Allen 1939: 64–66; Tunnell and Newcomb 1969: 162).

The military force left San Sabá in late September 1759 and traveled northeast without encountering any Natives until October 2, when they found a Yojuane village north of the Brazos River. A battle ensued, in which 55 Yojuane warriors were killed and 149 captured. Among the captives were some who knew the location of the Taovaya village; Parrilla used them as guides. On October 7, the guides told Parrilla that they would reach the Taovaya and Yscani village that day. They stated that they knew of a location with good pasture where the Spaniards could camp. The Apache warriors traveling with Parrilla, who knew the terrain, confirmed the information. After traveling 6 leagues (15.6 miles), the Spaniards were attacked by 60 or 70 Natives, followed by a second group of attackers. The Spaniards charged and the warriors dispersed, but the Spanish pursued them through the woods. When the Spaniards exited the woods they were faced with the fortified village (Allen 1939: 67–68; Tunnell and Newcomb 1969: 161).

It is obvious that the advance party of warriors was meant to lead the Spaniards straight to the fortified village and that they knew exactly when and how the Spaniards were arriving. The sheep were led to the slaughter! The Spaniards lost the advantage of surprise and were faced with a force and a military arrangement for which they were unprepared. A coalition of groups had gathered at the village and the number of warriors was large. The battle leader was a Taovaya. The battle tactics, bravery, and organization of the Native warriors deserved and received high praise from Parrilla, who had fought in many different places before coming to the Americas. Despite good intelligence and a large military force, the Spanish lost the battle. The Natives literally laughed at the Spaniards.

MISSION SAN LORENZO DE LA SANTA CRUZ AND MISSION NUESTRA SEÑORA DE LA CANDELARIA

Captain Parrilla was replaced by Captain Felipe de Rábago y Therán at the Presidio de las Amarillas. The improvements he made on the presidio seemed to rebuild the confidence of the Apache. Groups of Apache, especially the Lipan, camped in the area for extended periods. Displaced from the lands they had been using since moving into Texas, they experienced difficulty in obtaining buffalo. Captain Rábago provided gifts, protection, and sometimes military escorts to the buffalo hunts. The Apache appreciated the help (Tunnell and Newcomb 1969: 162). The Lipan told Rábago they wanted to settle in a mission. In October 1761, El Gran Cabezón, an Apache "chief," contacted Rábago and expressed his wish to settle in a mission. Rábago wrote to Fr. Ximenez at San Juan Bautista, and in November the friar came to San Sabá.

On November 3, 1761, a meeting was held with a Lipan chief (El Gran Cabezón?) (D. Ximenes 1761). He stated that ten other Apache "chiefs" were interested in living in a mission. Sometime later, El Gran Cabezón returned to San Sabá with other "chiefs" to discuss conditions. The Lipan agreed to accept the authority of El Cabezón as their spokesman. But these Apache groups did not want to reoccupy San Sabá. El Gran Cabezón, however, was amenable to the idea of settling on the San Joseph River, the Upper Nueces, but he stipulated some conditions. He wanted a military escort to go on a large buffalo hunt before entering the mission, and he asked for the release of the daughter of the Grande Capitán, a Natagé. He stated that the Grande Capitán was his relative and had promised to prevent the Mescalero (Natagé, see below) from committing robberies and depredations in Coahuila if he recovered his daughter. It appears that the Natagé and the Lipan shared family ties and continued to be closely allied (Tunnell and Newcomb 1969: 163), and that the Natagé (Mescalero) held leadership positions. El Cabezón also wanted a military escort to accompany him and his people on their forays against the Comanche during the prickly pear season. Rábago managed to dissuade him from this last demand.

The location on the Upper Nueces was known to Rábago because it was on the road traveled from Presidio San Juan Bautista to San Sabá. Fr. Jimenez managed to obtain supplies from the missions on the Rio Grande to speed up the process of establishing the mission on the Nueces; otherwise, the Lipan Apache would have to wait until official approval was granted. Fr. Ximenes knew that if the establishment of the mission was delayed, the Apache would change their minds. In December 1761, El Gran Cabezón returned to San Sabá from the buffalo hunt.

On January 3, 1762, Rábago, with a detachment of thirty soldiers, made the 100-mile journey from San Sabá to the Nueces. They arrived at the spring of El Canón on January 9. On January 16, Fr. Jimenez and Fr. Baños returned from the Rio Grande with supplies. These friars had been earlier at San Sabá but had left before the 1758 attack. Rábago surveyed the countryside and testified that the location had appropriate resources for establishing a mission.

On January 23, 1762, the military, the friars, and about three hundred of El Cabezón's people gathered for the ceremonies of official possession. There were other Apache Natives present who had not made a decision to join the mission. During the ceremony, El Cabezón and his people pulled grass, drew water, and watered stones picked up from the ground. He declared that these rituals symbolized the taking of possession of the lands (Tunnell and Newcomb 1969: 165–166; see Chapter 1). However, before September 1762, the northern groups attacked Apache *rancherías* on the Frio River, as well as Apache groups hunting near the Colorado River and on the San Sabá road to the Guadalupe River (Navarrete 1762).

Fr. Jimenez asked Rábago for more soldiers to protect the new mission and village. In his petition he made some important remarks about the Spanish perception of the Lipan. He stated that the Apache were courageous and proud, and had broad understanding. They were accustomed to living well on buffalo meat, raised their own crops, and had plenty of horses, clothing, and metal utensils, as well as a few firearms. The Apache were very different from the other Native groups the friars normally dealt with in the missions. The friars felt that their control over the Apache was slight, and the worldly ways and sophistication of the Lipan made the friars uneasy. Fr. Jimenez recognized that the Spanish worldview was very different from that of the Apache, and that Apache silence, or lack of argument, did not mean their agreement. He stated, "[W]hat seems inconsistent to us is not inconsistent to them regardless of the insufficient reasons they express" (Tunnell and Newcomb 1969: 167). Fr. Jimenez also mentioned that the shamans had a great deal of influence over the Lipan and were capable of stirring considerable unrest.

Mission San Lorenzo was essentially a way-station for a great number of Apache who came and went as they pleased. Captain Teja, who had been camped on the Llano River, joined the group at San Lorenzo in the summer of 1762. "Chief" Panocha promised to settle in a mission in about a year, and "Chief" El Turnio requested a mission for his group. By using grains of corn, he told Rábago that he had 114 warriors among his people and countless women and children. "Chief" El Turnio wanted to settle at a spring 4 leagues (10.4 miles—walking distance) from San Lorenzo on the western bank of the Nueces. The spring issued from a high spot on a plain amid a large pecan grove (Tunnell and Newcomb 1969: 167).

Rábago finally agreed to establish a mission for El Turnio, and on February 2, 1762, Rábago gave him possession of the lands requested. Turnio's family occupied ten tents. El Turnio made it clear that his people would leave the mission whenever the prickly-pear fruit and the *cogallitos* (?) were in season. He declared that many more people would join the village when the crops began to grow, and that his brother—who, he said, was more important than he—would join the mission once he saw him settled. Rábago called the village Nuestra Señora de la Candelaria. At about the same time, Fr. Ximenes and Fr. Baños reported that there were more than four hundred people at the mission and that five had been baptized (Tunnell and Newcomb 1969: 167–168).

In the spring of 1762, the fields were prepared and corn planted. Fr. Ximenes clearly knew that these missions represented the lesser of two evils, both to the Apache groups and to the military. As he stated on November 23, 1761, when the whole enterprise was still in the offing, he believed that these Natives accepted conversion with a divided will ("estos Yndios se reducen medio queriendo y no queriendo"), meaning that circumstances made them accept the unacceptable (D. Ximenes 1761a). He also expected little respite from the Comanche. In March, May, and June 1762, the Comanche attacked Lipan *rancherías* and camps in the area of the Upper Nueces, killing at least fifty-four people (Tunnell and Newcomb 1969: 168).

In June, the Apache people from the missions went on the buffalo hunt. While on the hunt they were told that the friars had abandoned the mission, taking their women and children as prisoners. Some of the Apache immediately returned to the mission to verify the rumor, only to realize that it was untrue (D. Ximenes 1762). In August, the friars reported that the Apache had gone to gather prickly-pear fruit, and in the fall they left again on the buffalo hunt (Tunnell and Newcomb 1969: 169). Five "chiefs," of what we may assume to have been five different *rancherías,* got permission to go hunting. These groups were under "chiefs" Gran Cabezón, Teja, Boruca, Bordado, and Cojo. El Turnio appears to have left the Nueces area before this date. His departure may have been connected with the earlier rumor that the friars had abandoned the mission. The Apache who went on the hunt were accompanied by a small escort of soldiers to prevent trouble from other Natives and from other Spanish soldiers.

On October 8, Fr. Ximenez and Fr. Manuel de Cuevas, who had joined the mission, wrote a Consulta, reporting that they were familiar with twelve different Apache groups. Apart from the groups headed by the individuals mentioned above, there were also the groups of "chiefs" Panocha, El Lumen, and four others whose names were not mentioned (Tunnell and Newcomb 1969: 169). Other Apache groups continued to hesitate to take up mission life, although a lot of people would come and go at will. The friars, who had limited provisions and could not have maintained the missions if the Apache had not procured much of their own food, did not insist that they remain.

In 1762, the following Apache spokespersons and their groups either were staying in the Nueces missions or visited the area frequently: Bordado, Boruca, Cojo, El Cabezón, El Lumen, El Turnio, Panocha, and the Teja. These would represent eight of the ten *rancherías* mentioned by El Cabezón on November 3, 1761. The other two might have been those of El Turnio's brother and the group of the Natagé Grande Capitán.

On October 28, Fr. Ximenes wrote to Fr. Manuel Naxera, the commissary general. He reported that since the establishment of the missions, three groups had joined. He had observed their mode of living and believed that there might be reason for hope because the Apache observed all the natural precepts of living (*los principales preceptos naturales*) (D. Ximenes 1762). He stated that the Comanche had made peace with the Tejas and had promised not to pursue the Apache from the missions. Fr. Ximenes, however, had not seen signs of this truce, and he did not believe that peace was possible between Apache and Comanche. He commented that not even Fr. Mariano de los Dolores understood how different the Apache were from the Comanche. On the other hand, he alluded to the private interests in San Antonio that might impede the success of the missions. He feared the enterprise would collapse if there was a great delay in the approval and delivery of supplies for the missions. He believed that, if the groups staying at the missions were kept apart from other proud Lipan (*altaneros*), who were always conveying disturbing news, the missions stood a chance. He thought the mission lands were very good and noted that they had already built an adobe church. He reported that the Apache had told him that among the enemies who were attacking them there were two Spaniards and four Natives from the missions of San Antonio. The presence of Spaniards and mission Natives among the attackers raised fears among the Apache that the Spaniards were playing a double game (D. Ximenes 1762).

Late in 1762, the Comanche attacked an Apache *ranchería,* killing several people and stealing horses. The settlers of San Antonio firmly believed that the only reason the Comanche were on their borders was the presence of the Apache. This belief, plus the attacks the Apache had been committing against civilians, led to a formal complaint against them. This complaint was largely based on the depredations the Apache were committing in Coahuila. Both Captain Phelipe Rábago of San Sabá and the friars pleaded that a distinction be made between the missionized Apache and those who were not, but they were well aware that this was a naive, if not disingenuous, request.

On December 19, 1762, the governor of Coahuila, Lorenzo Cancio, was informed that all the horses had been stolen from the Presidio de las Amarillas. There were persistent rumors that the Comanche were about to attack the presidio, but that did not happen (Cancio 1762). In January 1763, Esteban de Alderete led a campaign against the Apache from Coahuila, and in November of the same year another campaign was made against the Apache (Cancio 1763; 1763a).

Early in 1763, the friars at the Nueces missions noted that the Apache compliance with the rules of the mission had improved, and the level of trust between friars and Natives increased (Tunnell and Newcomb 1969: 171). In September 1763, the friars made some observations about the Apache. The Mescalero and the Lipan were very different from each other. The Apache proper (Natagé?) were known to the other groups as Apache, while they were known to the Spaniards as Mescalero. The two divisions had intermarried and maintained trade relations. The Apache (Mescalero or Natagé?) did not have friendly relations with the Spaniards and were always trying to entice the Lipan to join them. At one point, the Lipan tried to convince the Apache (Mescalero or Natagé) to join them, but the attempt backfired, strengthening instead the ties among the latter groups. However, some Mescalero (Natagé?) groups had joined the Lipan, among them the group led by "chief" Cabellos Largos that became part of Captain Boruca's group. There were also other individuals who, in the turmoil, preferred not to recognize the authority of any captain and remained unaffiliated (Tunnell and Newcomb 1969: 170).

In January 1764, the whole scenario of friends and foes was becoming ever more complex. The "nations" of the north had been bothering Texas and Coahuila, and a campaign was made against them in February (Cancio 1764). The Mescalero were said to be hiding near the Sierra Madre. On February 26, 1764, Fr. Ximenes wrote to the governor of Coahuila, stating that the friars expected an attack on the Presidio de las Amarillas sometime between February and April, because that was the time preferred by the Natives for attack. Some Apache, and other western groups he did not recognize, were also causing trouble. He added that a Lipan captain who participated in the founding of one of the missions, and who had been gone for over a year and a half, had returned (El Turnio?). He was a difficult person to deal with and had caused much trouble before. Fr. Ximenes was grateful for the presence of soldiers (D. Ximenes 1764).

In February 1764, Captain Manuel Rodríguez from the Presidio de San Juan Bautista informed Governor Cancio that a squadron of Apache from the *rancherías* of captains Casaca Colorada and Panocha, which was accompanying a supply convoy, had returned to its *ranchería* (mission) on February 25. The Apache reported that, on the east side of the Colorado River beyond the missions of San Xavier (Rockdale), they encountered three Comanche and killed one. The Apache took their five mares and one mule; they had caught the meat of the Comanche, as they put it, and celebrated the event with a dance. Many Apache joined the celebration, which took place between the missions of S. Lorenzo and Candelaria. During the dance, one woman parodied the Comanche by dressing up in a shirt and hat taken from a Comanche corpse. Captain Rodríguez was accompanied by a citizen of San Antonio who recognized the outfit as belonging to a young man who had been killed a few days before near the Puerto Viejo, 6 leagues (15.6 miles) north of San Antonio. Captain Rodríguez and his companion deduced that these had been the perpetrators of the attack at Puerto Viejo. When captains Boruca (a Mescalero or Natagé who joined the Apache) and Teja joined the celebration dance, the citizen from San Antonio recognized many people, and few of them belonged to Captain Turnio's group. Captain Rodríguez implied that although Captain Turnio (Lipan) was considered the troublemaker, he probably was not to blame for some of the problems caused by other Apache divisions (M. Rodríguez 1764).

On March 3, 1764, Governor Cancio informed Viceroy Marqués de Cruillas that the Comanche had made an attack on the presidio at San Sabá, and that some days later (January 26) Phelipe Ynguanzo and his servants had been attacked at Puerto Viejo, either by the Comanche or by the Apache or Mescalero (apparently by the Comanche). In this attack one Spaniard had been killed and two people had been wounded (Cancio 1764a).

In the summer of 1764, the Lipan were admitted to the Presidio de San Sabá to trade, and while there stole horses from the Comanche who were in the area under the protection of the Army. The Comanche pursued the Lipan toward El Cañón, but when they were about to catch up with them a large group of Lipan appeared. This group of Lipan was heading toward San Sabá accompanied by Spanish troops. When the Comanche saw Spanish troops accompanying the Lipan, the Comanche thought that Phelipe Rábago, commander at Las Amarillas, had betrayed them. Infuriated, the Comanche returned to San Sabá, got the few horses the Apache had not taken, picked up their tents, and left, enraged against Rábago. Cancio had no doubt the Comanche thought the Spanish had set a trap for them and would exact revenge. Cancio commented that Spanish protection of the Apache had brought only problems for the Spanish. He stated that time had gone by and no Apache had been reduced, nor had they ceased to commit depredations in Texas and Coahuila. He expressed the common feeling that the only reason the Comanche remained close to the borders of the province was the presence of the Apache. There were presidios closer to their lands that they did not attack because those presidios did not protect the Apache. They attacked San Sabá simply because of the union between Spaniards and Apaches, which the Comanche could not tolerate (Cancio 1764b).

In October 1764, Captain Rábago y Therán wrote to the governor of Coahuila, Diego Ortiz Parrilla. He stated that he had been ordered to help the Lipan with the buffalo hunt (*carneada*). He was concerned about attacks at the presidio during the months of November, December, and January, since this was the period often chosen for attack by the northern groups. He had learned from Domingo del Río, an officer at Orcoquisac in east Texas, that the Tejas were getting ready to set siege to the Presidio de las Amarillas. They had made it known they would hold the siege for at least a month in order to destroy the presidio (Rábago y Théran 1764). It should be noted that this was a siege and not a series of hit-and-run attacks.

In December 1764, Fr. Ximemes reported that the Lipan at the mission suffered a devastating smallpox epidemic. Most of the people at the missions had perished. He reported that the Natives were seeing an old man who appeared and disappeared. The old man told them to make continuous war on the neighboring nations and on the Spaniards. He told them not to receive baptism; those that did would soon die. This vision-man appeared in a battle in which he was killed (and disappeared), but later he reappeared. The old man promised the warriors life after death, a "paradise" where they would be reunited with their people. The vision-man changed forms to convince those in doubt, and he often appeared in the form of a woman. The oldest Native, who had seen the vision-man as a woman, stated that she never aged. The Apache shamans said that the vision-man should be believed (Tunnell and Newman 1969: 171).

The appearance of the vision-man was a clear indication of the internal and external tensions being suffered by the Apache. The psychic reassurance of the so-called nativistic movements revived the cultural tenets of groups, regrouping the individuals around certain goals and precepts that were essential for the survival of the social group. It provided a meta-vision beyond the messy realities of everyday life. The vision-man gave the Apache groups a rallying point and provided guidance that was free from particular group allegiances and personal frictions.

In 1765, the roads to San Sabá and the Nueces became risky. Early in the fall, El Turnio's group left Candelaria once more. In April 1766, there were troubles with the Natives at Las Amarillas and widespread rumors of a new invasion. Supplies were sent to Las Amarillas, even though the roads had become dangerous to travel (Jauregui 1766). In October 1766, about three hundred Comanche and their allies attacked El Canón. Thirty Spanish soldiers were present at the mission. The attack was repelled, but not before the intruders stole a herd of mares.

In November 1766, the Tejas, Tahuacana, Tancahue, Tahuya, Yiojuane, and other allied groups attacked the mission, but did not penetrate the compound. These groups had met at the Presidio de los Adaes earlier in August to discuss a plan to destroy the mission in retaliation for the attack they had suffered on January 24 on the Llano River Pass at the hands of Spanish troops. On that date, the Tejas had attacked the Lipan who had joined the missions. They killed some Lipan and made off with the horses belonging to both Lipan and Spaniards (Tunnell and Newcomb 1969: 173).

The spring of 1767 was a hard one for the people at Las Amarillas. Starting in February they were almost constantly under attack or siege. The attacking groups took most of the cattle. The supply convoys from S. Fernando de Austria and the Presidio de Santa Rosa could not reach the Presidio de las Amarillas because the Comanche controlled the roads and passes and had burned the pastureland. El Canón had also been attacked on April 18. The Apache were staying at Parage de las Moras near the Rio Grande (Jauregui 1767; 1767a; 1767b).

On April 22 the Presidio de las Amarillas was again attacked (Jauregui 1767c; Tun-nell and Newcomb 1969: 174). The frequency and persistence of these attacks left no doubt that the northern groups, as well as the Tejas and their allies, would not tolerate the Spanish support of the Apache, nor the presence of a presidio or missions in the area.

On May 5, 1767, Fr. Ximenes wrote to Barrios to recommend delay of the supply con-voys to San Sabá, because they had enough food for a few months and he had learned that a coalition of ten groups was preparing to attack. He suggested that, since the buf-falo went north in the hot weather, the herds would soon move northward of San Sabá. The Natives always furnished themselves with meat supplies before going on a campaign. If the military waited a while longer, the attacking groups would have no food supplies, and would tire and desist from the attack (Castilla y Théran 1767; D. Ximenes 1767).

THE MARQUÉS DE RUBÍ INSPECTION TOUR OF 1767

On August 7, 1765, Carlos III appointed Cayetano Maria Pignatelli Rubí Corbera y San Climent, Marqués de Rubí, to inspect the northern frontier of New Spain.[1] On this trip, Rubí was accompanied by an engineer, Nicolás Lafora, and by a cartographer, Joseph de Urrutia. Both the Marqués and Nicolás Lafora kept diaries of the expedition. This trip and Rubí's recommendations resulted in crucial and consistent changes in Native policy: relentless war on Apache groups, and alliances with the Comanche and other northern groups.

In the spring of 1767, the Marqués de Rubí left Nueva Vizcaya to inspect the military installations in Coahuila and Texas.[2] On June 15, 1767, Rubí's party arrived at Monclova. Between Monclova and the crossing of the Rio Grande, Rubí mentioned very few Na-tive groups. At Monclova, both diarists mentioned the Tlaxcaltecan pueblo. Lafora also mentioned the presence of Cohumero and Timamar at Mission San Miguel de Aguayo.

At the Santa Rosa presidio and the nearby town of S. Fernando de Austria, the diarists reported the presence of Lipan Apache. Lafora commented on the presence of Lipan in the mountains of Coahuila, and both diarists mentioned the trade between the Lipan and the citizens of the town and presidio. The Marqués considered this trade as the pri-mary reason for the robberies committed by the Lipan (Jackson and Foster 1995: 107). Both Rubí and Lafora (Jackson and Foster 1995: 107; Kinnaird 1958: 144–145) mentioned the spring and marshy drainage at a place called S. Ildefonso, located 1 league (2.6 miles) from the town of San Fernando de Austria (modern Zaragoza, Mexico). On July 12 Rubí departed S. Fernando de Austria for the missions on the Upper Nueces and the Presidio San Luis de las Amarillas at San Sabá.

The road they took to San Sabá had been well traveled since the establishment of the Apache missions of San Lorenzo de la Santa Cruz and Nuestra Señora de la Candelaria. The supply convoys for the Presidio de las Amarillas and the missions departed from the Presidio de Santa Rosa del Sacramento, the town of S. Fernando de Austria, and the Presidio San Juan Bautista on the Rio Grande. The Rubí expedition followed routes and camping spots that had been named and used for some time by supply convoys and couriers. After traveling 12 leagues (31.2 miles) from S. Fernando de Austria, they reached the Rio Grande. They forded the river near the modern town of Normandy, upstream from Eagle Pass, just as the Bosque-Larios expedition had done a century earlier.[3]

On the south bank of the Rio Grande, Rubí saw Lipan *rancherías* with cultivated fields (Jackson and Foster 1995: 108). According to Lafora, they used a Lipan canoe to ferry their luggage. After crossing the river, Rubí saw a large group of Lipan, who left the *ranchería* when the Spaniards approached. Their huts were made of branches. Rubí and his party remained at the river ford until the morning of the 17th (Jackson and Foster 1995: 108; Kinnaird 1958: 146).

On July 17, after traveling 14 leagues (36.4 miles), mostly north-northeast, they arrived at a place they named Cabecera de las Moras, 10 leagues (26 miles) below the headwaters of modern Las Moras Creek. Lafora's diary (Kinnaird 1958: 146) says the place was called Las Cabeceras del Ojo de las Moras. In a document dated March 24, 1767, this place was called Parage de las Moras (Jauregui 1767b). Halfway between Normandy and Las Moras Creek they saw another Apache camp. This camp was deserted, but they could see the stubble of the crops raised the previous year (Foster and Jackson 1995: 109; Kinnaird 1958: 146).

On July 18, they proceeded north-northeast and traveled about 15 leagues (39 miles) (Jackson and Foster 1995: 110; Kinnaird 1958: 146–147). They passed a spring or arroyo called El Cibolo, and traveled 4 leagues (10.4 miles) to the abandoned mission of La Candelaria. The ruins of the mission were at the foot of another spring of very pure and cold water. This was the site and spring chosen by the Apache "chief" El Turnio in 1762. On the way to Candelaria, they entered the valley of San Joseph on the Upper Nueces River. In the description of the buildings at Mission Candelaria, Lafora mentioned a house with a small chapel, and facing it a large hut "constructed by the Lipanes" (Kinnaird 1958: 146–147). This large hut could be one of the *parletones* referred to by Ugalde on May 8, 1788. Lafora commented (Kinnaird 1958: 146–147) on the gullibility of the friars, who believed that they could persuade the Lipan to live in the place. Mission Candelaria was located near the modern town of Montell in northwestern Uvalde County.

On July 19, they continued north-northeast, traveling through the canyon formed by the Nueces River. They traveled 2.5 leagues (6.5 miles) along the El Canōn River (the Nueces River), forded it, and continued northward for about 1.5 leagues (3.9 miles), until they arrived at Mission San Lorenzo de la Santa Cruz (at modern Camp Wood). There were no Apache or other Natives at the mission. Rubí commented (Jackson and Foster 1995: 111) that since January 1766, the Apache had been driven away by Comanche attacks and had abandoned the mission. Actually his information was incorrect, since the last major raid recorded at San Lorenzo took place in November 1766. Rubí described the San Lorenzo mission buildings, and Lafora drew a map of the settlement (Kinnaird 1958: 147–148).

On July 21, the expedition headed north with some detours to the northeast, but following the canyon of the Nueces River, which they forded four times before reaching camp. They were traveling close to the Edwards–Real County Line (Jackson and Foster 1995: 111–112; Kinnaird 1958: 148).

On July 22, they proceeded north and traveled about 10 leagues (26 miles). After covering 2 leagues (5.2 miles), they reached the headwaters of the Nueces River. From there they traveled about 8 leagues and reached the headwaters of the South Llano River (Río de los Janes or Chanas). Rubí stated (Jackson and Foster 1995: 112) that the Chana Natives were allied with the Comanche. Lafora, on the other hand, noted (Kinnaird 1958: 148) that the Chana had lived in the area, but had moved farther inland. They made camp on the right bank of the South Llano on a wooded hill, near a spring that Rubí named El Ojo. Before reaching their campsite they forded the South Llano three times (Jackson and Foster 1995: 112; Kinnaird 1958: 148).

On July 23, they headed northeast along the South Llano. They traveled 10 leagues (26 miles) that day. Passing through hilly country, they reached the Arroyo de las Lechugas, which ran west to east and flowed into the South Llano River. Continuing northward for half a league (1.3 miles), they reached the Arroyo de las Trancas, which joined the Arroyo de las Lechugas. The party sighted buffalo for the first time. The Arroyo de las Lechugas is most likely the North Llano River, and the Arroyo de las Trancas is Bear Creek (Jackson and Foster 1995: 112–113; Kinnaird 1958: 149).

On July 24, they traveled north-northeast for 11 leagues (28.6 miles), crossing the Arroyo de las Trancas four times before reaching Abuela Creek, where they camped. Lafora commented (Kinnaird 1958: 149–150) that the whole road from El Canón to San Sabá was exposed to Comanche attacks, especially as they approached the presidio. This situation had prevailed since the first attack at Las Amarillas in 1758, but especially since Captain Phelipe Rábago took command.

On July 25, they continued north along Abuela Creek and reached the San Sabá River, which they forded. They followed the course of the San Sabá and reached the Presidio de las Amarillas, having covered 2.25 leagues (5.85 miles). During their stay, they surveyed the country and dispatched scouts every day to look for signs of Natives. On the morning of the 26th, the scouts reported finding tracks of five Natives. They had seen smoke signals on the 25th and 26th, but the scouts could not locate their origin.

There were other false alarms, which indicated the state of alert at Las Amarillas. On the 29th, they sent some soldiers with two Julime Natives to explore the spring of San Lorenzo, 1.5 leagues (3.9 miles) away from the presidio. When they returned, they reported seeing three enemy Natives. Lafora stated (Kinnaird 1958: 150–151) that the soldiers went to verify the information but found it to be false. In their inspection they found only the remains of an old *ranchería* near the spring.

Rubí wrote that the presidio was badly constructed and stated: "[T]his fortification is as barbarous as the enemy who attacks it" (Jackson and Foster 1995: 114). He complained of being in danger of attack during the whole time spent at the presidio, and of having to keep constant guard on the horses. Despite all the caution, some horses were stolen by the Comanche (Jackson and Foster 1995: 114).

On August 4, they departed San Sabá heading for San Antonio de Béjar. They covered about 12 leagues (31.2 miles). They traveled southeast down the Oso valley and reached a spring that formed a small arroyo called Arroyo del Osito (Little Bear Creek). They passed La Cañada del Oso, reached again the Llano River, and camped on its right bank (Kinnaird 1958: 151–152). Rubí mentioned that they saw "enormous numbers of small bison herds" (Jackson and Foster 1995: 115). They killed four buffalo and three turkeys, and roped a bear—justifying the names of the geographic features crossed, since *oso* means "bear" in Spanish (Jackson and Foster 1995: 115). Jackson and Foster (1995: 50n) suggest that the Arroyo del Osito is modern Leon Creek, a tributary of the Llano.

On August 5, they proceeded east-southeast, first to the dry creek named La Lagita, and then to the Arroyo del Almagrito, which formed a valley. Rubí commented (Jackson and Foster 1995: 115) that this was a mineral region. Eight leagues (20.8 miles) from the Arroyo del Almagrito, they reached the Arroyo de los Pedernales and camped at its source, which was a bubbling spring. Jackson and Foster suggest that the Arroyo del Almagrito is the modern Saint James River near the Mason-Kimble-Gillespie county lines. The Rubí party camped on the headwaters of the modern Pedernales River (Jackson and Foster 1995: 115, 51n; Kinnaird 1958: 152).

On August 6, they headed south-southeast toward San Antonio. They traveled 16 leagues (41.6 miles) that day. After crossing the Pedernales, they crossed the Arroyo El Canóncito and followed its course until it emptied into the upper course of the Guadalupe River. They camped on its banks. The upper course of the Guadalupe River was often called the Alarcón River, and Rubí used both names. They saw great numbers of buffalo, deer, and other game. El Canóncito is likely to be modern Cypress Creek, which flows into the Guadalupe River near the town of Comfort (Jackson and Foster 1995: 116, 53n; Kinnaird 1958: 152).

On August 7, they traveled east-southeast for about 12 leagues (31.2 miles). They forded the upper Guadalupe River, and entered a series of hills to reach the Paso de los Balcones. Before reaching that pass, they crossed the arroyos El Rosario, Las Moharritas, and Atascosito. After exiting the Pass de los Balcones they entered a valley. At the foot of the Balcones Escarpment, they camped on the Arroyo de los Balcones, modern Balcones Creek (Jackson and Foster 1995: 116–117; Kinnaird 1958: 152–153).

On August 8, 1767, they headed east-southeast for 12 leagues (31.2 miles). They forded the Arroyo de los Balcones, and 2.5 leagues (6.5 miles) further on crossed the Arroyo de los Alamitos. After traveling 2 more leagues (5.8 miles), they went through the small pass of Puerto Viejo and then past El Devisero, reaching the town of San Antonio de Béjar. Puerto Viejo and El Devisero are spots frequently mentioned in historical records relating to San Antonio. Puerto Viejo was about 6 leagues (15.6 miles) from town, and El Devisero (the dividing line) was about 3 leagues (7.8 miles) from town. Quite likely Puerto Viejo was the small pass near modern Camp Bullis, as Jackson and Foster suggested (1995: 117, 56n; Kinnard 1958: 153).

FR. SOLIS'S INSPECTION TOUR
OF THE MISSIONS IN 1768

Coincidentally, but certainly not by chance, Fr. Gaspar de Solis made an inspection tour of the missions in Texas and Coahuila in 1767–1768 (Forrestal 1931). This inspection was ordered by the Guardian of the College of Guadalupe in Zacatecas, Fr. Tomas Cortez. The report is disparaging in tone and information about Native Americans, except for the southern missions of Rosario and La Bahía, in Texas. On February 5, 1768, Fr. Solis visited the mission of Punta de Lampazos (Coahuila), but he did not mention any Natives. On the south side of the Rio Grande he saw many "Carrizo" Natives, particularly at the Hacienda Las Estacas. On the north side of the Rio Grande Colonel Hugo O'Conor, governor of Texas, had a military escort to accompany the friar to the missions. Fr. Solis remarked (Forrestal 1931) that the Apache and the Lipan occupied the lands between the Rio Grande and the Nueces River, but he did not mention seeing any Apache. At the Nueces River stop he was supplied with provisions, showing that, although the roads were dangerous, pack trains utilized those routes.

In June 1768, Captain Phelipe Rábago, weary of the situation at Las Amarillas, moved without authorization to Mission S. Lorenzo de la Santa Cruz. In February 1769, Rábago was ordered to send twenty of his soldiers to reinforce the garrison at San Antonio, and by April 1, Rábago had been replaced by Captain Antonio Manuel de Oca. Captain Oca moved back to Las Amarillas, where he remained until 1770, at which time he returned to San Lorenzo. On June 1771, Jacobo de Ugarte y Loyola ordered the removal of the remainder of the garrison of Las Amarillas to San Fernando de Austria. The Presidio de San Sabá was reestablished at Aguaverde and became known by that name. These moves resulted from the recommendations made by the Marqués de Rubí.

1780s–1790s

To attempt to summarize the complexities of the last two decades of the eighteenth century is beyond the scope of this work, and would be foolhardy. The closing of the missions on the Nueces River, and the long period of inactivity at the Presidio de las Amarillas, resulted in the drying up of historical documentation connected with those outposts. Once the Spaniards had left the area, there was nothing to write about. The absence of mail to and from these installations leaves the researcher with fragmentary information that occurs only when the area is mentioned in relation to another subject. I shall, therefore, make some comments that seem pertinent to the activities and fate of the Apache and the Comanche. Although forced to address the various Spanish military campaigns, I focus on the tidbits that are indicative of the movements of the Apache as well as the utilization of the Edwards Plateau region.

As a result of the Marqués de Rubí's recommendations, the Crown implemented a series of military reforms and a change in Native policy. This was one of several attempts to restructure the military and deal with the Native problem, which by then meant

Apache, Comanche, and the northern groups (Norteños). The new policies heralded a different approach to war against any group perceived as an enemy. The military officers occupying leadership positions were a different breed of commanders, well trained and experienced, who fought surgical campaigns. Mercy and peace were obtained only by the force of arms.

One individual instrumental in implementing some of Rubí's reforms was Teniente Colonel Hugo O'Conor, who was ad interim governor of Texas in 1767. In September 1771, the Viceroy appointed O'Conor as commandant inspector of the internal presidios. In November 1773, after rousting the Mescalero from the Bolson de Mapimí (Moorhead 1968: 30), O'Conor decided to "clean up" some of the *rancherías* on the north side of the Rio Grande to guarantee that the presidios in the area would not be molested. He left La Junta de los Ríos and continued toward the Pecos River (which he called Colorado), and reached the Mountain Range of Mogano (or Movano). On November 27, O'Conor was attacked by about six hundred Apache, but he managed to control the situation, pursue them, and win the battle. The Mogano or Movano mountain range could be the Delaware Mountains.[4] In 1773, O'Conor made peace with the Lipan: that agreement was honored by the Lipan in Texas until the 1790s.

In 1777, O'Conor wrote a report to Teodoro de Croix about the state of the provinces. The report paints a grim picture of northern New Spain in 1771–1772. The fear the Apache instilled in the population led to the abandonment of towns and haciendas, and resulted in economic ruin (Cutter 1994: 35–40). O'Conor's endless list of devastations, and his determination to oust the Lipan from Coahuila, leads one to conclude that the Apache groups had won battles, but lost the war. O'Conor's campaigns in 1773 and the lasting peace with the Lipan turned the tide for the Spanish.

O'Conor recognized that minor troubles had arisen from time to time with small groups of Apache who could not be controlled by their captains. However, he also stated (Cutter 1994: 89–90) that many excesses had been committed by others, and these were unduly and consistently attributed to the Apache. He noted (Cutter 1994: 89–90) that the troubles in Nueva Vizcaya with the Native populations were due, in no small measure, to the cruel treatment of the Natives by the landowners and to the Natives' hunger, which forced them to steal in order to avoid starvation. Statements such as these from a resolute and implacable military commander are worth noting.

In a paragraph discussing the events that occurred at San Sabá in 1758, he referred to the east Texas groups as "the Indians who live under the protection of our presidios and pass for friends" (*y pasan por amigos*) (Cutter 1994: 91). As for the Tehuacane, Yscani, and Taovaya, he stated that they made up one people. These were the groups principally responsible for the attacks at San Sabá. These groups had also been "provoked . . . by oppression and other mistreatment" (Cutter 1994: 91).

Two other major players in the implementation of the Spanish military policy were Jacobo de Ugarte de Loyola, governor of Coahuila beginning in 1769, and Colonel Juan de Ugalde, who succeeded Jacobo de Ugarte as governor of Coahuila in 1777, when the latter was appointed governor of Sonora (Moorhead 1968: 24, 46).

Between 1767 and 1770, the area of modern west Texas–easternmost Coahuila seems to have been fairly quiet, but starting in April 1770, a series of attacks on ranches and convoys led to renewed military action (Navarro 1770; Ugarte 1771). The state of unrest could be related to the food shortages experienced at this time and to the hike in the prices of wheat and corn (Ugarte 1770).

In April 1770, a gathering of more than three thousand Natives on the north side of the Rio Grande made Captain Manuel Rodrígues, commander of Presidio San Juan Bautista, very nervous. It appeared that a big Junta was under way; it included Julimeños and Apache (Ugarte 1770a). Short of manpower, Jacobo de Ugarte requested that the soldiers of the old Presidio de las Amarillas, which had moved to El Cañon, be transferred to Coahuila. The old Presidio de San Sabá was finally moved to the lands near the town of San Fernando de Austria and became known as the Presidio de Aguaverde. At this time, El Cañon was within Coahuila's jurisdiction (Ugarte 1771; 1771a). On July 3, 1771, Natives attacked the Santa Rosa presidio, taking six hundred horses and mules. The army was left with no horses (Ugarte 1771a).

This situation continued throughout 1771, 1772, and 1773, culminating with Hugo O'Conor's campaigns against the Apache in 1773 (Ugarte 1773). The major Native groups said to be involved in the depredations were the Lipan and the Julimeños. One of the groups involved in some of the attacks and robberies was led by the Lipan captain Vigottes (Bigotes), together with some of his captains (Ugarte 1773a). These Lipan were not the Lipan in Texas, understood as the territory east of the Medina River, but the Lipan west of the Medina River and south of the Rio Grande. The Lipan in Texas were at peace and causing no trouble.

In 1775–1776, Jacobo de Ugarte led an expedition north of the Rio Grande to reconnoiter Apache positions and to dislodge the Apache groups in the area who were in violation of the peace accords or who had not signed them. This expedition included a series of military reconnaissance trips to areas where enemy Apache groups were thought to be hiding. After traveling about 60 leagues (156 miles) north and east from the Presidio de San Juan Bautista on his way to the San Sabá area, he met several Lipan groups under Cabellos Largos, a Lipan, with whom O'Conor had concluded a peace treaty in 1774. At this camp Ugarte also met the Lipan captains Poca Ropa, Boca Tuerta, El Cielo, El Flaco, Panocha, Rivera, Javielillo, Paxarito, and Manteca Mucha, who were hunting buffalo with their families (Ugarte 1776). Although Ugarte stated that on the trip to San Sabá they did not find any enemy groups, the diary of Alexo de la Garza Falcon (1776) stated that, near the Rio San Sabá, there were several *rancherías* of Apache enemies. When they saw the soldiers, they fled in all directions. Garza did not identify the Apache groups, except to say that these were the same people who previously had attacked the Spaniards on the Río San Pedro (Garza Falcon 1776).

A reconnaissance trip made from Santa Rosa to the confluence of the Pecos River and the Rio Grande found no sign of recent Apache encampments in the area (Ugarte 1776). Another excursion was taken upstream on the Pecos River to the Guadalupe Mountains. The tracks and signs indicated that Apache groups stayed in this area often and for prolonged periods of time (Ugarte 1776). Once again, the salines west of the Guadalupe Mountains were rediscovered (Ugarte 1776).

Ugarte and his soldiers did not encounter any other hostile groups until they reached the Río San Pedro (?), a tributary of the Pecos. In a skirmish with a group of about fifty Apache, three Native warriors were killed and others were wounded. The Spanish lost three men (Ugarte 1776). Despite these campaigns, during the following months the Lipan continued to make small raids in Coahuila and along the Rio Grande.

After the dismal results of Jacobo de Ugarte's campaign, the Spanish were afraid to use Lipan guides and warriors, believing them to be double agents who informed the enemy about the movements of the Spanish troops (Ugarte 1776a). In November 1776, a Spanish captive boy ran away from the Apache. Juan Domingo Ochoa, the fourteen-year-old captured by the Apache, stated (Bonilla 1776) that some of the Apache were being led by a Spaniard named Andres, who had fled from the prison in Durango. The Apache had *escopetas* (a weapon similar to a harquebus), lances, and bows (Bonilla 1776). In 1776, O'Conor again campaigned against the Apache in the Guadalupe Mountains, Sierra Blanca, and the Pecos areas. About this same time, the Comanche raided an Apache camp of about three hundred families, killing everyone. This surprise attack was made while the Apache were hunting buffalo (Moorhead 1968: 41).

The complexity of social mechanisms and ethnic arrangements during this period, just as during earlier periods, is exemplified by the case of an Apache who became the principal leader of the Tancagua in 1779. In a letter to the Viceroy, Atanasio de Mezieres reported that an Apache who had been a captive of the Tancagua became their leader at the death of the elderly Tancagua principal leader. This Apache, known to the Spaniards as Mocho (mutilated) because he had lost an ear in battle, obtained this position through his feats and eloquence. Mocho had a large following and was consistently anti-Spanish. Atanasio de Mezieres (1779) recognized the social and political fact that Mocho had dual ethnicity (Chapter 1) ("recayendo ahora la principal en un Apache que despues de cautivado gozo de la adopcion y enfin por sus proesas de la mayor acepcion y sequito. Este sujeto à quien conocemos por el burlesco epitetho de mocho por que perdio peleando una oreja se ha acreditado de inquieto, amante de alborotos, y mui capas de suscitarlos à impulzo de cierta elocuencia que sabe adaptar al genio de la Nacion en que se ha connaturalizado. Ninguno nos ha sido mas contrario segun se experimento con su asistencia y ferocidad en el sacrilejo saqueo la mision de Sāba . . .") (Mezieres 1779). Mezieres said that Mocho, an Apache but also a Tancagua, had participated in the San Sabá attack. This statement indicates that the political reasons that led to the San Sabá attack, as well as the involvement in it of particular individuals and groups, were far more complex than has been assumed.

The Baron de Ripperdá and Atanasio de Mezieres made a pact with three of Mocho's closest allies to entice him to travel to Natchitoches to receive gifts. Sometime during the trip, these individuals were to kill Mocho (*le diesen fin*). Atanasio de Mezieres (1779) commented that there were so many people with reasons to assassinate Mocho that no one would think that the Spaniards had been involved in the plot. Meanwhile, an epidemic must have killed Atanasio's Native co-conspirators, since he reported that the individuals the Spanish wished dead, including Mocho, had survived, while others had perished. The tide had turned, and Atanasio de Mezieres pretended to be Mocho's friend (*me revesti del de verdadero Amigo*) and went to visit him in order to conclude peace agreements with the Tancagua (Mezieres 1779).

In 1779, New Mexico governor Juan Bautista de Anza made a campaign against the Comanche in New Mexico and dealt them a serious blow. By 1785, Governor Anza established a firm working peace with the Comanche. In 1786, Governor Domingo Cabello of Texas concluded a peace agreement with the so-called Eastern Comanche, using basically the same stipulations as those included in the New Mexico agreement made by Governor Anza. One of the stipulations was that the Comanche would make relentless war on the Lipan, would inform San Antonio of the intelligence they obtained on the Lipan, and would be allowed to enter Coahuila to attack Lipan and Mescalero groups (Moorhead 1968: 145–147). The Comanche division that troubled Coahuila and Texas was known as Cuchantica and was headed by a very reputable man named Ecueracapa[5] (Leather Cape).

At the end of the 1780s, a series of controversies and power plays pitched Jacobo de Ugarte, then governor of Sinaloa, against Juan de Ugalde, commander general of the Eastern Provinces, which included Coahuila and Texas. Most of the troubles centered on peace agreements made with the Mescalero, Lipan, and Lipiyan, at the presidios of El Paso and Santa Rosa. Some Mescalero groups, including the groups of captains Volante (also known as Ligero), Alegre, Cuero Verde, Bigotes el Bermejo, Montera Blanca, Zapato Tuerto, Patule, and El Quemado, signed a peace agreement with Ugarte via the El Paso military commanders. The officials at El Paso were also waiting for captains El Calbo and El Natagé, who appeared to be willing to join in the peace treaty. These captains and their people had been delayed because they were hunting buffalo in the sand dunes east of the Pecos River (Diaz 1787). According to Captain Domingo Diaz, of the El Paso presidio, the Mescalero involved in the peace agreement signed at his presidio amounted to about three thousand people with four hundred warriors. These numbers represented ten Mescalero *rancherías*, or an average of three hundred people and forty warriors per *ranchería*.

It appears that after the Mescalero groups signed the agreement at El Paso, they went to hunt buffalo and deer in the Sierra del Carmen, where they were attacked by Juan de Ugalde's soldiers and dispossessed of their belongings. Most important, Ugalde captured many of their women and children. Juan de Ugalde's rationale for this campaign was that these groups were found on the north side of the Rio Grande, where their peace agreements did not apply (Rengel 1787a; Ugarte 1787). Despite warnings by Jacobo de Ugarte and the military officials at El Paso, Juan de Ugalde continued his campaigns against the Mescalero, attacking the *ranchería* of Cuerno Verde, near the El Paso presidio, and those of Bigotes el Bermejo and Montera Blanca (Diaz 1787a; 1787b).

The Mescalero captains Patule, Zapato Tuerto, and El Quemado followed Juan de Ugalde to Santa Rosa because Ugalde promised to release their kinfolk. These Mescalero captains and other Mescalero signed a peace treaty with Juan de Ugalde at the Santa Rosa presidio, in part to obtain the release of their captives (Ugalde 1787). Ugalde's raids and the capture of their families created great unrest among the Mescalero. Despite these events, the military officials at El Paso managed to avoid reprisals by assuring the Mescalero that they would try to get their families released and would provide them with a military escort to go on a buffalo hunt (Rengel 1787a).

The issue of providing Spanish military escorts to the Apache while on the buffalo hunt was very controversial. Some officials considered that it completely contradicted the policy of Native mutual destruction ("al empeñar a las naciones de Yndios en su destruccion reciproca") that had been laid out by the Viceroy Conde de Galvéz (Rengel 1787a). Part of the problem with these escorts was that the peace agreements made with the Comanche and the northern groups condoned and fostered any attack on Apache groups outside the Texas territory, which was understood as the lands east of the Medina River and west of the Colorado River. When Spanish soldiers were seen protecting the Apache, traveling or camping with them outside of Texas territory, it angered the Comanche and exposed the Spanish soldiers to Comanche attacks. On the other hand, as Diaz explained (Diaz 1787b), the Spanish military did not have the means to feed and clothe the Mescalero population near the presidio, nor did the Apache like the food supplied by the Spaniards (Diaz 1787b; Rengel 1787a).

The Spanish understood that the Apache were willing to enter into peace agreements only because of the pressure created by the Comanche attacks in the north. This pressure was partly achieved and maintained by the peace treaties the Spanish signed with the Comanche, particularly with the Comanche general Ecueracapa. These treaties placed the Spaniards in very awkward positions when they made treaties with Apache groups. Juan de Ugalde considered them unhealthy alliances, unworthy of the Spanish military, and a practice that would be very costly in the long run (Rengel 1787, Rengel 1787a).

In September 1787, the Mescalero gathered at the El Paso presidio went on their buffalo hunt accompanied by a military escort. According to Diaz (Diaz 1787b, 1787c), the buffalo hunt was to take place within Apache lands. When the Mescalero at Santa Rosa learned that the Mescalero at El Paso had been allowed to go hunting with a military escort, they complained bitterly to Juan de Ugalde, who conceded and provided them with an escort to go buffalo hunting on the Río San Pedro, a tributary of the Pecos. According to Ugalde, they would be hunting more than 200 leagues (520 miles) from the southernmost *rancherías* of the Comanche. Ugalde was so concerned that they might encounter the Comanche that he gave precise instructions to his soldiers in case of an encounter.

When they were about to return home, on December 21, 1787, the Comanche attacked the hunting camp and the Spanish troops. According to Juan de Ugalde (1788), the Comanche had spied on the camp and knew perfectly well that the Mescalero were accompanied by Spanish troops. When the Comanche saw that the soldiers and the Mescalero were prepared to fight, they waved a white flag, and the encounter did not produce any serious results, except for the forty horses taken by the Comanche. Juan de Ugalde commented on the restraint demonstrated by the Apache, and took the opportunity to belittle the peace agreements made with the Comanche. He stated that such a peace was purchased with gifts: the Comanche would attack the Spaniards if they found them outside of Texas territory and whenever the gifts stopped (Ugalde 1788).

After the agreements with captains Patule and El Quemado, Juan de Ugalde made a peace agreement with Captain Guifiegusya (Good Shoe), a Mescalero. He also initiated negotiations to establish a peace agreement with Picax-ende-Ynstixle, a Lipyiane leader of the most numerous and strange nation of the whole Apacheria ("de la Nacion Lipi-yana, pues este Yndio manda por si solo la parzialidade mas numerosa, y Bizarra de toda la Apacheria"), whose Native name meant Strong Arm. Picax-ende-Ynstixle was recognized as a leader by the Lipan, Mescalero, Sendi, Nit-ajende, and Cachu-ende divisions. Picax-ende-Ynstixle had contacted Juan de Ugalde to ask for peace, and planned to come to Santa Rosa at the end of the year to discuss peace terms. Ugalde asked the Viceroy to award the Lipyiane leader special recognition, and to name him Capitán Grande of the whole Apache nation. He requested that a special parchment be made to commemorate the awarding of the title to Picax-ende-Ynstixle. The proclamation document was to be made in the name of Manuel Picax-ende-Ynstixle de Ugalde and decorated with trophies and coats of arms. Ugalde considered this a fitting gift to a man of such character and accomplishments (Ugalde 1787).

In November 1787, the conditions for peace with the Lipiyane were approved by the Viceroy, and Ugalde commented that there had been no problems in Texas among the Lipan, the Comanche, and the nations of the north (Ugalde 1787a). In March 1788, the peace agreement with the Lipiyane was signed at the Presidio de Santa Rosa (Ugalde 1788a).

In April 1788, Juan de Ugalde made an inspection tour of Texas. Ugalde reached the Atascoso Arroyo on April 13, where he was welcomed by several Lipan captains and the people of their movable *ranchería* (*pueblo ambulante*). They had set up their *rancherías* 2 leagues (5.2 miles) east of the Camino Real (Ugalde 1788c). The Lipan were armed with firearms, bows with crested plumes, leather breastplates, and defensive trappings, and had leather armor on their horses.

Ugalde stayed two days with the Lipan, talking, eating, and attending their *mitotes*. The Lipan were deeply concerned with the Spanish policy to exterminate them (*pen-savamos en sus exterminios*) (Ugalde 1788f). The *pueblo ambulante* had about five hundred people of all ages and sexes. This was a little over half of the total number of Lipan in Texas: the others were away with their principal captain, Zapato Sas, who left their *ran-chería* to pursue horses that had stampeded. At sunset, the Lipan held a *mitote* to honor Ugalde. Juan de Ugalde stated that the *mitote* was a feast the Apache prepared for their guests. *Mitotes* were also held to celebrate war victories (Ugalde 1788f).

Juan de Ugalde continued on his trip and crossed the Medina River to reach San Antonio. Before entering the town Ugalde was welcomed by 109 Lipan Apache, accompanied by their principal captain, Zapato Sas, "the best looking man in all the Apacheria" (Ugalde 1788f). Zapato Sas, who was accompanied by other captains, women, and children, had not been in San Antonio for over a year because of some incident that happened there. It appears that Ugalde thought that the Lipan were blameless in the matter.

Zapato Sas asked to talk privately with Ugalde. For several hours they discussed the Lipan situation in Texas, particularly the problems raised after the peace agreements with the Comanche. According to Ugalde (1788f), the gist of Zapato Sas's justified complaints (see Spanish text below) was that the Lipan felt abandoned since the peace treaty with the Comanche, which gave the Comanche an open-door policy and complete freedom to molest the Lipan. The situation would be very different if this policy had not been adopted. If the Spaniards were at war with the Comanche, as they actually were, the Spanish would make sure that the Comanche would not penetrate the interior of the province, where the Lipan had lived for a very long time. If the Comanche did try to penetrate the province, the Apache would fight them alongside the Spanish as they had done many times before. The friendship between Lipan and Spaniard was an old one: all the Lipan present at this gathering had been born after the arrival of the Spanish. This historical relationship and intimacy did not exist, nor could it exist, with the Comanche and other nations of the north, even though the Spanish had given the Comanche more presents in one year than they had given to the Apache in all the time the Spanish and the Apache had known each other. But the most painful thing of all, said Zapato Sas, was that the Spanish were providing the Comanche with firearms, gunpowder, and bullets. These military supplies, which had always been denied to the Lipan, were the reason for the increased strength of the Comanche:

> [D]esprecio que se havia hecho con particularidad desde las Pazes celebradas con los Comanches, que los emos avandonado y abriendo a aquellos todas las Puertas para obstilizarles como lo estan haziendo, que no sucedería a no ser por essa causa pues teniendo nosotros Guerra con dichos Comanches procuraríamos no se introdujeran en lo interior de la Provincia adonde la maior parte de los Lipanes se hallan situados di largo tiempo y quando lo practicaran, como acontecio antes de las Pazes saldrían con los Españoles a castigarlos segundo lo han hecho infinitas vezes pues la época de la amistad de los Lipanes es mui antigua que no hay uno de los presentes que no haiga nacido, criado y muerto a la vista de los Españoles lo que no ha sucedido ni sucederia assi con los Comanches, y demas Naciones del Norte no obstante el que les regalan a estes en mas uno ano que lo que se ha echo con los Lipanes en tantos [años] que les tratan y lo mas doloroso el franquearles Armas de fuego, Polvora y balas con que se les augmentan las fuerzas y que siempre se les há negado a los Lipanes [Ugalde 1788f].

Zapato Sas told Ugalde that his people were leaving for their *rancherías* on the Nueces River and invited Ugalde to visit them on his return trip to Coahuila.

In his comments about the Lipan in Texas, Ugalde (1788b) said that the Lipan were the strongest group of all the Apacheria, that he had great love for them, and that the Apache held him in the highest admiration and trust ("congregacion mas fuerte de la Apacheria . . . se declara apasionado delos, le deven el más alto concepto y la mayor confianza").

Juan de Ugalde continued to state that the solution for the Mescalero problem was their destruction and extermination (*destrucción y exterminio*), but his clear appreciation of the behavior and expertise of the Lipan indicates that he viewed the extermination of enemies as the objective of war, while friends were to be treated fairly. On the other hand, Juan de Ugalde had proven to be merciless and unpredictable.

On the afternoon of April 22, 1788, Juan de Ugalde was visited by three Taguaya captains and twenty-six of their people. They remained at San Antonio until the 28th, and held long talks with Ugalde. They promised to be peaceful, but Ugalde commented that they often transgressed, attacking convoys and stealing horses when they came to San Antonio to get their gifts. He stated (Ugalde 1788d) that this was an expensive way to obtain peace, but he believed the system to be very lucrative for those who accepted and promoted it and preferred that course to war. The Taguaya offered to help Ugalde in the war against the Mescalero, and he told them he would let them know. The Taguaya brought a captive from New Mexico: Juan de Ugalde redeemed the captive by giving the Taguaya some horses (Ugalde 1788d).

On May 1, 1788, three Taguacana captains came to San Antonio, accompanied by forty-five Natives and their women. One of these captains was a very important man, who had given many proofs of his loyalty to the Spaniards. He had fought the Comanche on the Spanish side, and had been wounded in that battle. On their way to San Antonio, the Taguacana met the Taguaya, who were leaving, and learned about the campaigns Ugalde was preparing against the Mescalero. The Taguacana offered to help in the campaigns, and Juan de Ugalde was very tempted to accept, especially because of the captain, for whom he had great regard. The Taguacana asked Ugalde to give them some troops so they could bring back a large number of Natives who had run away from Mission Espiritu Santu and taken refuge with the Taguacana. Juan de Ugalde declined the offer because the state of the missions was so deplorable that he did not think it would do the Natives any good to be housed there. According to Ugalde, the friars were looking after their self-interest and were despotic toward the Natives. In the end, he did send an interpreter and five soldiers to see how the Natives felt about returning (Ugalde 1788d).

On May 18, Juan de Ugalde left San Antonio and traveled to the Presidio de la Bahía, which he left on June 2. On June 4, 1788, he arrived at the Nueces River to visit the Lipan, as he had promised. The Lipan met him on the way with great demonstrations of joy. The camp was made up of sixty-three large *parletones* (meeting lodges?) and seventy-five huts (*xacales*). Many of the Lipan did not have huts and found shelter in the thick woods by the river. He brought food supplies for a feast and set up camp at about the distance of a gunshot from the *pueblo ambulante,* which had about seven hundred people. On June 7, Ugalde departed toward the mouth of the Nueces with six Lipan guides. From there he proceeded down the coast and west to Laredo (Ugalde 1788e).

While Juan de Ugalde was in Texas, the Mescalero groups at Santa Rosa and on the Río Sabinas rebelled. Ugalde (1788g) believed that the Spanish officials and the Mescalero groups at El Paso had a hand in the insurrection. He asked his friend and namesake,

Manuel Picax-ende-Ynstixle de Ugalde, to keep him informed of the events and to find out what the Mescalero were planning. Picax-ende-Ynstixle promised to visit him in the winter.

On November 21, 1788, Alferez Casimiro informed Juan de Ugalde that his friend and ally Picax-ende-Ynstixle had been killed by the Comanche in the first days of August. His son Davinica-jaté-ende, who was now governing the *ranchería* of his deceased father, brought the news. Davinica-jaté-ende stated (Ugalde 1788h) that the Comanche had attacked while his father was camped between the San Sabá River and the Colorado. His father had a warrior's death: with his lance he had killed four Comanche captains, including one wearing the kind of uniform the Spanish gave the Comanche in San Antonio. Davinica-jaté-ende assured Juan de Ugalde of his continued friendship and alliance, and told Ugalde that if he wanted to find him, he would be on the east side of the Pecos River. Whenever his people moved from one area to another, Davinica-jaté-ende would leave behind a cross in order that Juan de Ugalde could follow his trail and know where he was (Ugalde 1788h).

The juggling of peace agreements between Spanish and Comanche, and between Spanish and Apache, which had to be common knowledge among the interested parties, guaranteed discontent and distrust. Peace agreements whereby Comanche attacks against the Apache were both sanctioned and required can be understood only if it is accepted that both the Spaniards and the Comanche aimed at the complete destruction of the Apache. Part of the Spanish rationale for making and keeping the agreements with the Comanche and their allies was the fact that they did abide by their commitments, while the Apache did not. According to these agreements, the Comanche were not to injure the mission Apache. The notion that the Comanche and the Spaniards could, or would, distinguish Apache friend from foe is ludicrous: the Spanish did not, and the Comanche would not.

For the Comanche, this was the best possible arrangement. They could proceed with the killing of their enemies and be rewarded for doing so. The Spanish consistently turned a blind eye to their misdeeds, and the Comanche enjoyed the benefits of safe-conduct in most places. During tough times, they could raid the Apache for supplies instead of having to harass the Spanish. The Apache would raid the Spanish, the Comanche would raid the Apache: the Comanche would reap the profits and the Apache would be blamed.

The military campaigns of Juan de Ugalde against the Apache were surgical, cruel, and single-minded. The enmities among Viceroy Manuel Antonio Flores, Jacobo de Ugarte, and Juan de Ugalde resulted in mixed and contradictory policy messages, and created severe confusion among the Natives, particularly the Apache. In the end, the aims of all three officials were the same: the destruction of the Apache. The difference lay in the means to the end. While Flores and Juan de Ugalde were bent on a war without mercy, with no allowance for voluntary peace treaties, Jacobo de Ugarte endorsed a policy of attrition through military campaigns that systematically disrupted the lives of the Apache. For Ugarte, warriors were either killed in battle or remanded to prison or labor houses.

Women and children were spared to serve in private houses or were shipped overseas (Moorhead 1968: 134). For the Apache, one wonders which strategy was more cruel.

Between August and December 1789, Juan de Ugalde's troops attacked Lipiyán and Mescalero camps at Piedras Negras on the Rio Grande, and between San Sabá and San Antonio in Texas. On January 9, 1790, a large group of Mescalero, Lipiyán, and Lipan suffered a serious attack by the northern groups. Before they could recover, Juan de Ugalde, with the help of 140 Comanche warriors, ambushed what was left of these Apache groups on the Frio River in Texas. The losses suffered by the Apache were considerable. Ugalde continued his campaign, attacking Lipan and Gileños in the Guadalupe Mountains during April 1790 (Moorhead 1968: 255).

The reprieve for Apache groups came in the form of a change of military leaders. Viceroy Flores was replaced by the Conde de Revillagigedo, who disagreed with the policy followed by Flores and Ugalde, and endorsed Jacobo de Ugarte's approach to the Apache problem. Revillagigedo was particularly upset by attacks against the Lipan (Moorhead 1968: 257). Jacobo de Ugarte was instructed to contact and gather the representatives of the various divisions of the Apache in order to reestablish the peace agreements and a measure of trust.

It is instructive to note, once again, where these groups were found. The Natagé were in the Organ and Sacramento mountains of New Mexico. Some of the Lipiyán were at Sierra Obscura, north of the Sacramento Mountains, while others were in the Sacramento Mountains. The Mescalero were at Sierra del Carmen and Sierra Rica. The Mescalero were asked to look for the Lipan and reported that they could not find them (Moorhead 1968: 258, 259, 267).

In October 1790, the Mescalero went on their buffalo hunt to the area between the Nueces and the Colorado rivers in Texas, accompanied by a Spanish military escort. Before departing they requested that some of their women who had been captured by Juan de Ugalde in his campaigns be allowed to join them on the hunt to help skin and butcher the buffalo. Their request was granted. Near the Nueces River they met a band of Comanche and apparently, due to an ironic series of misunderstandings, the Apache attacked and killed three Comanche while under the protection of Spanish soldiers (Moorhead 1968: 262–263). Episodes like this confirm the impossibility of maintaining an effective and coherent military policy. While the Mescalero were on the hunt, they saw a large group of Lipan butchering buffalo on the banks of the Nueces River. When the Mescalero approached, the Lipan left. Quite possibly these were the groups who had traveled from the Sacramento to the Nueces to hunt (see below).

On October 26, before the Mescalero left for their buffalo hunt, a Lipan couple came to the presidio at El Paso to find out about the peace agreement and its conditions. The couple explained that they had not been able to come to the presidio earlier because they had traveled from the Sacramento Mountains to the Nueces River to hunt buffalo. They reported that the Upper Lipan were camped between the Sacramento Mountains and Sierra Blanca. In general, the Lower Lipan continued to abide by the peace agree-

ments made in 1773 with Hugh O'Conor. Peace agreements between the Upper Lipan
and the Spanish were concluded in 1790. It was agreed that the Upper Lipan would reside near San Fernando de Austria and the Rio Grande, while the Lower Lipan would
remain between San Antonio and the Rio Grande (Moorhead 1968: 265, 267).

In 1791, the Upper Lipan broke the peace agreement when some of their envoys were
seized at Santa Rosa and at San Fernando de Austria, but they reopened negotiations in
1792. Sometime in 1792, the Comanche, under Ecueracapa, attacked the Lipan, Lipiyán,
and Llanero on the San Sabá and Nueces rivers. The uneasy peace between the Lipan
and the Spanish lasted until 1799, at which time the Spanish declared open war on the
Apache.

REFLECTIONS

During the period of the late eighteenth century, Apache groups, primarily the Lipan
and Mescalero, used the Spaniards as a buffer between themselves and the Comanche,
the northern groups, and the Tejas and their allies.

The Spanish missionary experiment with the Apache was a natural progression of their
policies, but a failure nonetheless. The friars had little to offer the Apache except relative protection. The resilience of the Apache (as a collective) resided in their cultural
precepts and their adherence to them. Unlike other groups, whose cultural core probably went underground when they entered missionary establishments, Apache groups
displayed their culture and their achievements. Fr. Ximenes recognized this difference
and comprehended that their worldview would allow them neither peace from their enemies nor the kind of submission that would satisfy the Spanish. The friar understood
that it was that same worldview that constituted them as Apache.

The Spanish envied Apache freedom and admired their horsemanship and warring
tactics, but they found the Apache unyielding and incapable of submission. The Spanish
citizens and the military resented the protection afforded the Apache, which brought the
Spanish few benefits and considerable trouble. The Spanish policy of protecting Apache
groups with missions and providing military escorts to their buffalo-hunting forays was
an affront to the Tejas and their allies, leading the Apache enemies to continual attacks
on San Sabá and on the missions on the Nueces. Captain Parrilla's major military blun-
der against the Norteños demonstrated the weakness of the Spanish and reinforced the
determination of the northern groups.

The shifts in policy and military strategy toward the Native populations that took
place in the last decades of the eighteenth century profoundly affected the lives of Native
Americans, particularly the Apache groups. The avowed policy of mutual destruction,
which utilized the Comanche and the northern groups as lethal weapons against the
Apache, was conceptually flawless. It should have gone like this: the Apache would fight
the Comanche; the Comanche would fight the Apache; eventually, they would eliminate
each other.

Under the conditions prescribed by the policy of mutual destruction, either the Apache were allied with the Spaniards or the wrath of both Spaniards and Comanche was un-leashed on them. However, if they were allied with the Spaniards, the Spanish military was forced to protect them. The Spanish had to ensure Apache safety while hunting be-cause they could not provide them with adequate food supplies, and they were compelled to use the Apache as spies, guides, warriors, and interpreters. To maintain their alliances with the Apache and the Comanche, the Spaniards were caught in a game of sleight-of-hand: there were times when the Apache were fair game for the Comanche and other times when they were off-limits.

The Comanche, by treaty, were not to molest the mission Apache. Assuming that the Comanche wanted to do so, how could they tell a mission Apache from a nonmission Apache? To get the cooperation of the Comanche and the northern groups against the Apache, as well as to guarantee that the Comanche would not molest the Spanish, the Spanish Crown paid them off with gifts, weapons, and ammunition. There was nothing covert about these dealings; all the groups involved knew what was at stake.

Notwithstanding the sophistry of these agreements, they had real impact on the lives of Native Americans. But the Spanish were involved in a colonial war, and it was in-cumbent upon them to win it. The policy of mutual destruction was coupled with very effective military campaigns, and these campaigns forced the Apache into a succession of peace agreements. The Comanche, empowered by dubious treaties with the Spanish, freed of the threat of the Apache, and well supplied with weaponry, became the nemesis of the nineteenth century, as Juan de Ugalde had predicted.

During the late eighteenth century the area of San Sabá, the Concho River drain-age, and the Nueces River continued to be the preferred hunting grounds of the Apache groups. Their presence continued, both in Texas, understood as the territory east of the Medina River, and in eastern Coahuila, understood as the territory west of the Medina River. When the pressure became too intense, Apache groups returned to the Guada-lupe, Organ, and Sacramento mountains of New Mexico. From the safety of that rugged terrain, which they had occupied intermittently for almost two centuries, they forayed to hunt buffalo on the Pecos, San Sabá, and Nueces rivers. The convoluted events of colonial history led most of them back home.

EIGHT

Ethnohistory and Archaeology

SETTING THE STAGE

The preceding chapters dealt with the ethnohistoric events that affected the lives of Native groups in the Edwards Plateau and related areas, as recorded by the European colonizers. This chapter deals, briefly, with the intersection of the ethnohistoric and the archaeological records, and with some ways in which the former can illuminate the latter.

The period of contact between Native Americans and Europeans refers, in present archaeological terms, to the two periods designated as Late Prehistoric and Historic. For this reason, no summary of prior archaeological time periods will be attempted. The Late Prehistoric is characterized by the Austin Interval, 1250 B.C.–A.D. 650 (Ricklis and Collins 1994: 14), and the Toyah Interval, between A.D. 1300–1320 and A.D. 1600–1650 or 1700 (Johnson 1994: 258). The dates for these intervals, particularly the Toyah Interval, vary somewhat according to site location, availability and reliability of radiocarbon assays, and the personal view of the researcher. The Historic period, as it stands, is rooted in the terminal dates for the Toyah Interval. For the purpose of this study, only the Toyah Interval and the period termed Historic are relevant.

In light of these stated objectives and temporal parameters, this chapter focuses on two main points, namely: (1) a pedestrian reflection on the meaning of *historical,* as well as the relationship between the evidence from the ethnohistoric and the archaeological records, and (2) a discussion of the location of some reported sites of the Late Prehistoric and Historic periods relative to the routes taken by the Spanish expeditions discussed in this work. In addition, I discuss the location of specific Native groups encountered during these expeditions.

THE MEANING OF HISTORY AND THE TOYAH INTERVAL

History "happened" at different times to different Native groups in the modern Texas territory. The type and duration of contact with Europeans, as recorded by the latter, varied in its earliest period between 1528 and the 1540s, principally with Cabeza de Vaca (1528–1535) and the Coronado and De Soto–Moscoso journeys of the 1540s. If by *history,* as defined by Western scholars, is meant the existence of written records resulting from contact, then almost half of the Prehistoric Toyah Interval falls into the Historic Period. If we accept that definition of history and the latest posting of possible time limits for the Toyah Interval (Johnson 1994: 258), it is apparent that the Toyah archaeological manifestations existed prior to contact and continued through contact. This raises important issues of continued Native cultural practices in the postcontact period (Hester, personal communication, 1998), acculturative choices, and culture change.

Obviously, the localized sporadic and limited contact between Native Americans and Europeans experienced between 1528 and 1542 is more likely to have affected Native life in concealed ways, such as the dispersion of pathogens, than in the cultural patterning of Native activities. The same, however, cannot be said for one case in particular, and quite possibly for others.

THE EVIDENCE

On August 7, 1583, Espejo met three Jumano Natives on the Pecos River near the modern town of Pecos (Hammond and Rey 1966: 209). These Jumano told Espejo that the Pecos River "came out far below the Conchos" and that they would take Espejo "by good trails" to the junction of the Rio Grande with the Río Conchos (Hammond and Rey 1966: 209). The information clearly indicates that before 1583, the Jumano traveled extensively and were very familiar with the course of the Pecos River from the modern town of Pecos to the Rio Grande and perhaps beyond.

On October 26, 1590, Castaño de Sosa reached the Pecos River. Two days later, traveling upstream on that river, he passed "many recently built rancherías" (Schroeder and Matson 1965: 55). On October 31, further upstream, Castaño de Sosa found the saline (Soda Lake) that Mendoza would encounter more than ninety-three years later, on January 14, 1684. Mendoza traveled about 26 miles downriver from that spot on the Pecos to the Gediondo *ranchería* in three days. It seems extremely likely that the *rancherías* Castaño de Sosa saw were near or at the *ranchería* of the Gediondo. The two locations were almost certainly near 41CX-3 and 41CX-4, since these two sites extend a combined distance of about 10 miles along the northeast side of the Pecos River. If this is correct, the course of the Pecos River, at this point, may have defined the boundaries of Jumano groups that lay eastward.

In 1632, Fr. Juan Salas visited the Jumano in their lands on the Nueces River (the Concho River in Texas). In 1650, captains Hernan Martin and Diego de Castillo traveled again to the Jumano lands in the Concho River drainage. These trips were discussed by Fr. Benavides (Ayer et al. 1965: 58), by Mendoza (in Fernandez Duro 1882: 57) in the 1600s, and in 1882 by Fernandez Duro (57–58). In 1654, Captain Diego de Guadalajara again visited the Jumano on the Concho River. Among the soldiers who accompanied him was Juan Dominguez de Mendoza (Chapter 4). However, the original documentation attesting to these trips has not been found, and it may have been lost during the upheaval of the 1680 Pueblo Revolt.

In 1683–1684, the Mendoza-Lopez expedition visited the Jumano in their lands and at their request. Between 1650 and 1680, small groups of Spanish individuals traveled to the Jumano lands to trade. In 1683, Juan Sabeata confirmed these visits and trade relations. Sabeata also mentioned that Captain Castillo had been contacted by a Tejas lieutenant sent as an envoy of the Tejas leader. Sabeata was born between 1630 and 1639 and may have been present at the time of Castillo's visit. This documentary evidence, provided by a Native American, confirms the presence of the Jumano in the Concho River drainage, certainly by 1650. It also verifies contacts between the Tejas (Caddo) and the Spanish as early as 1650, and confirms the friendship between Jumano groups and the Tejas.

During the Martin-Castillo (1650) and the Guadalajara (1654) trips, the Spanish encountered and engaged in battle three Native groups: the Cuitoa, the Escanjaque, and the Ayjado. Version M of the Mendoza-Lopez expedition (Chapter 4) indicates that Mendoza traveled to the general area where the Spanish had previously encountered the Cuitoa, Escanjaque, and Ayjado (campgrounds San Sebastian, San Roque, and Los Desamparados). Whoever these groups were, they were no longer occupying the same territory in 1684 under the same ethnic designations. Because the Jumano appear to have participated in the Cuitoa affair and to have informed on the Escanjaque, it is possible that the Jumano and their allies benefited from the Spanish actions against the Cuitoa, the Escanjaque, and the Ayjado, and possibly from the displacement of these groups, or even their loss of territory.

Basing my interpretation on Sabeata's 1683 statements and the events of Mendoza's journey, I take the Gediondo *ranchería* to have been near the western limits of the Jumano lands. These Jumano lands probably extended east of the Concho River drainage, east and west of San Angelo, and southward from that drainage over much of the Edwards Plateau. These limits may have been pushed, temporarily, eastward of the Concho River drainage toward the Colorado River after the Martin-Castillo and Guadalajara battles mentioned above. The 1684 westward limits of the Jumano lands may have been the same as in 1583, when Espejo met the Jumano near the Pecos.

There is no question that the visits of 1632, 1650, and 1654 fall within the Toyah Interval time span. There is also little question that Jumano groups inhabited both the region of La Junta de los Ríos and the Concho River drainage, since none other than Sabeata stated that his people lived in the two areas (Appendix). There is also little question that the Toyah components of the Buckhollow site (and other sites) fall within that period (Johnson 1994: 238). Whether the Jumano proper, or groups associated with the Jumano, can be linked with the archaeological material expression whose particular constituents are named Toyah Culture (or cultures) is altogether a different issue.

I have not researched the Toyah material culture as some scholars have (for example, Hester 1975, 1991, 1995; Johnson 1994; Ricklis and Collins 1994, to name a few); therefore, I do not presume to make an assessment of the validity of their respective positions.

My intent, as stated, is simply to provide solid ethnohistorical evidence of the presence of Native groups in the area, and to establish a dialogue between different sets of evidence to lead to the reevaluation of earlier research and point to further research considerations and possibilities.

The Toyah Interval is characterized by a predominance of Perdiz arrow points, although the dominance of Perdiz varies according to the area (Hester 1975: 115; 1995: 442–450). The other ubiquitous components of the Toyah material culture are end and side scrapers, two- and four-edged beveled knives, flake drills, and gravers. While some lithic tools were produced from flakes, others were produced from blades. Thus, the lithic tool kit includes a mixture of core and blade technologies (Hester 1975: 121; 1995: 444). Some sites have milling slabs and manos. Bone-tempered and sometimes sand-tempered ceramics are present at most Toyah sites, in varying percentages. The faunal remains include large game animals, such as buffalo, deer, and antelope, as well as a wide variety of smaller animals. The faunal remains indicate a subsistence strategy based on a broad utilization of environmental resources. The floral remains are, by their very nature, less informative about patterns of utilization, but hackberry seeds and sedges are sometimes present. The Toyah sites are generally open campsites or rock shelters, but Toyah materials have been found in and around Spanish mission compounds (Hester, personal communication, 1998).

In 1947, J. Charles Kelley (1947: 115–128) suggested that the artifacts recovered from the Lehman Rockshelter in the Llano River Drainage were connected with the Jumano (Kelley 1947: 122). The shelter provided Perdiz arrow points (21), four-edged beveled knives, and two thin sand- and bone-tempered pottery sherds. These sherds had "a red washed semi polished surface" (Kelley 1947: 123; 1986; see also Johnson 1994: 193). His statement linking the Jumano with the Lehman Rockshelter material culture resulted from his appraisal of archaeological remains from La Junta de los Ríos, near Presidio, Texas, and the connections between the area of La Junta and the Jumano.

In 1994, LeRoy Johnson (1994: 267) suggested that the high mobility of the Native Cibolo and Jumano groups made them unlikely candidates for association with Toyah materials. Alternatively, it might have been precisely their mobility and pattern of dual residency that placed the Jumano and their associated groups in the unique position of enablers, or promoters, of the Toyah techno-functional kit. Undoubtedly, the kit-set would not have been accepted wholesale. Different populations would mesh elements of the kit with particular needs and local traditions, introducing variability in the "pseudo-original" kit. Most of them, but not all, appear to have retained the ubiquitous Perdiz arrow point.

On the other hand, Johnson postulated the possibility, among several others, that the Toyah archaeological material expression might reflect influences from far western Texas or eastern Chihuahua (Johnson 1994: 277). These and other possible Toyah connections have also been discussed by Hester (1995) and Mallouf (1987), among other researchers.

The lands of the Jumano and affiliated groups, such as the Gediondo and the Arcos Tuertos, are completely encompassed by the area that LeRoy Johnson (1994: 243) de-

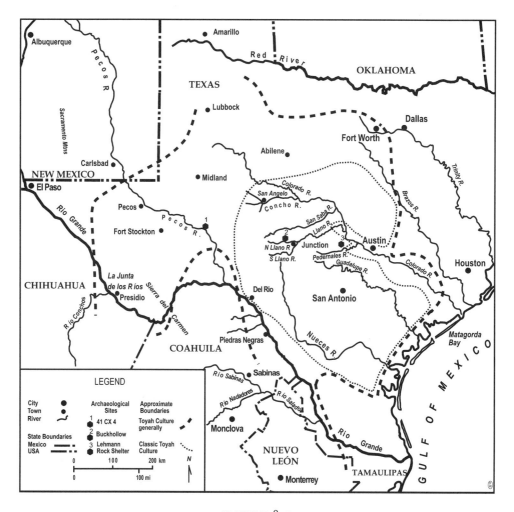

FIGURE 8.1
Map showing the approximate boundaries of the Toyah Culture. Adapted from LeRoy Johnson,
The Life and Times of Toyah-Culture Folk *(Office of the State Archeologist, Report 38,*
Texas Department of Transportation and Texas Historical Commission, Austin), figure 105.

picts as the area of the Classic Toyah Culture. The northwestern boundary of the Classic
Toyah area essentially coincides with the boundary I have suggested above for the Jumano
lands.

Whatever the case may be, neither the archaeological nor the ethnohistoric evidence
is sufficient to warrant conclusions. One thing appears evident, however: either the communities that used the Buckhollow site (and other sites in the region) were not Jumano
groups, or Jumano groups become the likeliest candidates for the honor of being called
"Toyah folk." That appears to be the most parsimonious explanation, since we do know
that, historically, these groups were living in those lands at the time apportioned for the
Buckhollow and other sites in the vicinity. If one assumes that they were not Jumano

groups, then we should find in the general area, if not on that specific site, material culture evidence that differs from that presented for the Toyah Interval.

On the other hand, if the Jumano, and some of the groups associated with them, were the agents of dispersion of a technological idea and tool kit, it is likely that they used at least pieces of that same tool kit. Often there is a considerable difference between the elements of a tool kit (in this case a set of lithic tools) and a site assemblage. Potentially, variability would be expressed in two ways: total site assemblage and lithic tool kit. The variability of the site assemblage would reflect the type of site and the group whose living activities produced it. The variability in the tool kit would reflect, presumably, the choices exercised by a given group when presented with the Toyah lithic options. Thus, it may prove advantageous to compare whole site assemblages as well as to compare, independently, the lithic assemblages.

It is a fact that Jumano groups were coeval with the Late Prehistoric (or Protohistoric) Toyah Interval in the Concho and Llano Rivers in the Edwards Plateau. Notwithstanding the scenarios presented above, it does not follow that Jumano groups introduced or were the carriers of the Toyah cultural expression. The presence of Jumano groups, taken together with the Toyah material culture archaeological expressions, may simply mean that these groups used the material culture kit, or elements of the kit, best adapted to their procurement activities and lifeways.

As far as I have been able to determine, Jumano groups hunted buffalo and deer, at least biannually, and processed deer and buffalo skins. The Xoman, as Jumano or a Jumano group, used animal fat, both rendered and nonrendered. The Bosque-Larios party was offered animal hides prepared for bedding and animal hides prepared for clothing, as well as animal fat (*sebo*) and rendered animal fat (*manteca*), by the Teaname, Teimammar, Teroodam, and Xoman. There is no mention of lithic tools or pottery being observed in any record I consulted. It is obvious, however, that they did manufacture lithic implements, since they had bows and arrows and processed and prepared hides.

The expression "Jumano groups" used here requires clarification. Judging from the research completed, it is very likely that the Jumano, in a broad sense, represented a series of groups that included (at least) the Jumano proper, the Cibolo, the Gediondo, the Machome, and Those Who Make Bows (or Arcos Fuertes, Arcos Tuertos, or Arcos Buenos), apparently related to the Suma, or the Suma proper. It is also possible that the word *Jumano* was often used to designate the *aggregate* of all the Jumano groups—in colonial Spanish parlance, the Jumano "nation"—and not a particular group designated as Jumano.

It is not clear whether the Xoman were a group of the Jumano or the Jumano proper. I am inclined to think that they were a group of the Jumano, because the Jumano were known since the 1580s as Jumano, and were known in Saltillo by the name Jumano and Juman from the 1630s or 1640s. Fr. Larios was familiar with them at least by 1673 (Chapter 3), and I do not think that Fr. Larios would mistake Juman for Xoman, even though the consonants *j* and *x* were interchangeable. Furthermore, the list compiled by Fr. Larios on December 30, 1674, lists the group as Jumanes (Chapter 1). On the other hand, the Xoman, who were first encountered on the Edwards Plateau, did not visit Balcarcel in Monclova, nor does their name appear in any of the earlier records except for those of the Bosque-Larios expedition. Quite likely, the set of groups associated with the Jumano changed through time, depending on the circumstances and the alliances made, but some of these were core-member groups because of kin affiliation, language, or both.

NATIVE GROUPS

This study has identified twenty-one Native groups that lived and used the Edwards Plateau, certainly in the 1670s and possibly during the last decades of the seventeenth century. These groups were the Ape, Arame, Bagname, Bobole, Ervipiame, Geniocane, Gueiquesale, Jumee, Mabibit (Bibit), Manos Prietas, Ocane, Pataguache, Pinanaca, Siano (Sana), Teaname, Tereoodan (Terecodam), Xaeser, and Xoman.

The lists of Native group names provided by the Mendoza-Lopez expedition include many names, but there is no evidence that those groups lived in the area of the Edwards Plateau in 1683–1684, except for the Arcos Tuertos, the Gediondo (Hutaca or Parugan), and the Jumano.

The Toyah Interval has been dated to between A.D. 1300–1320 and A.D. 1650–1700 (Johnson 1994: 258). Thus, the possible dates for the Jumano occupation of a major portion of the Edwards Plateau and the accepted dates for the terminal Toyah Interval overlap. Additional ethnohistorical research, combined with careful selection and excavation of sites within this region of the Edwards Plateau, may afford valid ties between the Jumano populations and the Toyah material culture and help to explain the variability in the ubiquitous Toyah tool kit, or, alternatively, highlight material culture manifestations that do not fit the Toyah profile. Sites along the Pecos River, between Girvin and Iraan, as well as sites along the Concho River drainage, deserve further evaluation for such a program. A comparison between the material culture remains from these sites and the materials obtained from sites in the La Junta area, where the Jumano are known to have lived, may also prove fruitful.

The expeditions of Fr. Manuel de la Cruz, Bosque-Larios, and Mendoza-Lopez (and the partial routes of Castaño de Sosa and Espejo-Lúxan) provide the modern researcher with a unique environmental record of a large portion of modern Texas territory, as well as with a glimpse at the Native people that inhabited these lands during that period. This portion of Texas territory would not be traversed again by Europeans until late in the eighteenth century, and by then Apache groups had transformed the human landscape.

REFLECTIONS

The ethnohistorical record is defined in reference to the recorded word, while the archaeological record is defined in terms of material culture expressions. Both records are bound by temporal parameters. The records are not that different: time and cultural manifestations define both, and both suffer, ultimately, from potentially biased interpretations. The ethnohistoric record provides evidence of events that can question, illuminate, or confirm the material culture evidence from the archaeological record. As records of evidence, neither should be privileged, nor should they stand in confrontation to each other. It is the tension established between both sets of evidence that can prove productive.

The idiosyncrasies of definition and classification have made it awkward to discuss ethnohistoric events in Late Prehistoric terms. This is especially true for the events connected with the Bosque-Larios and Mendoza-Lopez expeditions. These are historic expeditions that involve Late Prehistoric (or Protohistoric) Native groups! Although the issue is considerably more complicated than it may appear, it is probably time to reconsider the conceptual boundaries that determine what is prehistoric, protohistoric, and historic.

The evidence from archival documents locates twenty-one different Native American groups in the physiographic region of the Edwards Plateau. Several of the groups contacted by Fr. Larios and his coworkers lived in the Dacate or Yacatsol area, the dissected portion of the Edwards Plateau, the Hill Country. This area, Dacate and Yacatsol, was described in terms of several localized geographic features: arroyos, rivers, and mountains. Both the Native word *Dacate* and the Nahuatl-derived word *Yacatsol* were said to mean "noses" in Castilian ("stone noses" or "pointed things" in Nahuatl). Indeed, the Native descriptive words are appropriate: the broken edges of the Escarpment can be described as noses pointing *outward* from the face of the Edwards Plateau. In terms of features and micro-environments, this area would (and does) stand in contrast to the flat area of the Edwards Plateau to the north and the Coastal Plains to the south.[1]

Some of the groups associated with the Edwards Plateau appear on record as early as 1582–1583, and some in the 1670s and 1680s. The record confirms the presence of the Jumano proper, and possibly other groups affiliated with the Jumano, in the Edwards Plateau from the 1630s through the 1680s. These dates place the Jumano proper within the spatial and temporal grid postulated for the Toyah Interval, A.D. 1300–1320 and A.D. 1600–1650 or 1700 (Johnson 1994: 258). This evidence does not necessarily mean that the Jumano proper, or the groups affiliated with the Jumano, were connected with the archaeological material culture kit that characterizes the Toyah Interval. If the Jumano were not connected with the Toyah cultural manifestations, we should find other identifiable material culture expressions that diverge from the Toyah pattern, and can be associated with the Jumano and affiliated groups.

The evidence gathered in this study provides the basis for further ethnohistoric and archaeological research. It is incumbent upon archaeologists to reevaluate the material evidence for the Late Prehistoric, and ethnohistorians must continue a program of systematic archival research to attempt to clarify these issues.

NINE

Conclusions:

WEAVING THE THREADS

The recorded history of Native groups in Texas and Coahuila is woven into the fabric of European colonial history, particularly Spanish history. To pull the threads of Native history out of the weave of archival records constructed by Spanish officials and churchmen requires systematic and detailed research.

This work has gathered and analyzed documentary evidence about the Native American groups that, between 1582 and 1799, lived in and utilized the physiographic region called the Edwards Plateau and related areas. The evidence shows the impact of Native Americans in the colonization process and the sophistication and malleability of Native social arrangements. The following analysis focuses on the historical events presented in the book and how those events make manifest the roles and social sophistication of the Native groups in Texas and Coahuila.

In 1658, in Saltillo, some Babane and Jumano Natives, whose numbers were dwindling, attempted to shore up their ethnic viability and escape the confinement and social disruption of *encomiendas* and mining camps by organizing in pueblos. In 1673–1674 a large number of Native groups with members on both sides of the Rio Grande again requested permission to establish autonomous settlements. This time the project received the help of Franciscan friars, particularly Fr. Juan Larios, who enlisted the support of influential individuals such as Don Antonio Balcarcel. These requests were the primary reason for the trips of Fr. Manuel de la Cruz and Fr. Peñasco north of the Rio Grande, and they led to the Spanish resettlement of Monclova, the establishment of the Native pueblo of San Miguel de Luna, and the creation of several mission-settlements in Coahuila. When the Spanish realized they could not fulfill their settlement promises, Fernando del Bosque and Fr. Larios traveled north of the Rio Grande to quiet the groups and convince them to remain in their lands. By then, groups like the Yorica had moved out of their lands and to the south side of the Rio Grande.

In the attempt to obtain permission to settle and to co-opt some of the benefits provided to the Tlaxcaltecans by their settlement charter, the 1673 Native petitioners asked that Tlaxcaltecan families be allowed to share their settlement, and provided legal testimony of the military help given by the Bobole to the Spanish. While most Tlaxcaltecan pueblos persisted against all odds, the mission-settlements created for other Native groups faltered for a variety of reasons.

The Spanish settlers' progressive occupation of the best lands, the virulent conflicts among settlers, military, and clergy over the control of Native labor, and the enmities among Native groups combined to undermine the labors of friars and Native leaders. But the most important reason for the lackluster results of the mission-settlements was the different expectations held by the Natives and the friars. Neither group realized the magnitude of the changes involved or the time required to accomplish them. For the Natives, a change in subsistence practices implied a quantum change in the cycles of their lives. For the friars, the ethos of their work and commitment precluded an evaluation of the Natives' dilemma. From a long-term perspective the church efforts bore fruit in the belief syncretism imparted to later generations.

The events of the 1680s, the shifting of power structures in New Mexico, and the restlessness of the Apache put on notice the Spanish and the Native groups in Coahuila and Texas. The conjuncture of events that placed Juan Mendoza at El Paso in 1683 created the conditions for Juan Sabeata's bargain with the Spanish: without Sabeata and his allies it is unlikely the Spanish would have traveled to central Texas. Whatever really happened on that expedition—mutinous soldiers, conflicts between the Natives and the Spanish, or both—Sabeata and his allies had to feel abused and defrauded. In this bargain, the Native coalition treated the Spaniards as allies—not the other way around. As members of the Native coalition, the Spanish proved untrustworthy.

The Spanish did not heed the Jumano's warning about the Apache. The events of the first part of the eighteenth century may have made them wish they had. Pressed between Apache and Spaniard, local Native groups joined the Apache, entered missions, or fanned out into temporary ethnic strongholds: most died out. Without the Apache, some might have been able to survive the Spanish; without the Spanish, some might have been able to emerge from the Apache. The Spanish military campaigns of the 1730s and 1740s led the Apache in Texas to sign peace treaties that, for the most part, they honored. The Apache missions established at San Sabá, and later on the Nueces River, were missions only in name. The missions served as temporary campgrounds for the Apache when they came to hunt buffalo and wanted to broadcast their friendship with the Spanish. However, the history of the Apache west of the Medina River and in the Edwards Plateau is not altogether the history of the Lipan in Texas (east of the Medina River). The events in the area west of the Medina and northward into the Edwards Plateau involved other Apache groups, such as the Natagé and the Lipyiane.

In the second half of the eighteenth century, Spanish political and military policies placed the Apache in an untenable situation. The policy of mutual destruction, masterminded by the Conde de Galvé, supplied the Comanche and the northern groups with weapons and legal authorization to hunt the Apache. This policy, which aimed at the destruction of the Apache by the Comanche and vice-versa, was continually stoked by gifts to the Comanche and their allies. These gifts were procured and acquired by individuals who made considerable profits. Juan de Ugalde and Fr. Ximenez understood the economic interests that precluded a "fair" war or an accommodating peace. As Ugarte predicted, others, later, would reckon with the consequences of that policy.

EARLY SETTLEMENTS

The early attempts to settle permit four important observations. First, they originated from within the fold of Native societies. Second, they were completely unsolicited and vehemently opposed by the European settlers. Third, they were neither a result of the direct intervention of Catholic ministers, nor an attempt to bargain for rewards. Fourth, they were the result of a Native attempt to deal with social and cultural conditions that threatened the viability of their populations in ethnic terms. These attempts also underline three important issues. First, such adaptive sociocultural mechanisms had to be present in the panoply of solutions available to the Native communities, since social and cultural arrangements of this magnitude do not simply materialize when needed. Second, Native populations recognized population thresholds beyond which ethnic viability became questionable. And third, they were willing to forgo a traditional version of hunting and gathering practices to contemplate a mixed economy that relied on traditional patterns of hunting and gathering coupled with crop raising.

NATIVE GROUP COALITIONS

The establishment of Native group coalitions served very specific objectives. These coalitions were of different sizes and scales, and their dimensions reflected integrative factors, such as linguistic and kin ties, as well as broader commonality of interests, such as the threat posed by a common enemy. The evidence for these coalitions, often expressed in lists of allies, is overwhelming, as is the evidence for broader concerns that fostered the organization of the coalitions. These lists are indeed material and cultural evidence. The examples of the groupings of Don Esteban, Don Lacaro, Juan de la Cruz, and Captain Miguel, as well as Juan Sabeata, the Tejas, the Ranchería Grande, and Picax-ende-Ynstixle, testify to this broad pattern and its persistence. These coalitions, organized at a micro-social level, were quite likely determined by long-term relations between kinfolk, and possibly by regional concerns. The various macro-social and micro-social coalitions crosscut one another and interlocked among themselves. There are several perceptible examples of micro-social coalitions, such as those of the Yorica, Mabibit, and Jume, and possibly the Jeapa; the Bocora and the Pinanaca; the Gueiquezale and the Manos Prietas; the Jumano, Julime, Gediondo, and Arcos Tuertos; and the Jumano and the Cibolo.

The lifespan of the coalitions, particularly those that were brought about by singular events (e.g., Sabeata's coalition to get help from the Spanish against the Apache), very likely reflected the duration (and resolution) of the threat. The consensus that existed among members of a given coalition, and the level of importance the threat represented for each member, also determined the continued participation of individual members.

Quite likely, members who might not benefit greatly from the enterprise required incentives to participate.

What is new and remarkable is the associative process that permitted these groupings, as well as the regional extent of some coalitions. The number of groups included in Sabeata's coalition is a good measure of the importance of the Apache threat to local populations. The investment in social and economic resources required to entice the Spanish to join the Native cause against the Apache is worthy of notice. Some of these coalitions were fostered and maintained through trade, not just in goods, but also in services, such as the transmission of information.

DUAL ETHNICITY AND LADINOS

Two important and salient mechanisms, related to the pattern of social integration and adaptation, were the granting or adoption of dual ethnicity and the social role and importance of ladinos. Although these mechanisms sprung from different social and cultural realities, they represent two faces of the same coin.

Dual ethnicity was adopted by, or granted to, individuals who were born into one ethnic group and became recognized members of another ethnic group. This mechanism existed at least among the Bobole and the Tancagua. Thus far, I have documented four cases of this phenomenon: Don Lacaro Agustin, who was a Jumano by birth and became a Bobole governor; Juan de la Cruz, who was a Toboso, was brought up by the Contotore, and became a Bobole; Geronimillo, a Conian who was reported as being both a Conian and a Bobole; and Mocho, an Apache who became leader of the Tancagua. The best documentation for this mechanism is the case of Don Lacaro Agustin, since the archival documents state his birth ethnicity.

When I first came across Don Lacaro in the archival documents, he was always referred to as a Bobole: only later did I become aware that he had been born a Jumano. The Bobole were closely affiliated with the Jumano; therefore there appears to be a reasonable basis to justify the granting or adoption of Bobole ethnic status in the case of Don Lacaro. The same cannot be said for the Toboso or Contotore (Juan de la Cruz), or for the Conian (Geronimillo). None of these groups was allied with the Bobole during the historical period investigated. As a matter of fact, in 1655, the Bobole sided with the Spanish and fought the Contotore.

A later case may indicate some of the requirements that permitted the adoption and granting of dual ethnicity. In the case of the Apache known as Mocho, who became the leader of the Tancagua in 1779, his position of power was obtained through personal achievements and oratory. He had been a captive who was adopted by the Tancagua: at the death of the elderly Tancagua "leader," Mocho was chosen as his replacement. This is particularly noteworthy since the two groups were fierce enemies. The fact that enmity did not preclude adoption or concession of dual ethnicity may clarify the situation of the Contotore and the Bobole (see above). It is even possible that adoption or concession of dual ethnicity served as an alliance or conflict-resolution mechanism.

The sophistication of this social mechanism indicates that it existed in earlier times, and forces the realization that gathering and hunting societies did have a complex social organization that encompassed some mechanisms as elaborate as those of today. Further research may determine whether this pattern of dual ethnicity was particular to the Bobole and the Tancagua or was prevalent in other groups as well.

The other social mechanism relevant to the formation of coalitions, attempts to organize in settlements, and information networks is the role and influence of ladino Natives. Ladinos bridged the gap between Western and Native cultures and were, by definition, at least bilingual, and most often multilingual. These individuals facilitated the interchange between the two communities, but, depending on the issue and the perspective, were seen as both friends and foes.

Because they were cultural brokers who communicated with the Native populations and guided the contacts between European and Native, they were always necessary and sought after. They were the interpreters, the guides, the informers, the spokespersons, and the advisers. But they were also the manipulators, the unreliable, the double agents, and the troublemakers. The different Spanish appraisals of Don Lacaro Agustin and Juan Sabeata are good examples of the dual perception that the Spanish had of ladinos; they could not live with them and could not live without them. From the Native point of view, ladinos were essential in order to communicate with Europeans and to obtain information about them. The role of intermediary, or facilitator, was certainly in place before the arrival of the Europeans, but it must have gained considerable importance and expansion after contact.

NATIVE INFORMATION NETWORKS

The evidence for the existence of extensive information networks controlled and managed by Native Americans is overwhelming. Almost all the information the Spaniards obtained about other Native Americans, and certainly about the French (before the Spanish settled in Texas), was transmitted by Native Americans. Sabeata announced the presence of French traders in eastern Texas in 1683, two years before La Salle arrived on the coast of Texas. Sabeata informed the Spaniards at El Paso that other "Spaniards" were coming by boat to trade with the Tejas and other groups for pelts, tents, and other goods.

These information networks, which had to be in place before European arrival, were quite likely modified and revamped to accommodate the new demands and the location of Europeans. The networks connected most Native populations in Texas and other areas, and were tied to trade in goods and to trade fairs. Such networks conveyed cultural information and European trade items: this means that the circulation of the latter items went well beyond the recognizable boundaries of historical contact.

Ladinos were pivotal to the information networks after the arrival of the Europeans. The trade in information was translated into positions of leadership, gifts, prestige, and, most important, the acquisition of more and novel information. The position of ladinos as intermediaries between the two cultures (cultural brokers) made them invaluable for the Spanish and Native communities. Information was a resource that articulated most of the patterns revealed by this study.

In 1683, Sabeata mentioned that the Tejas were raising horses and already had large herds of these animals. Trade from New Mexico and Coahuila was well developed before the Spanish ever moved into Texas. The Pueblo Revolt affected the flux of goods considerably, but Sabeata and the members of his coalition were very interested in reactivating those networks.

SOCIAL AND SUBSISTENCE RESOURCES

The archival record points to the importance of certain social, subsistence, and exchange resources for Native communities. The evidence for the importance of social resources is always veiled, and as the archival record becomes more succinct about Native matters, the evidence becomes harder to obtain. However, the Bobosarigame, the Cabesa, the Tetecore, and probably others were extremely aggravated with the continued imprisonment of their women throughout the 1670s and 1680s. Capture of their womenfolk by Europeans caused tremendous disruption in their daily lives. Without women they could not procreate, raise the children they already had, and share the procurement and preparation of food. These facts impaired the capability of male warriors to dedicate time to warring activities and probably obliged them to capture women from other groups, forcing them into conflicts. While the selective capture and trade of young males appears to have served diplomatic and alliance needs (see below), wholesale capture of women and children by the Spanish deeply affected the morale as well as the social and cultural fabric of Native populations. The capture of slaves, under the guise of war captives, continued throughout the seventeenth and eighteenth centuries and reached some of its ugliest moments with the Apache.

Another resource with social and exchange dimensions was the giving of young males as gifts. These young men, who were both taken from and traded by other Native groups, could be either Native or European. They were not seen as slaves but as members of the group where they were raised, and were often considered family. Obviously, the attitudes toward and reasons for obtaining these young "captives" and their treatment by particular groups were not all equal. These gifts of individuals to other Native groups, to the Spanish, and to the French were a demonstration of friendship, diplomacy, and a currency for establishing alliances.

Several subsistence resources are mentioned in the records. The prickly-pear tuna, roots, nuts, and mescal are the floral resources most often mentioned. Agreements and alliances were made during the season when the tuna was available, and during hunting season, particularly at the time of the buffalo hunts.

From the beginning of the period covered by this study, Native preoccupation with the location of buffalo herds was a constant. The buffalo constituted an essential multi-resource with deep implications for the Native groups in terms of food supply, housing, clothing, weapons, alliances, and trade. Native Americans frequently mentioned the conflicts they experienced because of buffalo hunting rights, the way those conflicts restricted group movements, and the central role of the buffalo in trade and the establishment of alliances. If access to buffalo was not possible, most of these activities and social arrangements were curtailed. The statements made in 1675 by the Jeapa, Jumee, Mabibit, Yorica, and Geniocane relating their conflicts and difficulty in obtaining meat supplies; the statements of the Cibolo in 1688–1689 about the continual conflicts over buffalo hunting rights; the offer of foodstuffs and pelts made by Juan Sabeata and his coalition to the Spanish in exchange for help against the Apache; and the paramount Apache preoccupation with acquiring buffalo meat leave no doubt about the immense importance of the resource for Native Americans.

Only some items of European material culture interested the Native Americans in the early period. They were interested in clothing, horses, and symbolic elements, such as drawings, pages of books, and the cross. The widespread use and appropriation of the symbol of the cross is intriguing. The cross appears in a multitude of groups, including the Julime, Jumano, Gediondo, Tejas, Payaya, and Apache. The cross was used as a symbol of friendship, a talisman, and a standard in battle and in festive parades.

THE ETHNOHISTORIC AND THE ARCHAEOLOGICAL RECORDS

Several academic disciplines and subdisciplines require historical documentary evidence about the Native American populations that lived in Texas, *sensu lato,* to substantiate their research. Often the lack of historical evidence restricts and shortchanges the relevance of archaeological findings and the scope of interpretation. The fields of anthropology, history, ethnohistory, historical geography, and particularly Native American studies and archaeology require archival information to ground their assumptions.

One of the ultimate goals of archaeology is to link specific populations to archaeological material culture. This study has documented the presence of twenty-one Native groups that inhabited and used the area of the Edwards Plateau between the 1670s and the 1690s. Some of the groups appeared in the archival record in 1674–1675 and others in the 1680s. Quite likely, these groups were present in the areas where they were encountered at least for a few decades before the date of contact. The evidence shows that these Native populations had been exposed to European culture and diseases, if not to the presence of Europeans.

The Jumano were encountered on the Pecos River in 1582–1583. Jumano groups are documented to have been present in the Concho River drainage certainly from 1650 through the 1680s and probably from the 1630s through the end of the seventeenth century. The *ranchería* of the Gediondos, which Mendoza visited in 1684, was on the east side of the Pecos River, the western border of the lands of Jumano-affiliated groups. The area encompassed by the lands of the Jumano, taken as an umbrella concept that included several groups, would therefore incorporate the land area covered by the Mendoza route east of the Pecos River and southward to the Llano River drainage. Given the evidence presented, the range of broad historical dates for the Jumano groups extends from 1582 to 1583, 1630, 1650, 1654, the 1680s, and the 1690s.

The Toyah Interval, which spans the period 1600–1650 through 1700, places some of the Native groups, particularly the Jumano proper, within the spatial and temporal grid postulated for the Toyah folk. This does not mean that the Jumano proper, or the groups affiliated with the Jumano, are connected with the archaeological material culture kit that characterizes the Toyah Interval. Alternatively, if they are not, archaeology should find other identifiable material culture expressions that diverge from the Toyah pattern and can be associated with the Jumano and their affiliated groups. It may be that the Jumano proper, as well as the groups under the Jumano social umbrella, bordered the Toyah Classic Culture area as portrayed by Johnson (1994: 243 and Chapter 8), or that such a conclusion results from the distorted view presented by the evidence available from archaeological sites and radiocarbon dates.

The historical presence of the Native groups documented to have inhabited and used the Edwards Plateau, and the possible relationship between these groups and specific archaeological material culture expressions, may show that what the ethnohistoric and the archaeological records reflect is cultural change within cultural continuity.

A DIALOGUE

Culture change and cultural continuity have often been viewed as oppositional, the former precluding or inhibiting the latter. A series of recent articles (Lightfoot et al. 1998; McGuire and Saitta 1996, 1998; Rautman 1998), with varied emphasis and theoretical positions, attests to the relevance of the debate. Under the label of culture change and continuity are subsumed essential notions and questions about ethnicity, acculturation, social complexity, concepts of "band" and "tribe," social dynamics between colonizer and colonized, and a myriad of other issues. Theoretical postures and ethnohistoric interpretation of documents affect, if they do not direct, archaeological research and conclusions.

Culture change continuously shadows culture continuity: they are sociocultural twins. To state the obvious: in order to perceive change, one has to see and know what continuity looks like. But continuity is often harder to detect, particularly in the ethnohistoric record. In situations of culture change, communities and individuals assess, reevaluate, and modify their daily practices and social arrangements, but they build on structures already in place in the society.

Some of the social mechanisms discussed in this book (e.g., dual ethnicity, coalitions, ladinos, and information networks) were modified upon European contact, but they were already present in the colonized communities and were available to provide solutions to specific problems of contact. The flexibility of such social structures and their adaptability to novel situations is a measure of both culture change and cultural continuity.

It is probably not a misstatement to say that it is easier to see culture change in the ethnohistoric record and cultural continuity in the archaeological record. That is an obvious consequence of the manner in which both records were formed: the relatively short term of the former, versus the relatively long term of the latter. Because of these tempo-ral conditionings, what is perceptible in the ethnohistoric record may never register in the archaeological one. For this reason, if for no other, the two records must be made to cooperate and establish a dialogue. Together, these records may ultimately confirm the dialogue between the inevitability of change and the need for continuity.

A similar dialogue is necessary between previous ethnohistoric research and new ap-proaches to the subject. The fields of archaeology and ethnohistory, with their intrinsic links to anthropology and history, have changed considerably in the last two decades. Disciplinary introspection, new methodologies, and technical innovations have led to an awareness of how little we know, and have raised questions heretofore not contemplated.

The issue of social complexity among hunting and gathering populations, and the adequacy of anthropological concepts such as "bands" and "tribes," is a case in point. These days many scholars put terms such as "bands," "tribes," and "leaders" in quota-tion marks. I too have used that stratagem to express my uneasiness with the concepts and the state of our knowledge of the social organization of populations such as those in Texas and northeastern Mexico.

It should be apparent that the nature of social complexity among the various groups studied in this work, and classified as hunters and gatherers, was not the same. A classi-fication as "hunters and gatherers" places full weight on the ways these groups collected their food: it does not address the complexity of their social arrangements. The cultural achievements of hunters and gatherers resided in the elaboration and sophistication of their social systems. This is so because their lifeways depended on and revolved com-pletely around the interrelations between individuals. Such systems, and the adaptive mechanisms embedded in them, addressed the primary concerns of the individual and the group: the spiritual world and the environment. This apparent verbal trinity of social organization, spiritual world, and environment was a single web of practices, feelings, and experiences.

All history is a construct a posteriori. Historians and ethnohistorians of earlier decades provided a reading of archival documents that was meant to divulge a historical past that reflected its Western roots. The dynamic spur of archival sleuthing, research, and trans-lations that characterized the age of such scholars as Bolton, Bancroft, Castañeda, and Scholes was the basis for much of the work of subsequent scholars. However, in the ma-jority of cases, the primary focus continued to be the events and accomplishments in which Europeans were involved. Thus, while we have considerable knowledge about the activities of the Europeans, we know precious little about the Native populations.

The research methodology and the facts uncovered and presented in this book dem-onstrate to me, and, I hope, to the reader, that a history of Native American activities in Coahuila and Texas is possible, necessary, and rewarding. Such a history depends on colonial records and is a part of the history of colonization, but it does not have to be colonized by it. We too have to assess, reevaluate, modify, and build on cultural conti-nuity while enabling culture change.

APPENDIX

Translations of Documents

1. *Informe sent to the Audiencia de Guadalajara by Don Antonio de Balcarcel Rivadeneira y Soto-mayor,* July 3, 1675. The *Informe* was written at the town of Nuestra Señora de Guadalupe (Monclova). The Spanish transcript can be found in Esteban Portillo, *Apuntes para la Historia Antigua de Coahuila y Texas* (1886: 161–171).

The translation of this document skips some of the text because it does not relate to Native American issues. Words between brackets were introduced to make the text more comprehensible. Words between parentheses are in the original text. I have added a minimum of punctuation to facilitate reading, and I have followed the capitalization of the original.

Having seen and acknowledged the requests and documentation presented by the natives of [this province] of nueva extremadura [Coahuila] and the daily requests they make to settle, and for priests and since this is not possible at present, and [since] it is necessary to inform Your Excellency because of the delicacy of the matter, I thought it would be better to apprise you of what is necessary and convenient because I fear that, from the meeting I held with the Natives and which is included in the documentation, some irreparable damage may result from their rush decisions. I fear this because of my experience with some conflicts that have taken place between them spurred by some of the interested parties who are dissatisfied, which [conflicts] were difficult to quell. [With this intent] the Friars went back and forth to pacify them delivering different messages. This was all caused by the ladinos who live in this province and who are over four hundred from all nations. [The ladinos] use the simplicity and innocence of the Bozales to trick them, making them believe, with no effort, in their capricious [lies]. This I have experienced and it is necessary that [the ladinos] be controlled to keep [them] quiet and not to arouse the Bozales. [Also, I am fearful because] of another reason for their conflicts, which causes bloody wars among them in which they decimate each other and perish. Since it is not possible to arrange for their settlement in time [to avoid this] (as they request), because they are so poor and we have to supply them with food and all other necessary things to sustain them, which they do not possess as it is stated in their declarations, and since I know by personal experience that they [the Natives] have no other foods but roots and wild fruits which are abundant in the area surrounding this town, and since if I provide settlements for those who do not yet have pueblos there will be discord between both [groups of Natives]. For [this reason] I will not do so [establish other pueblos] until Your Excellency determines what should be done; and we should give them harnessed oxen teams, mattocks, axes, hoes, and the tools needed to build their pueblos, wheat and corn seed and for the first three years, some corn and meat to sustain them, and after [those three years] give them for a few more years, to be determined by

Your Excellency, meat [supplies], and for a limited period of time some clothing to cover their nudity, because both men and women use skins; the women cover their genitals with deerskins and the men with a buffalo skin. This is their permanent attire, and this is not available everywhere because to get buffalo they have to cross the rio del norte, where they have great wars and barbarous retaliations over the killing of buffalo—and it will be convenient to give each pueblo fifty sheep and fifty goats, [and] ten young cows with their bulls. They will care well for these animals since they are well inclined to the raising of animals—and because they are not used to the work [of farming] and have no experience in the cultivation of the land, it will be wise to incorporate in each pueblo [to be set up] ten families of indios tlaxcaltecos, because both groups [those requesting the pueblos and the Tlaxcaltecans] request it, and the tlaxcaltecos have said that when ordered to do so [live in those pueblos] they should be provided with some help to transport their families and belongings [there]. To that effect [the Tlaxcaltecans] ask that one hundred families be allowed to leave the pueblo of San Esteban de Tlaxcala in the Town of Saltillo, since at present, there are over five hundred [Tlaxcaltecans] from the [original] eighty that left Your City of Tlascala, and they wish [to leave] because they have neither [sufficient] land nor water [there]. With their example they [local Natives] can be reduced to [learn] land cultivation, [become] organized politically and socially, matters in which the said Tlaxcaltecos are well versed—and also [provide] fifty families of indios tarascos from Mechoacan all artisans because these have the capability to learn any craft that one teaches them, establishing with them [Tarascos] two pueblos where some of the people from the local nations will be incorporated with the young men of all [nations], in order that, just like in a school, they may learn a craft to make a living; and the women shall teach each other to make cloth, at which the tarascan women are so proficient in order that they [local Natives] can cover their nudity, because the land will provide cotton because I have experimented [with it] and have it [growing] in this city—and it will be convenient to have in each pueblo one person of wisdom and conscience who can supervise the sowing of seed and whatever [goods] Your Excellency determines [to give to the Natives] should be entrusted to this individual. He should make sure that enough seed is sown to sustain the indian community during the year since they will sow an insufficient amount because they are not accustomed to do it [to judge what they need] or understand it [the process] and these things I have experienced in this City. This person should keep a record and report all that is under his charge and he should be under the command of the person in charge of these pueblos and should follow his commands . . . [regarding the trip that Your Alferes Real made to the lands of the indians] . . . and as far as ministers, for the moment, fifteen will be needed, five for each chain of settlements because there is a large number of souls as I have recognized by the number of captains that have come to pay homage. Those that we have counted constitute a small number of those who are in this province. It will not be possible to count them all in the short term. We also do not have enough supplies to feed these people and if we take them out of their lands we will have to feed them. This will be very expensive, especially with the high cost of supplies in the area. [The number of people] is so large, that if I had not put a stop to it, these fields would be covered with indians. I have achieved this by using the ambassadors of their nations who come and go every day, since it is not convenient to have large congregations [of Natives] in this Town because of the enmities among the groups. I could not prevent the damage that would occur except for the presence of the army to intervene between groups and make them think twice. Many more nations would come [if we let them], because they all come to seek Your protection and they manifest a true desire to live under the protection of your Royal standard and the Catholic faith. This is clearly the work of the Lord. It is also not a good idea to establish another pueblo apart from the one in this town, until you supply troops. Then we can proceed with settlements for all; otherwise there will be many problems because of the eagerness and envy that exist between the Natives. This is visible with the Bobole and their allies, who are settled in this Town, but who do not want other groups to join them. The Bobole tell the others that this is their land, that God and King gave it to them, and that [others] will not eat from the crops of their land, that [if they want what they have] they can ask for the same as they [the Bobole] did, that they should go where they are given land, and pay with their labor as they [the Bobole] paid with theirs for so many years. Coming from barbarians this [reasoning] is cause for admiration and that is the reason I mention it to Your Excellency. This Captain Juan de la Cruz is the indian with greatest faith I have ever seen. His face seems like the face of an apostle, [and] it brings tears to one's eyes to see him at the doctrine, with the devotion and attention with which he attends it without ever missing [the doctrine] and night and day he preaches to his people, admonishing them about their bad habits and this is astonishing since he is a toboso. For this reason I have had Don Estevan Gueyquesale here for the last three months, since he is the key to peace all over the land; [they] all fear him because he is allied with the bobol and the spanish, and these [the Spaniards] fearful that the indians [who] little by little keep coming [into town since I] am not able to stop it [their move into the town], and [the Spaniards] say that now it is up to Your Excellency to stop it by force, because they cannot live without security [which they do not have because] of the many indians who come and go from this City every day. [These Natives] come to request settlements and missionaries and to establish [the pueblos they wish] it would be necessary [to have] over thirty Friars for the moment, because each day they request a separate pueblo with a separate friar, and they all ask for spaniards in their lands. For this reason it would be convenient if Your Excellency ordered that a City be established in the Valley of San Antonio with thirty spanish families and ten field soldiers for that City [of San Antonio] and ten soldiers for this City [of N.S. de Guadalupe]; at the catuxanos another ten [soldiers], and thirty [soldiers to be] at the place of Santa Cruz. Ten [soldiers] should accompany the person who travels to set up the [new] pueblos and these are not to be Presidial soldiers but field soldiers. All these [soldiers] should be under the command of the person who is the head of the [local] government in order that he can draft them whenever necessary . . . all this needs to be accomplished quickly because the matter demands it and if we delay action it will cause a great deal of sadness among the indians . . . in a circuit of about five hundred leagues there are many indians—the land is fertile, with good climate, good for all kinds of fruits, abundant in water, fish, buffalo although [the buffalo] are far from this city. . . . the Bozale indians are exceedingly innocent, both them and their children, [it] moves one to pity to see them attending the doctrine and they can soften the hardest hearts—the ladinos are the ones with bad tendencies who are always attempting to do evil. The ladinos know everything about land cultivation but they are lazy and do nothing; but considering the qualities [of the Bozales] if we have [military] forces we can mold them as we wish. They are not idolatrous, do not tolerate shamans and if they know of one they kill him right away be it a woman or a man, they marry only one woman, under the natural law, and she is not kin. The catuxana nations are different only in that they have two or three women and the brothers (brothers-in-law) can lay with all these women [the two or three] at the same time [they are coupled with another man]. These women do not feel jealous of each other. For this reason they [the Catujano groups and very likely the Tilijae] are shunned by the other nations who they fear very much [not clear who fears whom]. Although they enter into peace agreements they do not trust each other and when they establish peace [agreements] they celebrate with a dance [called] the *mitote*. This dance goes on for twenty-four hours and the individual who lasts the longest is considered the most valiant. They are very revengeful when someone kills one of them [Catujano and Tilijae groups]; they seek revenge in such a manner that the one who is caught they eat pieces of him while alive; they drink the blood saying that it is their blood that has been spilt by them [their enemies]. All the wars are because someone cannot pass [trespass] through the lands of others, they cannot [even] step on their [another group's] paths, they cannot reach [the areas] of the tuna and roots which are [located] at the boundaries [of each other's territories or places that are considered no-man's-land?]; regarding the buffalo there are many killings, [and] they eat each other. I sent embassies to the cabesos and [upon return] they said the [Cabesas] were all gathered at cuatro Cienegas and [they asked] that Your Governor from Nueva Vizcaya deliver back to them their families [which he has captured], and [they request] that Don Estevan and Fr. Larios go visit them and [if that happens] they will come to render obedience and [will] be peaceful. They will not dare to come any other way because they fear what they [Spanish officials] will do with them in Nueva Vizcaya [where] under the guise of peace they have tricked them and have killed and incarcerated them. If this is not done [the visit of Don Esteban and Fr. Larios and the return of their families] they will not be peaceful [and will fight] until they are decimated, and this was reported by an indian woman who traveled from their group to this city three days ago. I believe (with God's help) that if we return their families they will remain peaceful and if they do so will all the land—Don Esteban Gueiquesale [is] a great man of justice and a peace-loving [man] who wishes they all be in peace. This Juan de la Cruz and Don Miguel Catuxano his Governor [of the Catujano] are worthy of Your powerful intervention [on their behalf] and help because of how they care for their people and particularly Don Lazaro Agustin Governor of Your pueblo of San Miguel de Luna. They all acknowledge [Don Lazaro's authority] and they are thankful for the efforts he undertook to bring to them Friars and [people] who have defended them from the tyrannical measures that those interested in doing them harm [tried], which [things] as I have been told Don Lacaro did with great care and has been doing for over two years. He is a man among all and an arrogant indian (they all are) who is sensitive to what is said to him. . . .

2. Translation of the Declaration by Juan Sabeata before the Governor of New Mexico Don Antonio de Otermín made at El Paso del Rio del Norte on August 11, 1683. The original Spanish version of this document is in *Provincias Internas,* vol. 35, frames 77–80.

On the 11th of August 1683 at the Barracks of San Lorenzo at La Toma del Rio Grande [the point at which water was taken from the Rio Grande] Don Antonio de Otermín Governor and Captain General of the Kingdom and Province of New Mexico by order of His Majesty, declares that having arrived at these barracks twelve indians of the Jumanas nation, [who are] Captains of different *rancherias* with which [Jumana nation] we have always had relations of friendship and trade since [the time] of New Mexico [and these contacts between Spaniards and Jumano were conducted] with such security that spaniards [in groups] of six, eight, and ten went to their *rancherias* every year to trade with the indians mentioned and [since] these indians have always maintained [relations] of great loyalty [with the Spaniards] and having known of the rebellion of the apostate indians from New Mexico as well as that the spaniards who left after the rebellion were now here [at El Paso] they [the Jumano] came to find out what was the truth [about the Spaniards' situation] since the apache enemies, in the wars they [the Jumano] have had with them [the Apache], led them to understand that the spanish were finished; they [the Jumano] sent some days ago [to this town] one of their Captains, who came before me. This Captain demonstrated how pleased he was that the news he had received from the apaches was false and having talked with said Governor and having asked for help in the form of spanish people the Governor, being short of manpower and in great need because of the great hunger [suffered by the people at El Paso], led him to understand that a new Governor and General Captain was about to arrive and would be here in three months and that they could come to see him [the new Governor]. In view of this the said Captain and three others he brought with him said they understood [the situation] and that others would come to satisfy themselves [that the Spanish were not finished] and that he [the Jumano Captain] would call on them [to visit the Spanish Governor]. This is the reason these twelve [Jumano] are now present. Having asked them the reason for their visit they said they came to see the Governor and Captain General and the spanish in order that if they [the Spanish] wanted to go to their lands [Jumano lands] and *rancheria* and help them against the apaches, they would profit and they would trade as they had always done the things they [the Jumano] had, such as deer *gamusas,* shoes and buffalo skins. They declared that six days [travel] from these barracks there are many people on the margins of this rio del norte of the Jhulime farmers who have many [fields] sown with wheat, corn, beans, and other grains and [these Julime] are friends of the Jumanas and the other nations [who are also] their friends have offered [the Jumano] that if they convinced the spaniards to help them against the apache they [the Julimes, the Jumano, and the other nations] will give them the necessary food supplies in order that the spaniards can go and help them and [he said] that said nations of the Jumanas and [other] friends live very close to the Jhulimes. Having asked them many questions about the news [what news they had and] about the time in new Mexico they said that other spaniards very white and with red hair came by the sea in wooden houses that walk on the water and they bring them some earrings [and] things that amaze them much and with which they buy from them [the Jumano], the indians of the texas [Tejas] nation and others, deer skins, buffalo skins, shoes, tents and other things they [the Jumano and other nations] have. They also declared that on the river called of the nuts there are those shells from which small grains are taken which they call pearls and [they added that] from what they had [now] seen they were very pleased to see the Governor and Captain General. In what regards the spaniards they [the Jumano] are anxious that [the Spaniards] visit their lands as they did before and that they [the Jumano] will return as soon as they learn that the new Governor has arrived. They will give him [the new Governor] the same news and whatever other news they learn [may have learned in the meantime] and they will travel to their territories and find people [guides] capable and amenable in order that if any religious or any spaniard wants to go live with them [the Jumano] they will guide them to the texas [Tejas] who are settled people who raise crops and they [the Tejas] would let them [Spaniards] in [their lands] in order that they could baptize them [the Tejas]. In their territory [the Tejas] have good lands and great production [of crops]. They [the Jumano] will return to see the Governor and Captain general and they will have a long conversation with him, [to tell him] they want to reestablish the communication and friendship they had before and as a sign of friendship and to be sure they remained that way the Governor offered them twelve small machetes of those [made] in puebla and a dozen pairs of earrings for the women, one cow, tobacco, and corn with which they left very happy and saying they would return to see the Governor whom we are awaiting and to one of the Captains, who was the spokesperson among them, the Governor offered two red feathers and they said good-bye thankful and happy and in order that it may be recorded the Governor signed with the Maestro de Campo Francisco. . . .

3. Translation of the Declaration of Juan Sabeata before Governor Domingo Gironza Petriz de Cruzati made at N.S. de Guadalupe del Paso del Rio del Norte on October 20, 1683. The original Spanish version of this document is in *Províncias Internas,* vol. 35, frames 80–81.

In this declaration, when Sabeata says that a group is called by a given name, it is not clear who uses that name for that group. Whatever expression Sabeata used was translated as *que llaman,* which makes the subject undetermined. One cannot assume that the Jumano knew those groups by those names.

In consideration of having arrived at this pueblo an indian of the Humana nation whose name in his language is Sabeata and in the castilian language is [named] Juan who was baptized at San Joseph de Parral as he declared [and] who before my arrival had come to this place, [and having] returned to his land, which is as he said about six to eight days of travel from this pueblo, from where [his lands] he was sent [here] by all the Captains of different nations who have their territories toward the east and in order to inform His Excellency the Viceroy of New Spain of the declaration [made by] said indian named Don Juan and his companions, who are six [in number], I ordered him to appear before me and I appointed as interpreter Captain Fernando Martin Serrano a citizen of these provinces very fluent in the language that the indian Don Juan speaks. Don Juan swore by the sign of the cross and he promised to tell the [truth] about all he knows; who sent him, what he came for, what he has seen and heard in those territories, the distances between one territory and another, what nations trade and have relations of friendship with his own, and [in answer to those questions] he declared the following: that he is a Christian and he knows that if he speaks the [truth] God will help him and those who do not speak the [truth] are punished by God and [that] he lives with many people of the Humana nation at La Junta del Rio del Norte and the Concho [River] and that from this place [El Paso] to there [La Junta] there are [it takes] about eight days' travel. He declared that he was sent from there by six captains who are Christians and they are called Don Juan, Alonso, Bartholome, Luis, D. Francisco and Joseph; that these [Captains] and himself were unhappy because being Christians they do not have a Friar to teach them the things of God [and so] they resolved in a Junta they made that Juan Sabeata would come to the pueblo of El Passo to ask for a Friar in order that when they were ill he [the friar] could console them and when they died [they] would be buried as Christians and [the friar] would baptize the other people who are, as this witness says, over ten thousand souls asking for baptism and these people are the Julimes and the Humanas; and he was also sent by these people to ask for spanish families in order that they will defend them against their enemies the apaches who [are] in a *rancheria* very near theirs [Sabeata is now talking about the area on the Concho River in Texas and not La Junta] and that the very old friendship which his nation of the Humanas has had with the spanish since New Mexico gave them courage to come make this request. When asked what is the distance from where this witness lives to where the other peoples of his nation, the Humanas, live [the River of the Nuts or Concho River in Texas], he said that it will take six traveling days; that from where he [Sabeata] lives there are three days to where the buffalo [herds are or begin] and three more traveling days to the river they call of the nuts. There are so many nuts [there] that they are the sustenance of many nations who are friends and trade with his nation; these nations are: the one of the long penis which is a very widespread nation without a number, = and another nation which is the nation that grinds = and another of the ugly arrows (*flechas*) = and another called the people of the fish = and another called the people that eat = and another called the people of the dirty water = and another called tuxaxa = and another called the peñunde people = and another called the ti Jemu people (or tijemu) and another called the people of the nuts = and another called Tanaque = and another called tohojo and another called émiti = and another called the people of the caimanes = and another nation called Toapa and another called qui oboriqui = and another nation called Toapari = and another nation called geobori = and another called borobamo = and another called cocuma = and another called teanama = and another called obori = and another called *come casa* [eat house] = and another called bean = and another called ari human = and another called Ytaca = and another called tumpotoguas = and another called mana = and another which they call *los zurdos* [*sordos,* as "the deaf" and not as "left-handed"] = and another called quide = and the Great Kingdom of the Texas, and Those Who Make Bows, the Great Kingdom of quibira, the very widespread nation of the Yutes, [and] the widespread nation of Humanas which are [make] thirty-six nations without mentioning many others with which they trade and have firm friendships. He declared that he has no doubt they will welcome the Friars and the spaniards with great affection because they have all [nations] been waiting for them for some time and that because [the Spaniards?] were not going [to their lands] on that occasion they were greatly disconsolate and scattered [either literally or in the sense of upset and disorganized] at the place where this witness is [La Junta]. He said he had just left two indians of the tejas nation who were waiting for the [Spanish] response which this witness will convey to [the Tejas], who [in turn will take] the information to those of their nation. The Tejas have informed this witness that in the east there are spaniards who come in wooden houses on the water and they trade with the said nation [the Tejas]. In that Kingdom of the Tejas they sow great quantities and have abundant crops and there are many and different fruits; the acorns are the size of a large egg and the fields are full of plums of many diverse types and in the rivers there are grapevines which produce many grapes when it is the season. From where they were now living at La Junta de los Rios to the Kingdom of the Tejas takes about fifteen or twenty days taking the longest road and this witness thinks that, from what he has heard the people of that nation [Tejas] say, they will receive the spaniards and the Friars with great affection and love because they have been waiting for them since Sergeant Major Diego del castillo and other spaniards visited them; and the one that came to see Sergeant Major Castillo when he was there [in the Jumano lands] was not their King [of the Tejas] but his Lieutenant because the King never travels and rules with great authority; and this witness knows that among the texas [Tejas] there is an indian of the teguas nation of those from new Mexico very ladino in the castilian language who may serve as interpreter if the spaniards decide to go there. He [the Tegua] has been there for many years and knows the language of the texas [Tejas kingdom], which is a very powerful Kingdom with many people and they are ruled by this King; their Kingdom borders with La gran quibira and they communicate so often that almost every day they visit each other. [He also declared] that in the Kingdom of the texas [Tejas] so much food is produced that even the horses and the mares are fed on corn because they have many herds of mares which they have raised [Sabeata is now talking about Jumano people and not Tejas]; and that about four years ago when they were peaceful in their houses and fields they saw descending from the sky a cross [the cross shown to the Spanish at the Gediondo village] which was floating [in the air] but the day was very calm and it could not be the wind [to make it dance in the air] because there was none; [the cross] looked like something alive and the people were astonished and reasoning there was a God [that it was the work of God]; they stooped to admire the cross until it reached the ground and fell on some sticks where it remained for quite a while moving like something alive; [the cross] is about nine *quartas* in length and the color of fine gold and the mark that is in the margins of the manuscript and painted [or tattooed] in the hands of this witness is [the reproduction of the cross; see Figure 4.2]. The people watched the cross with great veneration and they saw that it was made of one piece and [with this sign] they understood that God wanted them to be Christians. On this occasion when the cross descended [from the sky] it happened that a great group of their enemies arrived in their lands and seeing themselves in this panic all of the people of his [Jumano] nation took courage and followed the trail [of their enemies] and when they got very near the *rancherias* of their enemies they strapped the cross to a tall piece of wood and tying it very securely they raised it as a flag and they all painted a cross on their foreheads [and] they began the attack on their enemies in their *rancheria* which was composed of seventy-eight tents destroying them all. This holy Cross has caused one of the greatest victories they ever had because [their enemies] feared the cross and they [the Jumano] did not lose a single man, He said that he is in possession of this cross and that the spanish can see it when they go to their lands. On another occasion after this one their enemies the apaches came to attack them in their lands and among the things they stole from them was the cross and when they [the Jumano] were returning from having followed their enemies and very sad because of the robbery of the cross, when they unfurled the flags [standards] which they had left in their lands they found the cross wrapped in one of the flags. They were extremely happy with this and since they have been in possession of this cross nothing bad has happened to them. Asked if [one] travels to all these places that he has mentioned, both the *rancherias* of their friends as well as those of the Kingdom of the tejas, what kind of lands [need to be traversed and if] there are water sources close enough to each other, he said that there are and in some areas they are very abundant even if you take a lot of horses and that [they came] only [because of] the love to request Friars and Spaniards [and] to be [able to become] Christians in order that [the Spanish come] and settle their land and that the cross he has on the colorado [Sabeata is talking about the Pecos, which has red beds at the Gediondo village, and not the modern Colorado River] is painted with different colors and that this is the [truth] and he swore by the Holy Cross and [since he] could not sign I the Governor and General Captain signed. . . .

4. Translation of *Certificazion Primera* made by Juan Dominguez de Mendoza at La Junta de los Ríos on June 12, 1684. The Spanish original is in *Províncias Internas,* vol. 37.

I certify while I can to D. Domingo Jironza petris de Cruzate Governor and Captain General of the provinces of New mexico and its presidio and to the other ministers of His Majesty who may see it [that] on June 12 having gathered all the Governors and Captains with more than five hundred indians from seven nations who have given obedience to His Majesty and being unanimously under the Catholic faith they requested, from the Reverend Fr. Nicolas Lopes Custodian and Ordinary Judge of the provinces of New Mexico, six Priests to administer to them the Sacraments saying that two Priests were not sufficient [for them] since their pueblos were not close to each other that they were so many [people] and it was too much labor for the two Priests. In order that this could be done they had already built six churches of wood and straw and that later they will build them of adobe. At the request of the Reverend Father Custodian I put this down; because the Reverend Father did not have paper to make the request in writing and in order that it be recorded I signed it as Corporal and Chief. . . .

4. Translation of *Certificazion Secunda* made by Juan Dominguez de Mendoza at La Junta de los Ríos on June 13, 1684. The Spanish original is in *Províncias Internas,* vol. 37.

At this place and new Conversions of La Junta of the Rio Conchos with the Rio del Norte on this other side of the Rio del norte on June 13, 1684, having gathered all the governors and Captains of this jurisdiction I asked them if they knew or had news that in the past other spaniards or ministers of justice had entered this jurisdiction who might have apprehended or taken possession [of the area], to which they answered unanimously that no one had. They only knew, because they saw it, that Fr. garsia de San Francisco and Fr. Juan de sumesta had come to their pueblos. The former said mass and left them. Sometime after arrived a Friar of the same order of San Francisco [Fr. Sumesta] who visited only the first pueblo and returned [home]. Since that occasion they had not seen spaniards or Friars except for those present. Considering this and seeing that it belonged to new mexico I apprehended and took possession [of this land] in the name of His Royal and Catholic Majesty, with all necessary ceremonies informing the said governors and Captains [of the act of possession], who asked me to appoint them Four Captains to better perform their Jobs for both majesties in whose name I gave them the staffs, and in order that it may be recorded I signed as Corporal and Chief. . . .

Notes

1. A MOVE TO SETTLE

1. The expedition of Fr. Augustin Rodríguez and Francisco Sanchez Chamuscado in 1581–1582 crossed the Rio Grande on its way to New Mexico. That trip does not provide any information relevant to this study. For further information see George P. Hammond and Agapito Rey (1927), *The Gallegos Relation of the Rodríguez Expedition to New Mexico*. The expedition of Antonio de Espejo and Diego Perez de Luxán (1582–1583) provides some information that can be connected with this study. During the return trip, on August 7, 1583, Espejo's party encountered three Jumano Natives, probably south of the modern town of Pecos near Toyah Lake. The Jumano guided the Spaniards to the junction of the Mexican Conchos River and the Rio Grande. On the way they stopped at two Jumano *rancherías* that were probably located 2 leagues (5.2 miles) south-southeast of the town of Pecos and 3 leagues (7.8 miles) upstream on Toyah Creek. These were large *rancherías* composed of tents (Hammond and Rey 1929: 124–125). Even though this expedition was probably never closer than 30 miles to the most western outliers of the Edwards Plateau, it confirms that the Jumano must have known well the western part of the Plateau because they knew the course of the Pecos and its point of entry into the Rio Grande. They were probably familiar with the canyon lands of southern Pecos, Terrell, and Val Verde counties, and therefore had probably traveled to the southern margin of the Plateau near Del Rio. At the very least, this expedition supports the view that the Jumano ranged over this area before the 1580s. For further information on this expedition see George P. Hammond and Agapito Rey (1929), *Expedition into New Mexico Made by Antonio de Espejo, 1582–1583*.

2. The *encomienda* system was "the delegation of the royal power to collect the tribute from, *and to use the personal services of,* the King's vassals (the Indians)" (Simpson 1982: xiii—italics in the original). Juridically, the *encomienda* system was characterized "por un sistema de trabajo forzoso, sin contrato de salariado" (Zavala 1973: 14).

3. Francisco Fernández de la Cueva, Duque de Albuquerque, was born in Barcelona in 1619 and died in Madrid in 1676. He held the post of Viceroy of New Spain between 1653 and 1660.

4. For an excellent account of the movements and settlements of the Tlaxcaltecans in northern Mexico and particularly in Coahuila, see Elisabeth Butzer, *Historia Social de una Comunidad Tlaxcalteca*.

5. The information provided by the testimony of those who participated in the battle differs somewhat from the information given by Juan Bautista Chapa (1995) in *Historia del Nuevo Reino de León de 1650 a 1690*, pp. 62, 63.

6. A *fanega* is a common unit of dry weight generally equivalent to 1.58 bushels (Haggard 1941: 76).

7. The settlements at S. Ildefonso and Santa Rosa are here called "mission-settlements" because there is a clear difference between these agglomerations of people and the mission system of later times. The former were often short-lived, unregulated, and dependent on minimal installations; the latter had at least some degree of permanency, were highly regulated, and were conspicuous for their installations. The word most often used in the early archival documents to designate these mission-settlements is *conversions,* a very apt word. Most of these early mission-settlements were destroyed or abandoned because of changes in the local physical environment or because the Native peoples deserted them.

8. *Agave lechuguilla.*

9. The word *tule* refers to a variety of cane (*scirpus lacustris* and *scirpus acutus*) with a tuberous root system.

10. Sotol: a plant of the lily family that resembles the yucca.

11. For a full discussion of the meaning of the word *dacate,* see Chapter 2, note 17.

12. The reader may wonder how Fr. Manuel could be so precise about the time since he did not have a watch. Fr. Manuel followed the sun (if possible) and the canonical hours of prayer, and 9:00 A.M. would have been Tierce.

13. Don Esteban stated that one hundred of his warriors were involved in the battle. Steck states that there were ninety-eight warriors (Steck 1932: 11). Don Esteban's testimony was confirmed by Fr. Manuel, and it is because of this testimony that we know the battle was waged against the Ervipiame (Portillo 1886: 79).

14. The word *ladino* has been often misinterpreted and even considered to be a group designation. *Ladino,* as used in the Spanish archival records, denotes any Native fluent in or capable of speaking other languages, particularly Spanish. It also denotes a Native who, having lived among Spaniards, had knowledge of their cultural ways and was relatively acculturated to them. Ladinos became influential among other Native Americans precisely because they understood the mores of Europeans and could speak their languages. By the same token, they became dangerous to Spaniards because they were used as interpreters, couriers, and informants, and so became privy to information they could use against the Spaniards. They were very much the enemy within. By contrast, the term *bozale* referred to a Native American who did not speak Spanish or another language, such as "Mexican," intelligible to his interlocutor, and who had not lived among the Spaniards, or, having lived with them, was not viewed as sufficiently acculturated. Sometimes the term *bozale* was applied to a particular group of Natives as a depreciative and generic term, but not as an ethnic designation.

15. The name of the Bagname captain was Mapo and his Siano relative was named Yosame carboan. The Bagname captain stated that they lived in a mountain called Dacate in his language. These are the two words known in the language the Bagname spoke: *mapo* and *dacate.* If the Siano are the same as the Sana, which appears highly probable, then Yosame carboan is a Sana personal name (Portillo 1886: 82–83). This assumption appears to be confirmed by the linguistic data, namely the word's initial *y,* the presence of *r,* and the morph *ame* (Johnson and Campbell 1992: 194, 196, 198, 200).

2. THE BOSQUE-LARIOS EXPEDITION

1. San Felipe de Jesus: (Mex) Nueva Rosita G14-1 (1979).

2. Given my very limited knowledge of fish species, I have used Eugene Bolton's translation of the types of fishes mentioned in the diaries. However, according to the Texas Memorial Museum, and thanks to the information provided by Christopher Jurgens, *mojarra* is a fish with a slab-sided body, akin to the sunfish.

3. San Francisco del Paso: (Mex) Nueva Rosita G14-1 (1979).

4. San Francisco del Paso: (Mex) Nueva Rosita G14-1 (1979).

5. Santa Crus: (Mex) Nueva Rosita G14-1 (1979).

6. Santa Catalina Martir: (Mex) Nueva Rosita G14-1 (1979).

7. S. Antonio de las Sabinas: (Mex) Nueva Rosita G14-1 (1979).

8. S. Ildefonso: (Mex) Nueva Rosita G14-1 (1979).

9. Señor Juan Evangelista: (Mex) Piedras Negras H14-10 (1980).

10. The problem of translating environmental information is a particularly thorny one. As discussed (Introduction), the recorder's background shapes his perception of the environment. The word *monte* and its definition are very problematic. The *Enciclopedia Universal Ilustrada* (EUI) (1968: 436–437) defines *monte* as "Grande elevación natural de terreno—Tierra inculta cubierta de árboles, arbustos ó matas," and gives as a typically Spanish connotation of the word *monte* "extension de tierra cubierta de plantas silvestres y espontáneas" (EUI 1968: 436–437). It adds that, according to the Academia de la Lengua, there is no difference between the word *monte* and the word *bosque* (EUI 1968: 436–437). Thus, the general and essential connotation is of a landscape perceived as uncultivated and in its natural state.

11. San Reymundo de Peña Fuerte de Fuertes Aires: (Mex) Piedras Negras H14-10 (1980).

12. Río de San Josefe: (Mex) Piedras Negras H14-10 (1980).

13. A vara is a unit of measurement that varied, and still varies, considerably, as Haggard showed (1941: 84–87). I have used 33.33 inches as the conversion for one vara.

14. San Buenaventura: (U.S.G.S.) (Mex) Piedras Negras H14-10 (1980).

15. A *tercio* was the third part (one-third) of something. The text could refer to the manner in which the meat cargo was divided, to its arrangement on the backs of the carriers, or to the fact that thirds of a buffalo were being carried. It could also mean that these Native Americans were carrying the cargo on mules or horses, but these animals were not mentioned. A *tercio* was often used to designate the cargo distribution on a mule.

16. The Omaha (Fletcher and La Flesche 1972 v. 1: 271) distinguished between wet meat and dry meat. Dry meat was meat that had been dried and prepared as jerky. It is likely that *aser carne,* "to make meat," referred both to the process of preparation and to the final product.

17. In 1916, Bolton suggested that the location named Dacate was Anacacho Mountain. The first mention of Dacate apparently occurs in 1674 with the trip of Fr. Manuel, who refers to the area as a mountain range with hills, mountains, and arroyos. The Dacate area is mentioned again in 1675 as the living area of the Bagname and the Siano. The third time Dacate is mentioned is in connection with the 1675 expeditionary orders of Bosque and Larios. The orders state that they are to travel to the sierra Dacate (Dacate mountains). On May 18, 1675, Bosque reached a place and a small river (*puesto y riachuelo*) that he said they called Dacate.

18. San Gregorio Nasianseno: (U.S.) Del Rio NH 14-7 (1958, revised 1969).

19. San Bisente Ferrer: (U.S.) Del Rio NH 14-7 (1958, revised 1969).

20. As mentioned (Chapter 1), there is a possible cultural connection between the Mabibit, Jumee (Humee), and even the Yorica groups and the Mariame and Iguase Native groups recorded by Cabeza de Vaca in 1535.

21. San Isidro Labrador: (U.S.) Del Rio NH 14-7 (1958, revised 1969).

22. The use of many Nahuatl words introduced in the general vocabulary is a small measure of the influence of that language. The adoptions of *tatuane* (for *tlatoani,* meaning "supreme ruler") (Portillo 1886: 39); *tlatoles* (for mischievous or conspiratory conversation and conflicts) (Portillo 1886: 161); *yacatsol* (meaning "stone noses," for the name of a hilly area); and *pinauana* (the name of a group, meaning "retired, bashful") are just a few of the examples encountered in the records. Apart from sign language, the most used form of communication appears to have been a corrupt version of Nahuatl or "Mexican." The friars had difficulty with other languages,

but most tried to learn Mexican (Burrus y Zubillaga 1982: 10n43, 12, 13; 1986: 57). Fr. Larios and certainly others preached in the Mexican or Nahuatl language (Peláez et al. 1994: 202–203, 210–212). The frequency of references to the Mexican language and its widespread use indicate that this idiom, whatever its word composition may have been, was used as a lingua franca. The adoption of Nahuatl words points out that a discussion about the acculturation of Native groups should first address the acculturation of Native groups to Aztec culture, and then the acculturation of Spaniards to Aztec and other Native cultures.

23. The gift-giving ceremonies were part of a hospitality behavior that was understood to be reciprocal (Wade 1999, 2001). This behavior, with its variants, was quite likely common to most groups living in Texas and Coahuila. The friars understood such offerings as *limosna,* or giving of alms.

24. Frederick H. Ruecking (1955: 103–106) thought that the word *clavo* meant nail, as it normally does, and portrayed the facial design as looking like a nail. However, the word *clavo* also means "beauty mark," in this case a black dot like a beauty mark, a *señal.*

25. There are several discrepancies between the two descriptions of the captive boy and the facts reported:

(1) Don Esteban and/or Larios did not mention the tattoos on the arms;
(2) Bosque said the boy appeared to be about twelve years of age, but Fr. Larios thought he was eighteen to twenty years old;
(3) Don Esteban (or Larios) did not mention the boy's sister;
(4) On or before March 20, 1675, the boy was with the Colorado.

The Colorado were among the following of Don Fabian in 1674 but recognized the authority of Don Esteban. In 1675, the Colorado were listed among the coalition of Don Esteban (Portillo 1886: 77). However, the Gueiquesale captain stated that his mother had raised the boy and that he considered him a brother.

There are many possible explanations for the fact that the boy was with the Colorado as of March 20, but all the scenarios have basically the same weight, since there is no further proof to confirm any of them. First, the Colorado's possession of the boy as of March 20 does not invalidate the fact that he had been raised by the mother of the Gueiquesale captain and that the captain considered him a brother: the boy could have been traded at a later time. Second, the Gueiquesale captain's mother, or father, could have been Colorado, in which case all the statements would be validated. In any case, these statements indicate a close relationship between the Gueiquesale and the Colorado, and imply the influence of the Gueiquesale over the Colorado.

Regardless of the validity of these scenarios, there are certain facts we can deduce from the sequence of events relating to the boy:

(1) Between 1655 and 1663 the Cabesa and Sibulo (Cibolo) were jointly engaged in raiding the area of Parral;
(2) About the same time the Cabesa (and Sibulo?) had close relations with the Gueiquesale;
(3) The Cabesa must have kept the boy long enough to tattoo him in a specific way because they believed him to be a wolf. The specific tattoos would therefore be culturally related to the Cabesa;
(4) Only Don Esteban connected the facial tattoos to the belief that the boy was a wolf;
(5) The Spanish boy, considered by the Spanish to be a captive and a slave, was viewed and treated as family by the Gueiquesale. He was liable to be given or traded between groups, as a special gift of friendship, but so were Native members of other groups. The Gueiquesale boy given to the Manos Prietas by the Yorica is a case in point. Kenmotsu (1994: 433) compiled a list of offspring exchanged between groups, probably with various motivations.

26. San Bernardo or San Bernardino: (U.S.) Del Rio NH 14-7 (1958, revised 1969).

27. San Jorje: (U.S.) Del Rio NH 14-7 (1958, revised 1969).

28. When the Spaniards referred to this coalition, it was almost always as the Catujano-Tilijae, which indicates that both groups participated in the "leadership" position but probably had different allied groups. At the macro-level they conjoined two spheres of influence, while at the micro-level they represented two or more sets of alliances and allegiances. The Catujano spokespersons who visited Balcarcel did not give any clues about these possible divisions.

29. San Pablo Ermitano: (U.S.) Sonora NH 14-4.

30. Rio Grande Crossing: (U.S.) Del Rio NH 14-7 (1958, revised 1969).

31. Santa Clara de las Nueses: (Mex) Piedras Negras H14-10 (1980).

32. San Diego: (Mex) Piedras Negras H14-10 (1980).

33. The record is unclear whether the one hundred Gueiquesale warriors who were supposed to be traveling with the Bosque-Larios party were included in this number.

34. San Ambrosio: (Mex) Nueva Rosita G14-1 (1979).

35. San Bartolome: (Mex) Monclova G14-4 (1979).

36. Los Baluartes: (Mex) Monclova G14-4 (1979).

37. Due to the length of the document it will be included in the Appendix.

3. A MOVE TO REVOLT

1. The distance given for Mission Ssmo Nombre de Jesus appears to be incorrect.

4. THE MENDOZA-LOPEZ EXPEDITION, 1683–1684

1. My interpretation of Mendoza's expedition route, according to Version L, agrees with that of Williams in general, but I disagree on three major issues. The first concerns the point on the Rio Grande at which Mendoza turned north and left the river, and the route he followed to reach the western boundary of the plains that extend eastward from the Davis Mountains. The reported travel distance (174 miles) from the first hot spring encountered (December 20, 1683), which is almost certainly Indian Hot Springs at the south end of the Quitman Mountains, to the hot spring reported when Mendoza turned north (January 1, 1684), exceeds by at least 50 miles, and more likely by over 75 miles, the travel distance to Ruidosa, near where Williams proposed Mendoza left the Rio Grande. The second issue concerns the location of La Nabidad en las Cruces. The friars, who preceded Mendoza to La Nabidad en las Cruces, joined the expedition there and came back to that area after the trip to the Jumano lands. Mendoza's Certifications and Version M confirm that they were in the La Junta area on both the outbound journey and the return trip. The third issue concerns Williams's belief that Mendoza did not follow Centralia Draw and the Middle Concho before turning south to San Clemente. On the other hand, my interpretation of Mendoza's route closely agrees with Connor's (1969), except for a few minor diversions that are not particularly significant to this study.

2. The Nueces River, or River of the Nuts, is the Concho River that flows through San Angelo, Texas. This was the first river named Nueces within the modern Texas territory.

3. The expedition of Castaño de Sosa (1590), from Monclova to New Mexico, crossed the Rio Grande into modern Texas territory on September 9, 1590. The diary gives few details, and does not provide directions or distances traveled. Hence the exact route cannot be determined with much certainty. However, sufficient information is given to indicate that the route was generally northward and that the point at which they reached the Rio Grande was probably between Ciu-

dad Acuña–Del Rio and the junction of the Rio Grande with the Devils River (now beneath the waters of Amistad Reservoir). On October 1, Castaño de Sosa's party set out for the Río Salado (Pecos River). On October 2, they crossed the Río de las Laxas (Devils River) and camped beside it. Between October 2 and October 18 they traveled in a generally north-northwest direction following the drainage divide (the route of the modern road between Comstock and Pandale as far as the point where this road turns west and traverses steep canyon terrain to reach Howard Draw and the town of Pandale) between the Pecos and the Devils River, to a location near the Val Verde–Crockett county line. On October 18, they were unable to find either the Pecos or the Devils River, which means they were beyond the point where the Pecos River turns toward the northwest and the Devils River bends to the northeast. Up to this location the rivers flow more or less parallel and are about 20 miles apart. At the county line they are about 40 miles apart and diverging. On October 24, the scouts returned to the main party and reported that the Salado (Pecos) River was about 4 leagues (10.4 miles) distant, and that the hills and sierras ended at that location on the river. This campsite was probably on a western tributary of Live Oak Creek and in the vicinity of the place Mendoza later named Corpus Christi on his return trip from San Clemente in 1684. On October 26, the party finally reached the Pecos, after a difficult, steep descent during which some of the wagons broke down. It is likely that Castaño de Sosa reached the Pecos River very near the spot Mendoza named San Juan de Dios on his outbound trip, and the point to which Mendoza returned on his way back to the junction of the Rio Grande and the Conchos River in Mexico. If this is correct, the expedition of Castaño de Sosa was about 4 miles west-northwest of the site of the Gediondo *ranchería* that Mendoza visited in January 1684. The probability that this was, in fact, where Castaño de Sosa reached the Pecos is supported by the diary report that on October 31, after three days of travel upriver on the northeast side of the Pecos, they found "some large salines with incredible amounts of very white salt" (Hammond and Rey 1966: 257). This is almost certainly Soda Lake, the saline Mendoza's party found on the east side of the Pecos in January 1684. The saline is about 22 miles from S. Juan de Dios, and thus about three days of the average distance traveled by the expedition. On their third day of travel, after finding the salines, they found "many rich salt beds" (Hammond and Rey 1966: 259). Juan Cordona Lake, with very rich salt beds, is about 16 miles northwest of Soda Lake, and thus should have been passed during their third day of travel. The following day, their fourth day of travel, they went through "some great dunes of sand" (Hammond and Rey 1966: 259)—the southern extension of the sand-dune belt in western Crane County, which begins about 3 miles west of Juan Cordona Lake. The sequence and distances of separation between these physiographic features strongly support the conclusion that Castaño de Sosa reached the Pecos very near its junction with Five Mile Creek on the Crockett-Pecos county line. On October 28, near the Val Verde–Crockett county line, they encountered a large number of Despeguan or Tepelguan Natives. Near the salt marshes northwest of Soda Lake, Castaño de Sosa's party saw some Native Americans traveling with dog-travois loaded with their belongings and pelts. Castaño de Sosa managed to bring to camp four Natives, two females and two males, but he was unable to communicate with them except through sign language (Schroeder and Matson 1965: 55–56).

4. For information about this period see a series of articles by France V. Scholes in the *New Mexico Historical Review,* particularly vols. XI, XII, XIII, XV, XIX, and XX.

5. For information about these groups see William W. Newcomb and T. N. Campbell (1982), "Southern Plains Ethnohistory: A Re-examination of the Escanjaques, Ahijados, and Cuitoas," in *Pathways to Plains Prehistory: Anthropological Perspectives of Plains Natives and Their Pasts.*

6. The godparents (*padrinos*) of a child are the *compadres* of that child's parents. This relationship was, and continues to be, very important in some Latin countries. It is still an accepted practice that if the parents of a child die, or for some reason cannot care for their offspring, the parenting responsibility will fall upon the godparents. The *compadre* relationship is often extended

to marriage godparents (*padrino de boda*). These were and are very important familial, economic, and political ties.

7. See Appendix. The first declaration does not make it explicit that Juan Sabeata was the spokesperson, but it is almost certain that he was.

8. The history of this cross is very important. Sabeata stated that after the miraculous appearance of the cross, the Jumano used it in battles in which they were victorious (Appendix). One element that is worth mentioning is the miracle or legend of the cross that had been erected at the entrance of the Mexican town of Sayula, where Fr. Larios was born. Between 1528 and 1633, this cross was said to have moved as if a strong wind or earthquake was making it move. The Sayula cross was erected by Franciscan friars (Figueroa Torres 1963: 16–17). The symbol of the cross was appropriated and used by the Tejas, the Jumano, the Julime, the Gediondo, the Payaya, and other groups, including the Apache.

9. According to Version M, Mendoza traveled on to the Colorado River and probably covered some of the terrain he knew from the trip he made in 1654 when the Spanish engaged in battle with the Cuitoa. Thus, it appears that freshwater pearls could be collected in the Concho River drainage and in the Colorado River in Texas.

10. The first request was made by twelve Jumano captains from different *rancherías,* which means that on August 11, 1683, the Jumano had at least twelve different *rancherías* that accepted Juan Sabeata as their spokesperson. The second request (October 20, 1683) was made by Juan Sabeata on behalf of the Jumano and thirty-five other groups.

11. San Bartolome: (Mex) Ciudad Juárez H13-1 (1979). I have used Mexican maps because (1) during most of Mendoza's trip from El Paso to La Junta he was traveling though Mexican territory, and (2) Mexican maps, unlike United States maps, show the territory on both sides of the U.S.-Mexico border.

12. Santissima Trenidad: (Mex) Porvenir H13-2 (1979).

13. N.S. del Pilar de Saragosa: (Mex) Porvenir H13-2 (1979).

14. Sabeata's declaration of October 20 clearly establishes that, like him, some Jumano lived at La Junta de los Ríos, while others lived in the area of the Texas Concho River.

15. N.S. de la Limpia Consepcion: (Mex) Porvenir H13-2 (1979).

16. N.S. de la Soledad: (Mex) San Antonio El Bravo H13-5 (1979).

17. N.S. del Transito: (Mex) San Antonio El Bravo H13-5 (1979).

18. N.S. del Buen Suseso: (Mex) San Antonio El Bravo H13-5 (1979).

19. N.S. del Rosario: (Mex) San Antonio El Bravo H13-5 (1979).

20. N.S. de Regla: (Mex) San Antonio El Bravo H13-5 (1979).

21. N.S. de Belen: (Mex) San Antonio El Bravo H13-5 (1979).

22. N.S. del Populo: (Mex) Ojinaga NH13-8 (1973).

23. N.S. de Atocha: (Mex) Ojinaga NH13-8 (1973).

24. N.S. de los Remedios: (Mex) Ojinaga NH13-8 (1973).

25. N.S. de Guadalupe: (Mex) Ojinaga NH13-8 (1973).

26. La Nabidad en las Cruces: (Mex) Ojinaga NH13-8 (1973).

27. El Apostol Santiago: (Mex) Ojinaga NH13-8 (1973).

28. N. Padre San Francisco: (Mex) Ojinaga NH13-8 (1973).

29. San Nicolas: (Mex) Ojinaga NH13-8 (1973).

30. N. Padre San Anttonio: (Mex) San Antonio El Bravo H13-5 (1979) or Marfa NH 13-6 (1973).

31. San Lorenso: (U.S.) Fort Stockton NH 13-6 (1973).

32. Parage de los Santos Reys: (U.S.) Fort Stockton NH 13-6 (1973).

33. San Pedro de Alcantara: (U.S.) Fort Stockton NH 13-6 (1973).

34. San Bernardino de Sena: (U.S.) Fort Stockton NH 13-6 (1973).

35. San Francisco Xavel: (U.S.) Fort Stockton NH 13-6 (1973).

36. San Juan del Río: (U.S.) Fort Stockton NH 13-6 (1973).

37. San Anselmo: (U.S.) Fort Stockton NH 13-6 (1973).

38. San Christoval: (U.S.) Pecos NH 13-3.

39. S. Domingo Soriano de la Noche Buena: (U.S.) Pecos NH 13-3.

40. San Juan de Dios: (U.S.) Fort Stockton NH 13-6 (1973).

41. There is little evidence for the use of or interest in firearms by Native Americans at this time. Sabeata was clearly sufficiently acquainted with these weapons to modify and use a harquebus. It is noteworthy that the Native reports of Jean Gery (Chapter 5) almost always refer to his disabled harquebus. One reason firearms may not have been of great interest to Native Americans is that they make noise. It is not possible to have a confrontation or an ambush without revealing one's position very early in the fray. Also, firearms were useless if one could not obtain reliable supplies of ammunition.

42. San Ygnacio de Loyola: (U.S.) Sonora NH 14-4 (1978).

43. La Conbercion de San Pablo: (U.S.) San Angelo NH 14-1 (1978).

44. Arcos Tuertos ("Twisted Bows") or Arcos Fuertes ("Strong Bows"), as the name appears in the two different versions of the diary, refers to a Native group and denotes bows that are both strong and twisted: different from all the other bows made by Natives in the area. Quite likely the group name Los que Hacen Arcos ("Those Who Make Bows") refers to the same group, since all the Natives probably made and fought with the bow and arrow; "Those Who Make Bows" made different bows from all the other groups. That distinction set them apart and resulted in the designation. If that is the case, the cultural connection between the group variously named Arcos Tuertos, Arcos Fuertes, and Los que Hacen Arcos and the groups encountered by the Espejo-Luxán expedition in 1582–1583 should not be dismissed. Luxán described these special bows as Turkish bows, which, for Europeans, would be the obvious parallel (Hammond and Rey 1929: 57–58). The groups referred to by Espejo-Luxán that used this particular weapon were variously called Otomoacos and Patarabueyes, the latter clearly a Spanish word (slang?) related to buffalo or cattle. Mendoza stated that the Arcos Tuertos or Arcos Fuertes were in all aspects like the Suma, who at this time were living at La Junta de los Ríos.

45. San Honofre: (U.S.) San Angelo NH 14-1 (1978).

46. San Marcos: (U.S.) San Angelo NH 14-1 (1978).

47. San Joseph: (U.S.) San Angelo NH 14-1 (1978).

48. N.S. de la Candelaria: (U.S.) San Angelo NH 14-1 (1978).

49. El Arcangel San Migel: (U.S.) San Angelo NH 14-1 (1978).

50. Señor San Diego: (U.S.) San Angelo NH 14-1 (1978).

51. The text actually says *gallinas montessas*. It is uncertain if this refers to prairie chickens, turkeys, or both.

52. According to the Texas Memorial Museum, *matalote* and *boquinete* refer to suckers, the latter being a smallmouth buffalo fish (see Chapter 2, note 2).

53. El Angel de Guarda: (U.S.) San Angelo NH 14-1 (1978).

54. San Bissente Ferrer: (U.S.) San Angelo NH 14-1 (1978).

55. Río del Señor San Pedro: (U.S.) San Angelo NH 14-1 (1978).

56. San Pablo: (U.S.) San Angelo NH 14-1 (1978).

57. San Isidro Labrador: (U.S.) Brownwood NH 14-2 (1978).

58. San Sebastian: (U.S.) Brownwood NH 14-2 (1978).

59. Los Desamparados: (U.S.) Brownwood NH 14-2 (1978).

60. San Roque: (U.S.) Brownwood NH 14-2 (1978).

61. When the Marqués de Rubí and his party traveled through some of this country in 1767 they killed buffalo and roped a bear.

62. Río del Glorioso San Clemente: (U.S.) Llano NH 14-5 (1975).

63. The actual Spanish transcript in Lino Canedo (1968: 156) reads: "Hallamos un indio ladino llamado Tomás, de la provincia de Coahuila, que entró con unos soldados y el custodio del Paso del Nuevo México hasta una sierra que está como doce leguas arriba del Paso del río Jondo [Hondo], los quales venian a los Texas y no se atrevieron a pasar de dicha sierra y lo enviaron a él para que viese y descubriese la población de los Texas, el cual, de indios en indios fue a dar allá al cabo de tiempo y ha más de un año que está en los Texas. . . ."

64. The only other problem we know the Apache to have caused was the theft of nine horses.

65. San Atanacio: (U.S.) Llano NH 14-5 (1978).

66. Santa Crus: (U.S.) Sonora NH 14-4 (1978).

67. San Agustin: (U.S.) Sonora NH 14-4 (1978).

68. La Hasencion del Señor: (U.S.) Sonora NH 14-4 (1978).

69. San Lazaro: (U.S.) Sonora NH 14-4 (1978).

70. N.S. de la Piedad: (U.S.) Sonora NH 14-4 (1978).

71. El Hespiritu Santo: (U.S.) Sonora NH 14-4 (1978).

72. San Geronimo: (U.S.) Sonora NH 14-4 (1978).

73. San Pantaleon: (U.S.) Sonora NH 14-4 (1978).

74. Corpus Christi: (U.S.) Sonora NH 14-4 (1978).

75. Santo Thomas de Villanueba: (U.S.) Fort Stockton NH 13-6 (1973).

76. A translation of both *certificaciones* appears in the Appendix.

77. Santa Catalina: (Mex) Ojinaga NH13-8 (1973).

78. Santa Polonia: (Mex) Ojinaga NH13-8 (1973).

79. Santa Teresa: (Mex) Ojinaga NH13-8 (1973).

80. Santa Brigida: (Mex) Ciudad Delicias H13-11 (1979).

81. Santa Monica: (Mex) Ciudad Delicias H13-11 (1979).

82. S. Anttonio de Julimes: (Mex) Ciudad Delicias H13-11 (1979).

83. El Tule: (Mex) Ciudad Delicias H13-11 (1979).

84. Tabalaopa: AAF Aeronautical Chart (470) Santiago Mountains, Scale 1:1,000,000, U.S. Coast and Geodetic Survey, May 1945 (hereafter shown as AAF Aeronautical Chart).

85. El Ojito: AAF Aeronautical Chart.

86. El Saúz: AAF Aeronautical Chart.

87. Las Ensinillas: AAF Aeronautical Chart.

88. Ojo Laguna: AAF Aeronautical Chart.

89. Gallego: AAF Aeronautical Chart.

90. Monteczuma: AAF Aeronautical Chart.

91. Ojo Caliente: AAF Aeronautical Chart.

92. Laguna de Patos: AAF Aeronautical Chart.

93. Ojo del Lucero: AAF Aeronautical Chart.

94. Los Medanos: AAF Aeronautical Chart.

5. A NEW FRONTIER

1. During the period covered by this work the expression *tierra adentro* was often used to signify the unknown interior. To travel *tierra adentro* was to go beyond the known frontier (*tierra afuera*). The *Diccionario de la lengua Castellana* defines *adentro* as: "Lo escondido y retirado del lúgar que está presente, y contrário à lo que es afuera" (1726: 81). *Tierra adentro* is defined as: "Phrase con que se explica la parte de un Réino, ò Província, que tiene alguna distáncia considerable de sus confines, especialmente del mar" (1726: 81). By contrast, *afuera* is defined as: "Lo que

está por la parte exterior de alguna cosa. Lo contrário de adentro" (1726: 112). Thus, the two terms and expressions are defined in opposition to each other even if, as oppositional expressions and concepts, they appear counterintuitive. *Tierra adentro,* that which is hidden and distant from the place within the known confines of the kingdom where the subject is located, is opposed to *tierra afuera,* the exterior of the hidden and distant territory, the known frontier.

2. In a letter to Don Carlos de Siguenza y Góngora (Lino Canedo 1968: 9–17), Fr. Massanet reported that he had informed Alonso de León of the presence and location of Jean Gery. The tone of the letter indicates that Massanet felt Alonso de León was hoarding all the glory from the capture of the Frenchman.

3. Native American reports of foreigners at this time consistently refer to them as Spaniards. They did not distinguish between Spaniard and French, and clearly did not, and probably could not, fathom the consequences of their reports. I think that the delivery of Jean Gery was the beginning of the understanding that the two groups of people with white skin and many other things in common were actually mutual enemies. This was a very costly error for Native groups in Texas. The reference to Jean Gery as the "moor" probably originated with the friars.

4. This estimate by the Spaniards may have been incorrect, because when one compares the travel time Sabeata estimated and the actual days of travel spent by the Mendoza expedition to cover the same distance, the ratio appears to be four days of travel by the Spanish for each day of travel by Native Americans (Chapter 4).

5. A gentile was a person who did not recognize the existence of the Christian God, a non-Christian. The word also often implied a person who had not been baptized.

6. Precontact gatherings for social intercourse and trade were held at times that reflected major ceremonial celebrations connected with hunting and harvest seasons, as well as with military campaigns. The timing of these gatherings would vary according to the geographic and climatic area where they were to take place. Postcontact gatherings held primarily for trade would have reflected at first the timing of the Spanish expeditions to Texas, and later the cycle of festivities of the Spanish population. For further information on the Native trade fairs in Texas, see Foster 1995, particularly pp. 219–220.

7. Some of the groups encountered by Salinas Varona had not appeared in the record for quite a while. One of these groups is the Cacaxtle (Chapter 1).

8. I included these population numbers because: (1) they are impressive, and these groups were presumably to be placed in pueblos at La Junta de los Ríos, and (2) the number of 2,500 people and the corresponding number of families result in an average of 16 to 19 members for each family. These numbers, if reliable, provide a very broad notion of extended family.

6. HARD CHOICES

1. Diego Ramón specified that the horse skins he saw were from mares. It is possible that mares were stolen more often because they would have been easier to control than stallions. Since Ramón was a very experienced soldier and frontiersman, his assessment should have been correct. Another possibility is that Native Americans, particularly ladinos, could be breeding horses just like the Tejas (Chapter 4).

2. If Captain Flores traveled for nineteen days at an average of 5 to 6 leagues per day, that results in 95 to 114 leagues, or 247 to 296.4 miles, for an average of 271.7 miles. Flores skirted the Balcones Escarpment on the east and proceeded northward to the area around Brownwood (Pecan Bayou); if he traveled more northwesterly, the battle could have taken place in the San Sabá area. East of the Colorado was the territory of the Tejas and their allies, and the Spaniards traveled that area frequently. Since Flores did not mention any of the usual roads or landmarks,

it is reasonable to assume that he traveled north and west. Both Flores and Bustillo y Zevallos emphasized that they traveled through unknown lands.

3. The information from the captive Apache women indicates that the small *ranchería* that was attacked was 70 leagues (182 miles) from Béjar by direct route. If one assumes an absolute straight-line distance and that the direction was northwesterly, the arc of possible maximum-distance locations extends from the northeast corner of Brown County (north-northeast of Brownwood) to Burnet, thence to Ballinger, and thence to San Angelo. If one assumes that straight-line distance is only 90 percent of the direct route in Native terms, the straight-line distance becomes 164 miles, and the arc of possible locations extends from Brownwood, thence to the Colorado River about 4 miles southeast of the southeast corner of Runnels County, thence to the town of Vick in westernmost Concho County, and thence to the headwaters of Pecan Creek, 22 miles south-southeast of San Angelo. The straight-line distance from San Sabá Mission (Menard) to San Antonio (Béjar) is 50 leagues (130 miles). During his inspection tour, the Marqués de Rubí traveled from San Sabá to Béjar by what probably was very close to the most direct route, and he reported traveling 67 leagues (174 miles). This distance, considering the terrain covered, makes the straight-line distance about 75 percent of the most direct route of travel. Using this percentage to determine straight-line distance from the battle site to Béjar yields 52.2 leagues (136.5 miles), and the arc of possible locations extends from the Colorado River 11 miles northeast of the modern town of San Sabá to a point 5 miles north of Brady, thence to a point about 6 miles north of Menard, the site of San Sabá Mission and the Presidio de las Amarillas, and thence to a point about 3 miles south of Ft. McKavett. Given the foregoing and the historical reports, the most likely site of the *ranchería* was on the north side of the San Sabá River near Menard.

4. The larger Lipan *ranchería* reported by the captive Apache women would be 70 leagues (182 miles) northwesterly from the battle site. The land northward from Menard is less rugged than the terrain traversed from San Antonio to Menard. Thus, a minimum straight-line distance would be 75 percent of the actual travel distance of 70 leagues, or 52.5 leagues (136.5 miles), and 90 percent of the distance, 63 leagues or 163.8 miles, is a reasonable maximum straight-line distance. The minimum arc at 137 miles begins at a point just south of the town of Stamford, thence parallels the Clear Fork of the Brazos River near its headwaters north and west of the town of Roby, thence to a point about 6 miles south of Snyder, thence to the Colorado River just below Lake J. B. Thomas, and thence to the city of Big Spring. The maximum arc at 164 miles would begin about 3 miles south of Weinert in Haskell County, extend to Claremont in Kent County, thence to a point about 5 miles southeast of Justiceburg in Garza County, and thence to a point on the headwaters of the Colorado River about 15 miles southeast of Lamesa near the Borden-Dawson county line. If it is assumed that the northwest azimuth from Béjar to San Sabá Mission and the site of the battle is also the same azimuth between the battle site and the site of the large *ranchería,* the latter's location would fall within a 12-mile radius of the northwest end of Lake J. B. Thomas, on the Colorado River. This site would also have several possible advantages, including proximity to the buffalo herd's migration routes on the southern portion of the Llano Estacado and on the Edwards Plateau and the Blackland Prairies. It would also be near several water sources, including the large springs for which the city of Big Spring is named, the Colorado River, the Double Mountain Fork of the Brazos River, and the headwaters of the Clear Fork of the Brazos River.

5. Several Native groups were, at different times, called Pelones as a descriptive term meaning "hairless," possibly referring to their shaved or partially shaved heads. It is often very difficult to tell to which group the recorder is referring. In this case, the Pelones may or may not have been Apache. On the other hand, according to Muñoz Camargo (1892: 9), the word *pellones* also meant clothing made of feathers and used by Tarasco Natives.

7. THE PRICE OF PEACE

1. The recently published *Imaginary Kingdom: Texas as Seen by the Rivera and Rubí Military Expeditions, 1727 and 1767,* edited by Jack Jackson and with annotations by William C. Foster (hereafter referred to as *IK*), gives extensive background information on the protagonists of the Marqués de Rubí inspection tour and provides the first English translation of the Rubí diary of the expedition. I refer often to this work. I have also used Nicolas Lafora's diary, translated and published by Lawrence Kinnaird in 1958.

2. The Marqués de Rubí tour was organized around visits to military installations. The route took him from the town of Saltillo to Monclova, thence to the Presidio de Santa Rosa, thence across the Rio Grande to the abandoned missions on the Nueces River, and from there to the Presidio de San Luis de las Amarillas in San Sabá. This work addresses only that part of the Rubí route from the Rio Grande crossing to San Antonio de Béjar, the route that traversed the lands of the Nueces River and the San Sabá area.

3. On page 108, note 36, Jackson (*IK*) notes that Lafora's estimate of 400 yards' width for the Rio Grande seemed exaggerated. In 1675, the Bosque-Larios expedition crossed the Rio Grande at basically the same point. Bosque estimated the width of the river at 400 varas, i.e., 1,111 feet (1 vara equals 33.33 inches). The 200 *toesas* compute to 1,100 feet (1 *toesa* equals 1 yard 30 inches, as in Haggard 1941: 84).

4. It is possible that the Mogano, or Movano, Mountain Range is the Delaware Mountains. In delineating the routes to be taken by various military detachments, O'Conor planned them in such a manner that the detachments would intercept each other's survey circuits. The third detachment was to head to the Sierra de Guadalupe, going by the Large Saline and the Guadalupe Mountains. Along the route they were to inspect the Mogano Mountain and its range. Before returning to their base, the soldiers were to wait for new orders at the Sierra de Guadalupe (Cutter 1994: 83–84).

5. For further information on the history of the Comanche in Texas and Ecueracapa see Kavanagh (1996).

8. ETHNOHISTORY AND ARCHAEOLOGY

1. This evidence confirms Thomas Campbell's conviction that the words *dacate* and *yacatsol* referred to the dissected edge of the Edwards Plateau (personal communication, 2001).

References Cited

UNPUBLISHED PRIMARY SOURCES

AGUAYO, MARQUES DE

1721   Certification, May 13. *Archivo General de la Nación* (hereafter referred to as *AGN*), *Províncias Internas* (hereafter referred to as *PI*), vol. 32, frames (hereafter fr.) 163–165. Microfilm at Latin American Collection, University of Texas at Austin.

1725   Aguayo to Viceroy, February. *AGN PI*, vol. 183, fr. 41–50. Microfilm at Latin American Collection, University of Texas at Austin.

1725a   Aguayo to Viceroy. *AGN PI*, vol. 32, fr. 181–186. Microfilm at Latin American Collection, University of Texas at Austin.

AGUIRRE, P., A. CORTINAS, B. FLORES, D. FLORES, N. FLORES, N. GUAJANDO, A. DE LUNA, D. DE MENCHACA, A. M. PEÑA, J. DE LOS SANTOS, AND OTHERS

1673   Testimony of Lacaro Agustin, July 29. *Documents for the Early History of Coahuila and Texas and the Approaches Thereto.* Box 2Q259, vol. 2, pp. 298–300. Center for American History, University of Texas at Austin.

1673a   Request of the *Junta de vecinos,* August 9. *Documents for the Early History of Coahuila and Texas and the Approaches Thereto.* Box 2Q259, vol. 2, p. 314. Center for American History, University of Texas at Austin.

1673b   Opinion of the Cabildo, August 9. *Documents for the Early History of Coahuila and Texas and the Approaches Thereto.* Box 2Q259, vol. 2, pp. 312–316. Center for American History, University of Texas at Austin.

AGUSTIN, LACARO (LAZARO)

1673   Request for a pueblo (Fr. Larios signed for Don Lacaro), April. *Documents for the Early History of Coahuila and Texas and the Approaches Thereto.* Box 2Q259, vol. 2, pp. 283–288. Center for American History, University of Texas at Austin.

1673a   Testimony, August 2. *Documents for the Early History of Coahuila and Texas and the Approaches Thereto.* Box 2Q259, vol. 2, pp. 300–304. Center for American History, University of Texas at Austin.

ALMAZAN, FERNANDO A. PERÉZ DE

1724   Report on attack, March 10. *AGN PI*, vol. 183, fr. 2–3. Microfilm at Latin American Collection, University of Texas at Austin.

1724a   Almazan to Cassafuerte, March 14. *AGN PI*, vol. 183, fr. 8. Microfilm at Latin American Collection, University of Texas at Austin.

1724b   Almazan to Cassafuerte, March 24. *AGN PI*, vol. 183, fr. 15–19. Microfilm at Latin American Collection, University of Texas at Austin.

1733   Almazan to Viceroy, February 10. *AGN PI,* vol. 32, fr. 347–351. Microfilm at Latin American Collection, University of Texas at Austin.

ANDREU, DR.

1755   Opinion, October 1. *Archivo General de Indias* (hereafter called AGI), *Audiencia de Mexico.* Box 2Q151, pp. 97–116. Center for American History, University of Texas at Austin.

ANNAYA, CHRISTOVAL

1663   Testimony to the Inquisition, April 20. *AGN Inquisición,* Siglo XVII, Tomo 595, p. 44. Center for Southwest Research, University Of New Mexico, Albuquerque.

ANONYMOUS

1746   Letter from a friar, n.d. *Documents for the Early History of Coahuila and Texas and the Approaches Thereto.* Box 2Q259, vol. 3, part 5, pp. 426–434. Center for American History, University of Texas at Austin.

ARANDA, FR. MIGUEL DE

1753   Letter to Fr. Mariano de los Dolores, July 19. *AGI Audiencia de Mexico.* Box 2Q151, p. 30. Center for American History, University of Texas at Austin.

ARDENOL, D. DE LA PARRA

1673   Autos and Informe. Box 121, *Legado 94,* no. 20, File 2. Catholic Archives of Texas, Austin.

1673a   Testimony. Box 121, *Legado 94,* no. 20, File 2. Catholic Archives of Texas, Austin.

AUDITOR

1750   Opinion, January 31. *AGN Historia* (hereafter *H*), vol. 28, fr. 125–130. Microfilm at Latin American Collection, University of Texas at Austin.

BAGA, FR. ANTONIO

1692   Report on the missions, May 17. *Documents for the Early History of Coahuila and Texas and the Approaches Thereto.* Box 2Q259, vol. 3, part 1, pp. 33–36. Center for American History, University of Texas at Austin.

BAGA, FR. ANTONIO, FR. NICOLAS PISSANO, FR. MARTIN PONCE,
AND FR. BERNARDO DE ROXAS

1692   Certification, July 12. *Documents for the Early History of Coahuila and Texas and the Approaches Thereto.* Box 2Q259, vol. 3, part 1, pp. 39–40. Center for American History, University of Texas at Austin.

1692a   Letter to Padre Boca Negra, July 24. *Documents for the Early History of Coahuila and Texas and the Approaches Thereto.* Box 2Q259, vol. 3, part 1, pp. 47–48. Center for American History, University of Texas at Austin.

BAGA, FR. ANTONIO, FR. JOSEPH S. BUENAVENTURA, FR. PEDRO GARCIA,
FR. XPTOVAL MEXIA, FR. NICOLAS PISSANO, FR. BERNARDO DE ROXAS,
AND FR. JUAN DE VELASCO

1693   Complaint against Governor Salinas Varona, January 31. *Documents for the Early History of Coahuila and Texas and the Approaches Thereto.* Box 2Q259, vol. 3, part 1, pp. 69–76. Center for American History, University of Texas at Austin.

BALCARCEL (BALCARSEL), ANTONIO DE (RIBADENEYRA Y SOTOMAYOR)

1675   *Documents for the Early History of Coahuila and Texas and the Approaches Thereto.* Box 2Q259, vol. 2, p. 779. Center for American History, University of Texas at Austin.

BALDES, NICOLAS FLORES

1724   Testimony, March 13. *AGN PI,* vol. 183, fr. 5–6. Microfilm at Latin American Collection, University of Texas at Austin.

1724a   Testimony, August 12. *AGN PI,* vol. 32, fr. 173–176. Microfilm at Latin American Collection, University of Texas at Austin.

BANEGAS, FR. ROQUE

1676   Resulta de Visita. *Documents for the Early History of Coahuila and Texas and the Ap-*

proaches Thereto. Box 2Q259, vol. 3, part 1, pp. 1–3. Center for American History, University of Texas at Austin.

BARBARIGO, CAPTAIN F.

1674 Petition to Barbarigo. Box 121, *Legado 94,* no. 7. Catholic Archives of Texas, Austin.

1674a Letter, July 19. Box 122, *Legado 94,* no. 11. Catholic Archives of Texas, Austin.

BLAS, DE LA PAZ

1724 Testimony of Juan de Santiago, July 12, 1724. *AGN PI,* vol. 32, fr. 168. Microfilm at Latin American Collection, University of Texas at Austin.

BOCA NEGRA, PADRE XPTOVAL DE ESTRADA

1692 Letter to Fr. Baga, July 28. *Documents for the Early History of Coahuila and Texas and the Approaches Thereto.* Box 2Q259, vol. 3, part 1, pp. 49–50. Center for American History, University of Texas at Austin.

BONILLA, ANTONIO

1776 Statement of Juan Domingo Ochoa, November 1. *AGN PI,* vol. 24, fr. 270. Microfilm at Latin American Collection, University of Texas at Austin.

BOSQUE, FERNANDO DEL

1675 Bosque-Larios Diary, Version B, May 16. *Documents for the Early History of Coahuila and Texas and the Approaches Thereto.* Box 2Q259, vol. 2, pp. 774–775. Center for American History, University of Texas at Austin.

1675a Bosque-Larios Diary, Version B, May 21. *Documents for the Early History of Coahuila and Texas and the Approaches Thereto.* Box 2Q259, vol. 2, pp. 775–776. Center for American History, University of Texas at Austin.

1675b Bosque-Larios Diary, Version B, June 1. *Documents for the Early History of Coahuila and Texas and the Approaches Thereto.* Box 2Q259, vol. 2, p. 776. Center for American History, University of Texas at Austin.

1675c Bosque-Larios Diary, Version B, June 5. *Documents for the Early History of Coahuila and Texas and the Approaches Thereto.* Box 2Q259, vol. 2, p. 776. Center for American History, University of Texas at Austin.

1675d Bosque-Larios Diary, Version B, June 10. *Documents for the Early History of Coahuila and Texas and the Approaches Thereto.* Box 2Q259, vol. 2, pp. 774–775. Center for American History, University of Texas at Austin.

BUSTAMANTE, JUAN DOMINGO

1723 Derrotero, November 8. *AGN H,* vol. 299, fr. 115. Microfilm at Latin American Collection, University of Texas at Austin.

BUSTILLO Y ZEVALLOS, JUAN ANTONIO

1732 Order of Bustillo y Zevallos, December 24. *AGN PI,* vol. 32, fr. 353–356. Microfilm at Latin American Collection, University of Texas at Austin.

1733 Bustillo y Zevallos to Conde de Galvé, January 31. *AGN PI,* vol. 32, fr. 356–375. Microfilm at Latin American Collection, University of Texas at Austin.

CADILLAC, LAMOTHE

1715 Letter, February 1. *French Activities in Spanish Southwest.* Box 2Q235, pp. 2–3. Center for American History, University of Texas at Austin.

CAH (CENTER FOR AMERICAN HISTORY)

1698 Various documents. *Documents for the Early History of Coahuila and Texas and the Approaches Thereto.* Box 2Q259, vol. 3, part 1. Center for American History, University of Texas at Austin.

CANCIO, LORENZO

1762 Letter, December 19. *AGN PI,* vol. 25, fr. 183, 191. Microfilm at Latin American Collection, University of Texas at Austin.

1763   Alderete's campaign on the Apache, June 25. *AGN PI,* vol. 25, fr. 189. Microfilm at Latin
              American Collection, University of Texas at Austin.

1763a   Letter, November 4. *AGN PI,* vol. 25, fr. 211. Microfilm at Latin American Collection,
              University of Texas at Austin.

1764   Letter, January 6. *AGN PI,* vol. 25, fr. 227. Microfilm at Latin American Collection,
              University of Texas at Austin.

1764a   Cancio to Cruillas, March 3. *AGN PI,* vol. 25, fr. 242–243. Microfilm at Latin American
              Collection, University of Texas at Austin.

1764b   Cancio to Cruillas, September 6. *AGN PI,* vol. 25, fr. 266–267. Microfilm at Latin
              American Collection, University of Texas at Austin.

CASTILLA Y THÉRAN, JOSEPH

1767   Dictamen, May. *AGN PI,* vol. 25, fr. 383. Microfilm at Latin American Collection, Uni-
              versity of Texas at Austin.

CEPEDA, YGNACIO DE

1756   Testimony, November 4. *Béxar Archives.* Box 2C19, vol. 30, pp. 74–76. Center for Ameri-
              can History, University of Texas at Austin.

CHIRINOS, DOMINGO

1761   Testimony, February 5. *Béxar Archives.* Box 2C20, vol. 37, pp. 78–81. Center for Ameri-
              can History, University of Texas at Austin.

CRUZATE, DOMINGO PETRIZ DE (CRUZATI)

1683   Request for military supplies, January 31. *AGN PI,* vol. 35, fr. 63. Microfilm at Latin
              American Collection, University of Texas at Austin.

1683a   Letter to the Viceroy, September 26. *AGN PI,* vol. 35, fr. 81–83. Microfilm at Latin
              American Collection, University of Texas at Austin.

1683b   Conveyance of Sabeata's declarations, October 30. *AGN PI,* vol. 35. Microfilm at Latin
              American Collection, University of Texas at Austin.

1683c   Commission as Commander of the Expedition to Texas, November 29. *France Scholes
              Collection,* MSS 360, Box 1, Folder 69. Center for Southwest Research, University of
              New Mexico, Albuquerque.

1684   Reference to the orders given to Dominguez Mendoza, July 25. *AGN PI,* vol. 35, fr. 68–
              71. Microfilm at Latin American Collection, University of Texas at Austin.

1684a   Letter to the Viceroy, October 7. *AGN H,* vol. 298, fr. 422. Microfilm at Latin American
              Collection, University of Texas at Austin.

1685   Request for military manpower, April 20. *AGN PI,* vol. 37, fr. 252. Microfilm at Latin
              American Collection, University of Texas at Austin.

1685a   Excerpt from a letter of Domingo Jironza Petriz de Cruzate to the Viceroy, August 26.
              F. Scholes translation. *France Scholes Collection,* MSS 360, Box 1, Folder 69. Center for
              Southwest Research, University of New Mexico, Albuquerque.

CUERBO Y VALDEZ, FRANCISCO

1698   Establishment of the pueblo and mission of San Antonio Galindo de Monteczuma,
              July 4, July 20, October 3, October 26, October 28. *AGI Audiencia de Guadalajara.* Box
              2Q136, vol. 17, pp. 93–107. Center for American History, University of Texas at Austin.

1698a   Establishment of the pueblo and mission of San Phelipe de Valladares, October 4, No-
              vember 2, November 15. *AGI Audiencia de Guadalajara.* Box 2Q136, vol. 17, pp. 192–204.
              Center for American History, University of Texas at Austin.

1698b   Establishment of the pueblo and mission of the Ssmo. nombre de Jesus, November 21.
              AGI Audiencia de Guadalajara. Box 2Q136, vol. 17, pp. 226–236. Center for American
              History, University of Texas at Austin.

1699 Establishment of the pueblo and mission San Francisco Jabier, November 24, December 14, 1698, January 5. *AGI Audiencia de Guadalajara.* Box 2Q136, vol. 17, pp. 216–224. Center for American History, University of Texas at Austin.

1699a Establishment of the pueblo and mission of San Juan Baptista in the Valle de Santo Domingo y Río de Savinas. *AGI Audiencia de Guadalajara.* Box 2Q136, vol. 17, pp. 238–249. Center for American History, University of Texas at Austin.

1699b Permission to Diego Rámon to go inland to find Natives for missions, December 16. *AGI Audiencia de Guadalajara.* Box 2Q136, vol. 17, pp. 251–252. Center for American History, University of Texas at Austin.

1700 Establishment of the pueblo and mission of S. Francisco Solano, March 27. *AGI Audiencia de Guadalajara.* Box 2Q136, vol. 17, pp. 252–257. Center for American History, University of Texas at Austin.

DE LA CRUZ, FR. MANUEL

1674 Letter, May 29. The letter describes the trip to the north side of the Rio Grande. Box 121, *Legado 94,* no. 9a. Catholic Archives of Texas, Austin.

1679 Report on the missions in Coahuila, April 10. Box 65, *Folder 1,* pp. 19–28. Catholic Archives of Texas, Austin.

DE SAN BUENAVENTURA, FR. DIONISIO

1674 Letter, October 31. Box 122, *Legado 94,* no. 13. Catholic Archives of Texas, Austin.

DIAZ, DOMINGO

1787 Diaz to Rengel, April 13. *AGN PI,* vol. III, fr. 26–27. Microfilm at Latin American Collection, University of Texas at Austin.

1787a Diaz to Rengel, April 21. *AGN PI,* vol. III, fr. 34. Microfilm at Latin American Collection, University of Texas at Austin.

1787b Diaz to Rengel, June 30. *AGN PI,* vol. III, fr. 41–44. Microfilm at Latin American Collection, University of Texas at Austin.

1787c Diaz to Rengel, August 30. *AGN PI,* vol. III, fr. 40. Microfilm at Latin American Collection, University of Texas at Austin.

DOLORES, FR. MARIANO DE LOS

1749 Letter to Thoribio Urrutia, November 25. *AGN H,* vol. 28, fr. 110. Microfilm at Latin American Collection, University of Texas at Austin.

ECHEBERZ Y SUBIÇA, A.

1673 Appointment of Fr. Larios as interpreter (incomplete), April. *Documents for the Early History of Coahuila and Texas and the Approaches Thereto.* Box 2Q259, vol. 2, p. 283. Center for American History, University of Texas at Austin.

1673a Order to Lacaro Agustin, August 3. *Documents for the Early History of Coahuila and Texas and the Approaches Thereto.* Box 2Q259, vol. 2, pp. 310–311. Center for American History, University of Texas at Austin.

1673b Order to convene a Junta of the Cabildo, August 3. *Documents for the Early History of Coahuila and Texas and the Approaches Thereto.* Box 2Q259, vol. 2, pp. 310–311. Center for American History, University of Texas at Austin.

ELIZONDO, FRANCISCO

1674 Autos en que se da cuenta de la entrada. Box 121, *Legado 94,* no. 3a. Catholic Archives of Texas, Austin.

FLORES, NICOLAS

1673 Testimony about the request for a pueblo made by Don Lacaro Agustin, June 27. *Documents for the Early History of Coahuila and Texas and the Approaches Thereto.* Box 2Q259, vol. 2, pp. 287–291. Center for American History, University of Texas at Austin.

GARCIA, JUAN BAUTISTA

1608   Testimony on the Urdiñola campaign. *AGI Audiencia de Guadalajara.* Box 2Q135, pp. 69–70. Center for American History, University of Texas at Austin.

GARZA FALCON, ALEJO

1776   Report to Ugalde, January 9. *AGN PI,* vol. 24, fr. 248. Microfilm at Latin American Collection, University of Texas at Austin.

GOMEZ, FR. PEDRO, FR. J. M. DE CASTRO, FR. D. DE MENDOÇA, FR. J. SABALETA, AND FR. F. VARGAS

1684   Petition to leave El Paso, September 19. *AGN PI,* vol. 37, fr. 210. Center Microfilm at Latin American Collection, University of Texas at Austin.

GONZALES, FR. JOSEPH

1724   Fr. Joseph Gonzales to Viceroy. *AGN PI,* vol. 32, fr. 156–161. Center Microfilm at Latin American Collection, University of Texas at Austin.

GUEMES Y HORCASITAS, JUAN FRANCISCO DE

1747   Approval, January 23. *Documents for the Early History of Coahuila and Texas and the Approaches Thereto.* Box 2Q259, vol. 3, part 5, p. 425. Center for American History, University of Texas at Austin.

1747a   Report of the Natives of Ranchería Grande, February 14. *Missions of Texas, Archivo del Colegio de Santa Cruz 1716–1749.* Box 2Q237, p. 121. Center for American History, University of Texas at Austin.

HIDALGO, FR. FRANCISCO

1716   Letter to the Viceroy, November 4. *French Activities in Spanish Southwest.* Box 2Q235, pp. 1–11. Center for American History, University of Texas at Austin.

ILLEGIBLE

1700   Rebuttal to Diego de Ramón, November 2. *Documents for the Early History of Coahuila and Texas and the Approaches Thereto.* Box 2Q259, vol. 3, part 2, pp. 185–197. Center for American History, University of Texas at Austin.

JAUREGUI, JACINTO B. DE

1766   Letter to Cruillas, April 9. *AGN PI,* vol. 25, fr. 339. Microfilm at Latin American Collection, University of Texas at Austin.

1767   Letter to Croix, March 9. *AGN PI,* vol. 25, fr. 380–382. Microfilm at Latin American Collection, University of Texas at Austin.

1767a   Letter to Croix, March 9. *AGN PI,* vol. 25, fr. 382–384. Microfilm at Latin American Collection, University of Texas at Austin.

1767b   Letter to Croix, April 8. *AGN PI,* vol. 25, fr. 384–387. Microfilm at Latin American Collection, University of Texas at Austin.

1767c   Letter to Croix, May 3. *AGN PI,* vol. 25, fr. 386. Microfilm at Latin American Collection, University of Texas at Austin.

LA BASTIDA, PEDRO DE

1684   Digest of the Fiscal, October 10. *AGN PI,* vol. 36, fr. 67–68. Center Microfilm at Latin American Collection, University of Texas at Austin.

1686   Fiscal's opinion, January 22. *AGN H,* vol. 298, fr. 422. Microfilm at Latin American Collection, University of Texas at Austin.

1686a   Opinion of the Fiscal, May 22. *AGN H,* vol. 298, fr. 419. Microfilm at Latin American Collection, University of Texas at Austin.

LARIOS, FR. JUAN

1674   Letter, September 15. Box 122, *Legado 94,* no. 12. Catholic Archives of Texas, Austin.

1674a   Letter, March 2. Box 121, *Legado 94,* no. 8. Catholic Archives of Texas, Austin.

1674b   Letter, December 30. Box 122, *Legado 94,* no. 14. Catholic Archives of Texas, Austin.

1674c   Memoria de las Naciones. Box 122, *Legado 94,* no. 15. Catholic Archives of Texas, Austin.

1675   Letter to Father Provincial, January 15. Box 122, *Legado 94,* no. 15. Catholic Archives of Texas, Austin.

1675a   Request to Don Antonio Balcarcel, July 5. *Documents for the Early History of Coahuila and Texas and the Approaches Thereto.* Box 2Q259, vol. 2, p. 778. Center for American History, University of Texas at Austin.

LLERENA, FR. LUCAS DE

1701   Letter to the Father Provincial, April 24. *Documents for the Early History of Coahuila and Texas and the Approaches Thereto.* Box 2Q259, vol. 3, part 2, pp. 198–200. Center for American History, University of Texas at Austin.

LEON, JOSEPH DE

1700   Report on Diego Ramón's trip, June 5. *AGN PI,* Box 2Q203, vol. 28, pp. 39–45. Center for American History, University of Texas at Austin.

LIZENCIADO BRIAL

1702   Respuesta fiscal dada en las dependencias del Reyno de el Parral, su fecha de 1 de Sept. de 1689. *AGI Audiencia de Guadalajara.* Box 2Q136, vol. 17, pp. 111–125. Center for American History, University of Texas at Austin.

LOPEZ, FR. NICOLAS

1684   Letter, September 19. *AGN PI,* vol. 37, fr. 210. Microfilm at Latin American Collection, University of Texas at Austin.

1685   Declaration to Viceroy, June 7. *AGN PI,* vol. 37, fr. 217–223. Microfilm at Latin American Collection, University of Texas at Austin.

1686   Declaration to Viceroy, March 26. *AGN PI,* vol. 37, fr. 259–261. Microfilm at Latin American Collection, University of Texas at Austin.

MADRID, L., JUAN SEVERINO, RODRIGO DE ZUBALLE, FRANCISCO DE ANAYA ALMAZÁN, JOSEPH TÉLLEZ GIRÓN, SEBASTIÁN GONZÁLEZ, AND PEDRO SEDILLO

1684   Certification of the personal appearance and services of the Maestro de Campo Don Juan Domínguez y Mendoza and his two sons Don Baltasar and Don Juan, October 8. *France Scholes Collection,* MSS 360, Box 1, Folder 69. Center for Southwest Research, University of New Mexico, Albuquerque.

MALDONADO, JUAN A.

1761   Testimony, October 31, 1762. *Béxar Archives.* Box 2C20, vol. 34, pp. 71–74. Center for American History, University of Texas at Austin.

MANZANAQUE, JOSEPH

ca. 1693 Memorial of Manzaneque. *AGI Audiencia de Guadalajara.* Box 2Q136, vol. 17, p. 127. Center for American History, University of Texas at Austin.

MARMOLEJO, FRANCISCO F.

1688   Declarations of Jean Gery. *AGI Audiencia de Mexico.* Box 2Q144, pp. 253–259, 263–277. Center for American History, University of Texas at Austin.

MARQUES DE LA LAGUNA, T. A.

1681   Approval for assistance to the Conversions of Coahuila, ca. August 5. *Documents for the Early History of Coahuila and Texas and the Approaches Thereto.* Box 2Q259, vol. 4, pp. 375–379. Center for American History, University of Texas at Austin.

1681a   Appointment of Fernando del Bosque and opinion of Fiscal, August 8. *Documents for the Early History of Coahuila and Texas and the Approaches Thereto.* Box 2Q259, vol. 4, pp. 339–349, 359. Center for American History, University of Texas at Austin.

1684   Approval of the Junta not to act against Mendoza and Duran y Chaves, October 11. *AGN PI*, vol. 35, fr. 82–83. Microfilm at Latin American Collection, University of Texas at Austin.

1686   Viceroy denies request for settlement in Texas and departure from El Paso, May 24. *AGN H*, vol. 298, fr. 419–420. Microfilm at Latin American Collection, University of Texas at Austin.

MENCHACA, DOMINGO DE

1673   Testimony, June 27. *Documents for the Early History of Coahuila and Texas and the Approaches Thereto*. Box 2Q259, vol. 2, pp. 291–293. Center for American History, University of Texas at Austin.

MENCHACA, FRANCISCO

1724   Testimony, March 10. *AGN PI*, vol. 183, fr. 2–3. Microfilm at Latin American Collection, University of Texas at Austin.

MENDOZA, JUAN DOMINGUEZ

1684   Derrotero of the trip to Texas. *AGN PI*, Box 2Q204, vol. 37, pp. 38–73 (typescript). Center for American History, University of Texas at Austin.

1684a   Derrotero of the trip to Texas. *AGN H*, vol. 298, fr. 173–188. Microfilm at Latin American Collection, University of Texas at Austin.

1684b   Derrotero of the trip to Texas. *AGN H*, vol. 299, fr. 377–398. Microfilm at Latin American Collection, University of Texas at Austin.

1684c   Derrotero of the trip to Texas, Version M. F. Scholes translation. *France Scholes Collection*, MSS 360, Box 1, Folder 69. Center for Southwest Research, University of New Mexico, Albuquerque.

MENDOZA, JUAN D. DE, D. L. DE GODOY, B. D. DE MENDOZA, AND H. SERRANO

1684   Certificación Primera, June 12. *AGN PI*, Box 2Q204, vol. 37, pp. 69–70. Center for American History, University of Texas at Austin.

1684a   Certificación Segunda, June 13. *AGN PI*, Box 2Q204, vol. 37, p. 70. Center for American History, University of Texas at Austin.

1684b   Declaration about the Discovery, June 23. *AGN PI*, vol. 37, fr. 214–215. Microfilm at Latin American Collection, University of Texas at Austin.

MEZIERES, ATHANASIO DE

1779   Letter to Viceroy, September 5. *AGN PI*, vol. 183, fr. 176–180. Microfilm at Latin American Collection, University of Texas at Austin.

MIRANDA, JUAN DE

1671   Commission as Maestro de Campo General of the Kingdom, July 27. *France Scholes Collection*, MSS 360, Box 1, Folder 69. Center for Southwest Research, University of New Mexico, Albuquerque.

MOHEDANO, FR. JUAN

1673   Authorization for Fr. Peñasco and Fr. Manuel de la Cruz, November 7. *Documents for the Early History of Coahuila and Texas and the Approaches Thereto*. Box 2Q259, vol. 2, pp. 770–772. Center for American History, University of Texas at Austin.

MORAÍN, JUAN A.

1756   Testimony, November 3. *Béxar Archives*. Box 2C19, vol. 30, pp. 66–68. Center for American History, University of Texas at Austin.

MORALES, LUIS DE

1658   Testimony, March 8. *Documents for the Early History of Coahuila and Texas and the Approaches Thereto*. Box 2Q259, vol. 4, pp. 320–324. Center for American History, University of Texas at Austin.

MUÑOZ, FR. ALONSO

1762   Letter to the Commissary General, February 10. *Documents for the Early History of Coahuila and Texas and the Approaches Thereto.* Box 2Q259, vol. 3, part 6, pp. 546–576. Center for American History, University of Texas at Austin.

NAVARRETE, ANGEL M. Y

1762   Declaration of Navarrete, September 15. *Béxar Archives.* Box 2C20, vol. 37, pp. 216–223. Center for American History, University of Texas at Austin.

NAVARRO, S. M.

1770   Letter, April 4. *AGN PI,* vol. 24, fr. 38. Microfilm at Latin American Collection, University of Texas at Austin.

OLIVARES, FR. ANTONIO S. B. Y

1700   Letter, May 6. *AGN PI,* Box 2Q203, vol. 28, pp. 34–35. Center for American History, University of Texas at Austin.

1700a   Letter to Fr. Felipe Galindo, December 13. *AGN PI,* Box 2Q203, vol. 28, pp. 48–51. Center for American History, University of Texas at Austin.

OTALONA, MIGUEL DE

1658   Conveyance, March 8. *Documents for the Early History of Coahuila and Texas and the Approaches Thereto.* Box 2Q259, vol. 4, pp. 331–337. Center for American History, University of Texas at Austin.

PEÑASCO, FR. FRANCISCO LOZANO

1674   Letter, July 7. Box 122, *Legado 94,* no. 10. Catholic Archives of Texas, Austin.

PEREZ, MATHEO, B. CARAVAJAL, D. FLORES, F. FLORES, J. A. FLORES, J. GALBAN, A. GUERRA, F. HERNANDEZ, J. MALDONADO, AND OTHERS

1732   Request of the soldiers, December 24. *AGN PI,* vol. 32, fr. 354–356. Microfilm at Latin American Collection, University of Texas at Austin.

1733   Request of soldiers, April 11. *AGN PI,* vol. 32, fr. 387–388. Microfilm at Latin American Collection, University of Texas at Austin.

RÁBAGO Y THERÁN, PEDRO DE

1746   Report to Guemes y Horcasitas, November 23. *Documents for the Early History of Coahuila and Texas and the Approaches Thereto.* Box 2Q259, vol. 3, part 5, pp. 412–424. Center for American History, University of Texas at Austin.

1755   Trip to San Sabá, January 20. *AGI Audiencia de Mexico.* Box 2Q151, pp. 63–65. Center for American History, University of Texas at Austin.

1755a   Letter to the Viceroy, January 31. *AGI Audiencia de Mexico.* Box 2Q151, pp. 69–90. Center for American History, University of Texas at Austin.

1764   Letter to Ortiz Parrilla, October 4. *AGN PI,* vol. 25, fr. 282–283. Microfilm at Latin American Collection, University of Texas at Austin.

RAMÓN, DIEGO

1692   Letter to Fr. Antonio de la Maneda, August 20. *Documents for the Early History of Coahuila and Texas and the Approaches Thereto.* Box 2Q259, vol. 3, part 1, pp. 51–52. Center for American History, University of Texas at Austin.

1692a   Letter to the Father Provincial, September 5. *Documents for the Early History of Coahuila and Texas and the Approaches Thereto.* Box 2Q259, vol. 3, part 1, pp. 63–65. Center for American History, University of Texas at Austin.

1698   Mission for the Chantaf and others, December 13. *AGI Audiencia de Guadalajara.* Box 2Q136, vol. 17, pp. 230–235. Center for American History, University of Texas at Austin.

1699-1700   Report about the Coahuila friars. *Documents for the Early History of Coahuila and Texas and the Approaches Thereto.* Box 2Q259, vol. 3, part 2, pp. 134–184. Center for American History, University of Texas at Austin.

1700   Foundation of Mission San Francisco Solano, March 1. *AGI Audiencia de Guadalajara.* Box 2Q136, vol. 17, pp. 252–255. Center for American History, University of Texas at Austin.

1707   Diario de la jornada, April 8. *AGN PI,* Box 2Q203, vol. 28, pp. 53–78. Center for American History, University of Texas at Austin.

REAL CEDULA

1681   Real Cedula and various Autos concerning the settlement in Coahuila. Documents include Bosque's request to the Viceroy (pp. 341–344), the opinions of the Fiscal Miranda de Solis (pp. 344–346), and the approval of the Viceroy Marques de la Laguna (pp. 352–353). *Documents for the Early History of Coahuila and Texas and the Approaches Thereto.* Box 2Q259, vol. 4, pp. 331–337. Center for American History, University of Texas at Austin.

RENGEL, JOSEPH A.

1787   Rengel to Diaz, September 7. *AGN PI,* vol. 3, fr. 49–52. Microfilm at Latin American Collection, University of Texas at Austin.

1787a   Rengel to Flores, December 31. *AGN PI,* vol. 3, fr. 5–19. Microfilm at Latin American Collection, University of Texas at Austin.

RODRÍGUEZ, BICENTE

1775   Reconnaissance, December. *AGN PI,* vol. 24, fr. 247. Microfilm at Latin American Collection, University of Texas at Austin.

RODRÍGUEZ, MANUEL

1764   Letter to Cancio, February 26. *AGN PI,* vol. 25, fr. 240–241. Microfilm at Latin American Collection, University of Texas at Austin.

SABEATA, JUAN

1683   Declaration of Juan Sabeata, August 11. *AGN PI,* vol. 35, fr. 77–78. Microfilm at Latin American Collection, University of Texas at Austin.

1683a   Declaration of Juan Sabeata, October 20. *AGN PI,* vol. 35, fr. 78–80. Microfilm at Latin American Collection, University of Texas at Austin.

SAINT-DENIS, LOUIS J. DE

1715   Route of Saint-Denis, November 7. *French Activities in Spanish Southwest.* Box 2Q235, p. 138. Center for American History, University of Texas at Austin.

SALAÇAR, MARTINEZ DE

1673   Testimony, June 27. *Documents for the Early History of Coahuila and Texas and the Approaches Thereto.* Box 2Q259, vol. 2, pp. 284–287. Center for American History, University of Texas at Austin.

SALINAS VARONA, GREGORIO

1717   Letter to the Viceroy, February 15. *Béxar Archives.* Box 2C14, vol. 1, pp. 57–61. Center for American History, University of Texas at Austin.

SANTA ANA, FR. BENITO F. DE

1750   Petition, February 20. *AGN H,* vol. 28, fr. 136–147. Microfilm at Latin American Collection, University of Texas at Austin.

SANTA CRUZ, JUAN J. DE LA

1756   Testimony, November 3. *Béxar Archives.* Box 2C19, vol. 30, pp. 88–90. Center for American History, University of Texas at Austin.

SANTO, E. J. DE

1684   Declaration, August 1. *AGN PI,* vol. 37. Microfilm at Latin American Collection, University of Texas at Austin.

SEVILLANO DE PAREDES, FR. MIGUEL

1726   Representation. *Missions of Texas, Archivo del Colegio de Santa Cruz.* Box 2Q237, pp. 39–41. Center for American History, University of Texas at Austin.

UGALDE, JUAN DE

1787   Ugalde to Flores, October 22. *AGN PI,* vol. 3, fr. 25–33. Microfilm at Latin American Collection, University of Texas at Austin.

1787a   Ugalde to Flores, November 19. *AGN PI,* vol. 3, fr. 42, 46. Microfilm at Latin American Collection, University of Texas at Austin.

1788   Ugalde to Flores, January 25. *AGN PI,* vol. 3, fr. 97–104. Microfilm at Latin American Collection, University of Texas at Austin.

1788a   Ugalde to Flores, March 10. *AGN PI,* vol. 3, fr. 106. Microfilm at Latin American Collection, University of Texas at Austin.

1788b   Military reconnaissance, April 13 to June 16. *AGN PI,* vol. 3, fr. 135–136. Microfilm at Latin American Collection, University of Texas at Austin.

1788c   Ugalde to Flores, April 14. *AGN PI,* vol. 3, fr. 126–127. Microfilm at Latin American Collection, University of Texas at Austin.

1788d   Ugalde to Flores, April 28. *AGN PI,* vol. 3, fr. 134–173. Microfilm at Latin American Collection, University of Texas at Austin.

1788e   Ugalde to Flores, June 20. *AGN PI,* vol. 3, fr. 173–175. Microfilm at Latin American Collection, University of Texas at Austin.

1788f   Ugalde to Flores, July 15. *AGN PI,* vol. 3, fr. 164–169. Microfilm at Latin American Collection, University of Texas at Austin.

1788g   Ugalde to Flores, September 24. *AGN PI,* vol. 3, fr. 205. Microfilm at Latin American Collection, University of Texas at Austin.

1788h   Ugalde to Flores, November 21. *AGN PI,* vol. 3, fr. 207–210. Microfilm at Latin American Collection, University of Texas at Austin.

UGARTE, JACOBO DE

1770   Ugarte to Viceroy, February 7. *AGN PI,* vol. 24, fr. 22–23. Microfilm at Latin American Collection, University of Texas at Austin.

1770a   Ugarte to Viceroy, April 17. *AGN PI,* vol. 24, fr. 48. Microfilm at Latin American Collection, University of Texas at Austin.

1771   Ugarte to Viceroy, June 8. *AGN PI,* vol. 24, fr. 54. Microfilm at Latin American Collection, University of Texas at Austin.

1771a   Ugarte to Viceroy, July 21. *AGN PI,* vol. 24, fr. 58–61. Microfilm at Latin American Collection, University of Texas at Austin.

1773   Ugarte to Viceroy, September 7. *AGN PI,* vol. 24, fr. 185–191. Microfilm at Latin American Collection, University of Texas at Austin.

1773a   Ugarte to Bucareli, May 11. *AGN PI,* vol. 24, fr. 156. Microfilm at Latin American Collection, University of Texas at Austin.

1776   Letter of Ugarte, January 24. *AGN PI,* vol. 24, fr. 235–240. Microfilm at Latin American Collection, University of Texas at Austin.

1776a   Ugarte to Bucareli, August 14. *AGN PI,* vol. 24, fr. 264. Microfilm at Latin American Collection, University of Texas at Austin.

1787   Ugarte to Ugalde, May 28. *AGN PI,* vol. III, fr. 37. Microfilm at Latin American Collection, University of Texas at Austin.

URDIÑOLA, FRANCISCO

1608   Copia de un capítulo de carta de Francisco Urdiñola. *AGI Audiencia de Guadalajara.* Box 2Q135, pp. 47–49. Center for American History, University of Texas at Austin.

URRUTIA, JOSEPH

1733   Declaration, July 4. *AGN PI,* vol. 32, fr. 400–403. Microfilm at Latin American Collection, University of Texas at Austin.

URRUTIA, THORIBIO

1741   Letter to the Auditor, December 17. *AGN PI,* vol. 32, fr. 118–123. Microfilm at Latin American Collection, University of Texas at Austin.

1747   Escrito sobre los 12 soldados. *Missions of Texas, Archivo del Colegio de Santa Cruz 1716–1749.* Box 2Q237, p. 139. Center for American History, University of Texas at Austin.

1755   Certification, January 12. *AGI Audiencia de Mexico.* Box 2Q151, p. 47. Center for American History, University of Texas at Austin.

VALCARCEL, DOMINGO DE

1755   Report to Viceroy, December 21. *AGI Audiencia de Mexico.* Box 2Q151, pp. 116–148. Center for American History, University of Texas at Austin.

VALLE, JUAN S. R. DEL

1684   Muster Roll at El Paso, September 11. *AGN PI,* Box 2Q204, vol. 37, pp. 87–102. Center for American History, University of Texas at Austin.

VARGAS, DIEGO DE

1692   Report to Viceroy, April 7. *AGN H,* vols. 36–37, fr. 155–160. Microfilm at Latin American Collection, University of Texas at Austin.

VILAR, L.

1695   Report on the Coahuila missions, November 3. *AGI Audiencia de Guadalajara.* Box 2Q136, vol. 17, pp. 19–39. Center for American History, University of Texas at Austin.

XIMENES, FR. DIEGO

1761   Letter to Fr. Manuel Naxera, November 4. *AGN H,* vol. 28, fr. 195–196. Microfilm at Latin American Collection, University of Texas at Austin.

1761a   Letter to Fr. Manuel Naxera, November 23. *AGN H,* vol. 28, fr. 196–197. Microfilm at Latin American Collection, University of Texas at Austin.

1762   Letter to Fr. Manuel Naxera, October 28. *AGN H,* vol. 28, fr. 198–200. Microfilm at Latin American Collection, University of Texas at Austin.

1764   Ximenes to Cancio, February 26. *AGN PI,* vol. 25, fr. 239. Microfilm at Latin American Collection, University of Texas at Austin.

1767   Ximenes to Jacinto Barrios, May 5. *AGN PI,* vol. 25, fr. 382–387, 393. Microfilm at Latin American Collection, University of Texas at Austin.

XIMENES, PEDRO

1658   Testimony, March 12. *Documents for the Early History of Coahuila and Texas and the Approaches Thereto.* Box 2Q259, vol. 4, pp. 324–327. Center for American History, University of Texas at Austin.

YBAÑES, LAZARO

1761   Testimony, February 30. *Béxar Archives.* Box 2C20, vol. 37, pp. 116–118. Center for American History, University of Texas at Austin.

PUBLISHED SECONDARY SOURCES

ALESSIO ROBLES, VITO

1938   Coahuila y Texas en la época colonial. Editorial Cultura, Mexico City.

ALLEN, HENRY E.

1939   The Parrilla Expedition to the Red River in 1759. *Southwestern Historical Quarterly* 43(1): 53–71. Texas Historical Association, Austin.

ANDERSON, EDWIN P.
1925   The Early Art of Terrestrial Measurement and Its Practice in Texas. *Southwestern Historical Quarterly* 29(2): 79–97.

AYER, E. E., F. W. HODGE, AND C. F. LUMMIS
1965   *The Memorial of Fray Alonso de Benavides 1630*. Horn and Wallace, Albuquerque.

BOLTON, HERBERT E.
1916   *Spanish Exploration in the Southwest, 1542–1706*. Charles Scribner's Sons, New York.

BRAUDEL, FERDINAND
1966   *The Mediterranean and the Mediterranean World in the Age of Philip II*. Vol. 1. Harper & Row, New York.

BUCKLEY, ELEANOR C.
1911   The Aguayo Expedition into Texas and Louisiana, 1719–1722. *Quarterly of the Texas Historical Association* 15(1): 1–65.

BURRUS, ERNEST J., AND F. ZUBILLAGA
1982   *Misiones mexicanas de la Compañia de Jesús, 1618–1745: Cartas y informes conservados en la Colección Mateu*. Colección "Chimalistac" de Libros y Documentos acerca de la Nueva España, no. 41. Ediciones José Porrua, Turanzas, S.A., Madrid.

BUTZER, ELISABETH
2001   *Historia social de una comunidad tlaxcalteca*. Archivo Municipal de Saltillo, Departamento de Geografía de la Universidad de Texas, Instituto Tlaxcalteca de la Cultura and Presidencia Municipal de Bustamante, Mexico.

CABEZA DE VACA, ALVAR N.
1971   *Naufragios y comentarios*. 5th ed. Espasa-Calpe, S.A., Madrid.

CAMARGO, DIEGO M.
1892   *Historia de Tlaxcala*. Publicada y anotada por Alfredo Chaveiro. Oficina Tip. de la Secretaría de Fomento, México.

CAMPBELL, THOMAS N.
1988   *The Indians of Southern Texas and Northeastern Mexico: Selected Writings of Thomas Nolan Campbell*. Texas Archeological Research Laboratory, University of Texas at Austin.

CARR, J. T.
1967   *The Climate and Physiography of Texas*. Texas Water Developmental Board, Report 53.

CHAPA, JUAN B., W. C. FOSTER (EDITOR), AND N. F. BRIERLEY (TRANSLATOR).
1995   *Texas & Northeastern Mexico 1630–1690*. University of Texas Press, Austin.

CHÁVEZ, FR. ANGÉLICO
1954   *Origins of New Mexico Families in the Spanish Colonial Period*. Historical Society of New Mexico, Santa Fe.

CHARDON, ROLAND
1980   The Linear League in North America. *Annals of the Association of American Geographers* 70(2): 129–143.

CONNOR, SEYMOUR V.
1969   The Mendoza-Lopez Expedition and the Location of San Clemente. *The West Texas Historical Association Year Book* 45: 1–29.

CORONA, E. S.
1988   Cosmogonía e ideología en la Relación Sociedad Naturaleza del Tlaxcala Prehispánico. *Historia y sociedad en Tlaxcala: Memorias del 4 y 5 Simposios Internacionales de Investigaciones Socio-Históricas sobre Tlascala*. Universidad Ibero-Americana, México.

CUTTER, DONALD C. (EDITOR AND TRANSLATOR)
1994   *The Defense of Northern New Spain*. Southern Methodist University Press, DeGolyer Library, Dallas.

DUNN, WILLIAM E.

1911   Apache Relations in Texas, 1718–1750. *Quarterly of the Texas Historical Association* 14(3): 198–274. Texas Historical Association, Austin.

1912   Missionary Activities among the Eastern Apaches Previous to the Founding of the San Sabá Mission. *Quarterly of the Texas Historical Association* 15(3): 186–200. Texas Historical Association, Austin.

1914   The Apache Mission on the San Sabá River; Its Founding and Failure. *Quarterly of the Texas Historical Association* 17(4): 379–414. Texas Historical Association, Austin.

EUI (*ENCICLOPEDIA UNIVERSAL ILUSTRADA*)

1968   *Enciclopedia Universal Ilustrada.* Vol. 36. Espasa-Calpe, S.A., Madrid.

EWERS, JOHN C.

1985   *The Horse in Blackfoot Indian Culture.* Smithsonian Institution Press, Washington, D.C.

FERNÁNDEZ DURO, CESAREO

1882   *Don Diego de Peñalosa y su descubrimiento del Reino de Quivira.* Imprenta y Fundición de Manuel Tello, Madrid.

FIGUEROA TORRES, J. J.

1963   *Fr. Juan Larios, defensor de los indios y fundador de Coahuila.* Editorial Jus, S.A., Mexico.

FIRTH, RAYMOND

1958   *Human Types: An Introduction to Social Anthropology.* New American Library, New York.

FLETCHER, ALICE C., AND F. LA FLESCHE

1972   *The Omaha Tribe.* Vols. 1 and 2. University of Nebraska Press, Lincoln.

FLORESCANO, ENRIQUE

1969   Colonización, ocupación del suelo y "frontera" en el norte de Nueva España, 1521–1750. *Tierras nuevas,* Alvaro Jara, editor. Centro de Estudios Históricos Nueva Serie 7, El Colegio de México.

FOIK, PAUL J.

1933   Captain Don Domingo Ramón's Diary of His Expedition into Texas in 1716. *Preliminary Studies of the Texas Catholic Historical Society* 2(5). Austin.

FORRESTAL, PETER P.

1931   The Solis Diary of 1767. *Preliminary Studies of the Texas Catholic Historical Society* 1(6). Austin.

1935   Peña's Diary of the Aguayo Expedition. *Preliminary Studies of the Texas Catholic Historical Society* 2(7): 3–68. Austin.

FOSTER, WILLIAM C.

1995   *Spanish Expeditions into Texas, 1689–1768.* University of Texas Press, Austin.

FRENCH, BENJAMIN F. (EDITOR)

1851   *Historical Collections of Louisiana.* Part III. D. Appleton & Company, New York.

GALAVIZ, MA. ELENA (SUAREZ) DEL REAL

1963   *Rebeliones indígenas en el norte de la Nueva España.* Tesis de Maestro, Facultad de Filosofía y Letras, Universidad Nacional Autónoma de México.

GALAVIZ, MA. ELENA DE CAPDEVIELLE

1967   *Rebeliones indígenas en el norte del Reino de la Nueva España (siglos XVI y XVII).* Editorial Campesina, Mexico.

GERALD, REX E.

1974   *Aboriginal use and occupation by Tigua, Manso, and Suma Indians.* Garland Publishing Inc., New York.

GILMORE, KATHLEEN K.

1967   *Documentary and Archaeological Investigation of Presidio San Luis de las Amarillas and*

Mission Santa Cruz de San Saba, Menard County, Texas. Archeological Program Report 8. State Building Commission, Austin.

GÓMEZGIL, IGNACIO R. S.

1997 Fray Juan de Larios Villela, pacificador y conquistador de Coahuila. In *La expansión del septentrión novohispano (1614–1723).* Tomo I, pp. 139–181. Instituto de Investigaciones Sociales, UNAM, and Instituto Estatal de Documentación de Coahuila. Saltillo, México.

GRIFFEN, WILLIAM B.

1969 *Culture Change and Shifting Populations in Central Northern Mexico.* University of Arizona Press, Tucson.

HACKETT, CHARLES W.

1926 *Historical Documents Relating to New Mexico, Nueva Vizcaya, and Approaches Thereto, to 1773.* Vol. II. Carnegie Institute of Washington, Washington, D.C.

1934 *Pichardo's Treatise on the Limits of Louisiana and Texas.* Vol. II. University of Texas Press, Austin.

HAGGARD, VILLASANA J.

1941 *Handbook for Translators of Spanish Historical Documents.* Photoprinted by Semco Color Press, Oklahoma.

HAMMOND, G. P., AND A. REY

1927 *The Gallegos Relation of the Rodriguez Expedition to New Mexico.* Historical Society of New Mexico, Publications in History, Santa Fe.

1929 *Expedition into New Mexico Made by Antonio de Espejo, 1582–1583.* Quivira Society, 1, Los Angeles.

1966 *The Rediscovery of New Mexico, 1580–1594.* University of New Mexico Press, Albuquerque.

HATCHER, MATTIE A.

1932 The Expedition of Don Domingo Terán de los Ríos into Texas. *Preliminary Studies of the Texas Catholic Historical Society* 2(1): 10–67.

HESTER, THOMAS R.

1975 Late Prehistoric Cultural Patterns along the Lower Rio Grande of Texas. *Bulletin of the Texas Archaeological Society* 46: 107–125.

1991 Preface. In *The Burned Rock Middens of Texas: An Archaeological Symposium,* edited by T. R. Hester, pp. v–vii. Studies in Archeology 13. Texas Research Laboratory, University of Texas at Austin.

1995 The Prehistory of South Texas. *Bulletin of the Texas Archeological Society* 66: 427–459.

HINDES, KAY V., M. R. WOLF, G. D. HALL, AND K. K. GILMORE

1995 *The Rediscovery of Santa Cruz de San Sabá, a Mission for the Apache in Spanish Texas.* San Saba Regional Survey Report 1, Texas Historical Foundation and Texas Tech University.

HOFFMANN, FRITZ L.

1935 *Diary of the Alarcón Expedition into Texas, 1718–1719, by Francisco Céliz.* Quivira Society Publications, Los Angeles.

1938 The Mezquía Diary of the Alarcón Expedition into Texas, 1718. *Southwestern Historical Quarterly* 41(3): 312–323.

HUGHES, ANNE E.

1914 *The Beginnings of Spanish Settlement in the El Paso District.* University of California Publications in History, University of California Press, California.

HUNT, LYNN

1986 French History in the Past Twenty Years: The Rise and the Fall of the Annales Paradigm. *Journal of Contemporary History* 21: 209–224.

JACKSON, JACK (EDITOR), AND W. C. FOSTER

1995   *Imaginary Kingdom: Texas as Seen by the Rivera and Rubí Military Expeditions, 1727 and 1767.* Texas State Historical Association, Austin.

JED, STEPHANIE H.

1989   *Chaste Thinking: The Rape of Lucretia and the Birth of Humanism.* Indiana University Press, Bloomington and Indianapolis.

JOHNSON, LEROY

1994   *The Life and Times of Toyah-Culture Folk.* Office of the State Archeologist, Report 38, Texas Department of Transportation and Texas Historical Commission, Austin.

JOHNSON, LEROY, AND T. N. CAMPBELL

1992   Sanan: Traces of a Previously Unknown Aboriginal Language in Colonial Coahuila and Texas. *Plains Anthropologist* 37(140): 185–212.

JOUTEL, HENRI

1998   *La Salle Expedition to Texas: The Journal of Henri Joutel, 1684–1687.* Edited by William S. Foster; translated by Johanna S. Warren. Texas Historical Commission, Austin.

KARTTUNEN, FRANCES, AND J. LOCKHART

1976   *Nahuatl in the Middle Years: Language Contact Phenomena in Texts of the Colonial Period.* University of California Publications in Linguistics 85. University of California Press, Berkeley.

KAVANAGH, THOMAS W.

1996   *Comanche Political History: An Ethnohistorical Perspective, 1706–1875.* University of Nebraska Press (in cooperation with the American Indian Studies Research Institute, Indiana University, Bloomington), Lincoln.

KELLEY, J. CHARLES

1947   The Lehman Rock Shelter: A Stratified Site of the Toyah, Uvalde, and Round Rock Foci. *Bulletin of the Texas Archeological and Paleontological Society* 18: 115–128.

1955   Juan Sabeata and Diffusion in Aboriginal Texas. *American Anthropologist* 57: 981–995.

1986   *Jumano and Patarabueye, Relations at La Junta de los Rios.* Anthropological Papers no. 77. Museum of Anthropology, University of Michigan.

KENMOTSU, N. A.

1994   Helping Each Other Out: A Study of the Mutualistic Relations of Small Scale Foragers and Cultivators in La Junta de los Rios Region, Texas and Mexico. Unpublished Ph.D. dissertation, University of Texas at Austin.

KINNAIRD, LAWRENCE (EDITOR AND TRANSLATOR)

1958   *The Frontiers of New Spain: Nicolás de Lafora's Description, 1766–1768.* Quivira Society Publications, Berkeley.

KRATZ, C.

1981   Are the Okiek Really Maasai? Or Kipsigis? Or Kikuyu? In *Cahiers d'Etudes Africaines* 79: 355–368.

LEE, RICHARD B.

1985   *The !Kung San: Men, Women and Work in a Foraging Society.* Cambridge University Press, Cambridge.

LIGHTFOOT, KENT G., A. MARTINEZ, AND A. M. SCHIFF

1998   Daily Practice and Material Culture in Pluralistic Social Settings: An Archaeological Study of Culture Change and Persistence from Fort Ross, California. *American Antiquity* 63: 199–222.

LINO CANEDO, G.

1968   *Primeras exploraciones y poblamiento de Texas (1686–1694).* Publicaciones del Instituto Tecnológico y de Estudios Superiores de Monterrey, Monterrey.

MALLOUF, ROBERT J.

1987   *Las Haciendas: A Cairn-Burial Assemblage from Northeastern Chihuahua, Mexico.* Office
        of the State Archeologist, Report 35, Texas Historical Commission, Austin.

MARGRY, PIERRE

1879   *Découvertes et établissements des Français dans l'ouest et dans le sud de l'Amérique septen-
        trionale, 1614–1698.* Troisième Partie. Maisonneuve et Cie, Libraires-Editeurs, Paris.

1888   *Exploration des affluents du Mississippi et découverte des montagnes Rocheuses, 1679–1754.*
        Sixième Partie. Maisonneuve et Cie, Libraires-Editeurs, Paris.

MCGUIRE, RANDALL H., AND D. J. SAITTA

1996   Although They Have Petty Captains, They Obey Them Badly: The Dialectics of Pre-
        hispanic Western Pueblo Social Organization. *American Antiquity* 61: 197–216.

1988   Dialectics, Heterarchy, and Western Pueblo Social Organization. *American Antiquity* 63:
        334–336.

MOLINA, FR. ALONSO DE

1977   (1551–1771) *Vocabulario en lengua castellana y mexicana y mexicana y castellana.* Segunda
        Edición. Editorial Porrua, S.A., Mexico.

MOORHEAD, MAX L.

1968   *The Apache Frontier: Jacobo Ugarte and Spanish-Indian Relations in Northern New Spain,
        1766–1791.* University of Oklahoma Press, Norman.

NATHAN, PAUL D. (TRANSLATOR), AND L. B. SIMPSON (EDITOR)

1959   *The San Saba Papers.* John Howell Books, San Francisco.

NEWCOMB, WILLIAM W., AND T. N. CAMPBELL

1982   Southern Plains Prehistory: A Re-examination of the Escanjaques, Ahijados, and Cui-
        toas. *Pathways to Plains Prehistory: Anthropological Perspectives of Plains Natives and Their
        Pasts,* pp. 29–43. Edited by D. G. Wyckoff and H. L. Hofman. Oklahoma Anthropo-
        logical Society, Memoir 3. Duncan, Oklahoma.

PATTEN, RODERICK B. (TRANSLATOR AND EDITOR)

1970   Miranda's Inspection of Los Almagres: His Journal, Report, and Petition. *Southwestern
        Historical Quarterly* 74(2): 223–254. Texas Historical Association, Austin.

PAYNE, DORIS L. (EDITOR)

1990   Introduction. *Amazonian Linguistics Studies in Lowland South American Languages.* Uni-
        versity of Texas Press, Austin.

PELÁEZ, A. C., H. B. ARÉVALO, G. C. PALACIOS, AND M. S. RAMÍREZ

1994   *El sur de Coahuila en el siglo XVII.* Enorme.

PORTILLO, ESTEBAN L.

1886   *Apuntes para la historia antigua de Coahuila y Texas.* Tip. "El Golfo de Mexico" de S. Fer-
        nández, Saltillo.

1984   *Apuntes para la historia antigua de Coahuila y Texas,* edited by Amado Prado. Biblioteca
        de la Universidad Autónoma de Coahuila, Saltillo.

PRATT, MARY L.

1992   *Imperial Eyes: Travel Writing and Transculturation.* Routledge, London.

RAUTMAN, A. E.

1988   Hierarchy and Heterarchy in the American Southwest: A Comment on McGuire and
        Saitta. *American Antiquity* 63: 325–333.

REAL ACADEMIA ESPAÑOLA (RAE)

1726   *Diccionario de la lengua castellana.* Tomo Primero. Imprenta de Francisco del Hierro,
        Madrid.

1739   *Diccionario de la Lengua Castellana.* Tomos Quinto y Sexto. Imprenta de los Herederos
        de Francisco del Hierro, Madrid.

RICKLIS, ROBERT A., AND M. B. COLLINS

1994   *Human Ecology in the Middle Onion Creek Valley, Hays County, Texas.* Studies in Archeology 19, vol. 1. Texas Archeological Research Laboratory, University of Texas at Austin.

ROE, FRANK G.

1970   *The North American Buffalo: A Critical Study of the Species in Its Wild State.* University of Toronto Press.

RUECKING, FREDERICK H., JR.

1955   The Coahuiltecan Indians of Southern Texas and Northeastern Mexico. Unpublished M.A. thesis, University of Texas at Austin.

SANTOS, RICHARD G.

1981   *Aguayo Expedition into Texas, 1721.* Jerkins Publishing Co., Austin.

SCHOLES, FRANCE V.

1936   Church and State in New Mexico. *New Mexico Historical Review* 11: 283–294.

SCHOLES, FRANCE V., AND L. B. BLOOM

1945   Friar Personnel and Mission Chronology. *New Mexico Historical Review* 20: 58–82.

SCHROEDER, ALBERT H.

1974   *Apache Indians I.* Garland Publishing Inc., New York.

SCHROEDER, ALBERT H., AND D. S. MATSON

1965   *A Colony on the Move: Gaspar Castaño de Sosa's Journal, 1590–1591.* Alphabet Printing Co., Salt Lake City.

SELLARDS, ELIAS H., W. S. ADKINS, AND F. B. PLUMMER

1954   *The Geology of Texas. Volume I, Stratigraphy.* The University of Texas Bulletin no. 3232. Austin.

SERVICE, ELMAN R.

1958   *A Profile of Primitive Culture.* Harper & Brothers, New York.

SHELBY, C. C.

1924   Saint Denis' Second Expedition to the Rio Grande, 1716–1719. *Southwestern Historical Quarterly* 27: 190–216.

SILVER, SHIRLEY, AND W. R. MILLER

1997   *American Indian Languages: Cultural and Social Contexts.* University of Arizona Press, Tucson.

SIMPSON, LESLEY B.

1982   *The Encomienda in New Spain.* University of Oklahoma Press, Berkeley.

STECK, FRANCIS B.

1932   Forerunners of Captain de Leon's Expedition to Texas, 1670–1675. *Southwestern Historical Quarterly* 36(1): 1–28.

TOUS, GABRIEL

1930   Ramon's Expedition: Espinosa's Diary of 1716. *Preliminary Studies of the Texas Catholic Historical Society* 1(4): 4–24.

TUNNELL, CURTIS D., AND W. W. NEWCOMB, JR.

1969   *A Lipan Apache Mission, San Lorenzo de la Santa Cruz, 1762–1771.* Bulletin 14. Texas Memorial Museum, University of Texas at Austin.

VALDÉS, CARLOS M., I. DÁVILA, M. DEL ROSARIO VILLARREAL, AND H. CARVALLO

1997–99   *Catálogo del Fondo Testamentos tomo I.* Archivo Municipal de Saltillo, Mexico.

WADE, MARIA F.

1998   The Native Americans of the Texas Edwards Plateau and Related Areas: 1582–1799. Unpublished Ph.D. dissertation, University of Texas at Austin.

1999   Go-Between: The Roles of Native American Women and Alvar Núñez Cabeza de Vaca in Southern Texas in the Sixteenth Century. *Journal of American Folklore* 112: 332–342.

2001   Cultural Fingerprints: The Native Americans of Texas, 1528–1687. *Bulletin of the Texas Archaeological Society* 72: 45–54.

WEDDLE, ROBERT S.
1991   *The French Thorn: Rival Explorers in the Spanish Sea, 1682–1762.* Texas A&M University Press, College Station.

WEST, ELIZABETH H.
1905   De León's Expedition of 1689. *Quarterly of the Texas State Historical Association* 8(3): 199–224.

WILLIAMS, J. W.
1962   New Conclusions on the Route of Mendoza, 1683–1684. *West Texas Historical Association Year Book* 38: 111–134.

ZAVALA, SILVIO A.
1973   *La Encomienda Indiana.* Editorial Porrua, S.A., Mexico.

Index

NA: Native American. NAG: Native American group.